DRIVER'S RECEIPT

This issue of the FMCSR Pocketbook includes all revisions issued on or before August 10, 2003.

I acknowledge receipt of this FEDERAL MOTOR CARRIER SAFETY REGULATIONS POCKETBOOK. In addition, I agree to familiarize myself with the Federal Motor Carrier Safety Regulations (FMCSR) of the U.S. Department of Transportation, Parts 40, 382, 383, 387, 390-396, Title 49 of the Code of Federal Regulations, as contained therein.

_____   _____
DRIVER'S SIGNATURE   DATE

_____
COMPANY

_____
COMPANY SUPERVISOR'S SIGNATURE

9/03
_____
NOTE: This receipt shall be read and signed by the driver. A responsible company supervisor shall countersign the receipt and place it in the driver's qualification file.
_____

Reserved

FEDERAL MOTOR CARRIER SAFETY REGULATIONS POCKETBOOK

This issue of the **FMCSR Pocketbook** includes all revisions issued on or before August 2003. Featured revisions include:

SECTION REVISED	SUBJECT	EFFECTIVE DATE
40	Drug and alcohol testing procedures	8/1/01
40	Alcohol screening devices	10/31/02
40	Dilute or substituted specimens	5/28/02
382	Controlled Substances and Alcohol Use and Testing	8/17/01
383	CDL improvements, noncommercial motor vehicle violations	9/30/02
390	Passenger-carrying vehicles	2/12/01
392	Registration enforcement	9/27/02
393	Performance-based brake testers	2/5/03
395	Hours of Service	6/27/03
397	Tire Checks	11/4/02

— Includes Appendix G - Minimum Periodic Inspection Standards —

Also included in this pocketbook is Part 655 of the **Federal Transit Authority Regulations**. It pertains strictly to mass transit operations and is **not** part of the FMCSRs.

© 2003

by: J. J. Keller & Associates, Inc.
Neenah, Wisconsin

Library of Congress Catalog Card Number 94-72842
ISBN 1-877798-33-9

19-ORS 9/03

SUBJECT INDEX

Federal Motor Carrier Safety Regulations

Federal Transit Authority Regulations

FEDERAL MOTOR CARRIER SAFETY REGULATIONS MOTORCOACH/BUS VERSION

This edited version of the Federal Motor Carrier Safety Regulations contains limited regulatory requirements, for use by the motorcoach/bus industry. Certain parts and sections of the FMCSR's have been omitted because they are not relevant to the overall needs of the passenger carrier. These omissions include all parts containing information on driveaway-towaway operations, coupling devices, transportation of migrant workers, and the transportation of hazardous materials.

Certain footnote references pertaining to specific manufacturing requirements, performance criteria, and testing of particular vehicle components have been omitted.

Title 49 CFR Parts 383 through 399, and 49 CFR Part 571 should be consulted for a complete listing of the regulatory requirements.

Also included in this pocketbook is Part 655 of the **Federal Transit Authority Regulations.** It pertains strictly to mass transit operations and is not part of the FMCSRs used by the motorcoach/bus industry.

D0752784

CONTENTS
PART 40 — PROCEDURES FOR TRANSPORTATION WORKPLACE DRUG AND ALCOHOL TESTING PROGRAMS

Subpart A — Administrative Provisions

Subpart B — Employer Responsibilities

Subpart C — Urine Collection Personnel

Subpart G — Medical Review Officers and the Verification Process

Subpart H — Split Specimen Tests

Subpart K — Testing Sites, Forms, Equipment and Supplies Used in Alcohol Testing

Subpart L — Alcohol Screening Tests

Subpart M — Alcohol Confirmation Tests

Subpart N — Problems in Alcohol Testing

Subpart R — Public Interest Exclusions

Appendix A to Part 40 — DOT Standards for Urine Collection Kits

Appendix B to Part 40 — DOT Drug Testing Semi-annual Laboratory Report

Appendix C to Part 40 — [Reserved]

Appendix D to Part 40 — Report Format: Split Specimen Failure to Reconfirm

Appendix E to Part 40 — SAP Equivalency Requirements for Certification Organizations

Appendix F to Part 40 — Drug and Alcohol Testing Information that C/TPAs May Transmit to Employers

Appendix G to Part 40 — Alcohol Testing Form (ATF)

Appendix H to Part 40 — DOT Drug and Alcohol Testing Management Information System (MIS) Data Collection Form

AUTHORITY: 49 U.S.C. 102, 301, 322, 5331, 20140, 31306, and 45101 *et seq.*

PART 382 — CONTROLLED SUBSTANCES AND ALCOHOL USE AND TESTING

Subpart A — General

PART 383 — COMMERCIAL DRIVER'S LICENSE STANDARDS; REQUIREMENTS AND PENALTIES

Subpart A — General

Subpart B — Single License Requirement

Subpart C — Notification Requirements and Employer Responsibilities

Subpart D — Driver Disqualifications and Penalties

Subpart E — Testing and Licensing Procedures

Subpart F — Vehicle Groups and Endorsements

Subpart G — Required Knowledge and Skills

PART 387 — MINIMUM LEVELS OF FINANCIAL RESPONSIBILITY FOR MOTOR CARRIERS

Subpart A — Motor Carriers of Property

Subpart B — Motor Carriers of Passengers

Subpart C — Surety Bonds and Policies of Insurance for Motor Carriers and Property Brokers

Subpart D — Surety Bonds and Policies of Insurance for Freight Forwarders

PART 390 — GENERAL

Subpart A — General Applicability and Definitions

Subpart B — General Requirements and Information

Subpart C — [Removed and Reserved]

PART 391 — QUALIFICATIONS OF DRIVERS

Subpart A — General

Subpart B — Qualification and Disqualification of Drivers

Subpart C —Background and Character

Subpart D — Examinations and Tests

Subpart E — Physical Qualifications and Examinations

Subpart F — Files and Records

PART 392 — DRIVING OF MOTOR VEHICLES

Subpart A — General

Subpart B — Driving of Vehicles

Subpart C — Stopped Vehicles

392.20	[Removed and reserved.]
392.21	[Removed and reserved.]
392.22	Emergency signals; stopped vehicles.
392.24	Emergency signals; flame-producing.
392.25	. . .

Subpart D — Use of Lighted Lamps and Reflectors

392.30	[Removed and reserved.]
392.31	[Removed and reserved.]
392.32	[Removed and reserved.]
392.33	Obscured lamps or reflectors.

Subpart E — Accidents and License Revocations; Duties of Driver

392.40	[Removed and reserved.]
392.41	[Removed and reserved.]
392.42	[Removed]

Subpart F — Fueling Precautions

392.50	Ignition of fuel; prevention.
392.51	Reserve fuel; materials of trade.
392.52	[Removed and reserved.]

Subpart G — Prohibited Practices

392.60	Unauthorized persons not to be transported.
392.61	[Removed and reserved.]
392.62	Safe operation, buses.
392.63	Towing or pushing loaded buses.
392.64	Riding within closed vehicles without proper exits.
392.65	[Removed and reserved.]
392.66	Carbon monoxide; use of vehicle when detected.
392.67	Heater, flame-producing; on vehicle in motion.
392.68	[Removed and reserved.]
392.69	[Removed and reserved.]
392.71	Radar detectors; use and/or possession.

PART 393 — PARTS AND ACCESSORIES NECESSARY FOR SAFE OPERATION

Subpart A — General

Subpart B — Lighting Devices, Reflectors, and Electrical Equipment

Subpart C — Brakes

PART 394
[REMOVED AND RESERVED]

PART 395 — HOURS OF SERVICE OF DRIVERS

PART 396 — INSPECTION, REPAIR, AND MAINTENANCE

PART 653 — [REMOVED]

PART 654 — [REMOVED]

PART 655 — PREVENTION OF ALCOHOL MISUSE AND PROHIITED DRUG USE IN TRANSIT OPERATIONS

Subpart A — General

Subpart B — Program Requirements

Subpart H — Administrative Requirements

Subpart I — Certifying Compliance

PART 40 — PROCEDURES FOR TRANSPORTATION WORKPLACE DRUG AND ALCOHOL TESTING PROGRAMS

Subpart A — Administrative Provisions

Subpart G — Medical Review Officers and the Verification Process

Subpart H — Split Specimen Tests

Subpart I — Problems in Drug Tests

Subpart J — Alcohol Testing Personnel

Subpart K — Testing Sites, Forms, Equipment and Supplies Used in Alcohol Testing

Subpart L — Alcohol Screening Tests

Subpart M — Alcohol Confirmation Tests

Subpart N — Problems in Alcohol Testing

Subpart O — Substance Abuse Professionals and the Return-to-Duty Process

Subpart R — Public Interest Exclusions

Appendix A to Part 40 — DOT Standards for Urine Collection Kits

Appendix B to Part 40 — DOT Drug Testing Semi-annual Laboratory Report

Appendix C to Part 40 — [Reserved]

Appendix D to Part 40 — Report Format: Split Specimen Failure to Reconfirm

Appendix E to Part 40 — SAP Equivalency Requirements for Certification Organizations

Appendix F to Part 40 — Drug and Alcohol Testing Information that C/TPAs May Transmit to Employers

Appendix G to Part 40 — Alcohol Testing Form (ATF)

Appendix H to Part 40 — DOT Drug and Alcohol Testing Management Information System (MIS) Data Collection Form

AUTHORITY: 49 U.S.C. 102, 301, 322, 5331, 20140, 31306, and 45101 *et seq.*

Subpart A — Administrative Provisions

§40.1 Who does this regulation cover?

(a) This part tells all parties who conduct drug and alcohol tests required by Department of Transportation (DOT) agency regulations how to conduct these tests and what procedures to use.

(b) This part concerns the activities of transportation employers, safety-sensitive transportation employees (including self-employed individuals, contractors and volunteers as covered by DOT agency regulations), and service agents.

(c) Nothing in this part is intended to supersede or conflict with the implementation of the Federal Railroad Administration's post-accident testing program (see 49 CFR 219.200).

§40.3 What do the terms used in this regulation mean?

In this part, the terms listed in this section have the following meanings:

Adulterated specimen. A specimen that contains a substance that is not expected to be present in human urine, or contains a substance expected to be present but is at a concentration so high that it is not consistent with human urine.

Affiliate. Persons are affiliates of one another if, directly or indirectly, one controls or has the power to control the other, or a third party controls or has the power to control both. Indicators of control include, but are not limited to: interlocking management or ownership; shared interest among family members; shared facilities or equipment; or common use of employees. Following the issuance of a public interest exclusion, an organization having the same or similar management, ownership, or principal employees as the service agent concerning whom a public interest exclusion is in effect is regarded as an affiliate. This definition is used in connection with the public interest exclusion procedures of Subpart R of this part.

Air blank. In evidential breath testing devices (EBTs) using gas chromatography technology, a reading of the device's internal standard. In all other EBTs, a reading of ambient air containing no alcohol.

Alcohol. The intoxicating agent in beverage alcohol, ethyl alcohol or other low molecular weight alcohols, including methyl or isopropyl alcohol.

Alcohol concentration. The alcohol in a volume of breath expressed in terms of grams of alcohol per 210 liters of breath as indicated by a breath test under this part.

Alcohol confirmation test. A subsequent test using an EBT, following a screening test with a result of 0.02 or greater, that provides quantitative data about the alcohol concentration.

Alcohol screening device (ASD). A breath or saliva device, other than an EBT, that is approved by the National Highway Traffic Safety Administration (NHTSA) and placed on a conforming products list (CPL) for such devices.

Alcohol screening test. An analytic procedure to determine whether an employee may have a prohibited concentration of alcohol in a breath or saliva specimen.

Alcohol testing site. A place selected by the employer where employees present themselves for the purpose of providing breath or saliva for an alcohol test.

Alcohol use. The drinking or swallowing of any beverage, liquid mixture or preparation (including any medication), containing alcohol.

Blind specimen or blind performance test specimen. A specimen submitted to a laboratory for quality control testing purposes, with a fictitious identifier, so that the laboratory cannot distinguish it from an employee specimen.

Breath Alcohol Technician (BAT). A person who instructs and assists employees in the alcohol testing process and operates an evidential breath testing device.

Cancelled test. A drug or alcohol test that has a problem identified that cannot be or has not been corrected, or which this part otherwise requires to be cancelled. A cancelled test is neither a positive nor a negative test.

Chain of custody. The procedure used to document the handling of the urine specimen from the time the employee gives the specimen to the collector until the specimen is destroyed. This procedure uses the Federal Drug Testing Custody and Control Form (CCF).

Collection container. A container into which the employee urinates to provide the specimen for a drug test.

Collection site. A place selected by the employer where employees present themselves for the purpose of providing a urine specimen for a drug test.

Collector. A person who instructs and assists employees at a collection site, who receives and makes an initial inspection of the specimen provided by those employees, and who initiates and completes the CCF.

Confirmation (or confirmatory) drug test. A second analytical procedure performed on a urine specimen to identify and quantify the presence of a specific drug or drug metabolite.

Confirmation (or confirmatory) validity test. A second test performed on a urine specimen to further support a validity test result.

Confirmed drug test. A confirmation test result received by an MRO from a laboratory.

Consortium/Third-party administrator (C/TPA). A service agent that provides or coordinates the provision of a variety of drug and alcohol testing services to employers. C/TPAs typically perform administrative tasks concerning the operation of the employers' drug and alcohol testing programs. This term includes, but is not limited to, groups of employers who join together to administer, as a single entity, the DOT drug and alcohol testing programs of its members. C/TPAs are not "employers" for purposes of this part.

Continuing education. Training for medical review officers (MROs) and substance abuse professionals (SAPs) who have completed qualification training and are performing MRO or SAP functions, designed to keep MROs and SAPs current on changes and developments in the DOT drug and alcohol testing program.

Designated employer representative (DER). An employee authorized by the employer to take immediate action(s) to remove employees from safety-sensitive duties or cause employees to be removed from these covered duties and to make required decisions in the testing and evaluation processes. The DER also receives test results and other communications for the employer, consistent with the requirements of this part. Service agents cannot act as DERs.

Dilute specimen. A specimen with creatinine and specific gravity values that are lower than expected for human urine.

DOT, The Department, DOT agency. These terms encompass all DOT agencies, including, but not limited to, the United States Coast Guard (USCG), the Federal Aviation Administration (FAA), the Federal Railroad Administration (FRA), the Federal Motor Carrier Safety Administration (FMCSA), the Federal Transit Administration (FTA), the National Highway Traffic Safety Administration (NHTSA), the Research and Special Programs Administration (RSPA), and the Office of the Secretary (OST). These terms include any designee of a DOT agency.

Drugs. The drugs for which tests are required under this part and DOT agency regulations are marijuana, cocaine, amphetamines, phencyclidine (PCP), and opiates.

Employee. Any person who is designated in a DOT agency regulation as subject to drug testing and/or alcohol testing. The term includes individuals currently performing safety-sensitive functions designated in DOT agency regulations and applicants for employment subject to pre-employment testing. For purposes of drug testing under this part, the term employee has the same meaning as the term "donor" as found on CCF and related guidance materials produced by the Department of Health and Human Services.

Employer. A person or entity employing one or more employees (including an individual who is self-employed) subject to DOT agency regulations requiring compliance with this part. The term includes an employer's officers, representatives, and management personnel. Service agents are not employers for the purposes of this part.

Error Correction Training. Training provided to BATs, collectors, and screening test technicians (STTs) following an error that resulted in the cancellation of a drug or alcohol test. Error correction training must be provided in person or by a means that provides real-time observation and interaction between the instructor and trainee.

Evidential Breath Testing Device (EBT). A device approved by NHTSA for the evidential testing of breath at the .02 and .04 alcohol concentrations, placed on NHTSA's Conforming Products List (CPL) for "Evidential Breath Measurement Devices" and identified on the CPL as conforming with the model specifications available from NHTSA's Traffic Safety Program.

HHS. The Department of Health and Human Services or any designee of the Secretary, Department of Health and Human Services.

Initial drug test. The test used to differentiate a negative specimen from one that requires further testing for drugs or drug metabolites.

Initial validity test. The first test used to determine if a specimen is adulterated, diluted, or substituted.

Invalid drug test. The result of a drug test for a urine specimen that contains an unidentified adulterant or an unidentified interfering substance, has abnormal physical characteristics, or has an endogenous substance at an abnormal concentration that prevents the laboratory from completing or obtaining a valid drug test result.

Laboratory. Any U.S. laboratory certified by HHS under the National Laboratory Certification Program as meeting the minimum standards of Subpart C of the HHS Mandatory Guidelines for Federal Workplace Drug Testing Programs; or, in the case of foreign laboratories, a laboratory approved for participation by DOT under this part. (The HHS Mandatory Guidelines for Federal Workplace Drug Testing Programs are available on the internet at *http://www.health.org/ workpl.htm* or from the Division of Workplace Programs, 5600 Fishers Lane, Rockwall II Building, Suite 815, Rockville, MD 20857.)

Medical Review Officer (MRO). A person who is a licensed physician and who is responsible for receiving and reviewing laboratory results generated by an employer's drug testing program and evaluating medical explanations for certain drug test results.

Office of Drug and Alcohol Policy and Compliance (ODAPC). The office in the Office of the Secretary, DOT, that is responsible for coordinating drug and alcohol testing program matters within the Department and providing information concerning the implementation of this part.

Primary specimen. In drug testing, the urine specimen bottle that is opened and tested by a first laboratory to determine whether the employee has a drug or drug metabolite in his or her system; and for the purpose of validity testing. The primary specimen is distinguished from the split specimen, defined in this section.

Qualification Training. The training required in order for a collector, BAT, MRO, SAP, or STT to be qualified to perform their functions in the DOT drug and alcohol testing program. Qualification training may be provided by any appropriate means (*e.g.,* classroom instruction, internet application, CD-ROM, video).

Refresher Training. The training required periodically for qualified collectors, BATs, and STTs to review basic requirements and provide instruction concerning changes in technology (*e.g.,* new testing methods that may be authorized) and amendments, interpretations, guidance, and issues concerning this part and DOT agency drug and alcohol testing regulations. Refresher training can be provided by any appropriate means (*e.g.,* classroom instruction, internet application, CD-ROM, video).

Screening Test Technician (STT). A person who instructs and assists employees in the alcohol testing process and operates an ASD.

Secretary. The Secretary of Transportation or the Secretary's designee.

Service agent. Any person or entity, other than an employee of the employer, who provides services specified under this part to employers and/or employees in connection with DOT drug and alcohol testing requirements. This includes, but is not limited to, collectors, BATs and STTs, laboratories, MROs, substance abuse professionals, and C/TPAs. To act as service agents, persons and organizations must meet the qualifications set forth in applicable sections of this part. Service agents are not employers for purposes of this part.

Shipping container. A container that is used for transporting and protecting urine specimen bottles and associated documents from the collection site to the laboratory.

Specimen bottle. The bottle that, after being sealed and labeled according to the procedures in this part, is used to hold the urine specimen during transportation to the laboratory.

Split specimen. In drug testing, a part of the urine specimen that is sent to a first laboratory and retained unopened,
and which is transported to a second laboratory in the event
that the employee requests that it be tested following a verified
positive test of the primary specimen or a verified adulterated
or substituted test result.

Stand-down. The practice of temporarily removing an employee from the performance of safety-sensitive functions based
only on a report from a laboratory to the MRO of a confirmed
positive test for a drug or drug metabolite, an adulterated test,
or a substituted test, before the MRO has completed verification
of the test result.

Substance Abuse Professional (SAP). A person who eval-
uates employees who have violated a DOT drug and alcohol regulation and makes recommendations concerning education,
treatment, follow-up testing, and aftercare.

Substituted specimen. A specimen with creatinine and
specific gravity values that are so diminished that they are not
consistent with human urine.

Verified test. A drug test result or validity testing result
from an HHS-certified laboratory that has undergone review
and final determination by the MRO.

§40.5 Who issues authoritative interpretations of this reg-ulation?

ODAPC and the DOT Office of General Counsel (OGC) provide written interpretations of the provisions of this part. These
written DOT interpretations are the only official and authorita-
tive interpretations concerning the provisions of this part. DOT
agencies may incorporate ODAPC/OGC interpretations in written guidance they issue concerning drug and alcohol testing
matters. Only Part 40 interpretations issued after August 1,
2001, are considered valid.

§40.7 How can you get an exemption from a requirement in this regulation?

(a) If you want an exemption from any provision of this part,
you must request it in writing from the Office of the Secretary of
Transportation, under the provisions and standards of 49 CFR
part 5. You must send requests for an exemption to the following
address: Department of Transportation, Deputy Assistant General Counsel for Regulation and Enforcement, 400 7th Street,

SW., Room 10424, Washington, DC 20590.

(b) Under the standards of 49 CFR part 5, we will grant the request only if the request documents special or exceptional circumstances, not likely to be generally applicable and not contemplated in connection with the rulemaking that established this part, that make your compliance with a specific provision of this part impracticable.

(c) If we grant you an exemption, you must agree to take steps we specify to comply with the intent of the provision from which an exemption is granted.

(d) We will issue written responses to all exemption requests.

Subpart B — Employer Responsibilities

§40.11 What are the general responsibilities of employers under this regulation?

(a) As an employer, you are responsible for meeting all applicable requirements and procedures of this part.

(b) You are responsible for all actions of your officials, representatives, and agents (including service agents) in carrying out the requirements of the DOT agency regulations.

(c) All agreements and arrangements, written or unwritten, between and among employers and service agents concerning the implementation of DOT drug and alcohol testing requirements are deemed, as a matter of law, to require compliance with all applicable provisions of this part and DOT agency drug and alcohol testing regulations. Compliance with these provisions is a material term of all such agreements and arrangements.

§40.13 How do DOT drug and alcohol tests relate to non-DOT tests?

(a) DOT tests must be completely separate from non-DOT tests in all respects.

(b) DOT tests must take priority and must be conducted and completed before a non-DOT test is begun. For example, you must discard any excess urine left over from a DOT test and collect a separate void for the subsequent non-DOT test.

(c) Except as provided in paragraph (d) of this section, you must not perform any tests on DOT urine or breath specimens other than those specifically authorized by this part or DOT agency regulations. For example, you may not test a DOT urine specimen for additional drugs, and a laboratory is prohibited from making a DOT urine specimen available for a DNA test or other types of specimen identity testing.

(d) The single exception to paragraph (c) of this section is when a DOT drug test collection is conducted as part of a physical examination required by DOT agency regulations. It is permissible to conduct required medical tests related to this physical examination (*e.g.,* for glucose) on any urine remaining in the collection container after the drug test urine specimens have been sealed into the specimen bottles.

(e) No one is permitted to change or disregard the results of DOT tests based on the results of non-DOT tests. For example, as an employer you must not disregard a verified positive DOT drug test result because the employee presents a negative test result from a blood or urine specimen collected by the employee's physician or a DNA test result purporting to question the identity of the DOT specimen.

(f) As an employer, you must not use the CCF or the ATF in your non-DOT drug and alcohol testing programs. This prohibition includes the use of the DOT forms with references to DOT programs and agencies crossed out. You also must always use the CCF and ATF for all your DOT-mandated drug and alcohol tests.

§40.15 May an employer use a service agent to meet DOT drug and alcohol testing requirements?

(a) As an employer, you may use a service agent to perform the tasks needed to comply with this part and DOT agency drug and alcohol testing regulations, consistent with the requirements of Subpart Q and other applicable provisions of this part.

(b) As an employer, you are responsible for ensuring that the service agents you use meet the qualifications set forth in this part (*e.g.,* §40.121 for MROs). You may require service agents to show you documentation that they meet the requirements of this part (*e.g.,* documentation of MRO qualifications required by §40.121(e)).

(c) You remain responsible for compliance with all applicable requirements of this part and other DOT drug and alcohol testing regulations, even when you use a service agent. If you violate this part or other DOT drug and alcohol testing regulations because a service agent has not provided services as our rules require, a DOT agency can subject you to sanctions. Your good faith use of a service agent is not a defense in an enforcement action initiated by a DOT agency in which your alleged noncompliance with this part or a DOT agency drug and alcohol regulation may have resulted from the service agent's conduct.

(d) As an employer, you must not permit a service agent to act as your DER.

§40.17 Is an employer responsible for obtaining information from its service agents?

Yes, as an employer, you are responsible for obtaining information required by this part from your service agents. This is true whether or not you choose to use a C/TPA as an intermediary in transmitting information to you. For example, suppose an applicant for a safety-sensitive job takes a pre-employment drug test, but there is a significant delay in your receipt of the test result from an MRO or C/TPA. You must not assume that "no news is good news" and permit the applicant to perform safety-sensitive duties before receiving the result. This is a violation of the Department's regulations.

§40.19 [Reserved]

§40.21 May an employer stand down an employee before the MRO has completed the verification process?

(a) As an employer, you are prohibited from standing employees down, except consistent with a waiver a DOT agency grants under this section.

(b) You may make a request to the concerned DOT agency for a waiver from the prohibition of paragraph (a) of this section. Such a waiver, if granted, permits you to stand an employee down following the MRO's receipt of a laboratory report of a confirmed positive test for a drug or drug metabolite, an adulterated test, or a substituted test pertaining to the employee.

(1) For this purpose, the concerned DOT agency is the one whose drug and alcohol testing rules apply to the majority of the covered employees in your organization. The concerned DOT agency uses its applicable procedures for considering requests for waivers.

(2) Before taking action on a waiver request, the concerned DOT agency coordinates with other DOT agencies that regulate the employer's other covered employees.

(3) The concerned DOT agency provides a written response to each employer that petitions for a waiver, setting forth the reasons for the agency's decision on the waiver request.

(c) Your request for a waiver must include, as a minimum, the following elements:

(1) Information about your organization:

(i) Your determination that standing employees down is necessary for safety in your organization and a statement of your basis for it, including any data on safety problems or incidents that could have been prevented if a stand-down procedure had been in place;

(ii) Data showing the number of confirmed laboratory positive, adulterated, and substituted test results for your employees over the two calendar years preceding your waiver request, and the number and percentage of those test results that were verified positive, adulterated, or substituted by the MRO;

(iii) Information about the work situation of the employees subject to stand-down, including a description of the size and organization of the unit(s) in which the employees work, the process through which employees will be informed of the stand-down, whether there is an in-house MRO, and whether your organization has a medical disqualification or stand-down policy for employees in situations other than drug and alcohol testing; and

(iv) A statement of which DOT agencies regulate your employees.

(2) Your proposed written company policy concerning stand-down, which must include the following elements:

(i) Your assurance that you will distribute copies of your written policy to all employees that it covers;

(ii) Your means of ensuring that no information about the confirmed positive, adulterated, or substituted test result or the reason for the employee's temporary removal from performance of safety-sensitive functions becomes available, directly or indirectly, to anyone in your organization (or subsequently to another employer) other than the employee, the MRO and the DER;

(iii) Your means of ensuring that all covered employees in a particular job category in your organization are treated the same way with respect to stand-down;

(iv) Your means of ensuring that a covered employee will be subject to stand-down only with respect to the actual performance of safety-sensitive duties;

(v) Your means of ensuring that you will not take any action adversely affecting the employee's pay and benefits pending the completion of the MRO's verification process. This includes continuing to pay the employee during the period of the stand-down in the same way you would have paid him or her had he or she not been stood down;

(vi) Your means of ensuring that the verification process will commence no later than the time an employee is temporarily removed from the performance of safety-sensitive functions and that the period of stand-down for any employee will not exceed five days, unless you are informed in writing by the MRO that a longer period is needed to complete the verification process; and

(vii) Your means of ensuring that, in the event that the MRO verifies the test negative or cancels it—

(A) You return the employee immediately to the performance of safety-sensitive duties;

(B) The employee suffers no adverse personnel or financial consequences as a result; and

(C) You maintain no individually identifiable record that the employee had a confirmed laboratory positive, adulterated, or substituted test result (*i.e.*, you maintain a record of the test only as a negative or cancelled test).

(d) The Administrator of the concerned DOT agency, or his or her designee, may grant a waiver request only if he or she determines that, in the context of your organization, there is a high probability that the procedures you propose will effectively enhance safety and protect the interests of employees in fairness and confidentiality.

(1) The Administrator, or his or her designee, may impose any conditions he or she deems appropriate on the grant of a waiver.

(2) The Administrator, or his or her designee, may immediately suspend or revoke the waiver if he or she determines that you have failed to protect effectively the interests of employees in fairness and confidentiality, that you have failed to comply with the requirements of this section, or that you have failed to comply with any other conditions the DOT agency has attached to the waiver.

(e) You must not stand employees down in the absence of a waiver, or inconsistent with the terms of your waiver. If you do, you are in violation of this part and DOT agency drug testing regulations, and you are subject to enforcement action by the DOT agency just as you are for other violations of this part and DOT agency rules.

§40.23 What actions do employers take after receiving verified test results?

(a) As an employer who receives a verified positive drug test result, you must immediately remove the employee involved from performing safety-sensitive functions. You must take this action upon receiving the initial report of the verified positive test result. Do not wait to receive the written report or the result of a split specimen test.

(b) As an employer who receives a verified adulterated or substituted drug test result, you must consider this a refusal to test and immediately remove the employee involved from performing safety-sensitive functions. You must take this action on receiving the initial report of the verified adulterated or substituted test result. Do not wait to receive the written report or the result of a split specimen test.

(c) As an employer who receives an alcohol test result of 0.04 or higher, you must immediately remove the employee involved from performing safety-sensitive functions. If you receive an alcohol test result of 0.02 — 0.39, you must temporarily remove the employee involved from performing safety-sensitive functions, as provided in applicable DOT agency regulations. Do not wait to receive the written report of the result of the test.

(d) As an employer, when an employee has a verified positive, adulterated, or substituted test result, or has otherwise violated a DOT agency drug and alcohol regulation, you must not return the employee to the performance of safety-sensitive functions until or unless the employee successfully completes the return-to-duty process of Subpart O of this part.

(e) As an employer who receives a drug test result indicating that the employee's specimen was dilute, take action as provided in §40.197.

(f) As an employer who receives a drug test result indicating that the employee's specimen was invalid and that a second collection must take place under direct observation—

(1) You must immediately direct the employee to provide a new specimen under direct observation.

(2) You must not attach consequences to the finding that the test was invalid other than collecting a new specimen under direct observation.

(3) You must not give any advance notice of this test requirement to the employee.

(4) You must instruct the collector to note on the CCF the

same reason (*e.g.* random test, post-accident test) as for the original collection.

(g) As an employer who receives a cancelled test result when a negative result is required (*e.g.*, pre-employment, return-to-duty, or follow-up test), you must direct the employee to provide another specimen immediately.

(h) As an employer, you may also be required to take additional actions required by DOT agency regulations (*e.g.*, FAA rules require some positive drug tests to be reported to the Federal Air Surgeon).

(i) As an employer, you must not alter a drug or alcohol test result transmitted to you by an MRO, BAT, or C/TPA.

§40.25 Must an employer check on the drug and alcohol testing record of employees it is intending to use to perform safety-sensitive duties?

(a) Yes, as an employer, you must, after obtaining an employee's written consent, request the information about the employee listed in paragraph (b) of this section. This requirement applies only to employees seeking to begin performing safety-sensitive duties for you for the first time (*i.e.*, a new hire, an employee transfers into a safety-sensitive position). If the employee refuses to provide this written consent, you must not permit the employee to perform safety-sensitive functions.

(b) You must request the information listed in this paragraph (b) from DOT-regulated employers who have employed the employee during any period during the two years before the date of the employee's application or transfer:

(1) Alcohol tests with a result of 0.04 or higher alcohol concentration;

(2) Verified positive drug tests;

(3) Refusals to be tested (including verified adulterated or substituted drug test results);

(4) Other violations of DOT agency drug and alcohol testing regulations; and

(5) With respect to any employee who violated a DOT drug and alcohol regulation, documentation of the employee's successful completion of DOT return-to-duty requirements (including follow-up tests). If the previous employer does not have information about the return-do-duty process (*e.g.*, an employer who did not hire an employee who tested positive on a pre-employment test), you must seek to obtain this information from the employee.

(c) The information obtained from a previous employer includes any drug or alcohol test information obtained from previous employers under this section or other applicable DOT agency regulations.

(d) If feasible, you must obtain and review this information before the employee first performs safety-sensitive functions. If this is not feasible, you must obtain and review the information as soon as possible. However, you must not permit the employee to perform safety-sensitive functions after 30 days from the date on which the employee first performed safety-sensitive functions, unless you have obtained or made and documented a good faith effort to obtain this information.

(e) If you obtain information that the employee has violated a DOT agency drug and alcohol regulation, you must not use the employee to perform safety-sensitive functions unless you also obtain information that the employee has subsequently complied with the return-to-duty requirements of Subpart O of this part and DOT agency drug and alcohol regulations.

(f) You must provide to each of the employers from whom you request information under paragraph (b) of this section written consent for the release of the information cited in paragraph (a) of this section.

(g) The release of information under this section must be in any written form (*e.g.*, fax, e-mail, letter) that ensures confidentiality. As the previous employer, you must maintain a written record of the information released, including the date, the party to whom it was released, and a summary of the information provided.

(h) If you are an employer from whom information is requested under paragraph (b) of this section, you must, after reviewing the employee's specific, written consent, immediately release the requested information to the employer making the inquiry.

(i) As the employer requesting the information required under this section, you must maintain a written, confidential record of the information you obtain or of the good faith efforts you made to obtain the information. You must retain this information for three years from the date of the employee's first performance of safety-sensitive duties for you.

(j) As the employer, you must also ask the employee whether he or she has tested positive, or refused to test, on any pre-employment drug or alcohol test administered by an employer to which the employee applied for, but did not obtain, safety-sensitive transportation work covered by DOT agency drug and alcohol testing rules during the past two years. If the employee admits that he or she had a positive test or a refusal to test, you must not use the employee to perform safety-sensitive functions for you, until and unless the employee documents successful completion of the return-to-duty process (see paragraphs (b)(5) and (e) of this section).

§40.27 May an employer require an employee to sign a consent or release in connection with the DOT drug and alcohol testing program?

No, as an employer, you must not require an employee to sign a consent, release, waiver of liability, or indemnification agreement with respect to any part of the drug or alcohol testing process covered by this part (including, but not limited to, collections, laboratory testing, MRO and SAP services).

§40.29 Where is other information on employer responsibilities found in this regulation?

You can find other information on the responsibilities of employers in the following sections of this part:

§40.3—Definition.

§40.35—Information about DERs that employers must provide collectors.

§40.45—Modifying CCFs, Use of foreign-language CCFs.

§40.47—Use of non-Federal forms for DOT tests or Federal CCFs for non-DOT tests.

§40.67—Requirements for direct observation.

§§40.103-40.105—Blind specimen requirements.

§40.173—Responsibility to ensure test of split specimen.

§40.193—Action in "shy bladder" situations.

§40.197—Actions following report of a dilute specimen.

§40.207—Actions following a report of a cancelled drug test.

§40.209—Actions following and consequences of non-fatal flaws in drug tests.

§40.215—Information about DERs that employers must provide BATs and STTs.

§40.225—Modifying ATFs; use of foreign-language ATFs.

§40.227—Use of non-DOT forms for DOT tests or DOT ATFs for non-DOT tests.

§40.235 (c) and (d)—responsibility to follow instructions for ASDs.

Subpart C — Urine Collection Personnel

§40.31 Who may collect urine specimens for DOT drug testing?

(a) Collectors meeting the requirements of this subpart are the only persons authorized to collect urine specimens for DOT drug testing.

(b) A collector must meet training requirements of §40.33.

(c) As the immediate supervisor of an employee being tested, you may not act as the collector when that employee is tested, unless no other collector is available and you are permitted to do so under DOT agency drug and alcohol regulations.

(d) You must not act as the collector for the employee being tested if you work for a HHS-certified laboratory (*e.g.*, as a technician or accessioner) and could link the employee with a urine specimen, drug testing result, or laboratory report.

§40.33 What training requirements must a collector meet?

To be permitted to act as a collector in the DOT drug testing program, you must meet each of the requirements of this section:

(a) **Basic information.** You must be knowledgeable about this part, the current "DOT Urine Specimen Collection Procedures Guidelines," and DOT agency regulations applicable to the employers for whom you perform collections, and you must keep current on any changes to these materials. The DOT Urine Specimen Collection Procedures Guidelines document is available from ODAPC (Department of Transportation, 400 7th Street, SW., Room 10403, Washington DC, 20590, 202-366-3784, or on the ODAPC web site (http:// www.dot.gov/ost/dapc).

(b) **Qualification training.** You must receive qualification training meeting the requirements of this paragraph. Qualification training must provide instruction on the following subjects:

(1) All steps necessary to complete a collection correctly and the proper completion and transmission of the CCF;

(2) "Problem" collections (*e.g.* situations like "shy bladder" and attempts to tamper with a specimen);

(3) Fatal flaws, correctable flaws, and how to correct problems in collections; and

(4) The collector's responsibility for maintaining the integrity of the collection process, ensuring the privacy of employees being tested, ensuring the security of the specimen, and avoiding conduct or statements that could be viewed as offensive or inappropriate;

(c) **Initial Proficiency Demonstration.** Following your completion of qualification training under paragraph (b) of this section, you must demonstrate proficiency in collections under this part by completing five consecutive error-free mock collections.

(1) The five mock collections must include two uneventful collection scenarios, one insufficient quantity of urine scenario, one temperature out of range scenario, and one scenario in which the employee refuses to sign the CCF and initial the specimen bottle tamper-evident seal.

(2) Another person must monitor and evaluate your performance, in person or by a means that provides real-time observation and interaction between the instructor and trainee, and attest in writing that the mock collections are "error-free."

This person must be a qualified collector who has demonstrated necessary knowledge, skills, and abilities by—

(i) Regularly conducting DOT drug test collections for a period of at least a year;

(ii) Conducting collector training under this part for a year; or

(iii) Successfully completing a "train the trainer" course.

(d) **Schedule for qualification training and initial proficiency demonstration.** The following is the schedule for qualification training and the initial proficiency demonstration you must meet:

(1) If you became a collector before August 1, 2001, and you have already met the requirements of paragraphs (b) and (c) of this section, you do not have to meet them again.

(2) If you became a collector before August 1, 2001, and have yet to meet the requirements of paragraphs (b) and (c) of this section, you must do so no later than January 31, 2003.

(3) If you become a collector on or after August 1, 2001, you must meet the requirements of paragraphs (b) and (c) of this section before you begin to perform collector functions.

(e) **Refresher training.** No less frequently than every five years from the date on which you satisfactorily complete the requirements of paragraphs (b) and (c) of this section, you must complete refresher training that meets all the requirements of paragraphs (b) and (c) of this section.

(f) **Error Correction Training.** If you make a mistake in the collection process that causes a test to be cancelled (*i.e.*, a fatal or uncorrected flaw), you must undergo error correction training. This training must occur within 30 days of the date you are notified of the error that led to the need for retraining.

(1) Error correction training must be provided and your proficiency documented in writing by a person who meets the requirements of paragraph (c)(2) of this section.

(2) Error correction training is required to cover only the subject matter area(s) in which the error that caused the test to be cancelled occurred.

(3) As part of the error correction training, you must demonstrate your proficiency in the collection procedures of this part by completing three consecutive error-free mock collections. The mock collections must include one uneventful scenario and two scenarios related to the area(s) in which your error(s) occurred. The person providing the training must monitor and evaluate your performance and attest in writing that the mock

collections were "error-free."

(g) **Documentation.** You must maintain documentation showing that you currently meet all requirements of this section. You must provide this documentation on request to DOT agency representatives and to employers and C/TPAs who are using or negotiating to use your services.

§40.35 What information about the DER must employers provide to collectors?

As an employer, you must provide to collectors the name and telephone number of the appropriate DER (and C/TPA, where applicable) to contact about any problems or issues that may arise during the testing process.

§40.37 Where is other information on the role of collectors found in this regulation?

You can find other information on the role and functions of collectors in the following sections of this part:

§40.3—Definition.
§40.43—Steps to prepare and secure collection sites.
§§40.45-40.47—Use of CCF.
§§40.49-40.51—Use of collection kit and shipping materials.
§§40.61-40.63—Preliminary steps in collections.
§40.65—Role in checking specimens.
§40.67—Role in directly observed collections.
§40.69—Role in monitored collections.
§40.71—Role in split specimen collections.
§40.73—Chain of custody completion and finishing the collection process.
§40.103—Processing blind specimens.
§40.191—Action in case of refusals to take test.
§40.193—Action in "shy bladder" situations.
§40.199-40.205—Collector errors in tests, effects, and means of correction.

Subpart D — Collection Sites, Forms, Equipment and Supplies Used in DOT Urine Collections

§40.41 Where does a urine collection for a DOT drug test take place?

(a) A urine collection for a DOT drug test must take place in a collection site meeting the requirements of this section.

(b) If you are operating a collection site, you must ensure that it meets the security requirements of §40.43.

(c) If you are operating a collection site, you must have all necessary personnel, materials, equipment, facilities and supervision to provide for the collection, temporary storage, and shipping of urine specimens to a laboratory, and a suitable clean surface for writing.

(d) Your collection site must include a facility for urination described in either paragraph (e) or paragraph (f) of this section.

(e) The first, and preferred, type of facility for urination that a collection site may include is a single-toilet room, having a full-length privacy door, within which urination can occur.

(1) No one but the employee may be present in the room during the collection, except for the observer in the event of a directly observed collection.

(2) You must have a source of water for washing hands, that, if practicable, should be external to the closed room where urination occurs. If an external source is not available, you may meet this requirement by securing all sources of water and other substances that could be used for adulteration and substitution (*e.g.,* water faucets, soap dispensers) and providing moist towelettes outside the closed room.

(f) The second type of facility for urination that a collection site may include is a multistall restroom.

(1) Such a site must provide substantial visual privacy (*e.g.,* a toilet stall with a partial-length door) and meet all other applicable requirements of this section.

(2) If you use a multi-stall restroom, you must either—

(i) Secure all sources of water and other substances that could be used for adulteration and substitution (*e.g.,* water faucets, soap dispensers) and place bluing agent in all toilets or secure the toilets to prevent access; or

(ii) Conduct all collections in the facility as monitored collections (see §40.69 for procedures). This is the only circumstance in which you may conduct a monitored collection.

(3) No one but the employee may be present in the multistall restroom during the collection, except for the monitor in the event of a monitored collection or the observer in the event of a directly observed collection.

(g) A collection site may be in a medical facility, a mobile facility (*e.g.,* a van), a dedicated collection facility, or any other location meeting the requirements of this section.

§40.43

§40.43 What steps must operators of collection sites take
to protect the security and integrity of urine
collections?

(a) Collectors and operators of collection sites must take the
steps listed in this section to prevent unauthorized access that
could compromise the integrity of collections.

(b) As a collector, you must do the following before each
collection to deter tampering with specimens:

(1) Secure any water sources or otherwise make them
unavailable to employees (e.g., turn off water inlet, tape handles
to prevent opening faucets);

(2) Ensure that the water in the toilet is blue;

(3) Ensure that no soap, disinfectants, cleaning agents, or
other possible adulterants are present;

(4) Inspect the site to ensure that no foreign or unauthorized
substances are present;

(5) Tape or otherwise secure shut any movable toilet tank
top, or put bluing in the tank;

(6) Ensure that undetected access (e.g., through a door not in
your view) is not possible;

(7) Secure areas and items (e.g., ledges, trash receptacles, paper towel holders, under-sink areas) that appear suitable for
concealing contaminants; and

(8) Recheck items in paragraphs (b)(1) through (7) of this
section following each collection to ensure the site's continued
integrity.

(c) If the collection site uses a facility normally used for other
purposes, like a public rest room or hospital examining room,
you must, as a collector, also ensure before the collection that:

(1) Access to collection materials and specimens is effectively
restricted; and

(2) The facility is secured against access during the procedure
to ensure privacy to the employee and prevent distraction of the
collector. Limited-access signs must be posted.

(d) As a collector, you must take the following additional
steps to ensure security during the collection process:

(1) To avoid distraction that could compromise security, you
are limited to conducting a collection for only one employee at a
time. However, during the time one employee is in the period for
drinking fluids in a "shy bladder" situation (see §40.193(b)), you
may conduct a collection for another employee

-59-

(2) To the greatest extent you can, keep an employee's collection container within view of both you and the employee between the time the employee has urinated and the specimen is sealed.

(3) Ensure you are the only person in addition to the employee who handles the specimen before it is poured into the bottles and sealed with tamper-evident seals.

(4) In the time between when the employee gives you the specimen and when you seal the specimen, remain within the collection site.

(5) Maintain personal control over each specimen and CCF throughout the collection process.

(e) If you are operating a collection site, you must implement a policy and procedures to prevent unauthorized personnel from entering any part of the site in which urine specimens are collected or stored.

(1) Only employees being tested, collectors and other collection site workers, DERs, employee and employer representatives authorized by the employer (*e.g.*, employer policy, collective bargaining agreement), and DOT agency representatives are authorized persons for purposes of this paragraph (e).

(2) Except for the observer in a directly observed collection or the monitor in the case of a monitored collection, you must not permit anyone to enter the urination facility in which employees provide specimens.

(3) You must ensure that all authorized persons are under the supervision of a collector at all times when permitted into the site.

(4) You or the collector may remove any person who obstructs, interferes with, or causes a delay in the collection process.

(f) If you are operating a collection site, you must minimize the number of persons handling specimens.

§40.45 What form is used to document a DOT urine collection?

(a) The Federal Drug Testing Custody and Control Form (CCF) must be used to document every urine collection required by the DOT drug testing program. The CCF must be a five-part carbonless manifold form. You may view this form on the Department's web site (http://www.dot.gov/ost/dapc) or the HHS web site (http://www.workplace.samhsa.gov).

(b) You must not use a non-Federal form or an expired Federal form to conduct a DOT urine collection. As a laboratory, C/TPA or other party that provides CCFs to employers, collection sites, or other customers, you must not provide copies of an expired Federal form to these participants. You must also affirmatively notify these participants that they must not use an expired Federal form (e.g., that beginning August 1, 2001, they may not use the old 7-part Federal CCF for DOT urine collections).

(c) As a participant in the DOT drug testing program, you are not permitted to modify or revise the CCF except as follows:

(1) You may include, in the area outside the border of the form, other information needed for billing or other purposes necessary to the collection process.

(2) The CCF must include the names, addresses, telephone numbers and fax numbers of the employer and the MRO, which may be preprinted, typed, or handwritten. The MRO information must include the specific physician's name and address, as opposed to only a generic clinic, health care organization, or company name. This information is required, and it is prohibited for an employer, collector, service agent or any other party to omit it. In addition, a C/TPA's name, address, fax number, and telephone number may be included, but is not required. The employer may use a C/TPA's address in place of its own, but must continue to include its name, telephone number, and fax number.

(3) As an employer, you may add the name of the DOT agency under whose authority the test occurred as part of the employer information.

(4) As a collector, you may use a CCF with your name, address, telephone number, and fax number preprinted, but under no circumstances may you sign the form before the collection event.

(d) Under no circumstances may the CCF transmit personal identifying information about an employee (other than a social security number (SSN) or other employee identification (ID) number) to a laboratory.

(e) As an employer, you may use an equivalent foreign-language version of the CCF approved by ODAPC. You may use such a non-English language form only in a situation where both the employee and collector understand and can use the form in that language.

§40.47 May employers use the CCF for non-Federal collections or non-Federal forms for DOT collections?

(a) No, as an employer, you are prohibited from using the CCF for non-Federal urine collections. You are also prohibited from using non-Federal forms for DOT urine collections. Doing either subjects you to enforcement action under DOT agency regulations.

(b) (1) In the rare case where the collector, either by mistake or as the only means to conduct a test under difficult circumstances (*e.g.*, post-accident or reasonable suspicion test with insufficient time to obtain the CCF), uses a non-Federal form for a DOT collection, the use of a non-Federal form does not present a reason for the laboratory to reject the specimen for testing or for an MRO to cancel the result.

(2) The use of the non-Federal form is a "correctable flaw." As an MRO, to correct the problem you must follow the procedures of §40.205(b)(2).

§40.49 What materials are used to collect urine specimens?

For each DOT drug test, you must use a collection kit meeting the requirements of Appendix A of this part.

§40.51 What materials are used to send urine specimens to the laboratory?

(a) Except as provided in paragraph (b) of this section, you must use a shipping container that adequately protects the specimen bottles from shipment damage in the transport of specimens from the collection site to the laboratory.

(b) You are not required to use a shipping container if a laboratory courier hand-delivers the specimens from the collection site to the laboratory.

Subpart E — Urine Specimen Collections

§40.61 What are the preliminary steps in the collection process?

As the collector, you must take the following steps before actually beginning a collection:

(a) When a specific time for an employee's test has been scheduled, or the collection site is at the employee's work site, and the employee does not appear at the collection site at the scheduled time, contact the DER to determine the appropriate interval within which the DER has determined the employee is authorized to arrive. If the employee's arrival is delayed beyond that time, you must notify the DER that the employee has not reported for testing. In a situation where a C/TPA has notified an owner/operator or other individual employee to report for testing and the employee does not appear, the C/TPA must notify the employee that he or she has refused to test (see §40.191(a)(1)).

(b) Ensure that, when the employee enters the collection site, you begin the testing process without undue delay. For example, you must not wait because the employee says he or she is not ready or is unable to urinate or because an authorized employer or employee representative is delayed in arriving.

(1) If the employee is also going to take a DOT alcohol test, you must, to the greatest extent practicable, ensure that the alcohol test is completed before the urine collection process begins.

Example to Paragraph (b)(1): An employee enters the test site for both a drug and an alcohol test. Normally, the collector would wait until the BAT had completed the alcohol test process before beginning the drug test process. However, there are some situations in which an exception to this normal practice would be reasonable. One such situation might be if several people were waiting for the BAT to conduct alcohol tests, but a drug testing collector in the same facility were free. Someone waiting might be able to complete a drug test without unduly delaying his or her alcohol test. Collectors and BATs should work together, however, to ensure that post-accident and reasonable suspicion alcohol tests happen as soon as possible (*e.g.,* by moving the employee to the head of the line for alcohol tests).

(2) If the employee needs medical attention (*e.g.,* an injured employee in an emergency medical facility who is required to have a post-accident test), do not delay this treatment to collect a specimen.

(3) You must not collect, by catheterization or other means, urine from an unconscious employee to conduct a drug test under this part. Nor may you catheterize a conscious employee. However, you must inform an employee who normally voids through self-catheterization that the employee is required to provide a specimen in that manner.

(4) If, as an employee, you normally void through self-catheterization, and decline to do so, this constitutes a refusal to test.

(c) Require the employee to provide positive identification. You must see a photo ID issued by the employer (other than in the case of an owner-operator or other self-employed individual) or a Federal, state, or local government (*e.g.*, a driver's license). You may not accept faxes or photocopies of identification. Positive identification by an employer representative (not a co-worker or another employee being tested) is also acceptable. If the employee cannot produce positive identification, you must contact a DER to verify the identity of the employee.

(d) If the employee asks, provide your identification to the employee. Your identification must include your name and your employer's name, but does not have to include your picture, address, or telephone number.

(e) Explain the basic collection procedure to the employee, including showing the employee the instructions on the back of the CCF.

(f) Direct the employee to remove outer clothing (*e.g.*, coveralls, jacket, coat, hat) that could be used to conceal items or substances that could be used to tamper with a specimen. You must also direct the employee to leave these garments and any briefcase, purse, or other personal belongings with you or in a mutually agreeable location. You must advise the employee that failure to comply with your directions constitutes a refusal to test.

(1) If the employee asks for a receipt for any belongings left with you, you must provide one.

(2) You must allow the employee to keep his or her wallet.

(3) You must not ask the employee to remove other clothing (*e.g.*, shirts, pants, dresses, underwear), to remove all clothing, or to change into a hospital or examination gown (unless the urine collection is being accomplished simultaneously with a DOT agency-authorized medical examination).

(4) You must direct the employee to empty his or her pockets and display the items in them to ensure that no items are present which could be used to adulterate the specimen. If nothing is there that can be used to adulterate a specimen, the employee can place the items back into his or her pockets. As the employee, you must allow the collector to make this observation.

(5) If, in your duties under paragraph (f)(4) of this section, you find any material that could be used to tamper with a specimen, you must:

(i) Determine if the material appears to be brought to the collection site with the intent to alter the specimen, and, if it is, conduct a directly observed collection using direct observation procedures (see §40.67); or

(ii) Determine if the material appears to be inadvertently brought to the collection site (*e.g.*, eye drops), secure and maintain it until the collection process is completed and conduct a normal (*i.e.*, unobserved) collection.

(g) You must instruct the employee not to list medications that he or she is currently taking on the CCF. (The employee may make notes of medications on the back of the employee copy of the form for his or her own convenience, but these notes must not be transmitted to anyone else.)

§40.63 What steps does the collector take in the collection process before the employee provides a urine specimen?

As the collector, you must take the following steps before the employee provides the urine specimen:

(a) Complete Step 1 of the CCF.

(b) Instruct the employee to wash and dry his or her hands at this time. You must tell the employee not to wash his or her hands again until after delivering the specimen to you. You must not give the employee any further access to water or other materials that could be used to adulterate or dilute a specimen.

(c) Select, or allow the employee to select, an individually wrapped or sealed collection container from collection kit materials. Either you or the employee, with both of you present, must unwrap or break the seal of the collection container. You must not unwrap or break the seal on any specimen bottle at this time. You must not allow the employee to take anything from the collection kit into the room used for urination except the collection container.

(d) Direct the employee to go into the room used for urination, provide a specimen of at least 45 mL, not flush the toilet, and return to you with the specimen as soon as the employee has completed the void.

(1) Except in the case of an observed or a monitored collection (see §§40.67 and 40.69), neither you nor anyone else may go into the room with the employee.

(2) As the collector, you may set a reasonable time limit for voiding.

(e) You must pay careful attention to the employee during the entire collection process to note any conduct that clearly indicates an attempt to tamper with a specimen (*e.g.*, substitute urine in plain view or an attempt to bring into the collection site an adulterant or urine substitute). If you detect such conduct, you must require that a collection take place immediately under direct observation (see §40.67) and note the conduct and the fact that the collection was observed in the "Remarks" line of the CCF (Step 2). You must also, as soon as possible, inform the DER and collection site supervisor that a collection took place under direct observation and the reason for doing so.

§40.65 What does the collector check for when the employee presents a specimen?

As a collector, you must check the following when the employee gives the collection container to you:

(a) **Sufficiency of specimen.** You must check to ensure that the specimen contains at least 45 mL of urine.

(1) If it does not, you must follow "shy bladder" procedures (see §40.193(b)).

(2) When you follow "shy bladder" procedures, you must discard the original specimen, unless another problem (*i.e.*, temperature out of range, signs of tampering) also exists.

(3) You are never permitted to combine urine collected from separate voids to create a specimen.

(4) You must discard any excess urine.

(b) **Temperature.** You must check the temperature of the specimen no later than four minutes after the employee has given you the specimen.

(1) The acceptable temperature range is 32-38 °C/90-100 °F.

(2) You must determine the temperature of the specimen by reading the temperature strip attached to the collection container.

(3) If the specimen temperature is within the acceptable range, you must mark the "Yes" box on the CCF (Step 2).

(4) If the specimen temperature is outside the acceptable range, you must mark the "No" box and enter in the "Remarks" line (Step 2) your findings about the temperature.

(5) If the specimen temperature is outside the acceptable range, you must immediately conduct a new collection using direct observation procedures (see §40.67).

(6) In a case where a specimen is collected under direct observation because of the temperature being out of range, you must process both the original specimen and the specimen collected using direct observation and send the two sets of specimens to the laboratory. This is true even in a case in which the original specimen has insufficient volume but the temperature is out of range. You must also, as soon as possible, inform the DER and collection site supervisor that a collection took place under direct observation and the reason for doing so.

(7) In a case where the employee refuses to provide another specimen (see §40.191(a)(3)) or refuses to provide another specimen under direct observation (see §40.191(a)(4)), you must notify the DER. As soon as you have notified the DER, you must discard any specimen the employee has provided previously during the collection procedure.

(c) **Signs of tampering.** You must inspect the specimen for unusual color, presence of foreign objects or material, or other signs of tampering (*e.g.*, if you notice any unusual odor).

(1) If it is apparent from this inspection that the employee has tampered with the specimen (*e.g.*, blue dye in the specimen, excessive foaming when shaken, smell of bleach), you must immediately conduct a new collection using direct observation procedures (see §40.67).

(2) In a case where a specimen is collected under direct observation because of showing signs of tampering, you must process both the original specimen and the specimen collected using direct observation and send the two sets of specimens to the laboratory. This is true even in a case in which the original specimen has insufficient volume but it shows signs of tampering. You must also, as soon as possible, inform the DER and collection site supervisor that a collection took place under direct observation and the reason for doing so.

(3) In a case where the employee refuses to provide a specimen under direct observation (see §40.191(a)(4)), you must discard any specimen the employee provided previously during the collection procedure. Then you must notify the DER as soon as practicable.

§40.67 When and how is a directly observed collection conducted?

(a) As an employer you must direct an immediate collection under direct observation with no advance notice to the employee, if:

(1) The laboratory reported to the MRO that a specimen is invalid, and the MRO reported to you that there was not an adequate medical explanation for the result;

(2) The MRO reported to you that the original positive, adulterated, or substituted test result had to be cancelled because the test of the split specimen could not be performed; or

(3) The laboratory reported to the MRO that the specimen was substituted with a creatinine concentration greater than or equal to 2 mg/dL and less than or equal to 5 mg/dL and the MRO reported the specimen to you as negative and dilute (see §§40.145(a)(1) and 40.197).

(b) As an employer, you may direct a collection under direct observation of an employee if the drug test is a return-to-duty test or a follow-up test.

(c) As a collector, you must immediately conduct a collection under direct observation if:

(1) You are directed by the DER to do so (see paragraphs (a) and (b) of this section); or

(2) You observed materials brought to the collection site or the employee's conduct clearly indicates an attempt to tamper with a specimen (see §§40.61(f)(5)(i) and 40.63(e)); or

(3) The temperature on the original specimen was out of range (see §40.65(b)(5)); or

(4) The original specimen appeared to have been tampered with (see §40.65(c)(1)).

(d)(1) As the employer, you must explain to the employee the reason for a directly observed collection under paragraph (a) or (b) of this section.

(2) As the collector, you must explain to the employee the reason, if known, under this part for a directly observed collection under paragraphs (c)(1) through (3) of this section.

(e) As the collector, you must complete a new CCF for the directly observed collection.

(1) You must mark the "reason for test" block (Step 1) the same as for the first collection.

(2) You must check the "Observed, (Enter Remark)" box and enter the reason (see §40.67(b)) in the "Remarks" line (Step 2).

(f) In a case where two sets of specimens are being sent to the laboratory because of suspected tampering with the specimen at the collection site, enter on the "Remarks" line of the CCF (Step 2) for each specimen a notation to this effect (*e.g.*, collection 1 of 2, or 2 of 2) and the specimen ID number of the other specimen.

(g) As the collector, you must ensure that the observer is the same gender as the employee. You must never permit an opposite gender person to act as the observer. The observer can be a different person from the collector and need not be a qualified collector.

(h) As the collector, if someone else is to observe the collection (*e.g.*, in order to ensure a same gender observer), you must verbally instruct that person to follow procedures at paragraphs (i) and (j) of this section. If you, the collector, are the observer, you too must follow these procedures.

(i) As the observer, you must watch the employee urinate into the collection container. Specifically, you are to watch the urine go from the employee's body into the collection container.

(j) As the observer but not the collector, you must not take the collection container from the employee, but you must observe the specimen as the employee takes it to the collector.

(k) As the collector, when someone else has acted as the observer, you must include the observer's name in the "Remarks" line of the CCF (Step 2).

(l) As the employee, if you decline to allow a directly observed collection required or permitted under this section to occur, this is a refusal to test.

(m) As the collector, when you learn that a directly observed collection should have been collected but was not, you must inform the employer that it must direct the employee to have an immediate recollection under direct observation.

§40.69 How is a monitored collection conducted?

(a) As the collector, you must secure the room being used for the monitored collection so that no one except the employee and the monitor can enter it until after the collection has been completed.

(b) As the collector, you must ensure that the monitor is the same gender as the employee, unless the monitor is a medical professional (e.g., nurse, doctor, physician's assistant, technologist, or technician licensed or certified to practice in the jurisdiction in which the collection takes place). The monitor can be a different person from the collector and need not be a qualified collector.

(c) As the collector, if someone else is to monitor the collection (e.g., in order to ensure a same-gender monitor), you must verbally instruct that person to follow the procedures of paragraphs (d) and (e) of this section. If you, the collector, are the monitor, you must follow these procedures.

(d) As the monitor, you must not watch the employee urinate into the collection container. If you hear sounds or make other observations indicating an attempt to tamper with a specimen, there must be an additional collection under direct observation (see §§40.63(e), 40.65(c), and 40.67(b)).

(e) As the monitor, you must ensure that the employee takes the collection container directly to the collector as soon as the employee has exited the enclosure.

(f) As the collector, when someone else has acted as the monitor, you must note that person's name in the "Remarks" line of the CCF (Step 2).

(g) As the employee being tested, if you decline to permit a collection authorized under this section to be monitored, it is a refusal to test.

§40.71 How does the collector prepare the specimens?

(a) All collections under DOT agency drug testing regulations must be split specimen collections.

(b) As the collector, you must take the following steps, in order, after the employee brings the urine specimen to you. You must take these steps in the presence of the employee.

(1) Check the box on the CCF (Step 2) indicating that this was a split specimen collection.

(2) You, not the employee, must first pour at least 30 mL of urine from the collection container into one specimen bottle, to be used for the primary specimen.

(3) You, not the employee, must then pour at least 15 mL of urine from the collection container into the second specimen bottle to be used for the split specimen.

(4) You, not the employee, must place and secure (*i.e.,* tighten or snap) the lids/caps on the bottles.

(5) You, not the employee, must seal the bottles by placing the tamper-evident bottle seals over the bottle caps/lids and down the sides of the bottles.

(6) You, not the employee, must then write the date on the tamper-evident bottle seals.

(7) You must then ensure that the employee initials the tamper-evident bottle seals for the purpose of certifying that the bottles contain the specimens he or she provided. If the employee fails or refuses to do so, you must note this in the "Remarks" line of the CCF (Step 2) and complete the collection process.

(8) You must discard any urine left over in the collection container after both specimen bottles have been appropriately filled and sealed. There is one exception to this requirement: you may use excess urine to conduct clinical tests (e.g., protein, glucose) if the collection was conducted in conjunction with a physical examination required by a DOT agency regulation. Neither you nor anyone else may conduct further testing (such as adulteration testing) on this excess urine and the employee has no legal right to demand that the excess urine be turned over to the employee.

§40.73 How is the collection process completed?

(a) As the collector, you must do the following things to complete the collection process. You must complete the steps called for in paragraphs (a)(1) through (a)(7) of this section in the employee's presence.

(1) Direct the employee to read and sign the certification statement on Copy 2 (Step 5) of the CCF and provide date of birth, printed name, and day and evening contact telephone numbers. If the employee refuses to sign the CCF or to provide date of birth, printed name, or telephone numbers, you must note this in the "Remarks" line (Step 2) of the CCF, and complete the collection. If the employee refuses to fill out any information, you must, as a minimum, print the employee's name in the appropriate place.

(2) Complete the chain of custody on the CCF (Step 5) by printing your name (note: you may pre-print your name), recording the time and date of the collection, signing the statement, and entering the name of the delivery service transferring the specimen to the laboratory.

(3) Ensure that all copies of the CCF are legible and complete.

(4) Remove Copy 5 of the CCF and give it to the employee.

(5) Place the specimen bottles and Copy 1 of the CCF in the appropriate pouches of the plastic bag.

(6) Secure both pouches of the plastic bag.

(7) Advise the employee that he or she may leave the collection site.

(8) To prepare the sealed plastic bag containing the specimens and CCF for shipment you must:

(i) Place the sealed plastic bag in a shipping container (*e.g.*, standard courier box) designed to minimize the possibility of damage during shipment. (More than one sealed plastic bag can be placed into a single shipping container if you are doing multiple collections.)

(ii) Seal the container as appropriate.

(iii) If a laboratory courier hand-delivers the specimens from the collection site to the laboratory, prepare the sealed plastic bag for shipment as directed by the courier service.

(9) Send Copy 2 of the CCF to the MRO and Copy 4 to the DER. You must fax or otherwise transmit these copies to the MRO and DER within 24 hours or during the next business day. Keep Copy 3 for at least 30 days, unless otherwise specified by applicable DOT agency regulations.

(b) As a collector or collection site, you must ensure that each specimen you collect is shipped to a laboratory as quickly as possible, but in any case within 24 hours or during the next business day.

Subpart F — Drug Testing Laboratories

§40.81 What laboratories may be used for DOT drug testing?

(a) As a drug testing laboratory located in the U.S., you are permitted to participate in DOT drug testing only if you are certified by HHS under the National Laboratory Certification Program (NLCP) for all testing required under this part.

(b) As a drug testing laboratory located in Canada or Mexico which is not certified by HHS under the NLCP, you are permitted to participate in DOT drug testing only if:

(1) The DOT, based on a written recommendation from HHS, has approved your laboratory as meeting HHS laboratory certification standards or deemed your laboratory fully equivalent to a laboratory meeting HHS laboratory certification standards for all testing required under this part; or

(2) The DOT, based on a written recommendation from HHS, has recognized a Canadian or Mexican certifying organization as having equivalent laboratory certification standards and procedures to those of HHS, and the Canadian or Mexican certifying organization has certified your laboratory under those equivalent standards and procedures.

(c) As a laboratory participating in the DOT drug testing program, you must comply with the requirements of this part. You must also comply with all applicable requirements of HHS in testing DOT specimens, whether or not the HHS requirements are explicitly stated in this part.

(d) If DOT determines that you are in noncompliance with this part, you could be subject to PIE proceedings under Subpart R of this part. If the Department issues a PIE with respect to you, you are ineligible to participate in the DOT drug testing program even if you continue to meet the requirements of paragraph (a) or (b) of this section.

§40.83 How do laboratories process incoming specimens?

As the laboratory, you must do the following when you receive a DOT specimen:

(a) You are authorized to receive only the laboratory copy of the CCF. You are not authorized to receive other copies of the CCF nor any copies of the alcohol testing form.

(b) You must comply with applicable provisions of the HHS Guidelines concerning accessioning and processing urine drug specimens.

(c) You must inspect each specimen and CCF for the following "fatal flaws:"

(1) The specimen ID numbers on the specimen bottle and the CCF do not match;

(2) The specimen bottle seal is broken or shows evidence of tampering, unless a split specimen can be redesignated (see paragraph (g) of this section);

(3) The collector's printed name *and* signature are omitted from the CCF; and

(4) There is an insufficient amount of urine in the primary bottle for analysis, unless the specimens can be redesignated (see paragraph (g) of this section).

(d) When you find a specimen meeting the criteria of paragraph (c) of this section, you must document your findings and stop the testing process. Report the result in accordance with §40.97(a)(3).

(e) You must inspect each CCF for the presence of the collector's signature on the certification statement in Step 4 of the CCF. Upon finding that the signature is omitted, document the flaw and continue the testing process.

(1) In such a case, you must retain the specimen for a minimum of 5 business days from the date on which you initiated action to correct the flaw.

(2) You must then attempt to correct the flaw by following the procedures of §40.205(b)(1).

(3) If the flaw is not corrected, report the result as rejected for testing in accordance with §40.97(a)(3).

(f) If you determine that the specimen temperature was not checked and the "Remarks" line did not contain an entry regarding the temperature being outside of range, you must then attempt to correct the problem by following the procedures of §40.208.

(1) In such a case, you must continue your efforts to correct the problem for five business days, before you report the result.

(2) When you have obtained the correction, or five business days have elapsed, report the result in accordance with §40.97(a).

(g) If you determine that a CCF that fails to meet the requirements of §40.45(a) (e.g., a non-Federal form or an expired Federal form was used for the collection), you must attempt to correct the use of the improper form by following the procedures of §40.205(b)(2).

(1) In such a case, you must retain the specimen for a minimum of 5 business days from the date on which you initiated action to correct the problem.

(2) During the period August 1-October 31, 2001, you are not required to reject a test conducted on an expired Federal CCF because this problem is not corrected. Beginning November 1, 2001, if the problem(s) is not corrected, you must reject the test and report the result in accordance with §40.97(a)(3).

(h) If the CCF is marked indicating that a split specimen collection was collected and if the split specimen does not accompany the primary, has leaked, or is otherwise unavailable for testing, you must still test the primary specimen and follow appropriate procedures outlined in §40.175(b) regarding the unavailability of the split specimen for testing.

(1) The primary specimen and the split specimen can be redesignated (*i.e.*, Bottle B is redesignated as Bottle A, and vice-versa) if:

(i) The primary specimen appears to have leaked out of its sealed bottle and the laboratory believes a sufficient amount of urine exists in the split specimen to conduct all appropriate primary laboratory testing; or

(ii) The primary specimen is labeled as Bottle B, and the split specimen as Bottle A; or

(iii) The laboratory opens the split specimen instead of the primary specimen, the primary specimen remains sealed, and the laboratory believes a sufficient amount of urine exists in the split specimen to conduct all appropriate primary laboratory testing; or

(iv) The primary specimen seal is broken but the split specimen remains sealed and the laboratory believes a sufficient amount of urine exists in the split specimen to conduct all appropriate primary laboratory testing.

(2) In situations outlined in paragraph (g)(1) of this section, the laboratory shall mark through the "A" and write "B," then initial and date the change. A corresponding change shall be made to the other bottle by marking through the "B" and writing "A," and initialing and dating the change.

(i) A notation shall be made on Copy 1 of the CCF (Step 5a) and on any laboratory internal chain of custody documents, as appropriate, for any fatal or correctable flaw.

§40.85 What drugs do laboratories test for?

As a laboratory, you must test for the following five drugs or classes of drugs in a DOT drug test. You must not test "DOT specimens" for any other drugs.

(a) Marijuana metabolites.

(b) Cocaine metabolites.

(c) Amphetamines.

(d) Opiate metabolites.

(e) Phencyclidine (PCP).

§40.87 What are the cutoff concentrations for initial and confirmation tests?

(a) As a laboratory, you must use the cutoff concentrations displayed in the following table for initial and confirmation drug tests. All cutoff concentrations are expressed in nanograms per milliliter (ng/mL). The table follows:

Type of drug or metabolite	Initial test	Confirmation test
(1) Marijuana metabolites	50	
(i) Delta-9-tetrahydrocanna-binol-9-car boxylic acid (THC)		15
(2) Cocaine metabolites (Benzoylecgo nine)....................	300	150
(3) Phencyclidine (PCP)	25	25

Type of drug or metabolite	Initial test	Confirmation test
(4) Amphetamines	1000	
(i) Amphetamine		500
(ii) Methamphetamine.................	....	500 (Specimen must also contain amphetamine at a concentration of greater than or equal to 200 ng/mL.)
(5) Opiate metabolites	2000	
(i) Codeine...........................	....	2000
(ii) Morphine	....	2000
(iii) 6-acetylmorphine (6-AM)	....	10 (Test for 6-AM in the specimen. Conduct this test only when specimen contains morphine at a concentration greater than or equal to 2000 ng/mL.)

(b) On an initial drug test, you must report a result below the cutoff concentration as negative. If the result is at or above the cutoff concentration, you must conduct a confirmation test.

(c) On a confirmation drug test, you must report a result below the cutoff concentration as negative and a result at or above the cutoff concentration as confirmed positive.

(d) You must report quantitative values for morphine or codeine at 15,000 ng/mL or above.

§40.89 What is validity testing, and are laboratories required to conduct it?

(a) Specimen validity testing is the evaluation of the specimen to determine if it is consistent with normal human urine. The purpose of validity testing is to determine whether certain adulterants or foreign substances were added to the urine, if the urine was diluted, or if the specimen was substituted.

(b) As a laboratory, you are authorized to conduct validity testing.

§40.91 What validity tests must laboratories conduct on primary specimens?

As a laboratory, when you conduct validity testing under §40.89, you must conduct it in accordance with the requirements of this section.

(a) You must test each primary specimen for creatinine. You must also determine its specific gravity if you find that the creatinine concentration is less than 20 mg/dL.

(b) You must measure the pH of each primary specimen.

(c) You must test each primary specimen to determine if it contains substances that may be used to adulterate the specimen. Your tests must have the capability of determining whether any substance identified in current HHS requirements or specimen validity guidance is present in the specimen.

(d) If you suspect the presence of an interfering substance/adulterant that could make a test result invalid, but you are unable to identify it (*e.g.*, a new adulterant), you must, as the first laboratory, send the specimen to another HHS certified laboratory that has the capability of doing so.

(e) If you identify a substance in a specimen that appears to be an adulterant, but which is not listed in current HHS requirements or guidance, you must report the finding in writing to ODAPC and the Division of Workplace Programs, HHS, within three business days. You must also complete testing of the specimen for drugs, to the extent technically feasible.

(f) You must conserve as much as possible of the specimen for possible future testing.

§40.93 What criteria do laboratories use to establish that a specimen is dilute or substituted?

(a) As a laboratory you must consider the primary specimen to be dilute if the creatinine concentration is less than 20 mg/dL and the specific gravity is less than 1.003, unless the criteria for a substituted specimen are met.

(b) As a laboratory you must consider the primary specimen to be substituted if the creatinine concentration is less than or equal to 5 mg/dL *and* the specific gravity is less than or equal to 1.001 or greater than or equal to 1.020.

§40.95 What criteria do laboratories use to establish that a specimen is adulterated?

(a) As a laboratory, you must consider the primary specimen to be adulterated if you determine that—

(1) A substance that is not expected to be present in human urine is identified in the specimen;

(2) A substance that is expected to be present in human urine is identified at a concentration so high that it is not consistent with human urine; or

(3) The physical characteristics of the specimen are outside the normal expected range for human urine.

(b) In making your determination under paragraph (a) of this section, you must apply the criteria in current HHS requirements or specimen validity guidance.

§40.97 What do laboratories report and how do they report it?

(a) As a laboratory, you must report the results for each primary specimen tested as one or more of the following:

(1) Negative;

(2) Negative—dilute;

(3) Rejected for testing, with remark(s);

(4) Positive, with drug(s)/metabolite(s) noted;

(5) Positive, with drug(s)/metabolite(s) noted— dilute;

(6) Adulterated, with remark(s);

(7) Substituted, with quantitative values for creatinine and specific gravity, and remarks; or

(8) Invalid result, with remark(s).

(b) As a laboratory, you must report laboratory results directly, and only, to the MRO at his or her place of business. You must not report results to or through the DER or a service agent (e.g., C/TPA).

(1) Negative results: You must fax, courier, mail, or electronically transmit a legible image or copy of the fully-completed Copy 1 of the CCF which has been signed by the certifying scientist, or you may provide the laboratory results report electronically (i.e., computer data file).

(i) If you elect to provide the laboratory results report, you must include the following elements, as a minimum, in the report format:

(A) Laboratory name and address;

(B) Employer's name (you may include I.D. or account number);

    (C) Medical review officer's name;

    (D) Specimen I.D. number;

    (E) Donor's SSN or employee I.D. number, if provided;

    (F) Reason for test, if provided;

    (G) Collector's name and telephone number;

    (H) Date of the collection;

    (I) Date received at the laboratory;

    (J) Date certifying scientist released the results;

    (K) Certifying scientist's name;

    (L) Results (e.g., positive, adulterated) as listed in paragraph (a) of this section; and

    (M) Remarks section, with an explanation of any situation in which a correctable flaw has been corrected.

    (ii) You may release the laboratory results report only after review and approval by the certifying scientist. It must reflect the same test result information as contained on the CCF signed by the certifying scientist. The information contained in the laboratory results report may not contain information that does not appear on the CCF.

    (iii) The results report may be transmitted through any means that ensures accuracy and confidentiality. You, as the laboratory, together with the MRO, must ensure that the information is adequately protected from unauthorized access or release, both during transmission and in storage.

    (2) Non-negative results: You must fax, courier, mail, or electronically transmit a legible image or copy of the fully-completed Copy 1 of the CCF that has been signed by the certifying scientist. In addition, you may provide the electronic laboratory results report following the format and procedures set forth in paragraphs (b)(1)(i) and (ii) of this section.

    (c) In transmitting laboratory results to the MRO, you, as the laboratory, together with the MRO, must ensure that the information is adequately protected from unauthorized access or release, both during transmission and in storage. If the results are provided by fax, the fax connection must have a fixed telephone number accessible only to authorized individuals.

    (d) You must transmit test results to the MRO in a timely manner, preferably the same day that review by the certifying scientist is completed.

    (e) (1) You must provide quantitative values for confirmed positive drug and adulterated test results to the MRO when the MRO requests you to do so in writing. The MRO's request may be either a general request covering all such results you send to the MRO or a specific case-by-case request.

(2) You must also provide to the MRO quantitative values for creatinine and specific gravity for all substituted test results when the result is above your detection limit. If the result is not above detection limit, you must report "creatinine not detected" to the MRO. You must make these reports for in all cases of substituted tests, without a request from the MRO.

(f) You must provide quantitative values for confirmed opiate results for morphine or codeine at 15,000 ng/mL or above, even if the MRO has not requested quantitative values for the test result.

§40.99 How long does the laboratory retain specimens after testing?

(a) As a laboratory testing the primary specimen, you must retain a specimen that was reported with positive, adulterated, substituted, or invalid results for a minimum of one year.

(b) You must keep such a specimen in secure, long-term, frozen storage in accordance with HHS requirements.

(c) Within the one-year period, the MRO, the employee, the employer, or a DOT agency may request in writing that you retain a specimen for an additional period of time (e.g., for the purpose of preserving evidence for litigation or a safety investigation). If you receive such a request, you must comply with it. If you do not receive such a request, you may discard the specimen at the end of the year.

(d) If you have not sent the split specimen to another laboratory for testing, you must retain the split specimen for an employee's test for the same period of time that you retain the primary specimen and under the same storage conditions.

(e) As the laboratory testing the split specimen, you must meet the requirements of paragraphs (a) through (d) of this section with respect to the split specimen.

§40.101 What relationship may a laboratory have with an MRO?

(a) As a laboratory, you may not enter into any relationship with an MRO that creates a conflict of interest or the appearance of a conflict of interest with the MRO's responsibilities for the employer. You may not derive any financial benefit by having an employer use a specific MRO.

(b) The following are examples of relationships between laboratories and MROs that the Department regards as creating conflicts of interest, or the appearance of such conflicts. This following list of examples is not intended to be exclusive or exhaustive:

(1) The laboratory employs an MRO who reviews test results produced by the laboratory;

(2) The laboratory has a contract or retainer with the MRO for the review of test results produced by the laboratory;

(3) The laboratory designates which MRO the employer is to use, gives the employer a slate of MROs from which to choose, or recommends certain MROs;

(4) The laboratory gives the employer a discount or other incentive to use a particular MRO;

(5) The laboratory has its place of business co-located with that of an MRO or MRO staff who review test results produced by the laboratory; or

(6) The laboratory permits an MRO, or an MRO's organization, to have a financial interest in the laboratory.

§40.103 What are the requirements for submitting blind specimens to a laboratory?

(a) As an employer or C/TPA with an aggregate of 2000 or more DOT-covered employees, you must send blind specimens to laboratories you use. If you have an aggregate of fewer than 2000 DOT-covered employees, you are not required to provide blind specimens.

(b) To each laboratory to which you send at least 100 specimens in a year, you must transmit a number of blind specimens equivalent to one percent of the specimens you send to that laboratory, up to a maximum of 50 blind specimens in each quarter (*i.e.*, January-March, April-June, July-September, October-December). As a C/TPA, you must apply this percentage to the total number of DOT-covered employees' specimens you send to the laboratory. Your blind specimen submissions must be evenly spread throughout the year. The following examples illustrate how this requirement works:

Example 1 to Paragraph (b). You send 2500 specimens to Lab X in Year 1. In this case, you would send 25 blind specimens to Lab X in Year 1. To meet the even distribution requirement, you would send 6 in each of three quarters and 7 in the other.

Example 2 to Paragraph (b). You send 2000 specimens to Lab X and 1000 specimens to Lab Y in Year 1. In this case, you would send 20 blind specimens to Lab X and 10 to Lab Y in Year 1. The even distribution requirement would apply in a similar way to that described in Example 1.

Example 3 to Paragraph (b). Same as Example 2, except that you also send 20 specimens to Lab Z. In this case, you would send blind specimens to Labs X and Y as in Example 2. You would not have to send any blind specimens to Lab Z, because you sent fewer than 100 specimens to Lab Z.

Example 4 to Paragraph (b). You are a C/ TPA sending 2000 specimens to Lab X in Year 1. These 2000 specimens represent 200 small employers who have an average of 10 covered employees each. In this case you—not the individual employers—send 20 blind specimens to Lab X in Year 1, again ensuring even distribution. The individual employers you represent are not required to provide any blind specimens on their own.

Example 5 to Paragraph (b). You are a large C/TPA that sends 40,000 specimens to Lab Y in Year 1. One percent of that figure is 400. However, the 50 blind specimen per quarter "cap" means that you need send only 50 blind specimens per quarter, rather than the 100 per quarter you would have to send to meet the one percent rate. Your annual total would be 200, rather than 400, blind specimens.

(c) Approximately 75 percent of the specimens you submit must be blank (*i.e.*, containing no drugs, nor adulterated or substituted). Approximately 15 percent must be positive for one or more of the five drugs involved in DOT tests, and approximately 10 percent must either be adulterated with a substance cited in HHS guidance or substituted (*i.e.*, having specific gravity and creatinine meeting the criteria of §40.93(b)).

(1) The blind specimens that you submit that contain drugs, that are adulterated with a substance cited in HHS guidance, or that are substituted must be validated as to their contents by the supplier using initial and confirmatory tests.

(2) The supplier must provide information regarding the shelf life of the blind specimens.

(3) If the blind specimen is drug positive, the concentration of drug it contains must be between 1.5 and 2 times the initial drug test cutoff concentration.

(4) If the blind specimen is adulterated with nitrite, the concentration of nitrite it contains must be between 1.5 and 2 times the initial validity test cutoff concentration.

(5) If the blind specimen is adulterated by altering pH, the pH must be less than or equal to 2, or greater than or equal to 12.

(6) If the blind specimen is substituted, the creatinine must be less than or equal to 2, and the specific gravity must be 1.000.

(d) You must ensure that each blind specimen is indistinguishable to the laboratory from a normal specimen.

(1) You must submit blind specimens to the laboratory using the same channels (*e.g.*, via a regular collection site) through which employees' specimens are sent to the laboratory.

(2) You must ensure that the collector uses a CCF, places fictional initials on the specimen bottle label/ seal, indicates for the MRO on Copy 2 that the specimen is a blind specimen, and discards Copies 4 and 5 (employer and employee copies).

(3) You must ensure that all blind specimens include split specimens.

§40.105 What happens if the laboratory reports a result different from that expected for a blind specimen?

(a) If you are an employer, MRO, or C/TPA who submits a blind specimen, and if the result reported to the MRO is different from the result expected, you must investigate the discrepancy.

(b) If the unexpected result is a false negative, you must provide the laboratory with the expected results (obtained from the supplier of the blind specimen), and direct the laboratory to determine the reason for the discrepancy.

(c) If the unexpected result is a false positive, you must provide the laboratory with the expected results (obtained from the supplier of the blind specimen), and direct the laboratory to determine the reason for the discrepancy. You must also notify ODAPC of the discrepancy by telephone (202-366-3784) or e-mail (addresses are listed on the ODAPC web site, http://www.dot.gov/ost/dapc). ODAPC will notify HHS who will take appropriate action.

§40.107 Who may inspect laboratories?

As a laboratory, you must permit an inspection, with or without prior notice, by ODAPC, a DOT agency, or a DOT-regulated employer that contracts with the laboratory for drug testing under the DOT drug testing program, or the designee of such an employer.

§40.109 What documentation must the laboratory keep, and for how long?

(a) As a laboratory, you must retain all records pertaining to each employee urine specimen for a minimum of two years.

(b) As a laboratory, you must also keep for two years employer-specific data required in §40.111.

(c) Within the two-year period, the MRO, the employee, the employer, or a DOT agency may request in writing that you retain the records for an additional period of time (*e.g.*, for the purpose of preserving evidence for litigation or a safety investigation). If you receive such a request, you must comply with it. If you do not receive such a request, you may discard the records at the end of the two-year period.

§40.111 When and how must a laboratory disclose statistical summaries and other information it maintains?

(a) As a laboratory, you must transmit an aggregate statistical summary, by employer, of the data listed in Appendix B to this part to the employer on a semi-annual basis.

(1) The summary must not reveal the identity of any employee.

(2) In order to avoid sending data from which it is likely that information about an employee's test result can be readily inferred, you must not send a summary if the employer has fewer than five aggregate tests results.

(3) The summary must be sent by January 20 of each year for July 1 through December 31 of the prior year.

(4) The summary must also be sent by July 20 of each year for January 1 through June 30 of the current year.

(b) When the employer requests a summary in response to an inspection, audit, or review by a DOT agency, you must provide it unless the employer had fewer than five aggregate test results. In that case, you must send the employer a report indicating that not enough testing was conducted to warrant a summary. You may transmit the summary or report by hard copy, fax, or other electronic means.

(c) You must also release information to appropriate parties as provided in §§40.329 and 40.331.

§40.113 Where is other information concerning laboratories found in this regulation?

You can find more information concerning laboratories in several sections of this part:

§40.3—Definition.

§40.13—Prohibition on making specimens available for other purposes.

§40.31—Conflicts of interest concerning collectors.

§40.47—Laboratory rejections of test for improper form.

§40.125—Conflicts of interest concerning MROs.

§40.175—Role of first laboratory in split specimen tests.

§40.177—Role of second laboratory in split specimen tests (drugs).

§40.179—Role of second laboratory in split specimen tests (adulterants).

§40.181—Role of second laboratory in split specimen tests (substitution).

§§40.183-40.185—Transmission of split specimen test results to MRO.

§§40.201-40.205—Role in correcting errors.

§40.329—Release of information to employees.

§40.331—Limits on release of information.

§40.355—Role with respect to other service agents.

Subpart G — Medical Review Officers and the Verification Process

§40.121 Who is qualified to act as an MRO?

To be qualified to act as an MRO in the DOT drug testing program, you must meet each of the requirements of this section:

(a) **Credentials.** You must be a licensed physician (Doctor of Medicine or Osteopathy). If you are a licensed physician in any U.S., Canadian, or Mexican jurisdiction and meet the other requirements of this section, you are authorized to perform MRO services with respect to all covered employees, wherever they are located. For example, if you are licensed as an M.D. in one state or province in the U.S., Canada, or Mexico, you are not limited to performing MRO functions in that state or province,

§40.121

and you may perform MRO functions for employees in other states or provinces without becoming licensed to practice medicine in the other jurisdictions.

(b) **Basic knowledge.** You must be knowledgeable in the following areas:

(1) You must be knowledgeable about and have clinical experience in controlled substances abuse disorders, including detailed knowledge of alternative medical explanations for laboratory confirmed drug test results.

(2) You must be knowledgeable about issues relating to adulterated and substituted specimens as well as the possible medical causes of specimens having an invalid result.

(3) You must be knowledgeable about this part, the DOT MRO Guidelines, and the DOT agency regulations applicable to the employers for whom you evaluate drug test results, and you must keep current on any changes to these materials. The DOT MRO Guidelines document is available from ODAPC (Department of Transportation, 400 7th Street, SW., Room 10403, Washington, DC 20590, 202-366-3784, or on the ODAPC web site (http://www.dot.gov/ost/dapc)).

(c) **Qualification training.** You must receive qualification training meeting the requirements of this paragraph (c).

(1) Qualification training must provide instruction on the following subjects:

(i) Collection procedures for urine specimens;

(ii) Chain of custody, reporting, and recordkeeping;

(iii) Interpretation of drug and validity tests results;

(iv) The role and responsibilities of the MRO in the DOT drug testing program;

(v) The interaction with other participants in the program (*e.g.,* DERs, SAPs); and

(vi) Provisions of this part and DOT agency rules applying to employers for whom you review test results, including changes and updates to this part and DOT agency rules, guidance, interpretations, and policies affecting the performance of MRO functions, as well as issues that MROs confront in carrying out their duties under this part and DOT agency rules.

(2) Following your completion of qualification training under paragraph (c)(1) of this section, you must satisfactorily complete an examination administered by a nationally-recognized MRO certification board or subspecialty board for medical practitioners in the field of medical review of DOT-mandated

drug tests. The examination must comprehensively cover all the elements of qualification training listed in paragraph (c)(1) of this section.

(3) The following is the schedule for qualification training you must meet:

(i) If you became an MRO before August 1, 2001, and have already met the qualification training requirement, you do not have to meet it again.

(ii) If you became an MRO before August 1, 2001, but have not yet met the qualification training requirement, you must do so no later than January 31, 2003.

(iii) If you become an MRO on or after August 1, 2001, you must meet the qualification training requirement before you begin to perform MRO functions.

(d) **Continuing Education.** During each three-year period from the date on which you satisfactorily complete the examination under paragraph (c)(2) of this section, you must complete continuing education consisting of at least 12 professional development hours (*e.g.*, Continuing Education Medical Units) relevant to performing MRO functions.

(1) This continuing education must include material concerning new technologies, interpretations, recent guidance, rule changes, and other information about developments in MRO practice, pertaining to the DOT program, since the time you met the qualification training requirements of this section.

(2) Your continuing education activities must include assessment tools to assist you in determining whether you have adequately learned the material.

(3) If you are an MRO who completed the qualification training and examination requirements prior to August 1, 2001, you must complete your first increment of 12 CEU hours before August 1, 2004.

(e) **Documentation.** You must maintain documentation showing that you currently meet all requirements of this section. You must provide this documentation on request to DOT agency representatives and to employers and C/TPAs who are using or negotiating to use your services.

§40.123 What are the MRO's responsibilities in the DOT drug testing program?

As an MRO, you have the following basic responsibilities:

(a) Acting as an independent and impartial "gatekeeper" and advocate for the accuracy and integrity of the drug testing process.

(b) Providing a quality assurance review of the drug testing process for the specimens under your purview. This includes, but is not limited to:

(1) Ensuring the review of the CCF on all specimen collections for the purposes of determining whether there is a problem that may cause a test to be cancelled (see §§40.199-40.203). As an MRO, you are not required to review laboratory internal chain of custody documentation. No one is permitted to cancel a test because you have not reviewed this documentation;

(2) Providing feedback to employers, collection sites and laboratories regarding performance issues where necessary; and

(3) Reporting to and consulting with the ODAPC or a relevant DOT agency when you wish DOT assistance in resolving any program issue. As an employer or service agent, you are prohibited from limiting or attempting to limit the MRO's access to DOT for this purpose and from retaliating in any way against an MRO for discussing drug testing issues with DOT.

(c) You must determine whether there is a legitimate medical explanation for confirmed positive, adulterated, substituted, and invalid drug tests results from the laboratory.

(d) While you provide medical review of employees' test results, this part does not deem that you have established a doctor-patient relationship with the employees whose tests you review.

(e) You must act to investigate and correct problems where possible and notify appropriate parties (e.g., HHS, DOT, employers, service agents) where assistance is needed, (e.g., cancelled or problematic tests, incorrect results, problems with blind specimens).

(f) You must ensure the timely flow of test results and other information to employers.

(g) You must protect the confidentiality of the drug testing information.

(h) You must perform all your functions in compliance with this part and other DOT agency regulations.

§40.125 What relationship may an MRO have with a laboratory?

As an MRO, you may not enter into any relationship with an employer's laboratory that creates a conflict of interest or the appearance of a conflict of interest with your responsibilities to that employer. You may not derive any financial benefit by having an employer use a specific laboratory. For examples of relationships between laboratories and MROs that the Department views as creating a conflict of interest or the appearance of such a conflict, see §40.101(b).

§40.127 What are the MRO's functions in reviewing negative test results?

As the MRO, you must do the following with respect to negative drug test results you receive from a laboratory, prior to verifying the result and releasing it to the DER:

(a) Review Copy 2 of the CCF to determine if there are any fatal or correctable errors that may require you to initiate corrective action or to cancel the test (see §§40.199 and 40.203).

(b) Review the negative laboratory test result and ensure that it is consistent with the information contained on the CCF.

(c) Before you report a negative test result, you must have in your possession the following documents:

(1) Copy 2 of the CCF, a legible copy of it, or any other CCF copy containing the employee's signature; and

(2) A legible copy (fax, photocopy, image) of Copy 1 of the CCF or the electronic laboratory results report that conveys the negative laboratory test result.

(d) If the copy of the documentation provided to you by the collector or laboratory appears unclear, you must request that the collector or laboratory send you a legible copy.

(e) On Copy 2 of the CCF, place a check mark in the "Negative" box (Step 6), provide your name, and sign, initial, or stamp and date the verification statement.

(f) Report the result in a confidential manner (see §§40.163-40.167).

(g) Staff under your direct, personal supervision may perform the administrative functions of this section for you, but only you can cancel a test. If you cancel a laboratory-confirmed negative result, check the "Test Cancelled" box (Step 6) on Copy 2 of the CCF, make appropriate annotation in the "Remarks" line, provide your name, and sign, initial or stamp and date the verification statement.

(1) On specimen results that are reviewed by your staff, you are responsible for assuring the quality of their work.

(2) You are required to personally review at least 5 percent of all CCFs reviewed by your staff on a quarterly basis, including all results that required a corrective action. However, you need not review more than 500 negative results in any quarter.

(3) Your review must, as a minimum, include the CCF, negative laboratory test result, any accompanying corrective documents, and the report sent to the employer. You must correct any errors that you discover. You must take action as necessary to ensure compliance by your staff with this part and document your corrective action. You must attest to the quality assurance review by initialing the CCFs that you review.

(4) You must make these CCFs easily identifiable and retrievable by you for review by DOT agencies.

§40.129 What are the MRO's functions in reviewing laboratory confirmed positive, adulterated, substituted, or invalid drug test results?

(a) As the MRO, you must do the following with respect to confirmed positive, adulterated, substituted, or invalid drug tests you receive from a laboratory, before you verify the result and release it to the DER:

(1) Review Copy 2 of the CCF to determine if there are any fatal or correctable errors that may require you to cancel the test (see §§40.199 and 40.203). Staff under your direct, personal supervision may conduct this administrative review for you, but only you may verify or cancel a test.

(2) Review Copy 1 of the CCF and ensure that it is consistent with the information contained on Copy 2, that the test result is legible, and that the certifying scientist signed the form. You are not required to review any other documentation generated by the laboratory during their analysis or handling of the specimen (*e.g.*, the laboratory internal chain of custody).

(3) If the copy of the documentation provided to you by the collector or laboratory appears unclear, you must request that the collector or laboratory send you a legible copy.

(4) Except in the circumstances spelled out in §40.133, conduct a verification interview. This interview must include direct contact in person or by telephone between you and the employee. You may initiate the verification process based on the laboratory results report.

(5) Verify the test result as either negative, positive, test cancelled, or refusal to test because of adulteration or substitution, consistent with the requirements of §§40.135-40.145 and 40.159.

(b) Before you report a verified negative, positive, test cancelled, refusal to test because of adulteration or substitution, you must have in your possession the following documents:

(1) Copy 2 of the CCF, a legible copy of it, or any other CCF copy containing the employee's signature; and

(2) A legible copy (fax, photocopy, image) of Copy 1 of the CCF, containing the certifying scientist's signature.

(c) With respect to verified positive test results, place a check mark in the "Positive" box (Step 6) on Copy 2 of the CCF, indicate the drug(s)/ metabolite(s) detected on the "Remarks" line, sign and date the verification statement.

(d) If you cancel a laboratory confirmed positive, adulterated, substituted, or invalid drug test report, check the "test cancelled" box (Step 6) on Copy 2 of the CCF, make appropriate annotation in the "Remarks" line, sign, provide your name, and date the verification statement.

(e) Report the result in a confidential manner (see §§40.163-40.167).

(f) With respect to adulteration or substitution test results, check the "refusal to test because:" box (Step 6) on Copy 2 of the CCF, check the "Adulterated" or "Substituted" box, as appropriate, make appropriate annotation in the "Remarks" line, sign and date the verification statement.

(g) As the MRO, your actions concerning reporting confirmed positive, adulterated, or substituted results to the employer before you have completed the verification process are also governed by the stand-down provisions of §40.21.

(1) If an employer has a stand-down policy that meets the requirements of §40.21, you may report to the DER that you have received an employee's laboratory confirmed positive, adulterated, or substituted test result, consistent with the terms of the waiver the employer received. You must not provide any further details about the test result (*e.g.,* the name of the drug involved).

(2) If the employer does not have a stand-down policy that meets the requirements of §40.21, you must not inform the employer that you have received an employee's laboratory confirmed positive, adulterated, or substituted test result until you verify the test result. For example, as an MRO employed directly by a company, you must not tell anyone on the company's staff or management that you have received an employee's laboratory confirmed test result.

§40.131 How does the MRO or DER notify an employee of the verification process after a confirmed positive, adulterated, substituted, or invalid test result?

(a) When, as the MRO, you receive a confirmed positive, adulterated, substituted with a creatinine concentration of less than 2 mg/dL, or invalid test result from the laboratory, you must contact the employee directly (*i.e.,* actually talk to the employee), on a confidential basis, to determine whether the employee wants to discuss the test result. In making this contact, you must explain to the employee that, if he or she declines to discuss the result, you will verify the test as positive or as a refusal to test because of adulteration or substitution, as applicable.

(b) As the MRO, staff under your personal supervision may conduct this initial contact for you.

(1) This staff contact must be limited to scheduling the discussion between you and the employee and explaining the consequences of the employee's declining to speak with you (*i.e.,* that the MRO will verify the test without input from the employee). If the employee declines to speak with you, the staff person must document the employee's decision, including the date and time.

(2) A staff person must not gather any medical information or information concerning possible explanations for the test result.

(3) A staff person may advise an employee to have medical information (*e.g.,* prescriptions, information forming the basis of a legitimate medical explanation for a confirmed positive test result) ready to present at the interview with the MRO.

(4) Since you are required to speak personally with the employee, face-to-face or on the phone, your staff must not inquire if the employee wishes to speak with you.

(c) As the MRO, you or your staff must make reasonable efforts to reach the employee at the day and evening telephone numbers listed on the CCF. Reasonable efforts include, as a minimum, three attempts, spaced reasonably over a 24-hour period, to reach the employee at the day and evening telephone numbers listed on the CCF. If you or your staff cannot reach the employee directly after making these efforts, you or your staff must take the following steps:

(1) Document the efforts you made to contact the employee, including dates and times. If both phone numbers are incorrect (*e.g.*, disconnected, wrong number), you may take the actions listed in paragraph (c)(2) of this section without waiting the full 24-hour period.

(2) Contact the DER, instructing the DER to contact the employee.

(i) You must simply direct the DER to inform the employee to contact you.

(ii) You must not inform the DER that the employee has a confirmed positive, adulterated, substituted, or invalid test result.

(iii) You must document the dates and times of your attempts to contact the DER, and you must document the name of the DER you contacted and the date and time of the contact.

(d) As the DER, you must attempt to contact the employee immediately, using procedures that protect, as much as possible, the confidentiality of the MRO's request that the employee contact the MRO. If you successfully contact the employee (*i.e.*, actually talk to the employee), you must document the date and time of the contact, and inform the MRO. You must inform the employee that he or she should contact the MRO immediately. You must also inform the employee of the consequences of failing to contact the MRO within the next 72 hours (see §40.133(a)(2)).

(1) As the DER, you must not inform anyone else working for the employer that you are seeking to contact the employee on behalf of the MRO.

(2) If, as the DER, you have made all reasonable efforts to contact the employee but failed to do so, you may place the employee on temporary medically unqualified status or medical leave. Reasonable efforts include, as a minimum, three at-

tempts, spaced reasonably over a 24-hour period, to reach the employee at the day and evening telephone numbers listed on the CCF.

(i) As the DER, you must document the dates and times of these efforts.

(ii) If, as the DER, you are unable to contact the employee within this 24-hour period, you must leave a message for the employee by any practicable means (*e.g.*, voice mail, e-mail, letter) to contact the MRO and inform the MRO of the date and time of this attempted contact.

§40.133 Under what circumstances may the MRO verify a test as positive, or as a refusal to test because of adulteration or substitution, without interviewing the employee?

(a) As the MRO, you normally may verify a confirmed positive test (for any drug or drug metabolite, including opiates), or as a refusal to test because of adulteration or substitution, only after interviewing the employee as provided in §§40.135-40.145. However, there are three circumstances in which you may verify such a result without an interview:

(1) You may verify a test result as a positive or refusal to test, as applicable, if the employee expressly declines the opportunity to discuss the test with you. You must maintain complete documentation of this occurrence, including notation of informing, or attempting to inform, the employee of the consequences of not exercising the option to speak with you.

(2) You may verify a test result as a positive or refusal to test, as applicable, if the DER has successfully made and documented a contact with the employee and instructed the employee to contact you and more than 72 hours have passed since the time the DER contacted the employee.

(3) You may verify a test result as a positive or refusal to test, as applicable, if neither you nor the DER, after making and documenting all reasonable efforts, has been able to contact the employee within ten days of the date on which the MRO receives the confirmed test result from the laboratory.

(b) As the MRO, when you verify a test result as a positive or refusal to test under this section, you must document the date, time and reason, following the instructions in §40.163.

(c) As the MRO, after you have verified a test result as a positive or refusal to test under this section and reported the result to the DER, you must allow the employee to present information to you within 60 days of the verification documenting that serious illness, injury, or other circumstances unavoidably precluded contact with the MRO and/or DER in the times provided. On the basis of such information, you may reopen the verification, allowing the employee to present information concerning whether there is a legitimate medical explanation for the confirmed test result.

§40.135 What does the MRO tell the employee at the beginning of the verification interview?

(a) As the MRO, you must tell the employee that the laboratory has determined that the employee's test result was positive, adulterated, substituted, or invalid, as applicable. You must also tell the employee of the drugs for which his or her specimen tested positive, or the basis for the finding of adulteration or substitution.

(b) You must explain the verification interview process to the employee and inform the employee that your decision will be based on information the employee provides in the interview.

(c) You must explain that, if further medical evaluation is needed for the verification process, the employee must comply with your request for this evaluation and that failure to do so is equivalent of expressly declining to discuss the test result.

(d) As the MRO, you must warn an employee who has a confirmed positive, adulterated, substituted or invalid test that you are required to provide to third parties drug test result information and medical information affecting the performance of safety-sensitive duties that the employee gives you in the verification process without the employee's consent (see §40.327).

(1) You must give this warning to the employee before obtaining any medical information as part of the verification process.

(2) For purposes of this paragraph (d), medical information includes information on medications or other substances affecting the performance of safety-sensitive duties that the employee reports using or medical conditions the employee reports having.

(3) For purposes of this paragraph (d), the persons to whom this information may be provided include the employer, a SAP evaluating the employee as part of the return to duty process (see §40.293(g)), DOT, another Federal safety agency (*e.g.*, the NTSB), or any state safety agency as required by state law.

(e) You must also advise the employee that, after informing any third party about any medication the employee is using pursuant to a legally valid prescription under the Controlled Substances Act, you will allow 5 days for the employee to have the prescribing physician contact you to determine if the medication can be changed to one that does not make the employee medically unqualified or does not pose a significant safety risk. If, as an MRO, you receive such information from the prescribing physician, you must transmit this information to any third party to whom you previously provided information about the safety risks of the employee's other medication.

§40.137 On what basis does the MRO verify test results involving marijuana, cocaine, amphetamines, or PCP?

(a) As the MRO, you must verify a confirmed positive test result for marijuana, cocaine, amphetamines, and/ or PCP unless the employee presents a legitimate medical explanation for the presence of the drug(s)/ metabolite(s) in his or her system.

(b) You must offer the employee an opportunity to present a legitimate medical explanation in all cases.

(c) The employee has the burden of proof that a legitimate medical explanation exists. The employee must present information meeting this burden at the time of the verification interview. As the MRO, you have discretion to extend the time available to the employee for this purpose for up to five days before verifying the test result, if you determine that there is a reasonable basis to believe that the employee will be able to produce relevant evidence concerning a legitimate medical explanation within that time.

(d) If you determine that there is a legitimate medical explanation, you must verify the test result as negative. Otherwise, you must verify the test result as positive.

(e) In determining whether a legitimate medical explanation exists, you may consider the employee's use of a medication from a foreign country. You must exercise your professional judgment consistently with the following principles:

(1) There can be a legitimate medical explanation only with respect to a substance that is obtained legally in a foreign country.

(2) There can be a legitimate medical explanation only with respect to a substance that has a legitimate medical use. Use of a drug of abuse (*e.g.*, heroin, PCP, marijuana) or any other substance (see §40.151(f) and (g)) that cannot be viewed as having a legitimate medical use can never be the basis for a legitimate medical explanation, even if the substance is obtained legally in a foreign country.

(3) Use of the substance can form the basis of a legitimate medical explanation only if it is used consistently with its proper and intended medical purpose.

(4) Even if you find that there is a legitimate medical explanation under this paragraph (e) and verify a test negative, you may have a responsibility to raise fitness-for-duty considerations with the employer (see §40.327).

§40.139 On what basis does the MRO verify test results involving opiates?

As the MRO, you must proceed as follows when you receive a laboratory confirmed positive opiate result:

(a) If the laboratory detects the presence of 6-acetylmorphine (6-AM) in the specimen, you must verify the test result positive.

(b) In the absence of 6-AM, if the laboratory detects the presence of either morphine or codeine at 15,000 ng/mL or above, you must verify the test result positive unless the employee presents a legitimate medical explanation for the presence of the drug or drug metabolite in his or her system, as in the case of other drugs (see §40.137). Consumption of food products (*e.g.*, poppy seeds) must not be considered a legitimate medical explanation for the employee having morphine or codeine at these concentrations.

(c) For all other opiate positive results, you must verify a confirmed positive test result for opiates only if you determine that there is clinical evidence, in addition to the urine test, of unauthorized use of any opium, opiate, or opium derivative (i.e., morphine, heroin, or codeine).

(1) As an MRO, it is your responsibility to use your best professional and ethical judgement and discretion to determine whether there is clinical evidence of unauthorized use of opiates. Examples of information that you may consider in making this judgement include, but are not limited to, the following:

(i) Recent needle tracks;

(ii) Behavioral and psychological signs of acute opiate intoxication or withdrawal;

(iii) Clinical history of unauthorized use recent enough to have produced the laboratory test result;

(iv) Use of a medication from a foreign country. See §40.137(e) for guidance on how to make this determination.

(2) In order to establish the clinical evidence referenced in paragraphs (c)(1)(i) and (ii) of this section, personal observation of the employee is essential.

(i) Therefore, you, as the MRO, must conduct, or cause another physician to conduct, a face-to-face examination of the employee.

(ii) No face-to-face examination is needed in establishing the clinical evidence referenced in paragraph (c)(1)(iii) or (iv) of this section.

(3) To be the basis of a verified positive result for opiates, the clinical evidence you find must concern a drug that the laboratory found in the specimen. (For example, if the test confirmed the presence of codeine, and the employee admits to unauthorized use of hydrocodone, you do not have grounds for verifying the test positive. The admission must be for the substance that was found).

(4) As the MRO, you have the burden of establishing that there is clinical evidence of unauthorized use of opiates referenced in this paragraph (c). If you cannot make this determination (*e.g.*, there is not sufficient clinical evidence or history), you must verify the test as negative. The employee does not need to show you that a legitimate medical explanation exists if no clinical evidence is established.

§40.141 How does the MRO obtain information for the verification decision?

As the MRO, you must do the following as you make the determinations needed for a verification decision:

(a) You must conduct a medical interview. You must review the employee's medical history and any other relevant biomedical factors presented to you by the employee. You may direct the employee to undergo further medical evaluation by you or another physician.

(b) If the employee asserts that the presence of a drug or drug metabolite in his or her specimen results from taking prescription medication, you must review and take all reasonable and necessary steps to verify the authenticity of all medical records the employee provides. You may contact the employee's physician or other relevant medical personnel for further information.

§40.143 [Reserved]

§40.145 On what basis does the MRO verify test results involving adulteration or substitution?

(a) As an MRO, when you receive a laboratory report that a specimen is adulterated or substituted, you must treat that report in the same way you treat the laboratory's report of a confirmed positive test for a drug or drug metabolite, unless the creatinine concentration for a subsituted specimen was reported by the laboratory to be equal to or more than 2 mg/dL.

(1) If the laboratory has reported the creatinine concentration for a substituted specimen as equal to or more than 2 mg/dL, you must report the specimen to the DER as being dilute, as provided in §40.155 of this part. Notwithstanding any other provision of this part, you must also instruct the DER that a second collection under direct observation must take place immediately.

(2) If the laboratory has reported the creatinine concentration for a substituted specimen as less than 2 mg/dL or "creatinine not detected," you must follow the procedures set forth in paragraphs (b) through (h) of this section.

(b) You must follow the same procedures used for verification of a confirmed positive test for a drug or drug metabolite (see §§40.129-40.135, 40.141, 40.151), except as otherwise provided in this section.

(c) In the verification interview, you must explain the laboratory findings to the employee and address technical questions or issues the employee may raise.

(d) You must offer the employee the opportunity to present a legitimate medical explanation for the laboratory findings with respect to presence of the adulterant in, or the creatinine and specific gravity findings for, the specimen.

(e) The employee has the burden of proof that there is a legitimate medical explanation.

(1) To meet this burden in the case of an adulterated specimen, the employee must demonstrate that the adulterant found

by the laboratory entered the specimen through physiological means.

(2) To meet this burden in the case of a substituted specimen, the employee must demonstrate that he or she did produce or could have produced urine, through physiological means, meeting criteria for creatinine of less than 2 mg/dL and for specific gravity of less than or equal to 1.001 or greater than or equal to 1.020.

(3) The employee must present information meeting this burden at the time of the verification interview. As the MRO, you have discretion to extend the time available to the employee for this purpose for up to five days before verifying the specimen, if you determine that there is a reasonable basis to believe that the employee will be able to produce relevant evidence supporting a legitimate medical explanation within that time.

(f) As the MRO or the employer, you are not responsible for arranging, conducting, or paying for any studies, examinations or analyses to determine whether a legitimate medical explanation exists.

(g) As the MRO, you must exercise your best professional judgment in deciding whether the employee has established a legitimate medical explanation.

(1) If you determine that the employee's explanation does not present a reasonable basis for concluding that there may be a legitimate medical explanation, you must report the test to the DER as a verified refusal to test because of adulteration or substitution, as applicable.

(2) If you believe that the employee's explanation may present a reasonable basis for concluding that there is a legitimate medical explanation, you must direct the employee to obtain, within the five-day period set forth in paragraph (e)(3) of this section, a further medical evaluation. This evaluation must be performed by a licensed physician (the "referral physician"), acceptable to you, with expertise in the medical issues raised by the employee's explanation. (The MRO may perform this evaluation if the MRO has appropriate expertise.)

(i) As the MRO or employer, you are not responsible for finding or paying a referral physician. However, on request of the employee, you must provide reasonable assistance to the employee's efforts to find such a physician. The final choice of the referral physician is the employee's, as long as the physician is acceptable to you.

(ii) As the MRO, you must consult with the referral physician, providing guidance to him or her concerning his or her responsibilities under this section. As part of this consultation, you must provide the following information to the referral physician:

(A) That the employee was required to take a DOT drug test, but the laboratory reported that the specimen was adulterated or substituted, which is treated as a refusal to test;

(B) The consequences of the appropriate DOT agency regulation for refusing to take the required drug test;

(C) That the referral physician must agree to follow the requirements of paragraphs (g)(3) through (g)(4) of this section; and

(D) That the referral physician must provide you with a signed statement of his or her recommendations.

(3) As the referral physician, you must evaluate the employee and consider any evidence the employee presents concerning the employee's medical explanation. You may conduct additional tests to determine whether there is a legitimate medical explanation. Any additional urine tests must be performed in an HHS-certified laboratory.

(4) As the referral physician, you must then make a written recommendation to the MRO about whether the MRO should determine that there is a legitimate medical explanation. As the MRO, you must seriously consider and assess the referral physician's recommendation in deciding whether there is a legitimate medical explanation.

(5) As the MRO, if you determine that there is a legitimate medical explanation, you must cancel the test and inform ODAPC in writing of the determination and the basis for it (e.g., referral physician's findings, evidence produced by the employee).

(6) As the MRO, if you determine that there is not a legitimate medical explanation, you must report the test to the DER as a verified refusal to test because of adulteration or substitution.

(h) The following are examples of types of evidence an employee could present to support an assertion of a legitimate medical explanation for a substituted result.

(1) Medically valid evidence demonstrating that the employee is capable of physiologically producing urine meeting the creatinine and specific gravity criteria of §40.93(b).

(i) To be regarded as medically valid, the evidence must have been gathered using appropriate methodology and controls to ensure its accuracy and reliability.

(ii) Assertion by the employee that his or her personal characteristics (*e.g.,* with respect to race, gender, weight, diet, working conditions) are responsible for the substituted result does not, in itself, constitute a legitimate medical explanation. To make a case that there is a legitimate medical explanation, the employee must present evidence showing that the cited personal characteristics actually result in the physiological production of urine meeting the creatinine and specific gravity criteria of §40.93(b).

(2) Information from a medical evaluation under paragraph (g) of this section that the individual has a medical condition that has been demonstrated to cause the employee to physiologically produce urine meeting the creatinine and specific gravity criteria of §40.93(b).

(i) A finding or diagnosis by the physician that an employee has a medical condition, in itself, does not constitute a legitimate medical explanation.

(ii) To establish there is a legitimate medical explanation, the employee must demonstrate that the cited medical condition actually results in the physiological production of urine meeting the creatinine and specific gravity criteria of §40.93(b).

§40.147 [Reserved]

§40.149 May the MRO change a verified positive drug test result or refusal to test?

(a) As the MRO, you may change a verified positive or refusal to test drug test result only in the following situations:

(1) When you have reopened a verification that was done without an interview with an employee (see §40.133(c)).

(2) If you receive information, not available to you at the time of the original verification, demonstrating that the laboratory made an error in identifying (*e.g.,* a paperwork mistake) or testing (*e.g.,* a false positive or negative) the employee's primary or split specimen. For example, suppose the laboratory originally reported a positive test result for Employee X and a negative result for Employee Y. You verified the test results as reported to you. Then the laboratory notifies you that it mixed up the two test results, and X was really negative and Y was really positive. You would change X's test result from positive to negative and contact Y to conduct a verification interview.

(3) If, within 60 days of the original verification decision—

(i) You receive information that could not reasonably have been provided to you at the time of the decision demonstrating that there is a legitimate medical explanation for the presence of drug(s)/metabolite(s) in the employee's specimen; or

(ii) You receive credible new or additional evidence that a legitimate medical explanation for an adulterated or substituted result exists.

Example to Paragraph (a)(3): If the employee's physician provides you a valid prescription that he or she failed to find at the time of the original verification, you may change the test result from positive to negative if you conclude that the prescription provides a legitimate medical explanation for the drug(s)/ metabolite(s) in the employee's specimen.

(4) If you receive the information in paragraph (a)(3) of this section after the 60-day period, you must consult with ODAPC prior to changing the result.

(5) When you have made an administrative error and reported an incorrect result.

(b) If you change the result, you must immediately notify the DER in writing, as provided in §§40.163-40.165.

(c) You are the only person permitted to change a verified test result, such as a verified positive test result or a determination that an individual has refused to test because of adulteration or substitution. This is because, as the MRO, you have the sole authority under this part to make medical determinations leading to a verified test (e.g., a determination that there was or was not a legitimate medical explanation for a laboratory test result). For example, an arbitrator is not permitted to overturn the medical judgment of the MRO that the employee failed to present a legitimate medical explanation for a positive, adulterated, or substituted test result of his or her specimen.

§40.151 What are MROs prohibited from doing as part of the verification process?

As an MRO, you are prohibited from doing the following as part of the verification process:

(a) You must not consider any evidence from tests of urine samples or other body fluids or tissues (*e.g.,* blood or hair samples) that are not collected or tested in accordance with this part. For example, if an employee tells you he went to his own physician, provided a urine specimen, sent it to a laboratory, and received a negative test result or a DNA test result questioning the identity of his DOT specimen, you are required to ignore this test result.

(b) It is not your function to make decisions about factual disputes between the employee and the collector concerning matters occurring at the collection site that are not reflected on the CCF (e.g., concerning allegations that the collector left the area or left open urine containers where other people could access them).

(c) It is not your function to determine whether the employer should have directed that a test occur. For example, if an employee tells you that the employer misidentified her as the subject of a random test, or directed her to take a reasonable suspicion or post-accident test without proper grounds under a DOT agency drug or alcohol regulation, you must inform the employee that you cannot play a role in deciding these issues.

(d) It is not your function to consider explanations of confirmed positive, adulterated, or substituted test results that would not, even if true, constitute a legitimate medical explanation. For example, an employee may tell you that someone slipped amphetamines into her drink at a party, that she unknowingly ingested a marijuana brownie, or that she traveled in a closed car with several people smoking crack. MROs are unlikely to be able to verify the facts of such passive or unknowing ingestion stories. Even if true, such stories do not present a legitimate medical explanation. Consequently, you must not declare a test as negative based on an explanation of this kind.

(e) You must not verify a test negative based on information that a physician recommended that the employee use a drug listed in Schedule I of the Controlled Substances Act. (e.g., under a state law that purports to authorize such recommendations, such as the "medical marijuana" laws that some states have adopted).

(f) You must not accept an assertion of consumption or other use of a hemp or other non-prescription marijuana-related product as a basis for verifying a marijuana test negative. You also must not accept such an explanation related to consumption of coca teas as a basis for verifying a cocaine test result as negative. Consuming or using such a product is not a legitimate medical explanation.

(g) You must not accept an assertion that there is a legitimate medical explanation for the presence of PCP or 6-AM in a specimen. There are no legitimate medical explanations for the presence of these substances.

(h) You must not accept, as a legitimate medical explanation for an adulterated specimen, an assertion that soap, bleach, or glutaraldehyde entered a specimen through physiological means. There are no physiological means through which these substances can enter a specimen.

(i) You must not accept, as a legitimate medical explanation for a substituted specimen, an assertion that an employee can produce urine with no detectable creatinine. There are no physiological means through which a person can produce a urine specimen having this characteristic.

§40.153 How does the MRO notify employees of their right to a test of the split specimen?

(a) As the MRO, when you have verified a drug test as positive for a drug or drug metabolite, or as a refusal to test because of adulteration or substitution, you must notify the employee of his or her right to have the split specimen tested. You must also notify the employee of the procedures for requesting a test of the split specimen.

(b) You must inform the employee that he or she has 72 hours from the time you provide this notification to him or her to request a test of the split specimen.

(c) You must tell the employee how to contact you to make this request. You must provide telephone numbers or other information that will allow the employee to make this request. As the MRO, you must have the ability to receive the employee's calls at all times during the 72 hour period (*e.g.*, by use of an answering machine with a "time stamp" feature when there is no one in your office to answer the phone).

(d) You must tell the employee that if he or she makes this request within 72 hours, the employer must ensure that the test takes place, and that the employee is not required to pay for the test from his or her own funds before the test takes place. You must also tell the employee that the employer may seek reimbursement for the cost of the test (see §40.173).

(e) You must tell the employee that additional tests of the specimen *e.g.*, (DNA tests) are not authorized.

§40.155 What does the MRO do when a negative or positive test result is also dilute?

(a) When the laboratory reports that a specimen is dilute or reports that a specimen is substituted with a creatinine quanitation of greater than or equal to 2 mg/dL, you must, as the MRO, report to the DER that the specimen, in addition to being negative or positive, is dilute.

(b) You must check the "dilute" box (Step 6) on Copy 2 of the CCF.

(c) When you report a dilute specimen to the DER, you must explain to the DER the employer's obligations and choices under §40.197.

§40.157 [Reserved]

§40.159 What does the MRO do when a drug test result is invalid?

(a) As the MRO, when the laboratory reports that the test result is an invalid result, you must do the following:

(1) Discuss the laboratory results with a certifying scientist to obtain more specific information.

(2) Contact the employee and inform the employee that the specimen was invalid or contained an unexplained interfering substance. In contacting the employee, use the procedures set forth in §40.131.

(3) After explaining the limits of disclosure (see §§40.135(d) and 40.327), you should inquire as to medications the employee may have taken that may interfere with some immunoassay tests.

(4) If the employee gives an explanation that is acceptable, you must:

(i) Place a check mark in the "Test Cancelled" box (Step 6) on Copy 2 of the CCF and enter "Invalid Result" and "direct observation collection not required" on the "Remarks" line.

(ii) Report to the DER that the test is cancelled, the reason for cancellation, and that no further action is required unless a negative test result is required (i.e., pre-employment, return-to-duty, or follow-up tests).

(5) If the employee is unable to provide an explanation and/or a valid prescription for a medication that interfered with the immunoassay test but denies having adulterated the specimen, you must:

(i) Place a check mark in the "Test Cancelled" box (Step 6) on Copy 2 of the CCF and enter "Invalid Result" and "direct observation collection required" on the "Remarks" line.

(ii) Report to the DER that the test is cancelled, the reason for cancellation, and that a second collection must take place immediately under direct observation.

(iii) Instruct the employer to ensure that the employee has the minimum possible advance notice that he or she must go to the collection site.

(b) You may only report an invalid test result when you are in possession of a legible copy of Copy 1 of the CCF. In addition, you must have Copy 2 of the CCF, a legible copy of it, or any other copy of the CCF containing the employee's signature.

(c) If the employee admits to having adulterated or substituted the specimen, you must, on the same day, write and sign your own statement of what the employee told you. You must then report a refusal to test in accordance with §40.163.

§40.161 What does the MRO do when a drug test specimen is rejected for testing?

As the MRO, when the laboratory reports that the specimen is rejected for testing (*e.g.,* because of a fatal or uncorrected flaw), you must do the following:

(a) Place a check mark in the "Test Cancelled" box (Step 6) on Copy 2 of the CCF and enter the reason on the "Remarks" line.

(b) Report to the DER that the test is cancelled and the reason for cancellation, and that no further action is required unless a negative test is required (*e.g.,* in the case of a pre-employment, return-to-duty, or follow-up test).

(c) You may only report a test cancelled because of a rejected for testing test result when you are in possession of a legible copy of Copy 1 of the CCF. In addition, you must have Copy 2 of the CCF, a legible copy of it, or any other copy of the CCF containing the employee's signature.

§40.163 How does the MRO report drug test results?

(a) As the MRO, it is your responsibility to report all drug test results to the employer.

(b) You may use a signed or stamped and dated legible photocopy of Copy 2 of the CCF to report test results.

(c) If you do not report test results using Copy 2 of the CCF for this purpose, you must provide a written report (e.g., a letter) for each test result. This report must, as a minimum, include the following information:

(1) Full name, as indicated on the CCF, of the employee tested;

(2) Specimen ID number from the CCF and the donor SSN or employee ID number;

(3) Reason for the test, if indicated on the CCF (e.g., random, post-accident);

(4) Date of the collection;

(5) Date you received Copy 2 of the CCF;

(6) Result of the test (i.e., positive, negative, dilute, refusal to test, test cancelled) and the date the result was verified by the MRO;

(7) For verified positive tests, the drug(s)/metabolite(s) for which the test was positive;

(8) For cancelled tests, the reason for cancellation; and

(9) For refusals to test, the reason for the refusal determination (e.g., in the case of an adulterated test result, the name of the adulterant).

(d) As an exception to the reporting requirements of paragraph (b) and (c) of this section, the MRO may report negative results using an electronic data file.

(1) If you report negatives using an electronic data file, the report must contain, as a minimum, the information specified in paragraph (c) of this section, as applicable for negative test results.

(2) In addition, the report must contain your name, address, and phone number, the name of any person other than you reporting the results, and the date the electronic results report is released.

(e) You must retain a signed or stamped and dated copy of Copy 2 of the CCF in your records. If you do not use Copy 2 for reporting results, you must maintain a copy of the signed or stamped and dated letter in addition to the signed or stamped and dated Copy 2. If you use the electronic data file to report negatives, you must maintain a retrievable copy of that report in a format suitable for inspection and auditing by a DOT representative.

(f) You must not use Copy 1 of the CCF to report drug test results.

(g) You must not provide quantitative values to the DER or C/TPA for drug or validity test results. However, you must provide the test information in your possession to a SAP who consults with you (see §40.293(g)).

§40.165 To whom does the MRO transmit reports of drug test results?

(a) As the MRO, you must report all drug test results to the DER, except in the circumstances provided for in §40.345.

(b) If the employer elects to receive reports of results through a C/TPA, acting as an intermediary as provided in §40.345, you must report the results through the designated C/TPA.

§40.167 How are MRO reports of drug results transmitted to the employer?

As the MRO or C/TPA who transmits drug test results to the employer, you must comply with the following requirements:

(a) You must report the results in a confidential manner.

(b) You must transmit to the DER on the same day the MRO verifies the result or the next business day all verified positive test results, results requiring an immediate collection under direct observation, adulterated or substituted specimen results, and other refusals to test.

(1) Direct telephone contact with the DER is the preferred method of immediate reporting. Follow up your phone call with appropriate documentation (see §40.163).

(2) You are responsible for identifying yourself to the DER, and the DER must have a means to confirm your identification.

(3) The MRO's report that you transmit to the employer must contain all of the information required by §40.163.

(c) You must transmit the MRO's report(s) of verified tests to the DER so that the DER receives it within two days of verification by the MRO.

(1) You must fax, courier, mail, or electronically transmit a legible image or copy of either the signed or stamped and dated Copy 2 or the written report (see §40.163(b) and (c)).

(2) Negative results reported electronically (i.e., computer data file) do not require an image of Copy 2 or the written report.

(d) In transmitting test results, you or the C/TPA and the employer must ensure the security of the transmission and limit access to any transmission, storage, or retrieval systems.

(e) MRO reports are not subject to modification or change by anyone other than the MRO, as provided in §40.149(c).

§40.169 Where is other information concerning the role of MROs and the verification process found in this regulation?

You can find more information concerning the role of MROs in several sections of this part:

§40.3—Definition.

§§40.47-40.49—Correction of form and kit errors.

§40.67—Role in direct observation and other atypical test situations.

§40.83—Laboratory handling of fatal and correctable flaws.

Subpart H — Split Specimen Tests

§40.171 How does an employee request a test of a split specimen?

(a) As an employee, when the MRO has notified you that you have a verified positive drug test or refusal to test because of adulteration or substitution, you have 72 hours from the time of notification to request a test of the split specimen. The request may be verbal or in writing. If you make this request to the MRO within 72 hours, you trigger the requirements of this section for a test of the split specimen.

(b)(1) If, as an employee, you have not requested a test of the split specimen within 72 hours, you may present to the MRO information documenting that serious injury, illness, lack of actual notice of the verified test result, inability to contact the MRO (*e.g.*, there was no one in the MRO's office and the answering machine was not working), or other circumstances unavoidably prevented you from making a timely request.

(2) As the MRO, if you conclude from the employee's information that there was a legitimate reason for the employee's failure to contact you within 72 hours, you must direct that the test of the split specimen take place, just as you would when there is a timely request.

(c) When the employee makes a timely request for a test of the split specimen under paragraphs (a) and (b) of this section, you must, as the MRO, immediately provide written notice to the laboratory that tested the primary specimen, directing the laboratory to forward the split specimen to a second HHS-certified laboratory. You must also document the date and time of the employee's request.

§40.173 Who is responsible for paying for the test of a split specimen?

(a) As the employer, you are responsible for making sure (e.g., by establishing appropriate accounts with laboratories for testing split specimens) that the MRO, first laboratory, and second laboratory perform the functions noted in §§40.175-40.185 in a timely manner, once the employee has made a timely request for a test of the split specimen.

(b) As the employer, you must not condition your compliance with these requirements on the employee's direct payment to the MRO or laboratory or the employee's agreement to reimburse you for the costs of testing. For example, if you ask the employee to pay for some or all of the cost of testing the split specimen, and the employee is unwilling or unable to do so, you must ensure that the test takes place in a timely manner, even though this means that you pay for it.

(c) As the employer, you may seek payment or reimbursement of all or part of the cost of the split specimen from the employee (e.g., through your written company policy or a collective bargaining agreement). This part takes no position on who ultimately pays the cost of the test, so long as the employer ensures that the testing is conducted as required and the results released appropriately.

§40.175 What steps does the first laboratory take with a split specimen?

(a) As the laboratory at which the primary and split specimen first arrive, you must check to see whether the split specimen is available for testing.

(b) If the split specimen is unavailable or appears insufficient, you must then do the following:

(1) Continue the testing process for the primary specimen as you would normally. Report the results for the primary specimen without providing the MRO information regarding the unavailable split specimen.

(2) Upon receiving a letter from the MRO instructing you to forward the split specimen to another laboratory for testing, report to the MRO that the split specimen is unavailable for testing. Provide as much information as you can about the cause of the unavailability.

(c) As the laboratory that tested the primary specimen, you are not authorized to open the split specimen under any circumstances (except when the split specimen is redesignated as provided in §40.83).

(d) When you receive written notice from the MRO instructing you to send the split specimen to another HHS-certified laboratory, you must forward the following items to the second laboratory:

(1) The split specimen in its original specimen bottle, with the seal intact;

(2) A copy of the MRO's written request; and

(3) A copy of Copy 1 of the CCF, which identifies the drug(s)/metabolite(s) or the validity criteria to be tested for.

(e) You must not send to the second laboratory any information about the identity of the employee. Inadvertent disclosure does not, however, cause a fatal flaw.

(f) This subpart does not prescribe who gets to decide which HHS-certified laboratory is used to test the split specimen. That decision is left to the parties involved.

§40.177 What does the second laboratory do with the split specimen when it is tested to reconfirm the presence of a drug or drug metabolite?

(a) As the laboratory testing the split specimen, you must test the split specimen for the drug(s)/drug metabolite(s) detected in the primary specimen.

(b) You must conduct this test without regard to the cutoff concentrations of §40.87.

(c) If the test fails to reconfirm the presence of the drug(s)/drug metabolite(s) that were reported positive in the primary specimen, you must conduct validity tests in an attempt to determine the reason for being unable to reconfirm the presence of the drug(s)/metabolite(s). You should conduct the same validity tests as you would conduct on a primary specimen set forth in §40.91.

(d) In addition, if the test fails to reconfirm the presence of the drugs/drugs metabolites or validity criteria that were reported in the primary specimen, you may transmit the specimen or an aliquot of it to another HHS-certified laboratory that will conduct another reconfirmation test.

§40.179 What does the second laboratory do with the split specimen when it is tested to reconfirm an adulterated test result?

As the laboratory testing the split specimen, you must test the split specimen for the adulterant detected in the primary specimen, using the criteria of §40.95 just as you would do for a primary specimen. The result of the primary specimen is reconfirmed if the split specimen meets these criteria.

§40.181 What does the second laboratory do with the split specimen when it is tested to reconfirm a substituted test result?

As the laboratory testing the split specimen, you must test the split specimen using the criteria of §40.93(b), just as you would do for a primary specimen. The result of the primary specimen is reconfirmed if the split specimen meets these criteria.

§40.183 What information do laboratories report to MROs regarding split specimen results?

(a) As the laboratory responsible for testing the split specimen, you must report split specimen test results by checking the "Reconfirmed" box or the "Failed to Reconfirm" box (Step 5(b)) on Copy 1 of the CCF.

(b) If you check the "Failed to Reconfirm" box, one of the following statements must be included (as appropriate) on the "Reason" line (Step 5(b)):

(1) "Drug(s)/Drug Metabolite(s) Not Detected."

(2) "Adulterant not found within criteria."

(3) "Specimen not consistent with substitution criteria [specify creatinine, specific gravity, or both]"

(4) "Specimen not available for testing."

(c) As the laboratory certifying scientist, enter your name, sign, and date the CCF.

§40.185 Through what methods and to whom must a laboratory report split specimen results?

(a) As the laboratory testing the split specimen, you must report laboratory results directly, and only, to the MRO at his or her place of business. You must not report results to or through the DER or another service agent (*e.g.*, a C/TPA).

(b) You must fax, courier, mail, or electronically transmit a legible image or copy of the fully-completed Copy 1 of the CCF, which has been signed by the certifying scientist.

(c) You must transmit the laboratory result to the MRO immediately, preferably on the same day or next business day as the result is signed and released.

§40.187 What does the MRO do with split specimen laboratory results?

As an MRO, you must take the following actions when a laboratory reports the following results of split specimen tests:

(a) **Reconfirmed.** (1) In the case of a reconfirmed positive test for a drug or drug metabolite, report the reconfirmation to the DER and the employee.

(2) In the case of a reconfirmed adulterated or substituted result, report to the DER and the employee that the specimen was adulterated or substituted, either of which constitutes a refusal to test. Therefore, "refusal to test" is the final result.

(3) In the case of a reconfirmed substituted result, in which the creatinine concentration for the primary specimen was less than 2 mg/dL and the creatinine concentration of the split specimen is between 2 and 5 mg/DL, inclusive, report the result to the employer as "dilute" and instruct the employer to conduct an immediate recollection under direct observation.

(b) **Failed to Reconfirm: Drug(s)/Drug Metabolite(s) Not Detected.** (1) Report to the DER and the employee that both tests must be cancelled.

(2) Using the format in Appendix D to this part, inform ODAPC of the failure to reconfirm.

(c) **Failed to Reconfirm: Adulteration or Substitution (as appropriate) Criteria Not Met.** (1) Report to the DER and the employee that both tests must be cancelled.

(2) Using the format in Appendix D to this part, inform ODAPC of the failure to reconfirm.

(d) **Failed to Reconfirm: Specimen not Available for Testing.** (1) Report to the DER and the employee that both tests must be cancelled and the reason for cancellation.

(2) Direct the DER to ensure the immediate collection of another specimen from the employee under direct observation, with no notice given to the employee of this collection requirement until immediately before the collection.

(3) Using the format in Appendix D to this part, notify

ODAPC of the failure to reconfirm.

(e) **Failed to Reconfirm: Specimen Results Invalid.**

(1) Report to the DER and the employee that both tests must be cancelled and the reason for cancellation.

(2) Direct the DER to ensure the immediate collection of another specimen from the employee under direct observation, with no notice given to the employee of this collection requirement until immediately before the collection.

(3) Using the format in Appendix D to this part, notify ODAPC of the failure to reconfirm.

(f) **Failed to Reconfirm: Split Specimen Adulterated.**

(1) Contact the employee and inform the employee that the laboratory has determined that his or her split specimen is adulterated.

(2) Follow the procedures of §40.145 to determine if there is a legitimate medical explanation for the laboratory finding of adulteration.

(3) If you determine that there is a legitimate medical explanation for the adulterated test result, report to the DER and the employee that the test is cancelled. Using the format in Appendix D to this part, notify ODAPC of the result.

(4) If you determine that there is not a legitimate medical explanation for the adulterated test result, take the following steps:

(i) Report the test to the DER and the employee as a verified refusal to test. Inform the employee that he or she has 72 hours to request a test of the primary specimen to determine if the adulterant found in the split specimen also is present in the primary specimen.

(ii) Except that the request is for a test of the primary specimen and is being made to the laboratory that tested the primary specimen, follow the procedures of §§40.153, 40.171, 40.173, 40.179, and 40.185.

(iii) As the laboratory that tests the primary specimen to reconfirm the presence of the adulterant found in the split specimen, report your result to the MRO on a photocopy (faxed, mailed, scanned, couriered) of Copy 1 of the CCF.

(iv) If the test of the primary specimen reconfirms the adulteration finding of the split specimen, as the MRO you must report the test result as a refusal as provided in §40.187(a)(2).

(v) If the test of the primary specimen fails to reconfirm the adulteration finding of the split specimen, as the MRO you cancel the test. Follow the procedures of paragraph (e) of this section in this situation.

(g) Enter your name, sign and date (Step 7) of Copy 2 of the CCF.

(h) Send a legible copy of Copy 2 of the CCF (or a signed and dated letter, see §40.163) to the employer and keep a copy for your records. Transmit the document as provided in §40.167.

§40.189 Where is other information concerning split specimens found in this regulation?

You can find more information concerning split specimens in several sections of this part:

§40.3—Definition.

§40.65—Quantity of split specimen.

§40.67—Directly observed test when split specimen is unavailable.

§§40.71-40.73—Collection process for split specimens.

§40.83—Laboratory accessioning of split specimens.

§40.99—Laboratory retention of split specimens.

§40.103—Blind split specimens.

§40.153—MRO notice to employees on tests of split specimen.

§§40.193 and 40.201—MRO actions on insufficient or unavailable split specimens.

Appendix D to Part 40 — Report format for split specimen failure to reconfirm.

Subpart I — Problems in Drug Tests

§40.191 What is a refusal to take a DOT drug test, and what are the consequences?

(a) As an employee, you have refused to take a drug test if you:

(1) Fail to appear for any test (except a pre-employment test) within a reasonable time, as determined by the employer, consistent with applicable DOT agency regulations, after being directed to do so by the employer. This includes the failure of an employee (including an owner-operator) to appear for a test when called by a C/TPA (see §40.61(a);

(2) *Fail to remain at the testing site until the testing process is complete; Provided,* That an employee who leaves the testing site before the testing process commences (see §40.63 (c)) for a pre-employment test is not deemed to have refused to test;

(3) Fail to provide a urine specimen for any drug test required by this part or DOT agency regulations; *Provided*, That an employee who does not provide a urine specimen because he or she has left the testing site before the testing process commences (see §40.63 (c)) for a pre-employment test is not deemed to have refused to test;

(4) In the case of a directly observed or monitored collection in a drug test, fail to permit the observation or monitoring of your provision of a specimen (see §§40.67(l) and 40.69(g));

(5) Fail to provide a sufficient amount of urine when directed, and it has been determined, through a required medical evaluation, that there was no adequate medical explanation for the failure (see §40.193(d)(2));

(6) Fail or decline to take an additional drug test the employer or collector has directed you to take (see, for instance, §40.197(b));

(7) Fail to undergo a medical examination or evaluation, as directed by the MRO as part of the verification process, or as directed by the DER under §40.193(d). In the case of a pre-employment drug test, the employee is deemed to have refused to test on this basis only if the pre-employment test is conducted following a contingent offer of employment; or

(8) Fail to cooperate with any part of the testing process (*e.g.*, refuse to empty pockets when so directed by the collector, behave in a confrontational way that disrupts the collection process).

(b) As an employee, if the MRO reports that you have a verified adulterated or substituted test result, you have refused to take a drug test.

(c) As an employee, if you refuse to take a drug test, you incur the consequences specified under DOT agency regulations for a violation of those DOT agency regulations.

(d) As a collector or an MRO, when an employee refuses to participate in the part of the testing process in which you are involved, you must terminate the portion of the testing process in which you are involved, document the refusal on the CCF (including in the case of the collector, printing the employee's name on Copy 2 of the CCF), immediately notify the DER by any means (*e.g.*, telephone or secure fax machine) that ensures that the refusal notification is immediately received. As a referral physician (*e.g.*, physician evaluating a "shy bladder" condition or a claim of a legitimate medical explanation in a validity testing situation), you must notify the MRO, who in turn will notify the DER.

§40.193

(1) As the collector, you must note the refusal in the "Remarks" line (Step 2), and sign and date the CCF.

(2) As the MRO, you must note the refusal by checking the "refused to test because" box (Step 6) on Copy 2 of the CCF, and add the reason on the "Remarks" line. You must then sign and date the CCF.

(e) As an employee, when you refuse to take a non-DOT test or to sign a non-DOT form, you have not refused to take a DOT test. There are no consequences under DOT agency regulations for refusing to take a non-DOT test.

§40.193 What happens when an employee does not provide a sufficient amount of urine for a drug test?

(a) This section prescribes procedures for situations in which an employee does not provide a sufficient amount of urine to permit a drug test (*i.e.*, 45 mL of urine).

(b) As the collector, you must do the following:

(1) Discard the insufficient specimen, except where the insufficient specimen was out of temperature range or showed evidence of adulteration or tampering (see §40.65(b) and (c)).

(2) Urge the employee to drink up to 40 ounces of fluid, distributed reasonably through a period of up to three hours, or until the individual has provided a sufficient urine specimen, whichever occurs first. It is not a refusal to test if the employee declines to drink. Document on the Remarks line of the CCF (Step 2), and inform the employee of, the time at which the three-hour peiod begins and ends.

(3) If the employee refuses to make the attempt to provide a new urine specimen or leaves the collection site before the collection process is complete, you must discontinue the collection, note the fact on the "Remarks" line of the CCF (Step 2), and immediately notify the DER. This is a refusal to test.

(4) If the employee has not provided a sufficient specimen within three hours of the first unsuccessful attempt to provide the specimen, you must discontinue the collection, note the fact on the "Remarks" line of the CCF (Step 2), and immediately notify the DER.

(5) Send Copy 2 of the CCF to the MRO and Copy 4 to the DER. You must send or fax these copies to the MRO and DER within 24 hours or the next business day.

(c) As the DER, when the collector informs you that the employee has not provided a sufficient amount of urine (see paragraph (b)(4) of this section), you must, after consulting with the MRO, direct the employee to obtain, within five working days, an evaluation from a licensed physician, acceptable to the MRO, who has expertise in the medical issues raised by the employee's failure to provide a sufficient specimen. (The MRO may perform this evaluation if the MRO has appropriate expertise.)

(1) As the MRO, if another physician will perform the evaluation, you must provide the other physician with the following information and instructions:

(i) That the employee was required to take a DOT drug test, but was unable to provide a sufficient amount of urine to complete the test;

(ii) The consequences of the appropriate DOT agency regulation for refusing to take the required drug test;

(iii) That the referral physician must agree to follow the requirements of paragraphs (d) through (g) of this section.

(2) [Reserved.]

(d) As the referral physician conducting this evaluation, you must recommend that the MRO make one of the following determinations:

(1) A medical condition has, or with a high degree of probability could have, precluded the employee from providing a sufficient amount of urine. As the MRO, if you accept this recommendation, you must:

(i) Check "Test Cancelled" (Step 6) on the CCF; and

(ii) Sign and date the CCF.

(2) There is not an adequate basis for determining that a medical condition has, or with a high degree of probability could have, precluded the employee from providing a sufficient amount of urine. As the MRO, if you accept this recommendation, you must:

(i) Check "Refusal to test because" (Step 6) on the CCF and enter reason in the remarks line; and

(ii) Sign and date the CCF.

(e) For purposes of this paragraph, a medical condition includes an ascertainable physiological condition (*e.g.*, a urinary system dysfunction) or a medically documented pre-existing psychological disorder, but does not include unsupported assertions of "situational anxiety" or dehydration.

(f) As the referral physician making the evaluation, after completing your evaluation, you must provide a written statement of your recommendations and the basis for them to the MRO. You must not include in this statement detailed information on the employee's medical condition beyond what is necessary to explain your conclusion.

(g) If, as the referral physician making this evaluation in the case of a pre-employment test, you determine that the employee's medical condition is a serious and permanent or long-term disability that is highly likely to prevent the employee from providing a sufficient amount of urine for a very long or indefinite period of time, you must set forth your determination and the reasons for it in your written statement to the MRO. As the MRO, upon receiving such a report, you must follow the requirements of §40.195, where applicable.

(h) As the MRO, you must seriously consider and assess the referral physician's recommendations in making your determination about whether the employee has a medical condition that has, or with a high degree of probability could have, precluded the employee from providing a sufficient amount of urine. You must report your determination to the DER in writing as soon as you make it.

(i) As the employer, when you receive a report from the MRO indicating that a test is cancelled as provided in paragraph (d)(1) of this section, you take no further action with respect to the employee. The employee remains in the random testing pool.

§40.195 **What happens when an individual is unable to provide a sufficient amount of urine for a pre-employment, follow-up, or return-to-duty test because of a permanent or long-term medical condition?**

(a) This section concerns a situation in which an employee has a medical condition that precludes him or her from providing a sufficient specimen for a pre-employment, follow-up, or return-to-duty test and the condition involves a permanent or long-term disability. As the MRO in this situation, you must do the following:

(1) You must determine if there is clinical evidence that the individual is an illicit drug user. You must make this determination by personally conducting, or causing to be conducted, a medical evaluation and through consultation with the em-

ployee's physician and/or the physician who conducted the evaluation under §40.193(d).

(2) If you do not personally conduct the medical evaluation, you must ensure that one is conducted by a licensed physician acceptable to you.

(3) For purposes of this section, the MRO or the physician conducting the evaluation may conduct an alternative test (*e.g.*, blood) as part of the medically appropriate procedures in determining clinical evidence of drug use.

(b) If the medical evaluation reveals no clinical evidence of drug use, as the MRO, you must report the result to the employer as a negative test with written notations regarding results of both the evaluation conducted under §40.193(d) and any further medical examination. This report must state the basis for the determination that a permanent or long-term medical condition exists, making provision of a sufficient urine specimen impossible, and for the determination that no signs and symptoms of drug use exist.

(1) Check "Negative" (Step 6) on the CCF.

(2) Sign and date the CCF.

(c) If the medical evaluation reveals clinical evidence of drug use, as the MRO, you must report the result to the employer as a cancelled test with written notations regarding results of both the evaluation conducted under §40.193(d) and any further medical examination. This report must state that a permanent or long-term medical condition exists, making provision of a sufficient urine specimen impossible, and state the reason for the determination that signs and symptoms of drug use exist. Because this is a cancelled test, it does not serve the purposes of a negative test (*i.e.*, the employer is not authorized to allow the employee to begin or resume performing safety-sensitive functions, because a negative test is needed for that purpose).

(d) For purposes of this section, permanent or long-term medical conditions are those physiological, anatomic, or psychological abnormalities documented as being present prior to the attempted collection, and considered not amenable to correction or cure for an extended period of time, if ever.

(1) Examples would include destruction (any cause) of the glomerular filtration system leading to renal failure; unrepaired traumatic disruption of the urinary tract; or a severe psychiatric disorder focused on genito-urinary matters.

(2) Acute or temporary medical conditions, such as cystitis, urethritis or prostatitis, though they might interfere with collection for a limited period of time, cannot receive the same exceptional consideration as the permanent or long-term conditions discussed in paragraph (d)(1) of this section.

§40.197 What happens when an employer receives a report of a dilute specimen?

(a) As the employer, if the MRO informs you that a positive drug test was dilute, you simply treat the test as a verified positive test. You must not direct the employee to take another test based on the fact that the specimen was dilute.

(b) As an employer, if the MRO informs you that a negative test was dilute, take the following action:

(1) If the MRO directs you to conduct a recollection under direct observation (i.e., because the creatinine concentration of the specimen was equal to or greater than 2mg/dL, but less than or equal to 5 mg/dL (see §40.145(a)(1)), you must do so immediately.

(2) Otherwise (i.e., if the creatinine concentration of the dilute specimen is greater than 5 mg/dL), you may, but are not required to, direct the employee to take another test immediately.

(i) Such recollections must not be collected under direct observation, unless there is another basis for use of direct observation (see §40.67 (b) and (c)).

(ii) You must treat all employees the same for this purpose. For example, you must not retest some employees and not others. You may, however, establish different policies for different types of tests (e.g., conduct retests in pre-employment situations, but not in random test situations). You must inform your employees in advance of your decisions on these matters.

(c) The following provisions apply to all tests you direct an employee to take under paragraph (b) of this section:

(1) You must ensure that the employee is given the minimum possible advance notice that he or she must go to the collection site;

(2) You must treat the result of the test you directed the employee to take under paragraph (b) of this section-and not a prior test-as the test result of record, on which you rely for purposes of this part;

(3) If the result of the test you directed the employee to take under paragraph (b) of this section is also negative and dilute, you are not permitted to make the employee take an additional test because the result was dilute. Provided, however, that if the MRO di-

rects you to conduct a recollection under direct observation under paragraph (b)(1) of this section, you must immediately do so.

(4) If the employee declines to take a test you directed him or her to take under paragraph (b) of this section, the employee has refused the test for purposes of this part and DOT agency regulations.

§40.199 What problems always cause a drug test to be cancelled?

(a) As the MRO, when the laboratory discovers a "fatal flaw" during its processing of incoming specimens (see §40.83), the laboratory will report to you that the specimen has been "Rejected for Testing" (with the reason stated). You must always cancel such a test.

(b) The following are "fatal flaws":

(1) There is no printed collector's name *and* no collector's signature;

(2) The specimen ID numbers on the specimen bottle and the CCF do not match;

(3) The specimen bottle seal is broken or shows evidence of tampering (and a split specimen cannot be redesignated, see §40.83(g)); and

(4) Because of leakage or other causes, there is an insufficient amount of urine in the primary specimen bottle for analysis and the specimens cannot be redesignated (see §40.83(g)).

(c) You must report the result as provided in §40.161.

§40.201 What problems always cause a drug test to be cancelled and may result in a requirement for another collection?

As the MRO, you must cancel a drug test when a laboratory reports that any of the following problems have occurred. You must inform the DER that the test was cancelled. You must also direct the DER to ensure that an additional collection occurs immediately, if required by the applicable procedures specified in paragraphs (a) through (e) of this section.

(a) The laboratory reports an "Invalid Result" You must follow applicable procedures in §40.159 (recollection under direct observation may be required).

(b) The laboratory reports the result as "Rejected for Testing" You must follow applicable procedures in §40.161 (a recollection may be required).

(c) The laboratory's test of the primary specimen is positive and the split specimen is reported by the laboratory as "Failure to Reconfirm: Drug(s)/Drug Metabolite(s) Not Detected" You must follow applicable procedures in §40.187(b) (no recollection is required in this case).

(d) The laboratory's test result for the primary specimen is adulterated or substituted and the split specimen is reported by the laboratory as "Adulterant not found within criteria," or specimen not consistent with substitution criteria, as applicable. You must follow applicable procedures in §40.187(c) (no recollection is required in this case).

(e) The laboratory's test of the primary specimen is positive, adulterated, or substituted and the split specimen is unavailable for testing. You must follow applicable procedures in §40.187(d) (recollection under direct observation is required in this case).

(f) The examining physician has determined that there is an acceptable medical explanation of the employee's failure to provide a sufficient amount of urine. You must follow applicable procedures in §40.193(d)(1) (no recollection is required in this case).

§40.203 What problems cause a drug test to be cancelled unless they are corrected?

(a) As the MRO, when a laboratory discovers a "correctable flaw" during its processing of incoming specimens (see §40.83), the laboratory will attempt to correct it. If the laboratory is unsuccessful in this attempt, it will report to you that the specimen has been "Rejected for Testing" (with the reason stated).

(b) The following is a "correctable flaw" that laboratories must attempt to correct: The collector's signature is omitted on the certification statement on the CCF.

(c) As the MRO, when you discover a "correctable flaw" during your review of the CCF, you must cancel the test unless the flaw is corrected.

(d) The following are correctable flaws that you must attempt to correct:

(1) The employee's signature is omitted from the certification statement, unless the employee's failure or refusal to sign is noted on the "Remarks" line of the CCF.

(2) The certifying scientist's signature is omitted on the laboratory copy of the CCF for a positive, adulterated, substituted, or invalid test result.

(3) The collector uses a non-Federal form or an expired Federal form for the test. This flaw may be corrected through the procedure set forth in §40.205(b)(2), provided that the collection

testing process has been conducted in accordance with the procedures of this part in an HHS-certified laboratory. During the period August 1–October 31, 2001, you are not required to cancel a test because of the use of an expired Federal form. Beginning November 1, 2001, if the problem is not corrected, you must cancel the test.

§40.205 How are drug test problems corrected?

(a) As a collector, you have the responsibility of trying to successfully complete a collection procedure for each employee.

(1) If, during or shortly after the collection process, you become aware of any event that prevents the completion of a valid test or collection (*e.g.*, a procedural or paperwork error), you must try to correct the problem promptly, if doing so is practicable. You may conduct another collection as part of this effort.

(2) If another collection is necessary, you must begin the new collection procedure as soon as possible, using a new CCF and a new collection kit.

(b) If, as a collector, laboratory, MRO, employer, or other person implementing these drug testing regulations, you become aware of a problem that can be corrected (see §40.203), but which has not already been corrected under paragraph (a) of this section, you must take all practicable action to correct the problem so that the test is not cancelled.

(1) If the problem resulted from the omission of required information, you must, as the person responsible for providing that information, supply in writing the missing information and a statement that it is true and accurate. For example, suppose you are a collector, and you forgot to make a notation on the "Remarks" line of the CCF that the employee did not sign the certification. You would, when the problem is called to your attention, supply a signed statement that the employee failed or refused to sign the certification and that your statement is true and accurate. You must supply this information on the same business day on which you are notified of the problem, transmitting it by fax or courier.

(2) If the problem is the use of a non-Federal form or an expired Federal form, you must provide a signed statement (i.e., a memorandum for the record). It must state that the incorrect form contains all the information needed for a valid DOT drug test, and that the incorrect form was used inadvertently or as the only means of conducting a test, in circumstances beyond

your control. The statement must also list the steps you have taken to prevent future use of non-Federal forms or expired Federal forms for DOT tests. For this flaw to be corrected, the test of the specimen must have occurred at a HHS-certified laboratory where it was tested consistent with the requirements of this part. You must supply this information on the same business day on which you are notified of the problem, transmitting it by fax or courier.

(3) You must maintain the written documentation of a correction with the CCF.

(4) You must mark the CCF in such a way (*e.g.*, stamp noting correction) as to make it obvious on the face of the CCF that you corrected the flaw.

(c) If the correction does not take place, as the MRO you must cancel the test.

§40.207 What is the effect of a cancelled drug test?

(a) A cancelled drug test is neither positive nor negative.

(1) As an employer, you must not attach to a cancelled test the consequences of a positive test or other violation of a DOT drug testing regulation (*e.g.*, removal from a safety-sensitive position).

(2) As an employer, you must not use a cancelled test for the purposes of a negative test to authorize the employee to perform safety-sensitive functions (*i.e.*, in the case of a pre-employment, return-to-duty, or follow-up test).

(3) However, as an employer, you must not direct a recollection for an employee because a test has been cancelled, except in the situations cited in paragraph (a)(2) of this section or other provisions of this part that require another test to be conducted (*e.g.*, §§40.159(a)(5) and 40.187(b)).

(b) A cancelled test does not count toward compliance with DOT requirements (*e.g.*, being applied toward the number of tests needed to meet the employer's minimum random testing rate).

(c) A cancelled DOT test does not provide a valid basis for an employer to conduct a non-DOT test (*i.e.*, a test under company authority).

§40.208 What problem requires corrective action but does not result in the cancellation of a test?

(a) If, as a laboratory, collector, employer, or other person implementing the DOT drug testing program, you become aware that the specimen temperature on the CCF was not checked and the "Remarks" line did not contain an entry regarding the temperature being out of range, you must take corrective action, including securing a memorandum for the record explaining the problem and taking appropriate action to ensure that the problem does not recur.

(b) This error does not result in the cancellation of the test.

(c) As an employer or service agent, this error, even though not sufficient to cancel a drug test result, may subject you to enforcement action under DOT agency regulations or Subpart R of this part.

§40.209 What procedural problems do not result in the cancellation of a test and do not require correction?

(a) As a collector, laboratory, MRO, employer or other person administering the drug testing process, you must document any errors in the testing process of which you become aware, even if they are not considered problems that will cause a test to be cancelled as listed in this subpart. Decisions about the ultimate impact of these errors will be determined by other administrative or legal proceedings, subject to the limitations of paragraph (b) of this section.

(b) No person concerned with the testing process may declare a test cancelled based on an error that does not have a significant adverse effect on the right of the employee to have a fair and accurate test. Matters that do not result in the cancellation of a test include, but are not limited to, the following:

(1) A minor administrative mistake (*e.g.,* the omission of the employee's middle initial, a transposition of numbers in the employee's social security number);

(2) An error that does not affect employee protections under this part (*e.g.,* the collector's failure to add bluing agent to the toilet bowl, which adversely affects only the ability of the collector to detect tampering with the specimen by the employee);

(3) The collection of a specimen by a collector who is required to have been trained (see §40.33), but who has not met this requirement;

(4) A delay in the collection process (see §40.61(a));

(5) Verification of a test result by an MRO who has the basic credentials to be qualified as an MRO (see §40.121(a) through (b)) but who has not met training and/or documentation requirements (see §40.121(c) through (e));

(6) The failure to directly observe or monitor a collection that the rule requires or permits to be directly observed or moni-

tored, or the unauthorized use of direct observation or monitoring for a collection;

(7) The fact that a test was conducted in a facility that does not meet the requirements of §40.41;

(8) If the specific name of the courier on the CCF is omitted or erroneous;

(9) Personal identifying information is inadvertently contained on the CCF (*e.g.,* the employee signs his or her name on the laboratory copy); or

(10) Claims that the employee was improperly selected for testing.

(c) As an employer or service agent these types of errors, even though not sufficient to cancel a drug test result, may subject you to enforcement action under DOT agency regulations or action under Subpart R of this part.

Subpart J — Alcohol Testing Personnel

§40.211 Who conducts DOT alcohol tests?

(a) Screening test technicians (STTs) and breath alcohol technicians (BATs) meeting their respective requirements of this subpart are the only people authorized to conduct DOT alcohol tests.

(b) An STT can conduct only alcohol screening tests, but a BAT can conduct alcohol screening and confirmation tests.

(c) As a BAT- or STT-qualified immediate supervisor of a particular employee, you may not act as the STT or BAT when that employee is tested, unless no other STT or BAT is available and DOT agency regulations do not prohibit you from doing so.

§40.213 What training requirements must STTs and BATs meet?

To be permitted to act as a BAT or STT in the DOT alcohol testing program, you must meet each of the requirements of this section:

(a) **Basic information.** You must be knowledgeable about the alcohol testing procedures in this part and the current DOT guidance. These documents and information are available from ODAPC (Department of Transportation, 400 7th Street, SW., Room 10403, Washington DC, 20590, 202-366-3784, or on the ODAPC web site, http://www.dot.gov/ost/dapc)).

(b) **Qualification training.** You must receive qualification training meeting the requirements of this paragraph (b).

§40.213

(1) Qualification training must be in accordance with the DOT Model BAT or STT Course, as applicable. The DOT Model Courses are available from ODAPC (Department of Transportation, 400 7th Street, SW., Room 10403, Washington DC, 20590, 202-366-3784, or on the ODAPC web site, http://www.dot.gov/ost/dapc). The training can also be provided using a course of instruction equivalent to the DOT Model Courses. On request, ODAPC will review BAT and STT instruction courses for equivalency.

(2) Qualification training must include training to proficiency in using the alcohol testing procedures of this part and in the operation of the particular alcohol testing device(s) (*i.e.,* the ASD(s) or EBT(s)) you will be using.

(3) The training must emphasize that you are responsible for maintaining the integrity of the testing process, ensuring the privacy of employees being tested, and avoiding conduct or statements that could be viewed as offensive or inappropriate.

(4) The instructor must be an individual who has demonstrated necessary knowledge, skills, and abilities by regularly conducting DOT alcohol tests as an STT or BAT, as applicable, for a period of at least a year, who has conducted STT or BAT training, as applicable, under this part for a year, or who has successfully completed a "train the trainer" course.

(c) **Initial Proficiency Demonstration.** Following your completion of qualification training under paragraph (b) of this section, you must demonstrate proficiency in alcohol testing under this part by completing seven consecutive error-free mock tests (BATs) or five consecutive error-free test (STTs).

(1) Another person must monitor and evaluate your performance, in person or by a means that provides real-time observation and interaction between the instructor and trainee, and attest in writing that the mock collections are "error-free." This person must be an individual who meets the requirements of paragraph (b)(4) of this section.

(2) These tests must use the alcohol testing devices (*e.g.,* EBT(s) or ASD(s)) that you will use as a BAT or STT.

(3) If you are an STT who will be using an ASD that indicates readings by changes, contrasts, or other readings in color, you must demonstrate as part of the mock test that you are able to discern changes, contrasts, or readings correctly.

(d) **Schedule for qualification training and initial proficiency demonstration.** The following is the schedule for qualification training and the initial proficiency demonstration you must meet:

(1) If you became a BAT or STT before August 1, 2001, you were required to have met the requirements set forth in paragraphs (b) and (c) of this section, and you do not have to meet them again.

(2) If you become a BAT or STT on or after August 1, 2001, you must meet the requirements of paragraphs (b) and (c) of this section before you begin to perform BAT or STT functions.

(e) **Refresher training.** No less frequently than every five years from the date on which you satisfactorily complete the requirements of paragraphs (b) and (c) of this section, you must complete refresher training that meets all the requirements of paragraphs (b) and (c) of this section. If you are a BAT or STT who completed qualification training before January 1, 1998, you are not required to complete refresher training until January 1, 2003.

(f) **Error Correction Training.** If you make a mistake in the alcohol testing process that causes a test to be cancelled (*i.e.,* a fatal or uncorrected flaw), you must undergo error correction training. This training must occur within 30 days of the date you are notified of the error that led to the need for retraining.

(1) Error correction training must be provided and your proficiency documented in writing by a person who meets the requirements of paragraph (b)(4) of this section.

(2) Error correction training is required to cover only the subject matter area(s) in which the error that caused the test to be cancelled occurred.

(3) As part of the error correction training, you must demonstrate your proficiency in the alcohol testing procedures of this part by completing three consecutive error-free mock tests. The mock tests must include one uneventful scenario and two scenarios related to the area(s) in which your error(s) occurred. The person providing the training must monitor and evaluate your performance and attest in writing that the mock tests were error-free.

(g) **Documentation.** You must maintain documentation showing that you currently meet all requirements of this section. You must provide this documentation on request to DOT agency representatives and to employers and C/TPAs who are negotiating to use your services.

(h) **Other persons who may serve as BATs or STTs.** (1) Anyone meeting the requirements of this section to be a BAT may act as an STT, provided that the individual has demonstrated initial proficiency in the operation of the ASD that he or she is using, as provided in paragraph (c) of this section.

(2) Law enforcement officers who have been certified by state or local governments to conduct breath alcohol testing are deemed to be qualified as BATs. They are not required to also complete the training requirements of this section in order to act as BATs. In order for a test conducted by such an officer to be accepted under DOT alcohol testing requirements, the officer must have been certified by a state or local government to use the EBT or ASD that was used for the test.

§40.215 What information about the DER do employers have to provide to BATs and STTs?

As an employer, you must provide to the STTs and BATs the name and telephone number of the appropriate DER (and C/TPA, where applicable) to contact about any problems or issues that may arise during the testing process.

§40.217 Where is other information on the role of STTs and BATs found in this regulation?

You can find other information on the role and functions of STTs and BATs in the following sections of this part:

§40.3—Definitions.

§40.223—Responsibility for supervising employees being tested.

§§40.225–40.227—Use of the alcohol testing form.

§§40.241–40.245—Screening test procedures with ASDs and EBTs.

§§40.251–40.255—Confirmation test procedures.

§40.261—Refusals to test.

§§40.263–40.265—Insufficient saliva or breath.

§40.267—Problems requiring cancellation of tests.

§§40.269–40.271—Correcting problems in tests.

Subpart K — Testing Sites, Forms, Equipment and Supplies Used in Alcohol Testing

§40.221 Where does an alcohol test take place?

(a) A DOT alcohol test must take place at an alcohol testing site meeting the requirements of this section.

(b) If you are operating an alcohol testing site, you must ensure that it meets the security requirements of §40.223.

§40.223

(c) If you are operating an alcohol testing site, you must ensure that it provides visual and aural privacy to the employee being tested, sufficient to prevent unauthorized persons from seeing or hearing test results.

(d) If you are operating an alcohol testing site, you must ensure that it has all needed personnel, materials, equipment, and facilities to provide for the collection and analysis of breath and/or saliva samples, and a suitable clean surface for writing.

(e) If an alcohol testing site fully meeting all the visual and aural privacy requirements of paragraph (c) is not readily available, this part allows a reasonable suspicion or post-accident test to be conducted at a site that partially meets these requirements. In this case, the site must afford visual and aural privacy to the employee to the greatest extent practicable.

(f) An alcohol testing site can be in a medical facility, a mobile facility (*e.g.*, a van), a dedicated collection facility, or any other location meeting the requirements of this section.

§40.223 What steps must be taken to protect the security of alcohol testing sites?

(a) If you are a BAT, STT, or other person operating an alcohol testing site, you must prevent unauthorized personnel from entering the testing site.

(1) The only people you are to treat as authorized persons are employees being tested, BATs, STTs, and other alcohol testing site workers, DERs, employee representatives authorized by the employer (*e.g.*, on the basis of employer policy or labor-management agreement), and DOT agency representatives.

(2) You must ensure that all persons are under the supervision of a BAT or STT at all times when permitted into the site.

(3) You may remove any person who obstructs, interferes with, or causes unnecessary delay in the testing process.

(b) As the BAT or STT, you must not allow any person other than you, the employee, or a DOT agency representative to actually witness the testing process (see §§40.241-40.255).

(c) If you are operating an alcohol testing site, you must ensure that when an EBT or ASD is not being used for testing, you store it in a secure place.

(d) If you are operating an alcohol testing site, you must ensure that no one other than BATs or other employees of the site have access to the site when an EBT is unsecured.

(e) As a BAT or STT, to avoid distraction that could compromise security, you are limited to conducting an alcohol test for only one employee at a time.

(1) When an EBT screening test on an employee indicates an alcohol concentration of 0.02 or higher, and the same EBT will be used for the confirmation test, you are not allowed to use the EBT for a test on another employee before completing the confirmation test on the first employee.

(2) As a BAT who will conduct both the screening and the confirmation test, you are to complete the entire screening and confirmation process on one employee before starting the screening process on another employee.

(3) You are not allowed to leave the alcohol testing site while the testing process for a given employee is in progress, except to notify a supervisor or contact a DER for assistance in the case an employee or other person who obstructs, interferes with, or unnecessarily delays the testing process.

§40.225 What form is used for an alcohol test?

(a) The DOT Alcohol Testing Form (ATF) must be used for every DOT alcohol test beginning February 1, 2002. The ATF must be a three-part carbonless manifold form. The ATF is found in Appendix G to this part. You may view this form on the ODAPC web site (http://www.dot.gov/ost/dapc).

(b) As an employer in the DOT alcohol testing program, you are not permitted to modify or revise the ATF except as follows:

(1) You may include other information needed for billing purposes, outside the boundaries of the form.

(2) You may use a ATF directly generated by an EBT which omits the space for affixing a separate printed result to the ATF, provided the EBT prints the result directly on the ATF.

(3) You may use an ATF that has the employer's name, address, and telephone number preprinted. In addition, a C/TPA's name, address, and telephone number may be included, to assist with negative results.

(4) You may use an ATF in which all pages are printed on white paper. You may modify the ATF by using colored paper, or have clearly discernable borders or designation statements on Copy 2 and Copy 3. When colors are used, they must be green for Copy 2 and blue for Copy 3.

(5) As a BAT or STT, you may add, on the "Remarks" line of the ATF, the name of the DOT agency under whose authority the test occurred.

(6) As a BAT or STT, you may use a ATF that has your name, address, and telephone number preprinted, but under no circumstances can your signature be preprinted.

(c) As an employer, you may use an equivalent foreign-language version of the ATF approved by ODAPC. You may use such a non-English language form only in a situation where both the employee and BAT/STT understand and can use the form in that language.

§40.227 May employers use the ATF for non-DOT tests, or non-DOT forms for DOT tests?

(a) No, as an employer, BAT, or STT, you are prohibited from using the ATF for non-DOT alcohol tests. You are also prohibited from using non-DOT forms for DOT alcohol tests. Doing either subjects you to enforcement action under DOT agency regulations.

(b) If the STT or BAT, either or by mistake, or as the only means to conduct a test under difficult circumstances (e.g., post-accident test with insufficient time to obtain the ATF), uses a non-DOT form for a DOT test, the use of a non-DOT form does not, in and of itself, require the employer or service agent to cancel the test. However, in order for the test to be considered valid, a signed statement must be obtained from the STT or BAT in accordance with §40.271(b).

§40.229 What devices are used to conduct alcohol screening tests?

EBTs and ASDs on the NHTSA conforming products lists (CPL) for evidential and non-evidential devices are the only devices you are allowed to use to conduct alcohol screening tests under this part. You may use an ASD that is on the NHTSA CPL for DOT alcohol tests only if there are instructions for its use in this part. An ASD can be used only for screening tests for alcohol, and may not be used for confirmation tests.

§40.231 What devices are used to conduct alcohol confirmation tests?

(a) EBTs on the NHTSA CPL for evidential devices that meet the requirements of paragraph (b) of this section are the only devices you may use to conduct alcohol confirmation tests under this part. Note that, among devices on the CPL for EBTs, only those devices listed without an asterisk (*) are authorized for use in confirmation testing in the DOT alcohol testing program.

(b) To conduct a confirmation test, you must use an EBT that has the following capabilities:

(1) Provides a printed triplicate result (or three consecutive identical copies of a result) of each breath test;

(2) Assigns a unique number to each completed test, which the BAT and employee can read before each test and which is printed on each copy of the result;

(3) Prints, on each copy of the result, the manufacturer's name for the device, its serial number, and the time of the test;

(4) Distinguishes alcohol from acetone at the 0.02 alcohol concentration level;

(5) Tests an air blank; and

(6) Performs an external calibration check.

§40.233 What are the requirements for proper use and care of EBTs?

(a) As an EBT manufacturer, you must submit, for NHTSA approval, a quality assurance plan (QAP) for your EBT before NHTSA places the EBT on the CPL.

(1) Your QAP must specify the methods used to perform external calibration checks on the EBT, the tolerances within which the EBT is regarded as being in proper calibration, and the intervals at which these checks must be performed. In designating these intervals, your QAP must take into account factors like frequency of use, environmental conditions (e.g., temperature, humidity, altitude) and type of operation (e.g., stationary or mobile).

(2) Your QAP must also specify the inspection, maintenance, and calibration requirements and intervals for the EBT.

(b) As the manufacturer, you must include, with each EBT, instructions for its use and care consistent with the QAP.

(c) As the user of the EBT (e.g., employer, service agent), you must do the following:

(1) You must follow the manufacturer's instructions (see paragraph (b) of this section), including performance of external calibration checks at the intervals the instructions specify.

(2) In conducting external calibration checks, you must use only calibration devices appearing on NHTSA's CPL for "Calibrating Units for Breath Alcohol Tests."

(3) If an EBT fails an external check of calibration, you must take the EBT out of service. You may not use the EBT again for DOT alcohol testing until it is repaired and passes an external calibration check.

(4) You must maintain records of the inspection, maintenance, and calibration of EBTs as provided in §40.333(a)(2).

(5) You must ensure that inspection, maintenance, and calibration of the EBT are performed by its manufacturer or a maintenance representative certified either by the manufacturer or by a state health agency or other appropriate state agency.

§40.235 What are the requirements for proper use and care of ASDs?

(a) As an ASD manufacturer, you must submit, for NHTSA approval, a QAP for your ASD before NHTSA places the ASD on the CPL. Your QAP must specify the methods used for quality control checks, temperatures at which the ASD must be stored and used, the shelf life of the device, and environmental conditions (*e.g.*, temperature, altitude, humidity) that may affect the ASD's performance.

(b) As a manufacturer, you must include with each ASD instructions for its use and care consistent with the QAP. The instructions must include directions on the proper use of the ASD, and, where applicable the time within which the device must be read, and the manner in which the reading is made.

(c) As the user of the ASD (*e.g.*, employer, STT), you must follow the QAP instructions.

(d) You are not permitted to use an ASD that does not pass the specified quality control checks or that has passed its expiration date.

(e) As an employer, with respect to breath ASDs, you must also follow the device use and care requirements of §40.233.

Subpart L — Alcohol Screening Tests

§40.241 What are the first steps in any alcohol screening test?

As the BAT or STT you will take the following steps to begin all alcohol screening tests, regardless of the type of testing device you are using:

(a) When a specific time for an employee's test has been scheduled, or the collection site is at the employee's worksite, and the employee does not appear at the collection site at the scheduled time, contact the DER to determine the appropriate interval within which the DER has determined the employee is authorized to arrive. If the employee's arrival is delayed beyond that time, you must notify the DER that the employee has not reported for testing. In a situation where a C/TPA has notified an owner/operator or other individual employee to report for testing and the employee does not appear, the C/TPA must notify the employee that he or she has refused to test.

(b) Ensure that, when the employee enters the alcohol testing site, you begin the alcohol testing process without undue delay. For example, you must not wait because the employee says he or she is not ready or because an authorized employer or employee representative is delayed in arriving.

(1) If the employee is also going to take a DOT drug test, you must, to the greatest extent practicable, ensure that the alcohol test is completed before the urine collection process begins.

(2) If the employee needs medical attention (*e.g.*, an injured employee in an emergency medical facility who is required to have a post-accident test), do not delay this treatment to conduct a test.

(c) Require the employee to provide positive identification. You must see a photo ID issued by the employer (other than in the case of an owner-operator or other self-employer individual) or a Federal, state, or local government (*e.g.*, a driver's license). You may not accept faxes or photocopies of identification. Positive identification by an employer representative (not a co-worker or another employee being tested) is also acceptable. If the employee cannot produce positive identification, you must contact a DER to verify the identity of the employee.

(d) If the employee asks, provide your identification to the employee. Your identification must include your name and your employer's name but is not required to include your picture, address, or telephone number.

(e) Explain the testing procedure to the employee, including showing the employee the instructions on the back of the ATF.

(f) Complete Step 1 of the ATF.

(g) Direct the employee to complete Step 2 on the ATF and sign the certification. If the employee refuses to sign this certification, you must document this refusal on the "Remarks" line of the ATF and immediately notify the DER. This is a refusal to test.

§40.243 What is the procedure for an alcohol screening test using an EBT or non-evidential breath ASD?

As the BAT or STT, you must take the following steps:

(a) Select, or allow the employee to select, an individually wrapped or sealed mouthpiece from the testing materials.

(b) Open the individually wrapped or sealed mouthpiece in view of the employee and insert it into the device in accordance with the manufacturer's instructions.

(c) Instruct the employee to blow steadily and forcefully into the mouthpiece for at least six seconds or until the device indicates that an adequate amount of breath has been obtained.

(d) Show the employee the displayed test result.

(e) If the device is one that prints the test number, testing device name and serial number, time, and result directly onto the ATF, you must check to ensure that the information has been printed correctly onto the ATF.

(f) If the device is one that prints the test number, testing device name and serial number, time and result, but on a separate printout rather than directly onto the ATF, you must affix the printout of the information to the designated space on the ATF with tamper-evident tape or use a self-adhesive label that is tamper-evident.

(g) If the device is one that does not print the test number, testing device name and serial number, time, and result, or it is a device not being used with a printer, you must record this information in Step 3 of the ATF.

§40.245 What is the procedure for an alcohol screening test using a saliva ASD or a breath tube ASD?

(a) As the STT or BAT, you must take the following steps when using the saliva ASD:

(1) Check the expiration date on the device or on the package containing the device and show it to the employee. You may not use the device after its expiration date.

(2) Open an individually wrapped or sealed package containing the device in the presence of the employee.

(3) Offer the employee the opportunity to use the device. If the employee uses it, you must instruct the employee to insert it into his or her mouth and use it in a manner described by the device's manufacturer.

(4) If the employee chooses not to use the device, or in all cases in which a new test is necessary because the device did not

activate (see paragraph (a)(7) of this section), you must insert the device into the employee's mouth and gather saliva in the manner described by the device's manufacturer. You must wear single-use examination or similar gloves while doing so and change them following each test.

(5) When the device is removed from the employee's mouth, you must follow the manufacturer's instructions regarding necessary next steps in ensuring that the device has activated.

(6)(i) If you were unable to successfully follow the procedures of paragraphs (a)(3) through (a)(5) of this section (*e.g.*, the device breaks, you drop the device on the floor), you must discard the device and conduct a new test using a new device.

(ii) The new device you use must be one that has been under your control or that of the employee before the test.

(iii) You must note on the "Remarks" line of the ATF the reason for the new test. (**Note:** You may continue using the same ATF with which you began the test.)

(iv) You must offer the employee the choice of using the device or having you use it unless the employee, in the opinion of the STT or BAT, was responsible (*e.g.*, the employee dropped the device) for the new test needing to be conducted.

(v) If you are unable to successfully follow the procedures of paragraphs (a)(3) through (a)(5) of this section on the new test, you must end the collection and put an explanation on the "Remarks" line of the ATF.

(vi) You must then direct the employee to take a new test immediately, using an EBT for the screening test.

(7) If you are able to successfully follow the procedures of paragraphs (a)(3)-(a)(5) of this section, but the device does not activate, you must discard the device and conduct a new test, in the same manner as provided in paragraph (a)(6) of this section. In this case, you must place the device into the employee's mouth to collect saliva for the new test.

(8) You must read the result displayed on the device no sooner than the device's manufacturer instructs. In all cases the result displayed must be read within 15 minutes of the test. You must then show the device and it's reading to the employee and enter the result on the ATF.

(9) You must never re-use devices, swabs, gloves or other materials used in saliva testing.

(10) You must note the fact that you used a saliva ASD in Step 3 of the ATF.

(b) As the STT or BAT, you must take the following steps when using the breath tube ASD:

(1) Check the expiration date on the device or on the package containing the device and show it to the employee. You must not use the device after its expiration date.

(2) Remove a device from the package and break the tube's ampule in the presence of the employee.

(3) Secure an inflation bag onto the appropriate end of the device, as directed by the manufacturer on the device's instructions.

(4) Offer the employee the opportunity to use the device. If the employee chooses to use (e.g. hold) the device, instruct the employee to blow forcefully and steadily into the blowing end of device until the inflation bag fills with air (approximately 12 seconds).

(5) If the employee chooses not to hold the device, you must hold it and provide the use instructions in paragraph (b)(4) of this section.

(6) When the employee completes the breath process, take the device from the employee (or if you were holding it, remove it from the employee's mouth); remove the inflation bag; and either hold the device or place it on a clean flat surface while waiting for the reading to appear.

(7)(i) If you were unable to successfully follow the procedures of paragraphs (b)(4) through (b)(6) of this section (*e.g.*, the device breaks apart, the employee did not fill the inflation bag), you must discard the device and conduct a new test using a new one.

(ii) The new device you use must be one that has been under your control or that of the employer before the test.

(iii) You must note on the "Remarks" line of the ATF the reason for the new test. (**Note:** You may continue using the same ATF with which you began the test.)

(iv) You must offer the employee the choice of holding the device or having you hold it unless the employee, in the your opinion, was responsible (e.g., the employee failed to fill the inflation bag) for the new test needing to be conducted.

(v) If you are unable to successfully follow the procedures of paragraphs (b)(4) through (b)(6) of this section on the new test, you must end the collection and put an explanation on the "Remarks" line of the ATF.

(vi) You must then direct the employee to take a new test immediately, using another type of ASD (*e.g.*, saliva device) or an EBT.

(8) If you were able to successfully follow the procedures of paragraphs (b)(4) through (b)(6) of this section, you must compare the color of the crystals in the device with the colored crystals on the manufacturer-produced control tube no sooner than the manufacturer instructs. In all cases color comparisons must take place within 15 minutes of the test.

(9) You must follow the manufacturer's instructions for determining the result of the test. You must then show both the device and the control tube side-by-side to the employee and record the result on the ATF.

(10) You must never re-use devices or gloves used in breath tube testing. The inflation bag must be voided of air following removal from a device. One inflation bag can be used for up to 10 breath tube tests.

(11) You must note the fact that you used a breath tube device in Step 3 of the ATF.

§40.247 What procedures does the BAT or STT follow after a screening test result?

(a) If the test result is an alcohol concentration of less than 0.02, as the BAT or STT, you must do the following:

(1) Sign and date Step 3 of the ATF; and

(2) Transmit the result to the DER in a confidential manner, as provided in §40.255.

(b) If the test result is an alcohol concentration of 0.02 or higher, as the BAT or STT, you must direct the employee to take a confirmation test.

(1) If you are the BAT who will conduct the confirmation test, you must then conduct the test using the procedures beginning at §40.251.

(2) If you are not the BAT who will conduct the confirmation test, direct the employee to take a confirmation test, sign and date Step 3 of the ATF, and give the employee Copy 2 of the ATF.

(3) If the confirmation test will be performed at a different site from the screening test, you must take the following additional steps:

(i) Advise the employee not to eat, drink, put anything (*e.g.,* cigarette, chewing gum) into his or her mouth, or belch;

(ii) Tell the employee the reason for the waiting period required by §40.251(a) (*i.e.,* to prevent an accumulation of mouth alcohol from leading to an artificially high reading);

(iii) Explain that following your instructions concerning the waiting period is to the employee's benefit;

(iv) Explain that the confirmation test will be conducted at the end of the waiting period, even if the instructions have not been followed;

(v) Note on the "Remarks" line of the ATF that the waiting period instructions were provided;

(vi) Instruct the person accompanying the employee to carry a copy of the ATF to the BAT who will perform the confirmation test; and

(vii) Ensure that you or another BAT, STT, or employer representative observe the employee as he or she is transported to the confirmation testing site. You must direct the employee not to attempt to drive a motor vehicle to the confirmation testing site.

(c) If the screening test is invalid, you must, as the BAT or STT, tell the employee the test is cancelled and note the problem on the "Remarks" line of the ATF. If practicable, repeat the testing process (see §40. 271).

Subpart M — Alcohol Confirmation Tests

§40.251 What are the first steps in an alcohol confirmation test?

As the BAT for an alcohol confirmation test, you must follow these steps to begin the confirmation test process:

(a) You must carry out a requirement for a waiting period before the confirmation test, by taking the following steps:

(1) You must ensure that the waiting period lasts at least 15 minutes, starting with the completion of the screening test. After the waiting period has elapsed, you should begin the confirmation test as soon as possible, but not more than 30 minutes after the completion of the screening test.

(i) If the confirmation test is taking place at a different location from the screening test (see §40.247(b)(3)) the time of transit between sites counts toward the waiting period if the STT or BAT who conducted the screening test provided the waiting period instructions.

(ii) If you cannot verify, through review of the ATF, that waiting period instructions were provided, then you must carry out the waiting period requirement.

(iii) You or another BAT or STT, or an employer representative, must observe the employee during the waiting period.

(2) Concerning the waiting period, you must tell the employee:

(i) Not to eat, drink, put anything (*e.g.,* cigarette, chewing gum) into his or her mouth, or belch;

(ii) The reason for the waiting period (*i.e.,* to prevent an accumulation of mouth alcohol from leading to an artificially high reading);

(iii) That following your instructions concerning the waiting period is to the employee's benefit; and

(iv) That the confirmation test will be conducted at the end of the waiting period, even if the instructions have not been followed.

(3) If you become aware that the employee has not followed the instructions, you must note this on the "Remarks" line of the ATF.

(b) If you did not conduct the screening test for the employee, you must require positive identification of the employee, explain the confirmation procedures, and use a new ATF. You must note on the "Remarks" line of the ATF that a different BAT or STT conducted the screening test.

(c) Complete Step 1 of the ATF.

(d) Direct the employee to complete Step 2 on the ATF and sign the certification. If the employee refuses to sign this certification, you must document this refusal on the "Remarks" line of the ATF and immediately notify the DER. This is a refusal to test.

(e) Even if more than 30 minutes have passed since the screening test result was obtained, you must begin the confirmation test procedures in §40.253, not another screening test.

(f) You must note on the "Remarks" line of the ATF the time that elapsed between the two events, and if the confirmation test could not begin within 30 minutes of the screening test, the reason why.

(g) Beginning the confirmation test procedures after the 30 minutes have elapsed does not invalidate the screening or confirmation tests, but it may constitute a regulatory violation subject to DOT agency sanction.

§40.253 What are the procedures for conducting an alcohol confirmation test?

As the BAT conducting an alcohol confirmation test, you must follow these steps in order to complete the confirmation test process:

(a) In the presence of the employee, you must conduct an air blank on the EBT you are using before beginning the confirmation test and show the reading to the employee.

(1) If the reading is 0.00, the test may proceed. If the reading is greater than 0.00, you must conduct another air blank.

(2) If the reading on the second air blank is 0.00, the test may proceed. If the reading is greater than 0.00, you must take the EBT out of service.

(3) If you take an EBT out of service for this reason, no one may use it for testing until the EBT is found to be within tolerance limits on an external check of calibration.

(4) You must proceed with the test of the employee using another EBT, if one is available.

(b) You must open a new individually wrapped or sealed mouthpiece in view of the employee and insert it into the device in accordance with the manufacturer's instructions.

(c) You must ensure that you and the employee read the unique test number displayed on the EBT.

(d) You must instruct the employee to blow steadily and forcefully into the mouthpiece for at least six seconds or until the device indicates that an adequate amount of breath has been obtained.

(e) You must show the employee the result displayed on the EBT.

(f) You must show the employee the result and unique test number that the EBT prints out either directly onto the ATF or onto a separate printout.

(g) If the EBT provides a separate printout of the result, you must attach the printout to the designated space on the ATF with tamper-evident tape, or use a self-adhesive label that is tamper-evident.

§40.255 What happens next after the alcohol confirmation test result?

(a) After the EBT has printed the result of an alcohol confirmation test, you must, as the BAT, take the following additional steps:

(1) Sign and date Step 3 of the ATF.

(2) If the alcohol confirmation test result is lower than 0.02, nothing further is required of the employee. As the BAT, you must sign and date Step 3 of the ATF.

(3) If the alcohol confirmation test result is 0.02 or higher, direct the employee to sign and date Step 4 of the ATF. If the employee does not do so, you must note this on the "Remarks" line of the ATF. However, this is not considered a refusal to test.

(4) If the test is invalid, tell the employee the test is cancelled and note the problem on the "Remarks" line of the ATF. If practicable, conduct a re-test. (see §40.271).

(5) Immediately transmit the result directly to the DER in a confidential manner.

(i) You may transmit the results using Copy 1 of the ATF, in person, by telephone, or by electronic means. In any case, you must immediately notify the DER of any result of 0.02 or greater by any means (*e.g.*, telephone or secure fax machine) that ensures the result is immediately received by the DER. You must not transmit these results through C/TPAs or other service agents.

(ii) If you do not make the initial transmission in writing, you must follow up the initial transmission with Copy 1 of the ATF.

(b) As an employer, you must take the following steps with respect to the receipt and storage of alcohol test result information:

(1) If you receive any test results that are not in writing (*e.g.*, by telephone or electronic means), you must establish a mechanism to establish the identity of the BAT sending you the results.

(2) You must store all test result information in a way that protects confidentiality.

Subpart N — Problems in Alcohol Testing

§40.261 What is a refusal to take an alcohol test, and what are the consequences?

(a) As an employee, you are considered to have refused to take an alcohol test if you:

(1) Fail to appear for any test (except a pre-employment test) within a reasonable time, as determined by the employer, consistent with applicable DOT agency regulations, after being directed to do so by the employer. This includes the failure of an employee (including an owner-operator) to appear for a test when called by a C/TPA (see §40.241(a));

(2) Fail to remain at the testing site until the testing process is complete; *Provided*, That an employee who leaves the testing site before the testing process commences (see §40.243(a)) for a pre-employment test is not deemed to have refused to test;

(3) Fail to provide an adequate amount of saliva or breath for any alcohol test required by this part or DOT agency regulations; *Provided*, That an employee who does not provide an ade-

quate amount of breath or saliva because he or she has left the testing site before the testing process commences (see §40.243(a)) for a pre-employment test is not deemed to have refused to test;

(4) Fail to provide a sufficient breath specimen, and the physician has determined, through a required medical evaluation, that there was no adequate medical explanation for the failure (see §40.265(c));

(5) Fail to undergo a medical examination or evaluation, as directed by the employer as part of the insufficient breath procedures outlined at §40.265(c);

(6) Fail to sign the certification at Step 2 of the ATF (see §§40.241 (g) and 40.251 (d)); or

(7) Fail to cooperate with any part of the testing process.

(b) As an employee, if you refuse to take an alcohol test, you incur the same consequences specified under DOT agency regulations for a violation of those DOT agency regulations.

(c) As a BAT or an STT, or as the physician evaluating a "shy lung" situation, when an employee refuses to test as provided in paragraph (a) of this section, you must terminate the portion of the testing process in which you are involved, document the refusal on the ATF (or in a separate document which you cause to be attached to the form), immediately notify the DER by any means (*e.g.*, telephone or secure fax machine) that ensures the refusal notification is immediately received. You must make this notification directly to the DER (not using a C/TPA as an intermediary).

(d) As an employee, when you refuse to take a non-DOT test or to sign a non-DOT form, you have not refused to take a DOT test. There are no consequences under DOT agency regulations for such a refusal.

§40.263 What happens when an employee is unable to provide a sufficient amount of saliva for an alcohol screening test?

(a) As the STT, you must take the following steps if an employee is unable to provide sufficient saliva to complete a test on a saliva screening device (*e.g.*, the employee does not provide sufficient saliva to activate the device).

(1) You must conduct a new screening test using a new screening device.

(2) If the employee refuses to make the attempt to complete the new test, you must discontinue testing, note the fact on the

"Remarks" line of the ATF, and immediately notify the DER. This is a refusal to test.

(3) If the employee has not provided a sufficient amount of saliva to complete the new test, you must note the fact on the "Remarks" line of the ATF and immediately notify the DER.

(b) As the DER, when the STT informs you that the employee has not provided a sufficient amount of saliva (see paragraph (a)(3) of this section), you must immediately arrange to administer an alcohol test to the employee using an EBT or other breath testing device.

§40.265 What happens when an employee is unable to provide a sufficient amount of breath for an alcohol test?

(a) If an employee does not provide a sufficient amount of breath to permit a valid breath test, you must take the steps listed in this section.

(b) As the BAT or STT, you must instruct the employee to attempt again to provide a sufficient amount of breath and about the proper way to do so.

(1) If the employee refuses to make the attempt, you must discontinue the test, note the fact on the "Remarks" line of the ATF, and immediately notify the DER. This is a refusal to test.

(2) If the employee again attempts and fails to provide a sufficient amount of breath, you may provide another opportunity to the employee to do so if you believe that there is a strong likelihood that it could result in providing a sufficient amount of breath.

(3) When the employee's attempts under paragraph (b)(2) of this section have failed to produce a sufficient amount of breath, you must note the fact on the "Remarks" line of the ATF and immediately notify the DER.

(4) If you are using an EBT that has the capability of operating manually, you may attempt to conduct the test in manual mode.

(5) If you are qualified to use a saliva ASD and you are in the screening test stage, you may change to a saliva ASD only to complete the screening test.

(c) As the employer, when the BAT or STT informs you that the employee has not provided a sufficient amount of breath, you must direct the employee to obtain, within five days, an evaluation from a licensed physician who is acceptable to you and who has expertise in the medical issues raised by the employee's failure to provide a sufficient specimen.

(1) You are required to provide the physician who will conduct the evaluation with the following information and instructions:

(i) That the employee was required to take a DOT breath alcohol test, but was unable to provide a sufficient amount of breath to complete the test;

(ii) The consequences of the appropriate DOT agency regulation for refusing to take the required alcohol test;

(iii) That the physician must provide you with a signed statement of his or her conclusions; and

(iv) That the physician, in his or her reasonable medical judgment, must base those conclusions on one of the following determinations:

(A) A medical condition has, or with a high degree of probability could have, precluded the employee from providing a sufficient amount of breath. The physician must not include in the signed statement detailed information on the employee's medical condition. In this case, the test is cancelled.

(B) There is not an adequate basis for determining that a medical condition has, or with a high degree of probability could have, precluded the employee from providing a sufficient amount of breath. This constitutes a refusal to test.

(C) For purposes of paragraphs (c)(1)(iv)(A) and (B) of this section, a medical condition includes an ascertainable physiological condition (e.g., a respiratory system dysfunction) or a medically documented pre-existing psychological disorder, but does not include unsupported assertions of "situational anxiety" or hyperventilation.

(2) As the physician making the evaluation, after making your determination, you must provide a written statement of your conclusions and the basis for them to the DER directly (and not through a C/TPA acting as an itermediary). You must not include in this statement detailed information on the employee's medical condition beyond what is necessary to explain your conclusion.

(3) Upon receipt of the report from the examining physician, as the DER you must immediately inform the employee and take appropriate action based upon your DOT agency regulations.

§40.267 What problems always cause an alcohol test to be cancelled?

As an employer, a BAT, or an STT, you must cancel an alcohol test if any of the following problems occur. These are "fatal flaws." You must inform the DER that the test was cancelled and must be treated as if the test never occurred. These problems are:

(a) In the case of a screening test conducted on a saliva ASD or a breath tube ASD:

(1) The STT or BAT reads the result either sooner than or later than the time allotted by the manufacturer and this Part (see §40.245(a)(8) for the saliva ASD and §40.245(b)(8) for the breath tube ASD).

(2) The saliva ASD does not activate (see §40.245(a)(7); or

(3) The device is used for a test after the expiration date printed on the device or on its package (see §40.245(a)(1) for the saliva ASD and §40.245(b)(1) for the breath tube ASD).

(b) In the case of a screening or confirmation test conducted on an EBT, the sequential test number or alcohol concentration displayed on the EBT is not the same as the sequential test number or alcohol concentration on the printed result (see §40.253(c), (e) and (f)).

(c) In the case of a confirmation test:

(1) The BAT conducts the confirmation test before the end of the minimum 15-minute waiting period (see §40.251(a)(1));

(2) The BAT does not conduct an air blank before the confirmation test (see §40.253(a));

(3) There is not a 0.00 result on the air blank conducted before the confirmation test (see §40.253(a)(1) and (2));

(4) The EBT does not print the result (see §40.253(f)); or

(5) The next external calibration check of the EBT produces a result that differs by more than the tolerance stated in the QAP from the known value of the test standard. In this case, every result of 0.02 or above obtained on the EBT since the last valid external calibration check is cancelled (see §40.233(a)(1) and (d)).

§40.269 What problems cause an alcohol test to be cancelled unless they are corrected?

As a BAT or STT, or employer, you must cancel an alcohol test if any of the following problems occur, unless they are corrected. These are "correctable flaws." These problems are:

(a) The BAT or STT does not sign the ATF (see §§40.247(a)(1) and 40.255(a)(1)).

(b) The BAT or STT fails to note on the "Remarks" line of the

ATF that the employee has not signed the ATF after the result is obtained (see §40.255(a)(2)).

(c) The BAT or STT uses a non-DOT form for the test (see §40.225(a)).

§40.271 How are alcohol testing problems corrected?

(a) As a BAT or STT, you have the responsibility of trying to complete successfully an alcohol test for each employee.

(1) If, during or shortly after the testing process, you become aware of any event that will cause the test to be cancelled (see §40.267), you must try to correct the problem promptly, if practicable. You may repeat the testing process as part of this effort.

(2) If repeating the testing process is necessary, you must begin a new test as soon as possible. You must use a new ATF, a new sequential test number, and, if needed, a new ASD and/or a new EBT. It is permissible to use additional technical capabilities of the EBT (*e.g.*, manual operation) if you have been trained to do so in accordance with §40.213(c).

(3) If repeating the testing process is necessary, you are not limited in the number of attempts to complete the test, provided that the employee is making a good faith effort to comply with the testing process.

(4) If another testing device is not available for the new test at the testing site, you must immediately notify the DER and advise the DER that the test could not be completed. As the DER who receives this information, you must make all reasonable efforts to ensure that the test is conducted at another testing site as soon as possible.

(b) If, as an STT, BAT, employer or other service agent administering the testing process, you become aware of a "correctable flaw" (see §40.269) that has not already been corrected, you must take all practicable action to correct the problem so that the test is not cancelled.

(1) If the problem resulted from the omission of required information, you must, as the person responsible for providing that information, supply in writing the missing information and a signed statement that it is true and accurate. For example, suppose you are a BAT and you forgot to make a notation on the "Remarks" line of the ATF that the employee did not sign the certification. You would, when the problem is called to your attention, supply a signed statement that the employee failed or refused to sign the certification after the result was obtained, and that your signed statement is true and accurate.

(2) If the problem is the use of a non-DOT form, you must, as the person responsible for the use of the incorrect form, certify in writing that the incorrect form contains all the information needed for a valid DOT alcohol test. You must also provide a signed statement that the incorrect form was used inadvertently or as the only means of conducting a test, in circumstances beyond your control, and the steps you have taken to prevent future use of non-DOT forms for DOT tests. You must supply this information on the same business day on which you are notified of the problem, transmitting it by fax or courier.

(c) If you cannot correct the problem, you must cancel the test.

§40.273 What is the effect of a cancelled alcohol test?

(a) A cancelled alcohol test is neither positive nor negative.

(1) As an employer, you must not attach to a cancelled test the consequences of a test result that is 0.02 or greater (*e.g.,* removal from a safety-sensitive position).

(2) As an employer, you must not use a cancelled test in a situation where an employee needs a test result that is below 0.02 (*e.g.,* in the case of a return-to-duty or follow-up test to authorize the employee to perform safety-sensitive functions).

(3) As an employer, you must not direct a recollection for an employee because a test has been cancelled, except in the situations cited in paragraph (a)(2) of this section or other provisions of this part.

(b) A cancelled test does not count toward compliance with DOT requirements, such as a minimum random testing rate.

(c) When a test must be cancelled, if you are the BAT, STT, or other person who determines that the cancellation is necessary, you must inform the affected DER within 48 hours of the cancellation.

(d) A cancelled DOT test does not provide a valid basis for an employer to conduct a non-DOT test (*i.e.,* a test under company authority).

§40.275 What is the effect of procedural problems that are not sufficient to cancel an alcohol test?

(a) As an STT, BAT, employer, or a service agent administering the testing process, you must document any errors in the testing process of which you become aware, even if they are not "fatal flaws" or "correctable flaws" listed in this subpart. Decisions about the ultimate impact of these errors will be determined by administrative or legal proceedings, subject to the limitation of paragraph (b) of this section.

(b) No person concerned with the testing process may declare a test cancelled based on a mistake in the process that does not have a significant adverse effect on the right of the employee to a fair and accurate test. For example, it is inconsistent with this part to cancel a test based on a minor administrative mistake (*e.g.*, the omission of the employee's middle initial) or an error that does not affect employee protections under this part. Nor does the failure of an employee to sign in Step 4 of the ATF result in the cancellation of the test. Nor is a test to be cancelled on the basis of a claim by an employee that he or she was improperly selected for testing.

(c) As an employer, these errors, even though not sufficient to cancel an alcohol test result, may subject you to enforcement action under DOT agency regulations.

§40.277 Are alcohol tests other than saliva or breath permitted under these regulations?

No, other types of alcohol tests (*e.g.*, blood and urine) are not authorized for testing done under this part. Only saliva or breath for screening tests and breath for confirmation tests using approved devices are permitted.

Subpart O — Substance Abuse Professionals and the Return-to-Duty Process

§40.281 Who is qualified to act as a SAP?

To be permitted to act as a SAP in the DOT drug testing program, you must meet each of the requirements of this section:

(a) **Credentials.** You must have one of the following credentials:

(1) You are a licensed physician (Doctor of Medicine or Osteopathy);

(2) You are a licensed or certified social worker;

(3) You are a licensed or certified psychologist;

(4) You are a licensed or certified employee assistance professional; or

(5) You are a drug and alcohol counselor certified by the National Association of Alcoholism and Drug Abuse Counselors Certification Commission (NAADAC) or by the International Certification Reciprocity Consortium/ Alcohol and Other Drug

Abuse (ICRC).

(b) **Basic knowledge.** You must be knowledgeable in the following areas:

(1) You must be knowledgeable about and have clinical experience in the diagnosis and treatment of alcohol and controlled substances-related disorders.

(2) You must be knowledgeable about the SAP function as it relates to employer interests in safety-sensitive duties.

(3) You must be knowledgeable about this part, the DOT agency regulations applicable to the employers for whom you evaluate employees, and the DOT SAP Guidelines, and you keep current on any changes to these materials. These documents are available from ODAPC (Department of Transportation, 400 7th Street, SW., Room 10403, Washington DC, 20590 (202-366-3784), or on the ODAPC web site (http:// www.dot.gov/ost/dapc).

(c) **Qualification training.** You must receive qualification training meeting the requirements of this paragraph (c).

(1) Qualification training must provide instruction on the following subjects:

(i) Background, rationale, and coverage of the Department's drug and alcohol testing program;

(ii) 49 CFR Part 40 and DOT agency drug and alcohol testing rules;

(iii) Key DOT drug testing requirements, including collections, laboratory testing, MRO review, and problems in drug testing;

(iv) Key DOT alcohol testing requirements, including the testing process, the role of BATs and STTs, and problems in alcohol tests;

(v) SAP qualifications and prohibitions;

(vi) The role of the SAP in the return-to-duty process, including the initial employee evaluation, referrals for education and/or treatment, the follow-up evaluation, continuing treatment recommendations, and the follow-up testing plan;

(vii) SAP consultation and communication with employers, MROs, and treatment providers;

(viii) Reporting and recordkeeping requirements;

(ix) Issues that SAPs confront in carrying out their duties under the program.

(2) Following your completion of qualification training under paragraph (c)(1) of this section, you must satisfactorily complete

an examination administered by a nationally-recognized professional or training organization. The examination must comprehensively cover all the elements of qualification training listed in paragraph (c)(1) of this section.

(3) The following is the schedule for qualification training you must meet:

(i) If you became a SAP before August 1, 2001, you must meet the qualification training requirement no later than December 31, 2003.

(ii) If you become a SAP between August 1, 2001, and December 31, 2003, you must meet the qualification training requirement no later than December 31, 2003.

(iii) If you become a SAP on or after January 1, 2004, you must meet the qualification training requirement before you begin to perform SAP functions.

(d) **Continuing education.** During each three-year period from the date on which you satisfactorily complete the examination under paragraph (c)(2) of this section, you must complete continuing education consisting of at least 12 professional development hours (*e.g.,* CEUs) relevant to performing SAP functions.

(1) This continuing education must include material concerning new technologies, interpretations, recent guidance, rule changes, and other information about developments in SAP practice, pertaining to the DOT program, since the time you met the qualification training requirements of this section.

(2) Your continuing education activities must include documentable assessment tools to assist you in determining whether you have adequately learned the material.

(e) **Documentation.** You must maintain documentation showing that you currently meet all requirements of this section. You must provide this documentation on request to DOT agency representatives and to employers and C/TPAs who are using or contemplating using your services.

§40.283 How does a certification organization obtain recognition for its members as SAPs?

(a) If you represent a certification organization that wants DOT to authorize its certified drug and alcohol counselors to be added to §40.281(a)(5), you may submit a written petition to DOT requesting a review of your petition for inclusion.

(b) You must obtain the National Commission for Certifying Agencies (NCCA) accreditation before DOT will act on your petition.

(c) You must also meet the minimum requirements of Appendix E to this part before DOT will act on your petition.

§40.285 When is a SAP evaluation required?

(a) As an employee, when you have violated DOT drug and alcohol regulations, you cannot again perform any DOT safety-sensitive duties for any employer until and unless you complete the SAP evaluation, referral, and education/treatment process set forth in this subpart and in applicable DOT agency regulations. The first step in this process is a SAP evaluation.

(b) For purposes of this subpart, a verified positive DOT drug test result, a DOT alcohol test with a result indicating an alcohol concentration of 0.04 or greater, a refusal to test (including by adulterating or substituting a urine specimen) or any other violation of the prohibition on the use of alcohol or drugs under a DOT agency regulation constitutes a DOT drug and alcohol regulation violation.

§40.287 What information is an employer required to provide concerning SAP services to an employee who has a DOT drug and alcohol regulation violation?

As an employer, you must provide to each employee (including an applicant or new employee) who violates a DOT drug and alcohol regulation a listing of SAPs readily available to the employee and acceptable to you, with names, addresses, and telephone numbers. You cannot charge the employee any fee for compiling or providing this list. You may provide this list yourself or through a C/TPA or other service agent.

§40.289 Are employers required to provide SAP and treatment services to employees?

(a) As an employer, you are not required to provide a SAP evaluation or any subsequent recommended education or treatment for an employee who has violated a DOT drug and alcohol regulation.

(b) However, if you offer that employee an opportunity to return to a DOT safety-sensitive duty following a violation, you must, before the employee again performs that duty, ensure that the employee receives an evaluation by a SAP meeting the requirements of §40.281 and that the employee successfully complies with the SAP's evaluation recommendations.

(c) Payment for SAP evaluations and services is left for employers and employees to decide and may be governed by existing management-labor agreements and health care benefits.

§40.291 What is the role of the SAP in the evaluation, referral, and treatment process of an employee who has violated DOT agency drug and alcohol testing regulations?

(a) As a SAP, you are charged with:

(1) Making a face-to-face clinical assessment and evaluation to determine what assistance is needed by the employee to resolve problems associated with alcohol and/or drug use;

(2) Referring the employee to an appropriate education and/or treatment program;

(3) Conducting a face-to-face follow-up evaluation to determine if the employee has actively participated in the education and/or treatment program and has demonstrated successful compliance with the initial assessment and evaluation recommendations;

(4) Providing the DER with a follow-up drug and/or alcohol testing plan for the employee; and

(5) Providing the employee and employer with recommendations for continuing education and/or treatment.

(b) As a SAP, you are not an advocate for the employer or employee. Your function is to protect the public interest in safety by professionally evaluating the employee and recommending appropriate education/treatment, follow-up tests, and aftercare.

§40.293 What is the SAP's function in conducting the initial evaluation of an employee?

As a SAP, for every employee who comes to you following a DOT drug and alcohol regulation violation, you must accomplish the following:

(a) Provide a comprehensive face-to-face assessment and clinical evaluation.

(b) Recommend a course of education and/or treatment with which the employee must demonstrate successful compliance prior to returning to DOT safety-sensitive duty.

(1) You must make such a recommendation for every individual who has violated a DOT drug and alcohol regulation.

(2) You must make a recommendation for education and/or treatment that will, to the greatest extent possible, protect public safety in the event that the employee returns to the performance of safety-sensitive functions.

(c) Appropriate education may include, but is not limited to, self-help groups (*e.g.,* Alcoholics Anonymous) and community lectures, where attendance can be independently verified, and bona fide drug and alcohol education courses.

(d) Appropriate treatment may include, but is not limited to, in-patient hospitalization, partial in-patient treatment, out-patient counseling programs, and aftercare.

(e) You must provide a written report directly to the DER highlighting your specific recommendations for assistance (see §40.311(c)).

(f) For purposes of your role in the evaluation process, you must assume that a verified positive test result has conclusively established that the employee committed a DOT drug and alcohol regulation violation. You must not take into consideration in any way, as a factor in determining what your recommendation will be, any of the following:

(1) A claim by the employee that the test was unjustified or inaccurate;

(2) Statements by the employee that attempt to mitigate the seriousness of a violation of a DOT drug or alcohol regulation (*e.g.,* related to assertions of use of hemp oil, "medical marijuana" use, "contact positives," poppy seed ingestion, job stress); or

(3) Personal opinions you may have about the justification or rationale for drug and alcohol testing.

(g) In the course of gathering information for purposes of your evaluation in the case of a drug-related violation, you may consult with the MRO. As the MRO, you are required to cooperate with the SAP and provide available information the SAP requests. It is not necessary to obtain the consent of the employee to provide this information.

§40.295 May employees or employers seek a second SAP evaluation if they disagree with the first SAP's recommendations?

(a) As an employee with a DOT drug and alcohol regulation violation, when you have been evaluated by a SAP, you must not seek a second SAP's evaluation in order to obtain another recommendation.

(b) As an employer, you must not seek a second SAP's evaluation if the employee has already been evaluated by a qualified SAP. If the employee, contrary to paragraph (a) of this section, has obtained a second SAP evaluation, as an employer you may not rely on it for any purpose under this part.

§40.297 Does anyone have the authority to change a SAP's initial evaluation?

(a) Except as provided in paragraph (b) of this section, no one (*e.g.,* an employer, employee, a managed-care provider, any service agent) may change in any way the SAP's evaluation or recommendations for assistance. For example, a third party is not permitted to make more or less stringent a SAP's recommendation by changing the SAP's evaluation or seeking another SAP's evaluation.

(b) The SAP who made the initial evaluation may modify his or her initial evaluation and recommendations based on new or additional information (*e.g.,* from an education or treatment program).

§40.299 What is the SAP's role and what are the limits on a SAP's discretion in referring employees for education and treatment?

(a) As a SAP, upon your determination of the best recommendation for assistance, you will serve as a referral source to assist the employee's entry into a education and/or treatment program.

(b) To prevent the appearance of a conflict of interest, you must not refer an employee requiring assistance to your private practice or to a person or organization from which you receive payment or to a person or organization in which you have a financial interest. You are precluded from making referrals to entities with which you are financially associated.

(c) There are four exceptions to the prohibitions contained in paragraph (b) of this section. You may refer an employee to any of the following providers of assistance, regardless of your relationship with them:

(1) A public agency (*e.g.,* treatment facility) operated by a state, county, or municipality;

(2) The employer or a person or organization under contract to the employer to provide alcohol or drug treatment and/or education services (*e.g.,* the employer's contracted treatment provider);

(3) The sole source of therapeutically appropriate treatment under the employee's health insurance program (*e.g.,* the single substance abuse in-patient treatment program made available by the employee's insurance coverage plan); or

(4) The sole source of therapeutically appropriate treatment reasonably available to the employee (*e.g.,* the only treatment

facility or education program reasonably located within the general commuting area).

§40.301 What is the SAP's function in the follow-up evaluation of an employee?

(a) As a SAP, after you have prescribed assistance under §40.293, you must re-evaluate the employee to determine if the employee has successfully carried out your education and/or treatment recommendations.

(1) This is your way to gauge for the employer the employee's ability to demonstrate successful compliance with the education and/or treatment plan.

(2) Your evaluation may serve as one of the reasons the employer decides to return the employee to safety-sensitive duty.

(b) As the SAP making the follow-up evaluation determination, you must:

(1) Confer with or obtain appropriate documentation from the appropriate education and/or treatment program professionals where the employee was referred; and

(2) Conduct a face-to-face clinical interview with the employee to determine if the employee demonstrates successful compliance with your initial evaluation recommendations.

(c) (1) If the employee has demonstrated successful compliance, you must provide a written report directly to the DER highlighting your clinical determination that the employee has done so with your initial evaluation recommendation (see §40.311(d)).

(2) You may determine that an employee has successfully demonstrated compliance even though the employee has not yet completed the full regimen of education and/or treatment you recommended or needs additional assistance. For example, if the employee has successfully completed the 30-day in-patient program you prescribed, you may make a "successful compliance" determination even though you conclude that the employee has not yet completed the out-patient counseling you recommended or should continue in an aftercare program.

(d)(1) As the SAP, if you believe, as a result of the follow-up evaluation, that the employee has not demonstrated successful compliance with your recommendations, you must provide written notice directly to the DER (see §40.311(e)).

(2) As an employer who receives the SAP's written notice that the employee has not successfully complied with the SAP's recommendations, you must not return the employee to the performance of safety-sensitive duties.

(3) As the SAP, you may conduct additional follow-up evaluation(s) if the employer determines that doing so is consistent with the employee's progress as you have reported it and with the employer's policy and/or labor-management agreements.

(4) As the employer, following a SAP report that the employee has not demonstrated successful compliance, you may take personnel action consistent with your policy and/or labor-management agreements.

§40.303 What happens if the SAP believes the employee needs additional treatment, aftercare, or support group services even after the employee returns to safety-sensitive duties?

(a) As a SAP, if you believe that ongoing services (in addition to follow-up tests) are needed to assist an employee to maintain sobriety or abstinence from drug use after the employee resumes the performance of safety-sensitive duties, you must provide recommendations for these services in your follow-up evaluation report (see §40.311(d)(10)).

(b) As an employer receiving a recommendation for these services from a SAP, you may, as part of a return-to-duty agreement with the employee, require the employee to participate in the recommended services. You may monitor and document the employee's participation in the recommended services. You may also make use of SAP and employee assistance program (EAP) services in assisting and monitoring employees' compliance with SAP recommendations. Nothing in this section permits an employer to fail to carry out its obligations with respect to follow-up testing (see §40.309).

(c) As an employee, you are obligated to comply with the SAP's recommendations for these services. If you fail or refuse to do so, you may be subject to disciplinary action by your employer.

§40.305 How does the return-to-duty process conclude?

(a) As the employer, if you decide that you want to permit the employee to return to the performance of safety-sensitive functions, you must ensure that the employee takes a return-to-duty test. This test cannot occur until after the SAP has determined that the employee has successfully complied with prescribed education and/or treatment. The employee must have a negative drug test result and/or an alcohol test with an alcohol concentration of less than 0.02 before resuming performance of safety-sensitive duties.

(b) As an employer, you must not return an employee to safety-sensitive duties until the employee meets the conditions of paragraph (a) of this section. However, you are not required to return an employee to safety-sensitive duties because the employee has met these conditions. That is a personnel decision that you have the discretion to make, subject to collective bargaining agreements or other legal requirements.

(c) As a SAP or MRO, you must not make a "fitness for duty" determination as part of this re-evaluation unless required to do so under an applicable DOT agency regulation. It is the employer, rather than you, who must decide whether to put the employee back to work in a safety-sensitive position.

§40.307 What is the SAP's function in prescribing the employee's follow-up tests?

(a) As a SAP, for each employee who has committed a DOT drug or alcohol regulation violation, and who seeks to resume the performance of safety-sensitive functions, you must establish a written follow-up testing plan. You do not establish this plan until after you determine that the employee has successfully complied with your recommendations for education and/or treatment.

(b) You must present a copy of this plan directly to the DER (see §40.311(d)(9)).

(c) You are the sole determiner of the number and frequency of follow-up tests and whether these tests will be for drugs, alcohol, or both, unless otherwise directed by the appropriate DOT agency regulation. For example, if the employee had a positive drug test, but your evaluation or the treatment program professionals determined that the employee had an alcohol problem as well, you should require that the employee have follow-up tests for both drugs and alcohol.

(d) However, you must, at a minimum, direct that the employee be subject to six unannounced follow-up tests in the first 12 months of safety-sensitive duty following the employee's return to safety-sensitive functions.

(1) You may require a greater number of follow-up tests during the first 12- month period of safety-sensitive duty (*e.g.*, you may require one test a month during the 12-month period; you may require two tests per month during the first 6-month period and one test per month during the final 6-month period).

(2) You may also require follow-up tests during the 48 months of safety-sensitive duty following this first 12-month period.

(3) You are not to establish the actual dates for the follow-up

tests you prescribe. The decision on specific dates to test is the employer's.

(4) As the employer, you must not impose additional testing requirements (*e.g.*, under company authority) on the employee that go beyond the SAP's follow-up testing plan.

(e) The requirements of the SAP's follow-up testing plan "follow the employee" to subsequent employers or through breaks in service.

Example 1 to Paragraph (e): The employee returns to duty with Employer A. Two months afterward, after completing the first two of six follow-up tests required by the SAP's plan, the employee quits his job with Employer A and begins to work in a similar position for Employer B. The employee remains obligated to complete the four additional tests during the next 10 months of safety-sensitive duty, and Employer B is responsible for ensuring that the employee does so. Employer B learns of this obligation through the inquiry it makes under §40.25.

Example 2 to Paragraph (e): The employee returns to duty with Employer A. Three months later, after the employee completes the first two of six follow-up tests required by the SAP's plan, Employer A lays the employee off for economic or seasonal employment reasons. Four months later, Employer A recalls the employee. Employer A must ensure that the employee completes the remaining four follow-up tests during the next nine months.

(f) As the SAP, you may modify the determinations you have made concerning follow-up tests. For example, even if you recommended follow-up testing beyond the first 12-months, you can terminate the testing requirement at any time after the first year of testing. You must not, however, modify the requirement that the employee take at least six follow-up tests within the first 12 months after returning to the performance of safety-sensitive functions.

§40.309 What are the employer's responsibilities with respect to the SAP's directions for follow-up tests?

(a) As the employer, you must carry out the SAP's follow-up testing requirements. You may not allow the employee to continue to perform safety-sensitive functions unless follow-up testing is conducted as directed by the SAP.

(b) You should schedule follow-up tests on dates of your own choosing, but you must ensure that the tests are unannounced with no discernable pattern as to their timing, and that the employee is given no advance notice.

(c) You cannot substitute any other tests (*e.g.*, those carried out under the random testing program) conducted on the employee for this follow-up testing requirement.

(d) You cannot count a follow-up test that has been cancelled as a completed test. A cancelled follow-up test must be recollected.

§40.311 What are the requirements concerning SAP reports?

(a) As the SAP conducting the required evaluations, you must send the written reports required by this section in writing directly to the DER and not to a third party or entity for forwarding to the DER (except as provided in §40.355(e)). You may, however, forward the document simultaneously to the DER and to a C/TPA.

(b) As an employer, you must ensure that you receive SAP written reports directly from the SAP performing the evaluation and that no third party or entity changed the SAP's report in any way.

(c) The SAP's written report, following an initial evaluation that determines what level of assistance is needed to address the employee's drug and/or alcohol problems, must be on the SAP's own letterhead (and not the letterhead of another service agent) signed and dated by the SAP, and must contain the following delineated items:

(1) Employee's name and SSN;

(2) Employer's name and address;

(3) Reason for the assessment (specific violation of DOT regulations and violation date);

(4) Date(s) of the assessment;

(5) SAP's education and/or treatment recommendation; and

(6) SAP's telephone number.

(d) The SAP's written report concerning a follow-up evaluation that determines the employee has demonstrated successful compliance must be on the SAP's own letterhead (and not the letterhead of another service agent), signed by the SAP and dated, and must contain the following items:

(1) Employee's name and SSN;

(2) Employer's name and address;

(3) Reason for the initial assessment (specific violation of DOT regulations and violation date);

(4) Date(s) of the initial assessment and synopsis of the treatment plan;

(5) Name of practice(s) or service(s) providing the recommended education and/or treatment;

(6) Inclusive dates of employee's program participation;

(7) Clinical characterization of employee's program participation;

(8) SAP's clinical determination as to whether the employee has demonstrated successful compliance;

(9) Follow-up testing plan;

(10) Employee's continuing care needs with specific treatment, aftercare, and/or support group services recommendations; and

(11) SAP's telephone number.

(e) The SAP's written report concerning a follow-up evaluation that determines the employee has not demonstrated successful compliance must be on the SAP's own letterhead (and not the letterhead of another service agent), signed by the SAP and dated, and must contain the following items:

(1) Employee's name and SSN;

(2) Employer's name and address;

(3) Reason for the initial assessment (specific DOT violation and date);

(4) Date(s) of initial assessment and synopsis of treatment plan;

(5) Name of practice(s) or service(s) providing the recommended education and/or treatment;

(6) Inclusive dates of employee's program participation;

(7) Clinical characterization of employee's program participation;

(8) Date(s) of the first follow-up evaluation;

(9) Date(s) of any further follow-up evaluation the SAP has scheduled;

(10) SAP's clinical reasons for determining that the employee has not demonstrated successful compliance; and

(11) SAP's telephone number.

(f) As a SAP, you must also provide these written reports directly to the employee if the employee has no current employer and to the gaining DOT regulated employer in the event the employee obtains another transportation industry safety-sensitive position.

(g) As a SAP, you are to maintain copies of your reports to employers for 5 years, and your employee clinical records in accordance with Federal, state, and local laws regarding record maintenance, confidentiality, and release of information. You must make these records available, on request, to DOT agency representatives (*e.g.*, inspectors conducting an audit or safety investigation) and representatives of the NTSB in an accident investigation.

(h) As an employer, you must maintain your reports from SAPs for 5 years from the date you received them.

§40.313 Where is other information on SAP functions and the return-to-duty process found in this regulation?

You can find other information on the role and functions of SAPs in the following sections of this part:

§40.3—Definition.

§40.347—Service agent assistance with SAP-required follow-up testing.

§40.355—Transmission of SAP reports.

§40.329(c)—Making SAP reports available to employees on request.

Appendix E to Part 40—SAP Equivalency Requirements for Certification Organizations.

Subpart P — Confidentiality and Release of Information

§40.321 What is the general confidentiality rule for drug and alcohol test information?

Except as otherwise provided in this subpart, as a service agent or employer participating in the DOT drug or alcohol testing process, you are prohibited from releasing individual test results or medical information about an employee to third parties without the employee's specific written consent.

(a) A "third party" is any person or organization to whom other subparts of this regulation do not explicitly authorize or require the transmission of information in the course of the drug or alcohol testing process.

(b) "Specific written consent" means a statement signed by the employee that he or she agrees to the release of a particular piece of information to a particular, explicitly identified, person or organization at a particular time. "Blanket releases," in which an employee agrees to a release of a category of information (*e.g.*, all test results) or to release information to a category of parties (*e.g.,* other employers who are members of a C/TPA, companies to which the employee may apply for employment), are prohibited under this part.

§40.323 May program participants release drug or alcohol test information in connection with legal proceedings?

(a) As an employer, you may release information pertaining to an employee's drug or alcohol test without the employee's consent in certain legal proceedings.

(1) These proceedings include a lawsuit (*e.g.,* a wrongful discharge action), grievance (*e.g.,* an arbitration concerning disciplinary action taken by the employer), or administrative proceeding (*e.g.,* an unemployment compensation hearing) brought by, or on behalf of, an employee and resulting from a positive DOT drug or alcohol test or a refusal to test (including, but not limited to, adulterated or substituted test results).

(2) These proceedings also include a criminal or civil action resulting from an employee's performance of safety-sensitive duties, in which a court of competent jurisdiction determines that the drug or alcohol test information sought is relevant to the case and issues an order directing the employer to produce the information. For example, in personal injury litigation following a truck or bus collision, the court could determine that a post-accident drug test result of an employee is relevant to determining whether the driver or the driver's employer was negligent. The employer is authorized to respond to the court's order to produce the records.

(b) In such a proceeding, you may release the information to the decision maker in the proceeding (*e.g.,* the court in a lawsuit). You may release the information only with a binding stipulation that the decision maker to whom it is released will make it available only to parties to the proceeding.

(c) If you are a service agent, and the employer requests its employee's drug or alcohol testing information from you to use in a legal proceeding as authorized in paragraph (a) of this section (*e.g.,* the laboratory's data package), you must provide the requested information to the employer.

(d) As an employer or service agent, you must immediately notify the employee in writing of any information you release under this section.

§40.325 [Reserved]

§40.327 When must the MRO report medical information gathered in the verification process?

(a) As the MRO, you must, except as provided in paragraph (c) of this section, report drug test results and medical information you learned as part of the verification process to third parties without the employee's consent if you determine, in your reasonable medical judgment, that:

(1) The information is likely to result in the employee being determined to be medically unqualified under an applicable DOT agency regulation; or

(2) The information indicates that continued performance by the employee of his or her safety-sensitive function is likely to pose a significant safety risk.

(b) The third parties to whom you are authorized to provide information by this section include the employer, a physician or other health care provider responsible for determining the medical qualifications of the employee under an applicable DOT agency safety regulation, a SAP evaluating the employee as part of the return to duty process (see §40.293(g)), a DOT agency, or the National Transportation Safety Board in the course of an accident investigation.

(c) If the law of a foreign country (*e.g.,* Canada) prohibits you from providing medical information to the employer, you may comply with that prohibition.

§40.329 What information must laboratories, MROs, and other service agents release to employees?

(a) As an MRO or service agent you must provide, within 10 business days of receiving a written request from an employee, copies of any records pertaining to the employee's use of alcohol and/or drugs, including records of the employee's DOT-mandated drug and/or alcohol tests. You may charge no more than the cost of preparation and reproduction for copies of these records.

(b) As a laboratory, you must provide, within 10 business days of receiving a written request from an employee, and made through the MRO, the records relating to the results of the employee's drug test (*i.e.,* laboratory report and data package). You may charge no more than the cost of preparation and reproduction for copies of these records.

(c) As a SAP, you must make available to an employee, on request, a copy of all SAP reports (see §40.311). However, you must redact follow-up testing information from the report before providing it to the employee.

§40.331 To what additional parties must employers and service agents release information?

As an employer or service agent you must release information under the following circumstances:

(a) If you receive a specific, written consent from an employee authorizing the release of information about that employee's drug or alcohol tests to an identified person, you must provide the information to the identified person. For example, as an employer, when you receive a written request from a former employee to provide information to a subsequent employer, you must do so. In providing the information, you must comply with the terms of the employee's consent.

(b) If you are an employer, you must, upon request of DOT agency representatives, provide the following:

(1) Access to your facilities used for this part and DOT agency drug and alcohol program functions.

(2) All written, printed, and computer-based drug and alcohol program records and reports (including copies of name-specific records or reports), files, materials, data, documents/documentation, agreements, contracts, policies, and statements that are required by this part and DOT agency regulations. You must provide this information at your principal place of business in the time required by the DOT agency.

(3) All items in paragraph (b)(2) of this section must be easily accessible, legible, and provided in an organized manner. If electronic records do not meet these standards, they must be converted to printed documentation that meets these standards.

(c) If you are a service agent, you must, upon request of DOT agency representatives, provide the following:

(1) Access to your facilities used for this part and DOT agency drug and alcohol program functions.

(2) All written, printed, and computer-based drug and alcohol program records and reports (including copies of name-specific records or reports), files, materials, data, documents/documentation, agreements, contracts, policies, and statements that are required by this part and DOT agency regulations. You must provide this information at your principal place of business in the time required by the DOT agency.

(3) All items in paragraph (c)(2) of this section must be easily

accessible, legible, and provided in an organized manner. If electronic records do not meet these standards, they must be converted to printed documentation that meets these standards.

(d) If requested by the National Transportation Safety Board as part of an accident investigation, you must provide information concerning post-accident tests administered after the accident.

(e) If requested by a Federal, state or local safety agency with regulatory authority over you or the employee, you must provide drug and alcohol test records concerning the employee.

(f) Except as otherwise provided in this part, as a laboratory you must not release or provide a specimen or a part of a specimen to a requesting party, without first obtaining written consent from ODAPC. If a party seeks a court order directing you to release a specimen or part of a specimen contrary to any provision of this part, you must take necessary legal steps to contest the issuance of the order (*e.g.,* seek to quash a subpoena, citing the requirements of §40.13). This part does not require you to disobey a court order, however.

§40.333 What records must employers keep?

(a) As an employer, you must keep the following records for the following periods of time:

(1) You must keep the following records for five years:

(i) Records of alcohol test results indicating an alcohol concentration of 0.02 or greater;

(ii) Records of verified positive drug test results;

(iii) Documentation of refusals to take required alcohol and/or drug tests (including substituted or adulterated drug test results);

(iv) SAP reports; and

(v) All follow-up tests and schedules for follow-up tests.

(2) You must keep records for three years of information obtained from previous employers under §40.25 concerning drug and alcohol test results of employees.

(3) You must keep records of the inspection, maintenance, and calibration of EBTs, for two years.

(4) You must keep records of negative and cancelled drug test results and alcohol test results with a concentration of less than 0.02 for one year.

(b) You do not have to keep records related to a program requirement that does not apply to you (*e.g.,* a maritime employer who does not have a DOT-mandated random alcohol testing program need not maintain random alcohol testing records).

(c) You must maintain the records in a location with controlled access.

(d) A service agent may maintain these records for you. However, you must ensure that you can produce these records at your principal place of business in the time required by the DOT agency. For example, as a motor carrier, when an FMCSA inspector requests your records, you must ensure that you can provide them within two business days.

(e) If you store records electronically, where permitted by this part, you must ensure that the records are easily accessible, legible, and formatted and stored in an organized manner. If electronic records do not meet these criteria, you must convert them to printed documentation in a rapid and readily auditable manner, at the request of DOT agency personnel.

Subpart Q — Roles and Responsibilities of Service Agents

§40.341 Must service agents comply with DOT drug and alcohol testing requirements?

(a) As a service agent, the services you provide to transportation employers must meet the requirements of this part and the DOT agency drug and alcohol testing regulations.

(b) If you do not comply, DOT may take action under the Public Interest Exclusions procedures of this part (see Subpart R of this part) or applicable provisions of other DOT agency regulations.

§40.343 What tasks may a service agent perform for an employer?

As a service agent, you may perform for employers the tasks needed to comply with DOT agency drug and alcohol testing regulations, subject to the requirements and limitations of this part.

§40.345 In what circumstances may a C/TPA act as an intermediary in the transmission of drug and alcohol testing information to employers?

(a) As a C/TPA or other service agent, you may act as an intermediary in the transmission of drug and alcohol testing information in the circumstances specified in this section only if the employer chooses to have you do so. Each employer makes the decision about whether to receive some or all of this information from you, acting as an intermediary, rather than directly from the service agent who originates the information (*e.g.*, an MRO or BAT).

(b) The specific provisions of this part concerning which you may act as an intermediary are listed in Appendix F to this part. These are the only situations in which you may act as an intermediary. You are prohibited from doing so in all other situations.

(c) In every case, you must ensure that, in transmitting information to employers, you meet all requirements (*e.g.*, concerning confidentiality and timing) that would apply if the service agent originating the information (*e.g.*, an MRO or collector) sent the information directly to the employer. For example, if you transmit drug testing results from MROs to DERs, you must transmit each drug test result to the DER in compliance with the MRO requirements set forth in §40.167.

§40.347 What functions may C/TPAs perform with respect to administering testing?

As a C/TPA, except as otherwise specified in this part, you may perform the following functions for employers concerning random selection and other selections for testing.

(a) You may operate random testing programs for employers and may assist (*i.e.*, through contracting with laboratories or collection sites, conducting collections) employers with other types of testing (*e.g.*, pre-employment, post-accident, reasonable suspicion, return-to-duty, and follow-up).

(b) You may combine employees from more than one employer or one transportation industry in a random pool if permitted by all the DOT agency drug and alcohol testing regulations involved.

(1) If you combine employees from more than one transportation industry, you must ensure that the random testing rate is at least equal to the highest rate required by each DOT agency.

(2) Employees not covered by DOT agency regulations may not be part of the same random pool with DOT covered employees.

(c) You may assist employers in ensuring that follow-up testing is conducted in accordance with the plan established by the SAP. However, neither you nor the employer are permitted to randomly select employees from a "follow-up pool" for follow-up testing.

§40.349 What records may a service agent receive and maintain?

(a) Except where otherwise specified in this part, as a service agent you may receive and maintain all records concerning DOT drug and alcohol testing programs, including positive, negative, and refusal to test individual test results. You do not need the employee's consent to receive and maintain these records.

(b) You may maintain all information needed for operating a drug/alcohol program (*e.g.,* CCFs, ATFs, names of employees in random pools, random selection lists, copies of notices to employers of selected employees) on behalf of an employer.

(c) If a service agent originating drug or alcohol testing information, such as an MRO or BAT, sends the information directly to the DER, he or she may also provide the information simultaneously to you, as a C/TPA or other service agent who maintains this information for the employer.

(d) If you are serving as an intermediary in transmitting information that is required to be provided to the employer, you must ensure that it reaches the employer in the same time periods required elsewhere in this part.

(e) You must ensure that you can make available to the employer within two business days any information the employer is asked to produce by a DOT agency representative.

(f) On request of an employer, you must, at any time on the request of an employer, transfer immediately all records pertaining to the employer and its employees to the employer or to any other service agent the employer designates. You must carry out this transfer as soon as the employer requests it. You are not required to obtain employee consent for this transfer. You must not charge more than your reasonable administrative costs for conducting this transfer. You may not charge a fee for the release of these records.

(g) If you are planning to go out of business or your organization will be bought by or merged with another organization, you must immediately notify all employers and offer to transfer all records pertaining to the employer and its employees to the employer or to any other service agent the employer designates. You must carry out this transfer as soon as the employer requests it. You are not required to obtain employee consent for this transfer. You must not charge more than your reasonable administrative costs for conducting this transfer. You may not charge a fee for the release of these records.

§40.351 What confidentiality requirements apply to service agents?

Except where otherwise specified in this part, as a service agent the following confidentiality requirements apply to you:

(a) When you receive or maintain confidential information about employees (*e.g.,* individual test results), you must follow the same confidentiality regulations as the employer with respect to the use and release of this information.

(b) You must follow all confidentiality and records retention requirements applicable to employers.

(c) You may not provide individual test results or other confidential information to another employer without a specific, written consent from the employee. For example, suppose you are a C/TPA that has employers X and Y as clients. Employee Jones works for X, and you maintain Jones' drug and alcohol test for X. Jones wants to change jobs and work for Y. You may not inform Y of the result of a test conducted for X without having a specific, written consent from Jones. Likewise, you may not provide this information to employer Z, who is not a C/TPA member, without this consent.

(d) You must not use blanket consent forms authorizing the release of employee testing information.

(e) You must establish adequate confidentiality and security measures to ensure that confidential employee records are not available to unauthorized persons. This includes protecting the physical security of records, access controls, and computer security measures to safeguard confidential data in electronic data bases.

§40.353 What principles govern the interaction between MROs and other service agents?

As a service agent other than an MRO (*e.g.,* a C/ TPA), the following principles govern your interaction with MROs:

(a) You may provide MRO services to employers, directly or through contract, if you meet all applicable provisions of this part.

(b) If you employ or contract for an MRO, the MRO must perform duties independently and confidentially. When you have a relationship with an MRO, you must structure the relationship to ensure that this independence and confidentiality are not compromised. Specific means (including both physical and operational measures, as appropriate) to separate MRO functions and other service agent functions are essential.

(c) Only your staff who are actually under the day-to-day supervision and control of an MRO with respect to MRO functions may perform these functions. This does not mean that those staff may not perform other functions at other times. However, the designation of your staff to perform MRO functions under MRO supervision must be limited and not used as a subterfuge to circumvent confidentiality and other requirements of this part and DOT agency regulations. You must ensure that MRO staff operate under controls sufficient to ensure that the independence and confidentiality of the MRO process are not compromised.

(d) Like other MROs, an MRO you employ or contract with must personally conduct verification interviews with employees and must personally make all verification decisions. Consequently, your staff cannot perform these functions.

§40.355 What limitations apply to the activities of service agents?

As a service agent, you are subject to the following limitations concerning your activities in the DOT drug and alcohol testing program.

(a) You must not require an employee to sign a consent, release, waiver of liability, or indemnification agreement with respect to any part of the drug or alcohol testing process covered by this part (including, but not limited to, collections, laboratory testing, MRO, and SAP services). No one may do so on behalf of a service agent.

(b) You must not act as an intermediary in the transmission of drug test results from the laboratory to the MRO. That is, the laboratory may not send results to you, with you in turn sending them to the MRO for verification. For example, a practice in which the laboratory transmits results to your computer system, and you then assign the results to a particular MRO, is not permitted.

(c) You must not transmit drug test results directly from the laboratory to the employer (by electronic or other means) or to a service agent who forwards them to the employer. All confirmed laboratory results must be processed by the MRO before they are released to any other party.

(d) You must not act as an intermediary in the transmission of alcohol test results of 0.02 or higher from the STT or BAT to the DER.

(e) Except as provided in paragraph (f) of this section, you must not act as an intermediary in the transmission of individual SAP reports to the actual employer. That is, the SAP may not send such reports to you, with you in turn sending them to the actual employer. However, you may maintain individual SAP summary reports and follow-up testing plans after they are sent to the DER, and the SAP may transmit such reports to you simultaneously with sending them to the DER.

(f) As an exception to paragraph (e) of this section, you may act as an intermediary in the transmission of SAP report from the SAP to an owner-operator or other self-employed individual.

(g) Except as provided in paragraph (h) of this section, you must not make decisions to test an employee based upon reasonable suspicion, post-accident, return-to-duty, and follow-up determination criteria. These are duties the actual employer cannot delegate to a C/ TPA. You may, however, provide advice and information to employers regarding these testing issues and how the employer should schedule required testing.

(h) As an exception to paragraph (g) of this section, you may make decisions to test an employee based upon reasonable suspicion, post-accident, return-to-duty, and follow-up determination criteria with respect to an owner-operator or other self-employed individual.

(i) Except as provided in paragraph (j) of this section, you must not make a determination that an employee has refused a drug or alcohol test. This is a non-delegable duty of the actual employer. You may, however, provide advice and information to employers regarding refusal-to-test issues.

(j) As an exception to paragraph (i) of this section, you may make a determination that an employee has refused a drug or alcohol test, if:

(1) You schedule a required test for an owner-operator or other self-employed individual, and the individual fails to appear for the test without a legitimate reason; or

(2) As an MRO, you determine that an individual has refused to test on the basis of adulteration or substitution.

(k) You must not act as a DER. For example, while you may be responsible for transmitting information to the employer about test results, you must not act on behalf of the employer in actions to remove employees from safety-sensitive duties.

(l) In transmitting documents to laboratories, you must ensure that you send to the laboratory that conducts testing only the laboratory copy of the CCF. You must not transmit other copies of the CCF or any ATFs to the laboratory.

(m) You must not impose conditions or requirements on employers that DOT regulations do not authorize. For example, as a C/TPA serving employers in the pipeline or motor carrier industry, you must not require employers to have provisions in their DOT plans that RSPA or FMCSA regulations do not require.

(n) You must not intentionally delay the transmission of drug or alcohol testing-related documents concerning actions you have performed, because of a payment dispute or other reasons.

Example 1 to Paragraph (n): A laboratory that has tested a specimen must not delay transmitting the documentation of the test result to an MRO because of a billing or payment dispute with the MRO or a C/TPA.

Example 2 to Paragraph (n): An MRO or SAP who has interviewed an employee must not delay sending a verified test result or SAP report to the employer because of such a dispute with the employer or employee.

Example 3 to Paragraph (n): A collector who has performed a urine specimen collection must not delay sending the drug specimen and CCF to the laboratory because of a payment or other dispute with the laboratory or a C/TPA.

Example 4 to Paragraph (n): A BAT who has conducted an alcohol test must not delay sending test result information to an employer or C/TPA because of a payment or other dispute with the employer or C/TPA.

(o) While you must follow the DOT agency regulations, the actual employer remains accountable to DOT for compliance, and your failure to implement any aspect of the program as required in this part and other applicable DOT agency regulations makes the employer subject to enforcement action by the Department.

Subpart R — Public Interest Exclusions

§40.361 What is the purpose of a public interest exclusion (PIE)?

(a) To protect the public interest, including protecting transportation employers and employees from serious noncompliance with DOT drug and alcohol testing rules, the Department's policy is to ensure that employers conduct business only with responsible service agents.

(b) The Department therefore uses PIEs to exclude from participation in DOT's drug and alcohol testing program any service agent who, by serious noncompliance with this part or other DOT agency drug and alcohol testing regulations, has shown that it is not currently acting in a responsible manner.

(c) A PIE is a serious action that the Department takes only to protect the public interest. We intend to use PIEs only to remedy situations of serious noncompliance. PIEs are not used for the purpose of punishment.

(d) Nothing in this subpart precludes a DOT agency or the Inspector General from taking other action authorized by its regulations with respect to service agents or employers that violate its regulations.

§40.363 On what basis may the Department issue a PIE?

(a) If you are a service agent, the Department may issue a PIE concerning you if we determine that you have failed or refused to provide drug or alcohol testing services consistent with the requirements of this part or a DOT agency drug and alcohol regulation.

(b) The Department also may issue a PIE if you have failed to cooperate with DOT agency representatives concerning inspections, complaint investigations, compliance and enforcement reviews, or requests for documents and other information about compliance with this part or DOT agency drug and alcohol regulations.

§40.365 What is the Department's policy concerning starting a PIE proceeding?

(a) It is the Department's policy to start a PIE proceeding only in cases of serious, uncorrected noncompliance with the provisions of this part, affecting such matters as safety, the outcomes of test results, privacy and confidentiality, due process and fairness for employees, the honesty and integrity of the testing program, and cooperation with or provision of information to DOT agency representatives.

(b) The following are examples of the kinds of serious noncompliance that, as a matter of policy, the Department views as appropriate grounds for starting a PIE proceeding. These examples are not intended to be an exhaustive or exclusive list of the grounds for starting a PIE proceeding. We intend them to illustrate the level of seriousness that the Department believes supports starting a PIE proceeding. The examples follow:

(1) For an MRO, verifying tests positive without interviewing the employees as required by this part or providing MRO services without meeting the qualifications for an MRO required by this part;

(2) For a laboratory, refusing to provide information to the Department, an employer, or an employee as required by this part; failing or refusing to conduct a validity testing program when required by this part; or a pattern or practice of testing errors that result in the cancellation of tests. (As a general matter of policy, the Department does not intend to initiate a PIE proceeding concerning a laboratory with respect to matters on which HHS initiates certification actions under its laboratory guidelines.);

(3) For a collector, a pattern or practice of directly observing collections when doing so is unauthorized, or failing or refusing to directly observe collections when doing so is mandatory;

(4) For collectors, BATs, or STTs, a pattern or practice of using forms, testing equipment, or collection kits that do not meet the standards in this part;

(5) For a collector, BAT, or STT, a pattern or practice of "fatal flaws" or other significant uncorrected errors in the collection process;

(6) For a laboratory, MRO or C/TPA, failing or refusing to report tests results as required by this part or DOT agency regulations;

(7) For a laboratory, falsifying, concealing, or destroying documentation concerning any part of the drug testing process, including, but not limited to, documents in a "litigation package";

(8) For SAPs, providing SAP services while not meeting SAP qualifications required by this part or performing evaluations without face-to-face interviews;

(9) For any service agent, maintaining a relationship with another party that constitutes a conflict of interest under this part (*e.g.,* a laboratory that derives a financial benefit from having an employer use a specific MRO);

(10) For any service agent, representing falsely that the service agent or its activities is approved or certified by the Department or a DOT agency;

(11) For any service agent, disclosing an employee's test result information to any party this part or a DOT agency regulation does not authorize, including by obtaining a "blanket" con-

sent from employees or by creating a data base from which employers or others can retrieve an employee's DOT test results without the specific consent of the employee;

(12) For any service agent, interfering or attempting to interfere with the ability of an MRO to communicate with the Department, or retaliating against an MRO for communicating with the Department;

(13) For any service agent, directing or recommending that an employer fail or refuse to implement any provision of this part; or

(14) With respect to noncompliance with a DOT agency regulation, conduct that affects important provisions of Department-wide concern (*e.g.,* failure to properly conduct the selection process for random testing).

§40.367 Who initiates a PIE proceeding?

The following DOT officials may initiate a PIE proceeding:

(a) The drug and alcohol program manager of a DOT agency;

(b) An official of ODAPC, other than the Director; or

(c) The designee of any of these officials.

§40.369 What is the discretion of an initiating official in starting a PIE proceeding?

(a) Initiating officials have broad discretion in deciding whether to start a PIE proceeding.

(b) In exercising this discretion, the initiating official must consider the Department's policy regarding the seriousness of the service agent's conduct (see §40.365) and all information he or she has obtained to this point concerning the facts of the case. The initiating official may also consider the availability of the resources needed to pursue a PIE proceeding.

(c) A decision not to initiate a PIE proceeding does not necessarily mean that the Department regards a service agent as being in compliance or that the Department may not use other applicable remedies in a situation of noncompliance.

§40.371 On what information does an initiating official rely in deciding whether to start a PIE proceeding?

(a) An initiating official may rely on credible information from any source as the basis for starting a PIE proceeding.

(b) Before sending a correction notice (see §40.373), the initiating official informally contacts the service agent to determine if there is any information that may affect the initiating official's

§40.373

determination about whether it is necessary to send a correction notice. The initiating official may take any information resulting from this contact into account in determining whether to proceed under this subpart.

§40.373 Before starting a PIE proceeding, does the initiating official give the service agent an opportunity to correct problems?

(a) If you are a service agent, the initiating official must send you a correction notice before starting a PIE proceeding.

(b) The correction notice identifies the specific areas in which you must come into compliance in order to avoid being subject to a PIE proceeding.

(c) If you make and document changes needed to come into compliance in the areas listed in the correction notice to the satisfaction of the initiating official within 60 days of the date you receive the notice, the initiating official does not start a PIE proceeding. The initiating official may conduct appropriate fact finding to verify that you have made and maintained satisfactory corrections. When he or she is satisfied that you are in compliance, the initiating official sends you a notice that the matter is concluded.

§40.375 How does the initiating official start a PIE proceeding?

(a) As a service agent, if your compliance matter is not correctable (see §40.373(a)), or if have not resolved compliance matters as provided in §40.373(c), the initiating official starts a PIE proceeding by sending you a notice of proposed exclusion (NOPE). The NOPE contains the initiating official's recommendations concerning the issuance of a PIE, but it is not a decision by the Department to issue a PIE.

(b) The NOPE includes the following information:

(1) A statement that the initiating official is recommending that the Department issue a PIE concerning you;

(2) The factual basis for the initiating official's belief that you are not providing drug and/or alcohol testing services to DOT-regulated employers consistent with the requirements of this part or are in serious noncompliance with a DOT agency drug and alcohol regulation;

(3) The factual basis for the initiating official's belief that your noncompliance has not been or cannot be corrected;

(4) The initiating official's recommendation for the scope of the PIE;

(5) The initiating official's recommendation for the duration of the PIE; and

(6) A statement that you may contest the issuance of the proposed PIE, as provided in §40.379.

(c) The initiating official sends a copy of the NOPE to the ODAPC Director at the same time he or she sends the NOPE to you.

§40.377 Who decides whether to issue a PIE?

(a) The ODAPC Director, or his or her designee, decides whether to issue a PIE. If a designee is acting as the decision-maker, all references in this subpart to the Director refer to the designee.

(b) To ensure his or her impartiality, the Director plays no role in the initiating official's determination about whether to start a PIE proceeding.

(c) There is a "firewall" between the initiating official and the Director. This means that the initiating official and the Director are prohibited from having any discussion, contact, or exchange of information with one another about the matter, except for documents and discussions that are part of the record of the proceeding.

§40.379 How do you contest the issuance of a PIE?

(a) If you receive a NOPE, you may contest the issuance of the PIE.

(b) If you want to contest the proposed PIE, you must provide the Director information and argument in opposition to the proposed PIE in writing, in person, and/or through a representative. To contest the proposed PIE, you must take one or more of the steps listed in this paragraph (b) within 30 days after you receive the NOPE.

(1) You may request that the Director dismiss the proposed PIE without further proceedings, on the basis that it does not concern serious noncompliance with this part or DOT agency regulations, consistent with the Department's policy as stated in §40.365.

(2) You may present written information and arguments, consistent with the provisions of §40.381, contesting the proposed PIE.

(3) You may arrange with the Director for an informal meeting to present your information and arguments.

(c) If you do not take any of the actions listed in paragraph (b) of this section within 30 days after you receive the NOPE, the matter proceeds as an uncontested case. In this event, the Director makes his or her decision based on the record provided by the initiating official (*i.e.*, the NOPE and any supporting information or testimony) and any additional information the Director obtains.

§40.381 What information do you present to contest the proposed issuance of a PIE?

(a) As a service agent who wants to contest a proposed PIE, you must present at least the following information to the Director:

(1) Specific facts that contradict the statements contained in the NOPE (see §40.375(b)(2) and (3)). A general denial is insufficient to raise a genuine dispute over facts material to the issuance of a PIE;

(2) Identification of any existing, proposed or prior PIE; and

(3) Identification of your affiliates, if any.

(b) You may provide any information and arguments you wish concerning the proposed issuance, scope and duration of the PIE (see §40.375(b)(4) and (5)).

(c) You may provide any additional relevant information or arguments concerning any of the issues in the matter.

§40.383 What procedures apply if you contest the issuance of a PIE?

(a) DOT conducts PIE proceedings in a fair and informal manner. The Director may use flexible procedures to allow you to present matters in opposition. The Director is not required to follow formal rules of evidence or procedure in creating the record of the proceeding.

(b) The Director will consider any information or argument he or she determines to be relevant to the decision on the matter.

(c) You may submit any documentary evidence you want the Director to consider. In addition, if you have arranged an informal meeting with the Director, you may present witnesses and confront any person the initiating official presents as a witness against you.

(d) In cases where there are material factual issues in dispute, the Director or his or her designee may conduct additional fact-finding.

(e) If you have arranged a meeting with the Director, the Director will make a transcribed record of the meeting available to you on your request. You must pay the cost of transcribing and copying the meeting record.

§40.385 Who bears the burden of proof in a PIE proceeding?

(a) As the proponent of issuing a PIE, the initiating official bears the burden of proof.

(b) This burden is to demonstrate, by a preponderance of the evidence, that the service agent was in serious noncompliance with the requirements of this part for drug and/or alcohol testing-related services or with the requirements of another DOT agency drug and alcohol testing regulation.

§40.387 What matters does the Director decide concerning a proposed PIE?

(a) Following the service agent's response (see §40.379(b)) or, if no response is received, after 30 days have passed from the date on which the service agent received the NOPE, the Director may take one of the following steps:

(1) In response to a request from the service agent (see §40.379(b)(1)) or on his or her own motion, the Director may dismiss a PIE proceeding if he or she determines that it does not concern serious noncompliance with this part or DOT agency regulations, consistent with the Department's policy as stated in §40.365.

(i) If the Director dismisses a proposed PIE under this paragraph (a), the action is closed with respect to the noncompliance alleged in the NOPE.

(ii) The Department may initiate a new PIE proceeding against you on the basis of different or subsequent conduct that is in noncompliance with this part or other DOT drug and alcohol testing rules.

(2) If the Director determines that the initiating official's submission does not have complete information needed for a decision, the Director may remand the matter to the initiating official. The initiating official may resubmit the matter to the Director when the needed information is complete. If the basis for the proposed PIE has changed, the initiating official must send an amended NOPE to the service agent.

(b) The Director makes determinations concerning the following matters in any PIE proceeding that he or she decides on the merits:

(1) Any material facts that are in dispute;

(2) Whether the facts support issuing a PIE;

(3) The scope of any PIE that is issued; and

(4) The duration of any PIE that is issued.

§40.389 What factors may the Director consider?

This section lists examples of the kind of mitigating and aggravating factors that the Director may consider in determining whether to issue a PIE concerning you, as well as the scope and duration of a PIE. This list is not exhaustive or exclusive. The Director may consider other factors if appropriate in the circumstances of a particular case. The list of examples follows:

(a) The actual or potential harm that results or may result from your noncompliance;

(b) The frequency of incidents and/or duration of the noncompliance;

(c) Whether there is a pattern or prior history of noncompliance;

(d) Whether the noncompliance was pervasive within your organization, including such factors as the following:

(1) Whether and to what extent your organization planned, initiated, or carried out the noncompliance;

(2) The positions held by individuals involved in the noncompliance, and whether your principals tolerated their noncompliance; and

(3) Whether you had effective standards of conduct and control systems (both with respect to your own organization and any contractors or affiliates) at the time the noncompliance occurred;

(e) Whether you have demonstrated an appropriate compliance disposition, including such factors as the following:

(1) Whether you have accepted responsibility for the noncompliance and recognize the seriousness of the conduct that led to the cause for issuance of the PIE;

(2) Whether you have cooperated fully with the Department during the investigation. The Director may consider when the cooperation began and whether you disclosed all pertinent information known to you;

(3) Whether you have fully investigated the circumstances of the noncompliance forming the basis for the PIE and, if so, have made the result of the investigation available to the Director;

(4) Whether you have taken appropriate disciplinary action against the individuals responsible for the activity that constitutes the grounds for issuance of the PIE; and

(5) Whether your organization has taken appropriate corrective actions or remedial measures, including implementing actions to prevent recurrence;

(f) With respect to noncompliance with a DOT agency regulation, the degree to which the noncompliance affects matters common to the DOT drug and alcohol testing program;

(g) Other factors appropriate to the circumstances of the case.

§40.391 What is the scope of a PIE?

(a) The scope of a PIE is the Department's determination about the divisions, organizational elements, types of services, affiliates, and/or individuals (including direct employees of a service agent and its contractors) to which a PIE applies.

(b) If, as a service agent, the Department issues a PIE concerning you, the PIE applies to all your divisions, organizational elements, and types of services that are involved with or affected by the noncompliance that forms the factual basis for issuing the PIE.

(c) In the NOPE (see §40.375(b)(4)), the initiating official sets forth his or her recommendation for the scope of the PIE. The proposed scope of the PIE is one of the elements of the proceeding that the service agent may contest (see §40.381(b)) and about which the Director makes a decision (see §40.387(b)(3)).

(d) In recommending and deciding the scope of the PIE, the initiating official and Director, respectively, must take into account the provisions of paragraphs (e) through (j) of this section.

(e) The pervasiveness of the noncompliance within a service agent's organization (see §40.389(d)) is an important consideration in determining the scope of a PIE. The appropriate scope of a PIE grows broader as the pervasiveness of the noncompliance increases.

(f) The application of a PIE is not limited to the specific location or employer at which the conduct that forms the factual basis for issuing the PIE was discovered.

(g) A PIE applies to your affiliates, if the affiliate is involved with or affected by the conduct that forms the factual basis for issuing the PIE.

(h) A PIE applies to individuals who are officers, employees, directors, shareholders, partners, or other individuals associated with your organization in the following circumstances:

(1) Conduct forming any part of the factual basis of the PIE occurred in connection with the individual's performance of duties by or on behalf of your organization; or

(2) The individual knew of, had reason to know of, approved, or acquiesced in such conduct. The individual's acceptance of benefits derived from such conduct is evidence of such knowledge, acquiescence, or approval.

(i) If a contractor to your organization is solely responsible for the conduct that forms the factual basis for a PIE, the PIE does not apply to the service agent itself unless the service agent knew or should have known about the conduct and did not take action to correct it.

(j) PIEs do not apply to drug and alcohol testing that DOT does not regulate.

(k) The following examples illustrate how the Department intends the provisions of this section to work:

Example 1 to §40.391. Service Agent P provides a variety of drug testing services. P's SAP services are involved in a serious violation of this Part 40. However, P's other services fully comply with this part, and P's overall management did not plan or concur in the noncompliance, which in fact was contrary to P's articulated standards. Because the noncompliance was isolated in one area of the organization's activities, and did not pervade the entire organization, the scope of the PIE could be limited to SAP services.

Example 2 to §40.391. Service Agent Q provides a similar variety of services. The conduct forming the factual basis for a PIE concerns collections for a transit authority. As in Example 1, the noncompliance is not pervasive throughout Q's organization. The PIE would apply to collections at all locations served by Q, not just the particular transit authority or not just in the state in which the transit authority is located.

§40.391

Example 3 to §40.391. Service Agent R provides a similar array of services. One or more of the following problems exists: R's activities in several areas—collections, MROs, SAPs, protecting the confidentiality of information—are involved in serious noncompliance; DOT determines that R's management knew or should have known about serious noncompliance in one or more areas, but management did not take timely corrective action; or, in response to an inquiry from DOT personnel, R's management refuses to provide information about its operations. In each of these three cases, the scope of the PIE would include all aspects of R's services.

Example 4 to §40.391. Service Agent W provides only one kind of service (e.g., laboratory or MRO services). The Department issues a PIE concerning these services. Because W only provides this one kind of service, the PIE necessarily applies to all its operations.

Example 5 to §40.391. Service Agent X, by exercising reasonably prudent oversight of its collection contractor, should have known that the contractor was making numerous "fatal flaws" in tests. Alternatively, X received a correction notice pointing out these problems in its contractor's collections. In neither case did X take action to correct the problem. X, as well as the contractor, would be subject to a PIE with respect to collections.

Example 6 to §40.391. Service Agent Y could not reasonably have known that one of its MROs was regularly failing to interview employees before verifying tests positive. When it received a correction notice, Y immediately dismissed the erring MRO. In this case, the MRO would be subject to a PIE but Y would not.

Example 7 to §40.391. The Department issues a PIE with respect to Service Agent Z. Z provides services for DOT-regulated transportation employers, a Federal agency under the HHS-regulated Federal employee testing program, and various private businesses and public agencies that DOT does not regulate. The PIE applies only to the DOT-regulated transportation employers with respect to their DOT-mandated testing, not to the Federal agency or the other public agencies and private businesses. The PIE does not prevent the non-DOT regulated entities from continuing to use Z's services.

§40.393

§40.393 How long does a PIE stay in effect?

(a) In the NOPE (see §40.375(b)(5)), the initiating official proposes the duration of the PIE. The duration of the PIE is one of the elements of the proceeding that the service agent may contest (see §40.381(b)) and about which the Director makes a decision (see §40.387(b)(4)).

(b) In deciding upon the duration of the PIE, the Director considers the seriousness of the conduct on which the PIE is based and the continued need to protect employers and employees from the service agent's noncompliance. The Director considers factors such as those listed in §40.389 in making this decision.

(c) The duration of a PIE will be between one and five years, unless the Director reduces its duration under §40.407.

§40.395 Can you settle a PIE proceeding?

At any time before the Director's decision, you and the initiating official can, with the Director's concurrence, settle a PIE proceeding.

§40.397 When does the Director make a PIE decision?

The Director makes his or her decision within 60 days of the date when the record of a PIE proceeding is complete (including any meeting with the Director and any additional fact-finding that is necessary). The Director may extend this period for good cause for additional periods of up to 30 days.

§40.399 How does the Department notify service agents of its decision?

If you are a service agent involved in a PIE proceeding, the Director provides you written notice as soon as he or she makes a PIE decision. The notice includes the following elements:

(a) If the decision is not to issue a PIE, a statement of the reasons for the decision, including findings of fact with respect to any material factual issues that were in dispute.

(b) If the decision is to issue a PIE—

(1) A reference to the NOPE;

(2) A statement of the reasons for the decision, including findings of fact with respect to any material factual issues that were in dispute;

(3) A statement of the scope of the PIE; and

(4) A statement of the duration of the PIE.

§40.401 How does the Department notify employers and the public about a PIE?

(a) The Department maintains a document called the "List of Excluded Drug and Alcohol Service Agents." This document may be found on the Department's web site (http://www.dot.gov/ost/dapc). You may also request a copy of the document from ODAPC.

(b) When the Director issues a PIE, he or she adds to the List the name and address of the service agent, and any other persons or organizations, to whom the PIE applies and information about the scope and duration of the PIE.

(c) When a service agent ceases to be subject to a PIE, the Director removes this information from the List.

(d) The Department also publishes a *Federal Register* notice to inform the public on any occasion on which a service agent is added to or taken off the List.

§40.403 Must a service agent notify its clients when the Department issues a PIE?

(a) As a service agent, if the Department issues a PIE concerning you, you must notify each of your DOT-regulated employer clients, in writing, about the issuance, scope, duration, and effect of the PIE. You may meet this requirement by sending a copy of the Director's PIE decision or by a separate notice. You must send this notice to each client within three business days of receiving from the Department the notice provided for in §40.399(b).

(b) As part of the notice you send under paragraph (a) of this section, you must offer to transfer immediately all records pertaining to the employer and its employees to the employer or to any other service agent the employer designates. You must carry out this transfer as soon as the employer requests it.

§40.405 May the Federal courts review PIE decisions?

The Director's decision is a final administrative action of the Department. Like all final administrative actions of Federal agencies, the Director's decision is subject to judicial review under the Administrative Procedure Act (5 U.S.C. 551 *et. seq*).

§40.407 May a service agent ask to have a PIE reduced or terminated?

(a) Yes, as a service agent concerning whom the Department has issued a PIE, you may request that the Director terminate a PIE or reduce its duration and/or scope. This process is limited to the issues of duration and scope. It is not an appeal or reconsideration of the decision to issue the PIE.

(b) Your request must be in writing and supported with documentation.

(c) You must wait at least nine months from the date on which the Director issued the PIE to make this request.

(d) The initiating official who was the proponent of the PIE may provide information and arguments concerning your request to the Director.

(e) If the Director verifies that the sources of your noncompliance have been eliminated and that all drug or alcohol testing-related services you would provide to DOT-regulated employers will be consistent with the requirements of this part, the Director may issue a notice terminating or reducing the PIE.

§40.409 What does the issuance of a PIE mean to transportation employers?

(a) As an employer, you are deemed to have notice of the issuance of a PIE when it appears on the List mentioned in §40.401(a) or the notice of the PIE appears in the *Federal Register* as provided in §40.401(d). You should check this List to ensure that any service agents you are using or planning to use are not subject to a PIE.

(b) As an employer who is using a service agent concerning whom a PIE is issued, you must stop using the services of the service agent no later than 90 days after the Department has published the decision in the *Federal Register* or posted it on its web site. You may apply to the ODAPC Director for an extension of 30 days if you demonstrate that you cannot find a substitute service agent within 90 days.

(c) Except during the period provided in paragraph (b) of this section, you must not, as an employer, use the services of a service agent that are covered by a PIE that the Director has issued under this subpart. If you do so, you are in violation of the Department's regulations and subject to applicable DOT agency sanctions (*e.g.*, civil penalties, withholding of Federal financial assistance).

(d) You also must not obtain drug or alcohol testing services through a contractor or affiliate of the service agent to whom the PIE applies.

Example to Paragraph (d): Service Agent R was subject to a PIE with respect to SAP services. As an employer, not only must you not use R's own SAP services, but you also must not use SAP services you arrange through R, such as services provided by a subcontractor or affiliate of R or a person or organization that receives financial gain from its relationship with R.

(e) This section's prohibition on using the services of a service agent concerning which the Director has issued a PIE applies to employers in all industries subject to DOT drug and alcohol testing regulations.

Example to Paragraph (e): The initiating official for a PIE was the FAA drug and alcohol program manager, and the conduct forming the basis of the PIE pertained to the aviation industry. As a motor carrier, transit authority, pipeline, railroad, or maritime employer, you are also prohibited from using the services of the service agent involved in connection with the DOT drug and alcohol testing program.

(f) The issuance of a PIE does not result in the cancellation of drug or alcohol tests conducted using the service agent involved before the issuance of the Director's decision or up to 90 days following its publication in the *Federal Register* or posting on the Department's web site, unless otherwise specified in the Director's PIE decision or the Director grants an extension as provided in paragraph (b) of this section.

Example to Paragraph (f): The Department issues a PIE concerning Service Agent N on September 1. All tests conducted using N's services before September 1, and through November 30, are valid for all purposes under DOT drug and alcohol testing regulations, assuming they meet all other regulatory requirements.

§40.411 What is the role of the DOT Inspector General's office?

(a) Any person may bring concerns about waste, fraud, or abuse on the part of a service agent to the attention of the DOT Office of Inspector General.

(b) In appropriate cases, the Office of Inspector General may pursue criminal or civil remedies against a service agent.

(c) The Office of Inspector General may provide factual information to other DOT officials for use in a PIE proceeding.

§40.413 How are notices sent to service agents?

(a) If you are a service agent, DOT sends notices to you, including correction notices, notices of proposed exclusion, decision notices, and other notices, in any of the ways mentioned in paragraph (b) or (c) of this section.

(b) DOT may send a notice to you, your identified counsel, your agent for service of process, or any of your partners, officers, directors, owners, or joint venturers to the last known street address, fax number, or e-mail address. DOT deems the notice to have been received by you if sent to any of these persons.

(c) DOT considers notices to be received by you—

(1) When delivered, if DOT mails the notice to the last known street address, or five days after we send it if the letter is undeliverable;

(2) When sent, if DOT sends the notice by fax or five days after we send it if the fax is undeliverable; or

(3) When delivered, if DOT sends the notice by e-mail or five days after DOT sends it if the e-mail is undeliverable.

Appendix A to Part 40—DOT Standards for Urine Collection Kits

The Collection Kit Contents
1. *Collection Container*

a. Single-use container, made of plastic, large enough to easily catch and hold at least 55 mL of urine voided from the body.

b. Must have graduated volume markings clearly noting levels of 45 mL and above.

c. Must have a temperature strip providing graduated temperature readings 3238 ° C/90- 100 ° F, that is affixed or can be affixed at a proper level on the outside of the collection container. Other methodologies (*e.g.,* temperature device built into the wall of the container) are acceptable provided the temperature measurement is accurate and such that there is no potential for contamination of the specimen.

d. Must be individually wrapped in a sealed plastic bag or shrink wrapping; or must have a peelable, sealed lid or other easily visible tamper-evident system.

e. May be made available separately at collection sites to address shy bladder situations when several voids may be required to complete the testing process.

2. *Plastic Specimen Bottles*

a. Each bottle must be large enough to hold at least 35 mL; or alternatively, they may be two distinct sizes of specimen bottles provided that the bottle designed to hold the primary specimen holds at least 35 mL of urine and the bottle designed to hold the split specimen holds at least 20 mL.

b. Must have screw-on or snap-on caps that prevent seepage of the urine from the bottles during shipment.

c. Must have markings clearly indicating the appropriate levels (30 mL for the primary specimen and 15 mL for the split) of urine that must be poured into the bottles.

d. Must be designed so that the required tamper-evident bottle seals made available on the CCF fit with no damage to the seal when the employee initials it nor with the chance that the seal overlap would conceal printed information.

e. Must be wrapped (with caps) together in a sealed plastic bag or shrink wrapping separate from the collection container; or must be wrapped (with cap) individually in sealed plastic bags or shrink wrapping; or must have peelable, sealed lid or other easily visible tamper-evident system

f. Plastic material must be leach resistant.

3. *Leak-Resistant Plastic Bag*

a. Must have two sealable compartments or pouches which are leak-resistant; one large enough to hold two specimen bottles and the other large enough to hold the CCF paperwork.

b. The sealing methodology must be such that once the compartments are sealed, any tampering or attempts to open either compartment will be evident.

4. *Absorbent material*

Each kit must contain enough absorbent material to absorb the entire contents of both specimen bottles. Absorbent material must be designed to fit inside the leak-resistant plastic bag pouch into which the specimen bottles are placed.

5. *Shipping Container*

a. Must be designed to adequately protect the specimen bottles from shipment damage in the transport of specimens from the collection site to the laboratory (*e.g.,* standard courier box, small cardboard box, plastic container).

b. May be made available separately at collection sites rather than being part of an actual kit sent to collection sites.

c. A shipping container is not necessary if a laboratory courier hand-delivers the specimen bottles in the plastic leak-proof bags from the collection site to the laboratory.

Appendix B to Part 40—DOT Drug Testing

Semi-Annual Laboratory Report

The following items are required on each report:

Reporting Period: (inclusive dates)

Laboratory Identification: (name and address)

Employer Identification: (name; may include billing code or ID code)

C/C/TPA Identification: (where applicable; name and address)

1. Number of specimen results reported: (total number)

By test type:

(a) Pre-employment testing: (number)

(b) Post-accident testing: (number)

(c) Random testing: (number)

(d) Reasonable suspicion/cause testing: (number)

(e) Return-to-duty testing: (number)

(f) Follow-up testing: (number)
(g) Type not noted on CCF: (number)
2. Number of specimens reported as
(a) Negative: (total number)
(b) Negative-dilute: (number)
3. Number of specimens reported as Rejected for Testing: (total number)
By reason:
(a) Fatal flaw: (number)
(b) Uncorrected flaw: (number)
4. Number of specimens reported as Positive: (total number)
By drug:
(a) Marijuana Metabolite: (number)
(b) Cocaine Metabolite: (number)
(c) Opiates:
(1) Codeine: (number)
(2) Morphine: (number)
(3) 6-AM: (number)
(d) Phencyclidine: (number)
(e) Amphetamines: (number)
(1) Amphetamine: (number)
(2) Methamphetamine: (number):
5. Adulterated: (number)
6. Substituted: (number)
7. Invalid results: (number)

Appendix C to Part 40—[Reserved]

Appendix D to Part 40—Report Format: Split
Specimen Failure to Reconfirm

Fax or mail to: Department of Transportation, Office of Drug and Alcohol Policy and Compliance, 400 7th Street, SW., Room 10403, Washington, DC 20590 (fax) 202-366-3897.
1. MRO name, address, phone number, and fax number.
2. Collection site name, address, and phone number.
3. Date of collection.
4. Specimen I.D. number.

5. Laboratory accession number.

6. Primary specimen laboratory name, address, and phone number.

7. Date result reported or certified by primary laboratory.

8. Split specimen laboratory name, address, and phone number.

9. Date split specimen result reported or certified by split specimen laboratory.

10. Primary specimen results (*e.g.*, name of drug, adulterant) in the primary specimen.

11. Reason for split specimen failure-to-reconfirm result (*e.g.*, drug or adulterant not present, specimen invalid, split not collected, insufficient volume).

12. Actions taken by the MRO (*e.g.*, notified employer of failure to reconfirm and requirement for recollection).

13. Additional information explaining the reason for cancellation.

14. Name of individual submitting the report (if not the MRO).

Appendix E to Part 40—SAP Equivalency

Requirements for Certification Organizations

1. *Experience:* Minimum requirements are for three years of full-time supervised experience or 6,000 hours of supervised experience as an alcoholism and/or drug abuse counselor. The supervision must be provided by a licensed or certified practitioner. Supervised experience is important if the individual is to be considered a professional in the field of alcohol and drug abuse evaluation and counseling.

2. *Education:* There exists a requirement of 270 contact hours of education and training in alcoholism and/or drug abuse or related training. These hours can take the form of formal education, in-service training, and professional development courses. Part of any professional counselor's development is participation in formal and non-formal education opportunities within the field.

3. *Continuing Education:* The certified counselor must receive at least 40-60 hours of continuing education units (CEU) during each two year period. These CEUs are important to the counselor's keeping abreast of changes and improvements in the field.

4. *Testing:* A passing score on a national test is a requirement. The test must accurately measure the application of the knowledge, skills, and abilities possessed by the counselor. The test establishes a national standard that must be met to practice.

5. *Testing Validity:* The certification examination must be reviewed by an independent authority for validity (examination reliability and relationship to the knowledge, skills, and abilities required by the counseling field). The reliability of the exam is paramount if counselor attributes are to be accurately measured. The examination passing score point must be placed at an appropriate minimal level score as gauged by statistically reliable methodology.

6. *Measurable Knowledge Base:* The certification process must be based upon measurable knowledge possessed by the applicant and verified through collateral data and testing. That level of knowledge must be of sufficient quantity to ensure a high quality of SAP evaluation and referral services.

7. *Measurable Skills Base:* The certification process must be based upon measurable skills possessed by the applicant and verified through collateral data and testing. That level of skills must be of sufficient quality to ensure a high quality of SAP evaluation and referral services.

8. *Quality Assurance Plan:* The certification agency must ensure that a means exists to determine that applicant records are verified as being true by the certification staff. This is an important check to ensure that true information is being accepted by the certifying agency.

9. *Code of Ethics:* Certified counselors must pledge to adhere to an ethical standard for practice. It must be understood that code violations could result in de-certification. These standards are vital in maintaining the integrity of practitioners. High ethical standards are required to ensure quality of client care and confidentiality of client information as well as to guard against inappropriate referral practices.

10. *Re-certification Program:* Certification is not just a one-time event. It is a continuing privilege with continuing requirements. Among these are continuing education, continuing state certification, and concomitant adherence to the code of ethics. Re-certification serves as a protector of client interests by removing poor performers from the certified practice.

11. *Fifty State Coverage:* Certification must be available to qualified counselors in all 50 states and, therefore, the test must be available to qualified applicants in all 50 states. Because many companies are multi-state operators, consistency in SAP evaluation quality and opportunities is paramount. The test need not be given in all 50 states but should be accessible to candidates from all states.

12. *National Commission for Certifying Agencies (NCCA) Accreditation:* Having NCCA accreditation is a means of demonstrating to the Department of Transportation that your certification has been reviewed by a panel of impartial experts that have determined that your examination(s) has met stringent and appropriate testing standards.

Appendix F to Part 40—Drug and Alcohol Testing Information that C/TPAs May Transmit to Employers

1. If you are a C/TPA, you may, acting as an intermediary, transmit the information in the following sections of this part to the DER for an employer, if the employer chooses to have you do so. These are the only items that you are permitted to transmit to the employer as an intermediary. The use of C/TPA intermediaries is prohibited in all other cases, such as transmission of laboratory drug test results to MROs, the transmission of medical information from MROs to employers, the transmission of SAP reports to employers, the transmission of positive alcohol test results, and the transmission of medical information from MROs to employers.

2. In every case, you must ensure that, in transmitting the information, you meet all requirements (*e.g.*, concerning confidentiality and timing) that would apply if the party originating the information (*e.g.*, an MRO or collector) sent the information directly to the employer. For example, if you transmit MROs' drug testing results to DERs, you must transmit each drug test result to the DER in compliance with the requirements for MROs set forth in §40.167.

Drug Testing Information

§40.25: Previous two years' test results

§40.35: Notice to collectors of contact information for DER

§40.61(a): Notification to DER that an employee is a "no show" for a drug test

§40.63(e): Notification to DER of a collection under direct observation

§40.65(b)(6) and (7) and (c)(2) and (3): Notification to DER of a refusal to provide a specimen or an insufficient specimen

§40.73(a)(9): Transmission of CCF copies to DER (However, MRO copy of CCF must be sent by collector directly to the MRO, not through the C/TPA.)

§40.111(a): Transmission of laboratory statistical report to employer

§40.127(f): Report of test results to DER

§§40.127(g), 40.129(d), 40.159(a)(4)(ii); 40.161(b): Reports to DER that test is cancelled

§40.129 (d): Report of test results to DER

§40.129(g)(1): Report to DER of confirmed positive test in stand-down situation

§§40.149(b): Report to DER of changed test result

§40.155(a): Report to DER of dilute specimen

§40.167(b) and (c): Reports of test results to DER

§40.187(a)-(f) Reports to DER concerning the reconfirmation of tests

§40.191(d): Notice to DER concerning refusals to test

§40.193(b)(3): Notification to DER of refusal in shy bladder situation

§40.193(b)(4): Notification to DER of insufficient specimen

§40.193(b)(5): Transmission of CCF copies to DER (not to MRO)

§40.199: Report to DER of cancelled test and direction to DER for additional collection

§40.201: Report to DER of cancelled test

Alcohol Testing Information

§40.215: Notice to BATs and STTs of contact information for DER

§40.241(b)(1): Notification to DER that an employee is a "no show" for an alcohol test

§40.247(a)(2): Transmission of alcohol screening test results only when the test result is less than 0.02

§40.255(a)(4): Transmission of alcohol confirmation test results only when the test result is less than 0.02

§40.263(a)(3) and 263(b)(3): Notification of insufficient saliva and failure to provide sufficient amount of breath

Appendix G to Part 40—Alcohol Testing Form

The following form is the alcohol testing form required for use in the DOT alcohol testing program beginning August 1, 2001. Use of the form is authorized beginning January 18, 2001.

U.S. Department of Transportation (DOT)
Alcohol Testing Form
(The instructions for completing this form are on the back of Copy 3)

Affix
Or
Print
Screening Results
Here

Affix
With
Tamper Evident Tap

Step 1: TO BE COMPLETED BY ALCOHOL TECHNICIAN

A: Employee Name _____
(Print) (First, M.I., Last)

B: SSN or Employee ID No. _____

C: Employer Name _____
Street _____
City, ST ZIP _____

DER Name and
Telephone No. _____
DER Name   (   )   DER Phone Number

D: Reason for Test: ☐Random ☐Reasonable Susp ☐Post-Accident ☐Return to Duty ☐Follow-up ☐Pre-employment

STEP 2: TO BE COMPLETED BY EMPLOYEE

I certify that I am about to submit to alcohol testing required by US Department of Transportation regulations and that the identifying information provided on the form is true and correct.

_____   ___/___/___
Signature of Employee   Date Month Day Year

Affix
Or
Print
Confirmation Result
Here

Affix
With
Tamper Evident
Tape

STEP 3: TO BE COMPLETED BY ALCOHOL TECHNICIAN

(If the technician conducting the rescreening test is not the same technician who will be conducting the confirmation test, each technician must complete their own form.) I certify that I have conducted alcohol testing on the above named individual in accordance with the procedures established in the US Department of Transportation regulation, 49 CFR Part 40, that I am qualified to operate the testing device(s) identified, and that the results are as recorded.

TECHNICIAN: ☐BAT ☐STT   DEVICE: ☐SALIVA ☐BREATH* 15-Minute Wait: ☐ Yes ☐ No

SCREENING TEST: *(For BREATH DEVICE* write in the space below only if the testing device is not designed to print.)*

Test #	Testing Device Name	Device Serial # OR Lot # & Exp Date	Activation Time	Reading Time	Result

CONFIRMATION TEST: *Results MUST be affixed to each copy of this form or printed directly onto the form.*

REMARKS:
_____
_____
_____

Affix
Or
Print
Additional Results
Here

Affix
With
Tamper Evident
Tape

_____   _____
Alcohol Technician's Company   Company Street Address

_____   _____ (   )
(PRINT) Alcohol Technician's Name (First, M.I., Last)   Company City, State, Zip   Phone Number

_____   ___/___/___
Signature of Alcohol Technician   Date Month Day Year

STEP 4: TO BE COMPLETED BY EMPLOYEE IF TEST RESULT IS 0.02 OR HIGHER

I certify that I have submitted to the alcohol test, the results of which are accurately recorded on this form. I understand that I must not drive, perform safety-sensitive duties, or operate heavy equipment because the results are 0.02 or greater.

_____   ___/___/___
Signature of Employee   Date Month Day Year

COPY 1 – ORIGINAL – FORWARD TO THE EMPLOYER

U.S. Department of Transportation (DOT)
Alcohol Testing Form
(The instructions for completing this form are on the back of Copy 3)

Step 1: TO BE COMPLETED BY ALCOHOL TECHNICIAN

A: Employee Name _____
(Print)   (First, M.I., Last)

B: SSN or Employee ID No. _____

C: Employer Name _____
Street
City, ST ZIP

DER Name and
Telephone No. _____
DER Name   ( ) DER Phone Number

D: Reason for Test: ☐Random ☐Reasonable Susp ☐Post-Accident ☐Return to Duty ☐Follow-up ☐Pre-employment

STEP 2: TO BE COMPLETED BY EMPLOYEE

I certify that I am about to submit to alcohol testing required by US Department of Transportation regulations and that the identifying information provided on the form is true and correct.

Signature of Employee _____   Date ___/___/___ Month Day Year

STEP 3: TO BE COMPLETED BY ALCOHOL TECHNICIAN

(If the technician conducting the screening test is not the same technician who will be conducting the confirmation test, each technician must complete their own form.) I certify that I have conducted alcohol testing on the above named individual in accordance with the procedures established in the US Department of Transportation regulation, 49 CFR Part 40, that I am qualified to operate the testing device(s) identified, and that the results are as recorded.

TECHNICIAN: ☐BAT ☐STT   DEVICE: ☐SALIVA ☐BREATH* 15-Minute Wait: ☐ Yes ☐ No

SCREENING TEST: *(For BREATH DEVICE* write in the space below only if the testing device is not designed to print.)*

Test #   Testing Device Name   Device Serial # OR Lot # & Exp Date   Activation Time   Reading Time   Result

CONFIRMATION TEST: *Results MUST be affixed to each copy of this form or printed directly onto the form.*

REMARKS:

Alcohol Technician's Company _____   Company Street Address _____

(PRINT) Alcohol Technician's Name (First, M.I., Last)   Company City, State, Zip   Phone Number ( )

Signature of Alcohol Technician _____ Date ___/___/___ Month Day Year

STEP 4: TO BE COMPLETED BY EMPLOYEE IF TEST RESULT IS 0.02 OR HIGHER

I certify that I have submitted to the alcohol test, the results of which are accurately recorded on this form. I understand that I must not drive, perform safety-sensitive duties, or operate heavy equipment because the results are 0.02 or greater.

Signature of Employee _____   Date ___/___/___ Month Day Year

Sidebar:
Affix Or Print Screening Results Here
Affix With Tamper Evident Tap
Affix Or Print Confirmation Result Here
Affix With Tamper Evident Tape
Affix Or Print Additional Results Here
Affix With Tamper Evident Tape

COPY 2 – EMPLOYEE RETAINS

U.S. Department of Transportation (DOT)
Alcohol Testing Form
(The instructions for completing this form are on the back of Copy 3)

Affix Or Print Screening Results Here

Affix With Tamper Evident Tap

Step 1: TO BE COMPLETED BY ALCOHOL TECHNICIAN

A: Employee Name _____
(Print)   (First, M.I., Last)

B: SSN or Employee ID No. _____

C: Employer Name
Street
City, ST ZIP

DER Name and
Telephone No. _____
DER Name   (   )   DER Phone Number

D: Reason for Test: ☐Random ☐Reasonable Susp ☐Post-Accident ☐Return to Duty ☐Follow-up ☐Pre-employment

STEP 2: TO BE COMPLETED BY EMPLOYEE

I certify that I am about to submit to alcohol testing required by US Department of Transportation regulations and that the identifying information provided on the form is true and correct.

Signature of Employee _____   ___/___/___
Date   Month Day Year

Affix Or Print Confirmation Results Here

Affix With Tamper Evident Tape

STEP 3: TO BE COMPLETED BY ALCOHOL TECHNICIAN

(If the technician conducting the screening test is not the same technician who will be conducting the confirmation test, each technician must complete their own form.) I certify that I have conducted alcohol testing on the above named individual in accordance with the procedures established in the US Department of Transportation regulation, 49 CFR Part 40, that I am qualified to operate the testing device(s) identified, and that the results are as recorded.

TECHNICIAN: ☐BAT ☐STT   DEVICE: ☐SALIVA ☐BREATH*   15-Minute Wait: ☐Yes ☐No

SCREENING TEST: *(For BREATH DEVICE* write in the space below only if the testing device is not designed to print.)*

Test #	Testing Device Name	Device Serial # OR Lot # & Exp Date	Activation Time	Reading Time	Result

CONFIRMATION TEST: *Results MUST be affixed to each copy of this form or printed directly onto the form.*

REMARKS:

Affix Or Print Additional Results. Here

_____   _____
Alcohol Technician's Company   Company Street Address

_____   _____   (   )
(PRINT) Alcohol Technician's Name (First, M.I., Last)   Company City, State, Zip   Phone Number

Signature of Alcohol Technician _____   ___/___/___
Date   Month Day Year

Affix With Tamper Evident Tape

STEP 4: TO BE COMPLETED BY EMPLOYEE IF TEST RESULT IS 0.02 OR HIGHER

I certify that I have submitted to the alcohol test, the results of which are accurately recorded on this form. I understand that I must not drive, perform safety-sensitive duties, or operate heavy equipment because the results are 0.02 or greater.

Signature of Employee _____   ___/___/___
Date   Month Day Year

COPY 3 – ALCOHOL TECHNICIAN RETAINS

PAPERWORK REDUCTION ACT NOTICE (as required by 5 CFR 1320.21)

Public reporting burden for this collection of information is estimated for each respondent to average: 1 minute/employee, 4 minutes/Breath Alcohol Technician. Individuals may send comments regarding these burden estimates, or any other aspect of this collection of information, including suggestions for reducing the burden, to U.S. Department of Transportation, Drug and alcohol Policy and Compliance, Room 10403, 400 Seventh St., SW, Washington, D.C. 20590 or Office of Management and Budget, Paperwork Reduction Project, Room 3001, 725 Seventeenth St., NW, Washington, D.C. 20503.

BACK OF PAGES 1 and 2

INSTRUCTIONS FOR COMPLETING THE U.S. DEPARTMENT OF TRANSPORTATION ALCOHOL TESTING FORM

NOTE   Use a ballpoint pen, press hard, and check all copies for legibility.

STEP 1   The Breath Alcohol Technician (BAT) or Screening Test Technician (STT) completes the information required in this step Be sure to print the employee's name and check the box identifying the reason for the test.

NOTE   If the employee refuses to provide SSN or I.D. number, be sure to indicate this in the remarks section in STEP 3. Proceed with STEP 2.

STEP 2   Instruct the employee to read, sign, and date the employee certification statement in STEP 2

NOTE   If the employee refuses to sign the certification statement, do not proceed with the alcohol test Contact the designated employer representative.

STEP 3   The BAT or STT completes the information required in this step and checks the type of device (saliva or breath) being used. After conducting the alcohol screening test, do the following (as appropriate):

Enter the information for the screening test (test number, testing device name, testing device serial number or lot number and expiration date, time of test with any device-dependent activation times, and the results). on the front of the ATF. For a breath testing device capable of printing, the information may be part of the printed record.

NOTE   Be sure to enter the result of the test exactly as it is indicated on the breath testing device, e.g., 0.00, 0.02, 0.04, etc.

Affix the printed information in the space provided, in a tamper-evident manner (e.g., tape), or the device may print the results directly on the ATF. If the results of the screening test are less than 0.02, print, sign your name, and enter today's date in the space provided. The test process is complete.

If the results of the screening test are 0.02 or greater, a confirmation test must be administered in accordance with DOT regulations. An EVIDENTIAL BREATH TESTING device that is capable of printing confirmation test information must be used in conducting this test.

After conducting the alcohol confirmation test, affix the printed information in the space provided, in a tamper-evident manner (e.g., tape), or the device may print the results directly on the ATF. Print, sign your name, and enter the date in the space provided Go to STEP 4.

STEP 4   If the employee has a breath alcohol confirmation test result of 0.02 or higher, instruct the employee to read, sign, and date the employee certification statement in STEP 4.

NOTE   If the employee refuses to sign the certification statement in STEP 4, be sure to indicate this in the remarks line in STEP 3.

Immediately notify the DER if the employee has a breath alcohol confirmation test result of 0.02 or higher.

Forward Copy 1 to the employer Give Copy 2 to the employee Retain Copy 3 for BAT/STT records.

BACK OF PAGE 3

BILLING CODE 4910-62-C

Appendix H to Part 40 — DOT Drug and Alcohol Testing Management Information System (MIS) Data Collection Form

The following form and instructions must be used when an employer is required to report MIS data to a DOT agency.

Editor's Note: Form not included due to legibility concerns.

PART 382 — CONTROLLED SUBSTANCES AND ALCOHOL USE AND TESTING

Subpart A — General

Subpart B — Prohibitions

Subpart C — Tests Required

Subpart D — Handling of Test Results, Record Retention, and Confidentiality

Subpart E — Consequences for Drivers Engaging in Substance Use-Related Conduct

Subpart F — Alcohol Misuse and Controlled Substances Use Information, Training, and Referral

Authority: 49 U.S.C. 31133, 31136, 31301 *et seq*., 31502; 49 CFR 1.73.

Subpart A — General

§382.101 Purpose.

The purpose of this part is to establish programs designed to help prevent accidents and injuries resulting from the misuse of alcohol or use of controlled substances by drivers of commercial motor vehicles.

§382.103 Applicability.

(a) This part applies to every person and to all employers of such persons who operate a commercial motor vehicle in commerce in any State, and is subject to:

(1) The commercial driver's license requirements of part 383 of this subchapter;

(2) The Licencia Federal de Conductor (Mexico) requirements; or

(3) The commercial drivers license requirements of the Canadian National Safety Code.

(b) An employer who employs himself/herself as a driver must comply with both the requirements in this part that apply to employers and the requirements in this part that apply to drivers. An employer who employs only himself/herself as a driver shall implement a random alcohol and controlled substances testing program of two or more covered employees in the random testing selection pool.

(c) The exceptions contained in §390.3(f) of this subchapter do not apply to this part. The employers and drivers identified in §390.3(f) of this subchapter must comply with the requirements of this part, unless otherwise specifically provided in paragraph (d) of this section.

(d) **Exceptions.** This part shall not apply to employers and their drivers:

(1) Required to comply with the alcohol and/or controlled substances testing requirements of part 655 of this title (Federal Transit Administration alcohol and controlled substances testing regulations); or

(2) Who a State must waive from the requirements of part 383 of this subchapter. These individuals include active duty military personnel; members of the reserves; and members of the national guard on active duty, including personnel on full-time national guard duty, personnel on part-time national guard training and national guard military technicians (civilians who are required to wear military uniforms), and active duty U.S. Coast Guard personnel; or

(3) Who a State has, at its discretion, exempted from the requirements of part 383 of this subchapter. These individuals may be:

(i) Operators of a farm vehicle which is:

(A) Controlled and operated by a farmer;

(B) Used to transport either agricultural products, farm machinery, farm supplies, or both to or from a farm;

(C) Not used in the operations of a common or contract motor carrier; and

(D) Used within 241 kilometers (150 miles) of the farmer's farm.

(ii) Firefighters or other persons who operate commercial motor vehicles which are necessary for the preservation of life or property or the execution of emergency governmental functions, are equipped with audible and visual signals, and are not subject to normal traffic regulation.

§382.105 Testing procedures.

Each employer shall ensure that all alcohol or controlled substances testing conducted under this part complies with the procedures set forth in part 40 of this title. The provisions of part 40 of this title that address alcohol or controlled substances testing are made applicable to employers by this part.

§382.107 Definitions.

Words or phrases used in this part are defined in §§386.2 and 390.5 of this subchapter, and §40.3 of this title, except as provided in this section—

Actual knowledge for the purpose of subpart B of this part, means actual knowledge by an employer that a driver has used alcohol or controlled substances based on the employer's direct observation of the employee, information provided by the driver's previous employer(s), a traffic citation for driving a CMV while under the influence of alcohol or controlled substances or an employee's admission of alcohol or controlled substance use, except as provided in §382.121. Direct observation as used in this definition means observation of alcohol or controlled substances use and does not include observation of employee behavior or physical characteristics sufficient to warrant reasonable suspicion testing under §382.307.

Alcohol means the intoxicating agent in beverage alcohol, ethyl alcohol, or other low molecular weight alcohols including methyl and isopropyl alcohol.

Alcohol concentration (or content) means the alcohol in a volume of breath expressed in terms of grams of alcohol per 210 liters of breath as indicated by an evidential breath test under this part.

Alcohol use means the drinking or swallowing of any beverage, liquid mixture or preparation (including any medication), containing alcohol.

Commerce means:

(1) Any trade, traffic or transportation within the jurisdiction of the United States between a place in a State and a place outside of such State, including a place outside of the United States; and

(2) Trade, traffic, and transportation in the United States which affects any trade, traffic, and transportation described in paragraph (1) of this definition.

Commercial motor vehicle means a motor vehicle or combination of motor vehicles used in commerce to transport passengers or property if the vehicle—

(1) Has a gross combination weight rating of 11,794 or more kilograms (26,001 or more pounds) inclusive of a towed unit with a gross vehicle weight rating of more than 4,536 kilograms (10,000 pounds); or

(2) Has a gross vehicle weight rating of 11,794 or more kilograms (26,001 or more pounds); or

(3) Is designed to transport 16 or more passengers, including the driver; or

(4) Is of any size and is used in the transportation of materials found to be hazardous for the purposes of the Hazardous Materials Transportation Act (49 U.S.C. 5103(b)) and which require the motor vehicle to be placarded under the Hazardous Materials Regulations (49 CFR part 172, subpart F).

Confirmation (or confirmatory) drug test means a second analytical procedure performed on a urine specimen to identify and quantify the presence of a specific drug or drug metabolite.

Confirmation (or confirmatory) validity test means a second test performed on a urine specimen to further support a validity test result.

Confirmed drug test means a confirmation test result received by an MRO from a laboratory.

Consortium/Third party administrator (C/TPA) means a service agent that provides or coordinates one or more drug and/or alcohol testing services to DOT-regulated employers. C/TPAs typically provide or coordinate the provision of a number of such services and perform administrative tasks concerning the operation of the employers' drug and alcohol testing programs. This term includes, but is not limited to, groups of employers who join together to administer, as a single entity, the DOT drug and alcohol testing programs of its members (e.g., having a combined random testing pool). C/TPAs are not "employers" for purposes of this part.

Controlled substances mean those substances identified in §40.85 of this title.

Designated employer representative (DER) is an individual identified by the employer as able to receive communications and test results from service agents and who is authorized to take immediate actions to remove employees from safety-sensitive duties and to make required decisions in the testing and evaluation processes. The individual must be an employee of the company. Service agents cannot serve as DERs.

Disabling damage means damage which precludes departure of a motor vehicle from the scene of the accident in its usual manner in daylight after simple repairs.

(1) **Inclusions.** Damage to motor vehicles that could have been driven, but would have been further damaged if so driven.

(2) **Exclusions.**

(i) Damage which can be remedied temporarily at the scene of the accident without special tools or parts.

(ii) Tire disablement without other damage even if no spare tire is available.

(iii) Headlight or taillight damage.

(iv) Damage to turn signals, horn, or windshield wipers which make them inoperative.

DOT Agency means an agency (or "operating administration") of the United States Department of Transportation administering regulations requiring alcohol and/or drug testing (14 CFR parts 61, 63, 65, 121, and 135; 49 CFR parts 199, 219, 382, and 655), in accordance with part 40 of this title.

Driver means any person who operates a commercial motor vehicle. This includes, but is not limited to: Full time, regularly employed drivers; casual, intermittent or occasional drivers; leased drivers and independent owner-operator contractors.

Employer means a person or entity employing one or more employees (including an individual who is self-employed) that is subject to DOT agency regulations requiring compliance with this part. The term, as used in this part, means the entity responsible for overall implementation of DOT drug and alcohol program requirements, including individuals employed by the entity who take personnel actions resulting from violations of this part and any applicable DOT agency regulations. Service agents are not employers for the purposes of this part.

Licensed medical practitioner means a person who is licensed, certified, and/or registered, in accordance with applicable Federal, State, local, or foreign laws and regulations, to prescribe controlled substances and other drugs.

Performing (a safety-sensitive function) means a driver is considered to be performing a safety-sensitive function during any period in which he or she is actually performing, ready to perform, or immediately available to perform any safety-sensitive functions.

Positive rate means the number of positive results for random controlled substances tests conducted under this part plus the number of refusals of random controlled substances tests required by this part, divided by the total of random controlled substances tests conducted under this part plus the number of refusals of random tests required by this part.

Refuse to submit (to an alcohol or controlled substances test) means that a driver:

(1) Fail to appear for any test (except a pre-employment test) within a reasonable time, as determined by the employer, consistent with applicable DOT agency regulations, after being directed to do so by the employer. This includes the failure of an employee (including an owner-operator) to appear for a test when called by a C/TPA (see §40.61(a) of this title);

(2) Fail to remain at the testing site until the testing process is complete. Provided, that an employee who leaves the testing site before the testing process commences (see §40.63(c) of this title) a pre-employment test is not deemed to have refused to test;

(3) Fail to provide a urine specimen for any drug test required by this part or DOT agency regulations. Provided, that an employee who does not provide a urine specimen because he or she has left the testing site before the testing process commences (see §40.63(c) of this title) for a pre-employment test is not deemed to have refused to test;

(4) In the case of a directly observed or monitored collection in a drug test, fails to permit the observation or monitoring of the driver's provision of a specimen (see §§40.67(l) and 40.69(g) of this title);

(5) Fail to provide a sufficient amount of urine when directed, and it has been determined, through a required medical evaluation, that there was no adequate medical explanation for the failure (see §40.193(d)(2) of this title);

(6) Fail or declines to take a second test the employer or collector has directed the driver to take;

(7) Fail to undergo a medical examination or evaluation, as directed by the MRO as part of the verification process, or as directed by the DER under §40.193(d) of this title. In the case of a pre-employment drug test, the employee is deemed to have refused to test on this basis only if the pre-employment test is conducted following a contingent offer of employment;

(8) Fail to cooperate with any part of the testing process (e.g., refuse to empty pockets when so directed by the collector, behave in a confrontational way that disrupts the collection process); or

(9) Is reported by the MRO as having a verified adulterated or substituted test result.

Safety-sensitive function means all time from the time a driver begins to work or is required to be in readiness to work until the time he/she is relieved from work and all responsibility for performing work. Safety-sensitive functions shall include:

(1) All time at an employer or shipper plant, terminal, facility, or other property, or on any public property, waiting to be dispatched, unless the driver has been relieved from duty by the employer;

(2) All time inspecting equipment as required by §§392.7 and 392.8 of this subchapter or otherwise inspecting, servicing, or conditioning any commercial motor vehicle at any time;

(3) All time spent at the driving controls of a commercial motor vehicle in operation;

(4) All time, other than driving time, in or upon any commercial motor vehicle except time spent resting in a sleeper berth (a berth conforming to the requirements of §393.76 of this subchapter);

(5) All time loading or unloading a vehicle, supervising, or assisting in the loading or unloading, attending a vehicle being loaded or unloaded, remaining in readiness to operate the vehicle, or in giving or receiving receipts for shipments loaded or unloaded; and

(6) All time repairing, obtaining assistance, or remaining in attendance upon a disabled vehicle.

Screening test (or initial test) means:

(1) In drug testing, a test to eliminate "negative" urine specimens from further analysis or to identify a specimen that requires additional testing for the presence of drugs.

(2) In alcohol testing, an analytical procedure to determine whether an employee may have a prohibited concentration of alcohol in a breath or saliva specimen.

Stand-down means the practice of temporarily removing an employee from the performance of safety-sensitive functions based only on a report from a laboratory to the MRO of a confirmed positive test for a drug or drug metabolite, an adulterated test, or a substituted test, before the MRO has completed verification of the test results.

Violation rate means the number of drivers (as reported under §382.305) found during random tests given under this part to have an alcohol concentration of 0.04 or greater, plus the number of drivers who refuse a random test required by this part, divided by the total reported number of drivers in the industry given random alcohol tests under this part plus the total reported number of drivers in the industry who refuse a random test required by this part.

§382.109 Preemption of State and local laws.

(a) Except as provided in paragraph (b) of this section, this part preempts any State or local law, rule, regulation, or order to the extent that:

(1) Compliance with both the State or local requirement in this part is not possible; or

(2) Compliance with the State or local requirement is an obstacle to the accomplishment and execution of any requirement in this part.

(b) This part shall not be construed to preempt provisions of State criminal law that impose sanctions for reckless conduct leading to actual loss of life, injury, or damage to property, whether the provisions apply specifically to transportation employees, employers, or the general public.

§382.111 Other requirements imposed by employers.

Except as expressly provided in this part, nothing in this part shall be construed to affect the authority of employers, or the rights of drivers, with respect to the use of alcohol, or the use of controlled substances, including authority and rights with respect to testing and rehabilitation.

§382.113 Requirement for notice.

Before performing each alcohol or controlled substances test under this part, each employer shall notify a driver that the alcohol or controlled substances test is required by this part. No employer shall falsely represent that a test is administered under this part.

§382.115 Starting date for testing programs.

(a) All domestic-domiciled employers must implement the requirements of this part on the date the employer begins commercial motor vehicle operations.

(b) All foreign-domiciled employers must implement the requirements of this part on the date the employer begins commercial motor vehicle operations in the United States.

§382.117 Public interest exclusion.

No employer shall use the services of a service agent who is subject to public interest exclusion in accordance with 49 CFR part 40, Subpart R.

§382.119 Stand-down waiver provision.

(a) Employers are prohibited from standing employees down, except consistent with a waiver from the Federal Motor Carrier Safety Administration as required under this section.

(b) An employer subject to this part who seeks a waiver from the prohibition against standing down an employee before the MRO has completed the verification process shall follow the procedures in 49 CFR 40.21. The employer must send a written request, which includes all of the information required by that section to the Federal Motor Carrier Safety Administrator (or the Administrator's designee), U.S. Department of Transportation, 400 Seventh Street, SW., Washington, DC 20590.

(c) The final decision whether to grant or deny the application for a waiver will be made by the Administrator or the Administrator's designee.

(d) After a decision is signed by the Administrator or the Administrator's designee, the employer will be sent a copy of the decision, which will include the terms and conditions for the waiver or the reason for denying the application for a waiver.

(e) Questions regarding waiver applications should be directed to the Office of Enforcement and Compliance, Federal Motor Carrier Safety Administration, 400 Seventh Street, SW., Washington, DC 20590. The telephone number is (202) 366-5720.

§382.121 Employee admission of alcohol and controlled substances use.

(a) Employees who admit to alcohol misuse or controlled substances use are not subject to the referral, evaluation and treatment requirements of this part and part 40 of this title, provided that:

(1) The admission is in accordance with a written employer-established voluntary self-identification program or policy that meets the requirements of paragraph (b) of this section;

(2) The driver does not self-identify in order to avoid testing under the requirements of this part;

(3) The driver makes the admission of alcohol misuse or controlled substances use prior to performing a safety sensitive function (i.e., prior to reporting for duty); and

§382.201

(4) The driver does not perform a safety sensitive function until the employer is satisfied that the employee has been evaluated and has successfully completed education or treatment requirements in accordance with the self-identification program guidelines.

(b) A qualified voluntary self-identification program or policy must contain the following elements:

(1) It must prohibit the employer from taking adverse action against an employee making a voluntary admission of alcohol misuse or controlled substances use within the parameters of the program or policy and paragraph (a) of this section;

(2) It must allow the employee sufficient opportunity to seek evaluation, education or treatment to establish control over the employee's drug or alcohol problem;

(3) It must permit the employee to return to safety sensitive duties only upon successful completion of an educational or treatment program, as determined by a drug and alcohol abuse evaluation expert, i.e., employee assistance professional, substance abuse professional, or qualified drug and alcohol counselor;

(4) It must ensure that:

(i) Prior to the employee participating in a safety sensitive function, the employee shall undergo a return to duty test with a result indicating an alcohol concentration of less than 0.02; and/or

(ii) Prior to the employee participating in a safety sensitive function, the employee shall undergo a return to duty controlled substance test with a verified negative test result for controlled substances use; and

(5) It may incorporate employee monitoring and include non-DOT follow-up testing.

Subpart B - Prohibitions

§382.201 Alcohol concentration.

No driver shall report for duty or remain on duty requiring the performance of safety-sensitive functions while having an alcohol concentration of 0.04 or greater. No employer having actual knowledge that a driver has an alcohol concentration of 0.04 or greater shall permit the driver to perform or continue to perform safety-sensitive functions.

§382.205 On-duty use.

No driver shall use alcohol while performing safety-sensitive functions. No employer having actual knowledge that a driver is using alcohol while performing safety-sensitive functions shall permit the driver to perform or continue to perform safety-sensitive functions.

§382.207 Pre-duty use.

No driver shall perform safety-sensitive functions within four hours after using alcohol. No employer having actual knowledge that a driver has used alcohol within four hours shall permit a driver to perform or continue to perform safety-sensitive functions.

§382.209 Use following an accident.

No driver required to take a post-accident alcohol test under §382.303 shall use alcohol for eight hours following the accident, or until he/she undergoes a post-accident alcohol test, whichever occurs first.

§382.211 Refusal to submit to a required alcohol or controlled substances test.

No driver shall refuse to submit to a post-accident alcohol or controlled substances test required under §382.303, a random alcohol or controlled substances test required under §382.305, a reasonable suspicion alcohol or controlled substances test required under §382.307, or a follow-up alcohol or controlled substances test required under §382.311. No employer shall permit a driver who refuses to submit to such tests to perform or continue to perform safety-sensitive functions.

§382.213 Controlled substances use.

(a) No driver shall report for duty or remain on duty requiring the performance of safety-sensitive functions when the driver uses any controlled substance, except when the use is pursuant to the instructions of a licensed medical practitioner, as defined in §382.107, who has advised the driver that the substance will not adversely affect the driver's ability to safely operate a commercial motor vehicle.

(b) No employer having actual knowledge that a driver has used a controlled substance shall permit the driver to perform or continue to perform a safety-sensitive function.

(c) An employer may require a driver to inform the employer of any therapeutic drug use.

§382.215 Controlled substances testing.

No driver shall report for duty, remain on duty or perform a safety-sensitive function, if the driver tests positive or has adulterated or substituted a test specimen for controlled substances. No employer having actual knowledge that a driver has tested positive or has adulterated or substituted a test specimen for controlled substances shall permit the driver to perform or continue to perform safety-sensitive functions.

Subpart C — Tests Required

§382.301 Pre-employment testing.

(a) Prior to the first time a driver performs safety-sensitive functions for an employer, the driver shall undergo testing for controlled substances as a condition prior to being used, unless the employer uses the exception in paragraph (b) of this section. No employer shall allow a driver, who the employer intends to hire or use, to perform safety-sensitive functions unless the employer has received a controlled substances test result from the MRO or C/TPA indicating a verified negative test result for that driver.

(b) An employer is not required to administer a controlled substances test required by paragraph (a) of this section if:

(1) The driver has participated in a controlled substances testing program that meets the requirements of this part within the previous 30 days; and

(2) While participating in that program, either:

(i) Was tested for controlled substances within the past 6 months (from the date of application with the employer), or

(ii) Participated in the random controlled substances testing program for the previous 12 months (from the date of application with the employer); and

(3) The employer ensures that no prior employer of the driver of whom the employer has knowledge has records of a violation of this part or the controlled substances use rule of another DOT agency within the previous six months.

(c)(1) An employer who exercises the exception in paragraph (b) of this section shall contact the controlled substances testing program(s) in which the driver participates or participated and shall obtain and retain from the testing program(s) the following information:

(i) Name(s) and address(es) of the program(s).

(ii) Verification that the driver participates or participated in the program(s).

(iii) Verification that the program(s) conforms to part 40 of this title.

(iv) Verification that the driver is qualified under the rules of this part, including that the driver has not refused to be tested for controlled substances.

(v) The date the driver was last tested for controlled substances.

(vi) The results of any tests taken within the previous six months and any other violations of subpart B of this part.

(2) An employer who uses, but does not employ a driver more than once a year to operate commercial motor vehicles must obtain the information in paragraph (c)(1) of this section at least once every six months. The records prepared under this paragraph shall be maintained in accordance with §382.401. If the employer cannot verify that the driver is participating in a controlled substances testing program in accordance with this part and part 40 of this title, the employer shall conduct a pre-employment controlled substances test.

(d) An employer may, but is not required to, conduct pre-employment alcohol testing under this part. If an employer chooses to conduct pre-employment alcohol testing, it must comply with the following requirements:

(1) It must conduct a pre-employment alcohol test before the first performance of safety-sensitive functions by every covered employee (whether a new employee or someone who has transferred to a position involving the performance of safety-sensitive functions).

(2) It must treat all safety-sensitive employees performing safety-sensitive functions the same for the purpose of pre-employment alcohol testing (i.e., it must not test some covered employees and not others).

(3) It must conduct the pre-employment tests after making a contingent offer of employment or transfer, subject to the employee passing the pre-employment alcohol test.

(4) It must conduct all pre-employment alcohol tests using the alcohol testing procedures of 49 CFR part 40 of this title.

(5) It must not allow a covered employee to begin performing safety-sensitive functions unless the result of the employee's test indicates an alcohol concentration of less than 0.04.

§382.303 Post-accident testing.

(a) As soon as practicable following an occurrence involving a commercial motor vehicle operating on a public road in commerce, each employer shall test for alcohol for each of its surviving drivers:

(1) Who was performing safety-sensitive functions with respect to the vehicle, if the accident involved the loss of human life; or

(2) Who receives a citation within 8 hours of the occurrence under State or local law for a moving traffic violation arising from the accident, if the accident involved:

(i) Bodily injury to any person who, as a result of the injury, immediately receives medical treatment away from the scene of the accident; or

(ii) One or more motor vehicles incurring disabling damage as a result of the accident, requiring the motor vehicle to be transported away from the scene by a tow truck or other motor vehicle.

(b) As soon as practicable following an occurrence involving a commercial motor vehicle operating on a public road in commerce, each employer shall test for controlled substances for each of its surviving drivers:

(1) Who was performing safety-sensitive functions with respect to the vehicle, if the accident involved the loss of human life; or

(2) Who receives a citation within thirty-two hours of the occurrence under State or local law for a moving traffic violation arising from the accident, if the accident involved:

(i) Bodily injury to any person who, as a result of the injury, immediately receives medical treatment away from the scene of the accident; or

(ii) One or more motor vehicles incurring disabling damage as a result of the accident, requiring the motor vehicle to be transported away from the scene by a tow truck or other motor vehicle.

(c) The following table notes when a post-accident test is required to be conducted by paragraphs (a)(1), (a)(2), (b)(1), and (b)(2) of this section:

TABLE FOR §382.303 (A) AND (B)		
Type of accident involved	Citation issued to the CMV driver	Test must be performed by employer
i. Human fatality	YES	YES
	NO	YES
ii. Bodily injury with immediate medical treatment away from the scene	YES	YES
	NO	NO
iii. Disabling damage to any motor vehicle requiring tow away	YES	YES
	NO	NO

(d)(1) **Alcohol tests.** If a test required by this section is not administered within two hours following the accident, the employer shall prepare and maintain on file a record stating the reasons the test was not promptly administered. If a test required by this section is not administered within eight hours following the accident, the employer shall cease attempts to administer an alcohol test and shall prepare and maintain the same record. Records shall be submitted to the FMCSA upon request.

(2) **Controlled substance tests.** If a test required by this section is not administered within 32 hours following the accident, the employer shall cease attempts to administer a controlled substances test, and prepare and maintain on file a record stating the reasons the test was not promptly administered. Records shall be submitted to the FMCSA upon request.

(e) A driver who is subject to post-accident testing shall remain readily available for such testing or may be deemed by the employer to have refused to submit to testing. Nothing in this section shall be construed to require the delay of necessary medical attention for injured people following an accident or to prohibit a driver from leaving the scene of an accident for the period necessary to obtain assistance in responding to the accident, or to obtain necessary emergency medical care.

(f) An employer shall provide drivers with necessary post-accident information, procedures and instructions, prior to the driver operating a commercial motor vehicle, so that drivers will be able to comply with the requirements of this section.

(g)(1) The results of a breath or blood test for the use of alcohol, conducted by Federal, State, or local officials having independent authority for the test, shall be considered to meet the requirements of this section, provided such tests conform to the applicable Federal, State or local alcohol testing requirements, and that the results of the tests are obtained by the employer.

(2) The results of a urine test for the use of controlled substances, conducted by Federal, State, or local officials having independent authority for the test, shall be considered to meet the requirements of this section, provided such tests conform to the applicable Federal, State or local controlled substances testing requirements, and that the results of the tests are obtained by the employer.

(h) **Exception.** This section does not apply to:

(1) An occurrence involving only boarding or alighting from a stationary motor vehicle; or

(2) An occurrence involving only the loading or unloading of cargo; or

(3) An occurrence in the course of the operation of a passenger car or a multipurpose passenger vehicle (as defined in §571.3 of this title) by an employer unless the motor vehicle is transporting passengers for hire or hazardous materials of a type and quantity that require the motor vehicle to be marked or placarded in accordance with §177.823 of this title.

§382.305 Random testing.

(a) Every employer shall comply with the requirements of this section. Every driver shall submit to random alcohol and controlled substance testing as required in this section.

(b)(1) Except as provided in paragraphs (c) through (e) of this section, the minimum annual percentage rate for random alcohol testing shall be 10 percent of the average number of driver positions.

(2) Except as provided in paragraphs (f) through (h) of this section, the minimum annual percentage rate for random controlled substances testing shall be 50 percent of the average number of driver positions.

(c) The FMCSA Administrator's decision to increase or decrease the minimum annual percentage rate for alcohol testing is based on the reported violation rate for the entire industry. All information used for this determination is drawn from the alcohol management information system reports required by §382.403. In order to ensure reliability of the data, the FMCSA Administrator considers the quality and completeness of the reported data, may obtain additional information or reports from employers, and may make appropriate modifications in calculating the industry violation rate. In the event of a change in the annual percentage rate, the FMCSA Administrator will publish in the *Federal Register* the new minimum annual percentage rate for random alcohol testing of drivers. The new minimum annual percentage rate for random alcohol testing will be applicable starting January 1 of the calendar year following publication in the *Federal Register*.

(d)(1) When the minimum annual percentage rate for random alcohol testing is 25 percent or more, the FMCSA Administrator may lower this rate to 10 percent of all driver positions if the FMCSA Administrator determines that the data received under the reporting requirements of §382.403 for two consecutive calendar years indicate that the violation rate is less than 0.5 percent.

(2) When the minimum annual percentage rate for random alcohol testing is 50 percent, the FMCSA Administrator may lower this rate to 25 percent of all driver positions if the FMCSA Administrator determines that the data received under the reporting requirements of §382.403 for two consecutive calendar years indicate that the violation rate is less than 1.0 percent but equal to or greater than 0.5 percent.

(e)(1) When the minimum annual percentage rate for random alcohol testing is 10 percent, and the data received under the reporting requirements of §382.403 for that calendar year indicate that the violation rate is equal to or greater than 0.5 percent, but less than 1.0 percent, the FMCSA Administrator will increase the minimum annual percentage rate for random alcohol testing to 25 percent for all driver positions.

(2) When the minimum annual percentage rate for random alcohol testing is 25 percent or less, and the data received under the reporting requirements of §382.403 for that calendar year indicate that the violation rate is equal to or greater than 1.0 percent, the FMCSA Administrator will increase the minimum annual percentage rate for random alcohol testing to 50 percent for all driver positions.

(f) The FMCSA Administrator's decision to increase or decrease the minimum annual percentage rate for controlled substances testing is based on the reported positive rate for the entire industry. All information used for this determination is drawn from the controlled substances management information system reports required by §382.403. In order to ensure reliability of the data, the FMCSA Administrator considers the quality and completeness of the reported data, may obtain additional information or reports from employers, and may make appropriate modifications in calculating the industry positive rate. In the event of a change in the annual percentage rate, the FMCSA Administrator will publish in the *Federal Register* the new minimum annual percentage rate for controlled substances testing of drivers. The new minimum annual percentage rate for random controlled substances testing will be applicable starting January 1 of the calendar year following publication in the *Federal Register*.

(g) When the minimum annual percentage rate for random controlled substances testing is 50 percent, the FMCSA Administrator may lower this rate to 25 percent of all driver positions if the FMCSA Administrator determines that the data received under the reporting requirements of §382.403 for two consecutive calendar years indicate that the positive rate is less than 1.0 percent.

(h) When the minimum annual percentage rate for random controlled substances testing is 25 percent, and the data received under the reporting requirements of §382.403 for any calendar year indicate that the reported positive rate is equal to or greater than 1.0 percent, the FMCSA Administrator will increase the minimum annual percentage rate for random controlled substances testing to 50 percent of all driver positions.

(i)(1) The selection of drivers for random alcohol and controlled substances testing shall be made by a scientifically valid method, such as a random number table or a computer-based random number generator that is matched with drivers' Social Security numbers, payroll identification numbers, or other comparable identifying numbers.

(2) Each driver selected for random alcohol and controlled substances testing under the selection process used, shall have an equal chance of being tested each time selections are made.

(3) Each driver selected for testing shall be tested during the selection period.

(j) The employer shall randomly select a sufficient number of drivers for testing during each calendar year to equal an annual rate not less than the minimum annual percentage rate for random alcohol and controlled substances testing determined by the FMCSA Administrator. If the employer conducts random testing for alcohol and/or controlled substances through a C/TPA, the number of drivers to be tested may be calculated for each individual employer or may be based on the total number of drivers covered by the C/TPA who are subject to random alcohol and/or controlled substances testing at the same minimum annual percentage rate under this part.

(k)(1) Each employer shall ensure that random alcohol and controlled substances tests conducted under this part are unannounced.

(2) Each employer shall ensure that the dates for administering random alcohol and controlled substances tests conducted under this part are spread reasonably throughout the calendar year.

(l) Each employer shall require that each driver who is notified of selection for random alcohol and/or controlled substances testing proceeds to the test site immediately; provided, however, that if the driver is performing a safety-sensitive function, other than driving a commercial motor vehicle, at the time of notification, the employer shall instead ensure that the driver ceases to perform the safety-sensitive function and proceeds to the testing site as soon as possible.

(m) A driver shall only be tested for alcohol while the driver is performing safety-sensitive functions, just before the driver is to perform safety-sensitive functions, or just after the driver has ceased performing such functions.

(n) If a given driver is subject to random alcohol or controlled substances testing under the random alcohol or controlled substances testing rules of more than one DOT agency for the same employer, the driver shall be subject to random alcohol and/or controlled substances testing at the annual percentage rate established for the calendar year by the DOT agency regulating more than 50 percent of the driver's function.

(o) If an employer is required to conduct random alcohol or controlled substances testing under the alcohol or controlled substances testing rules of more than one DOT agency, the employer may—

(1) Establish separate pools for random selection, with each pool containing the DOT-covered employees who are subject to testing at the same required minimum annual percentage rate; or

(2) Randomly select such employees for testing at the highest minimum annual percentage rate established for the calendar year by any DOT agency to which the employer is subject.

§382.307 Reasonable suspicion testing.

(a) An employer shall require a driver to submit to an alcohol test when the employer has reasonable suspicion to believe that the driver has violated the prohibitions of subpart B of this part concerning alcohol. The employer's determination that reasonable suspicion exists to require the driver to undergo an alcohol test must be based on specific, contemporaneous, articulable observations concerning the appearance, behavior, speech or body odors of the driver.

(b) An employer shall require a driver to submit to a controlled substances test when the employer has reasonable suspicion to believe that the driver has violated the prohibitions of subpart B of this part concerning controlled substances. The employer's determination that reasonable suspicion exists to require the driver to undergo a controlled substances test must be based on specific, contemporaneous, articulable observations concerning the appearance, behavior, speech or body odors of the driver. The observations may include indications of the chronic and withdrawal effects of controlled substances.

(c) The required observations for alcohol and/or controlled substances reasonable suspicion testing shall be made by a supervisor or company official who is trained in accordance with §382.603. The person who makes the determination that reasonable suspicion exists to conduct an alcohol test shall not conduct the alcohol test of the driver.

(d) Alcohol testing is authorized by this section only if the observations required by paragraph (a) of this section are made during, just preceding, or just after the period of the work day that the driver is required to be in compliance with this part. A driver may be directed by the employer to only undergo reasonable suspicion testing while the driver is performing safety-sensitive functions, just before the driver is to perform safety-sensitive functions, or just after the driver has ceased performing such functions.

(e)(1) If an alcohol test required by this section is not administered within two hours following the determination under paragraph (a) of this section, the employer shall prepare and maintain on file a record stating the reasons the alcohol test was not promptly administered. If an alcohol test required by this section is not administered within eight hours following the determination under paragraph (a) of this section, the employer shall cease attempts to administer an alcohol test and shall state in the record the reasons for not administering the test.

(2) Notwithstanding the absence of a reasonable suspicion alcohol test under this section, no driver shall report for duty or remain on duty requiring the performance of safety-sensitive functions while the driver is under the influence of or impaired by alcohol, as shown by the behavioral, speech, and performance indicators of alcohol misuse, nor shall an employer permit the driver to perform or continue to perform safety-sensitive functions, until:

(i) An alcohol test is administered and the driver's alcohol concentration measures less than 0.02; or

(ii) Twenty four hours have elapsed following the determination under paragraph (a) of this section that there is reasonable suspicion to believe that the driver has violated the prohibitions in this part concerning the use of alcohol.

(3) Except as provided in paragraph (e)(2) of this section, no employer shall take any action under this part against a driver based solely on the driver's behavior and appearance, with respect to alcohol use, in the absence of an alcohol test. This does not prohibit an employer with independent authority of this part from taking any action otherwise consistent with law.

(f) A written record shall be made of the observations leading to an alcohol or controlled substances reasonable suspicion test, and signed by the supervisor or company official who made the observations, within 24 hours of the observed behavior or before the results of the alcohol or controlled substances tests are released, whichever is earlier.

§382.309 Return-to-duty testing.

The requirements for return-to-duty testing must be performed in accordance with 49 CFR part 40, Subpart O.

§382.311 Follow-up testing.

The requirements for follow-up testing must be performed in accordance with 49 CFR part 40, Subpart O.

Subpart D — Handling of Test Results, Record Retention and Confidentiality

§382.401 Retention of records.

(a) **General requirement.** Each employer shall maintain records of its alcohol misuse and controlled substances use prevention programs as provided in this section. The records shall be maintained in a secure location with controlled access.

(b) **Period of retention.** Each employer shall maintain the records in accordance with the following schedule:

(1) **Five years.** The following records shall be maintained for a minimum of five years:

(i) Records of driver alcohol test results indicating an alcohol concentration of 0.02 or greater,

(ii) Records of driver verified positive controlled substances test results,

(iii) Documentation of refusals to take required alcohol and/or controlled substances tests,

(iv) Driver evaluation and referrals,

(v) Calibration documentation,

(vi) Records related to the administration of the alcohol and controlled substances testing programs, and

(vii) A copy of each annual calendar year summary required by §382.403.

(2) **Two years.** Records related to the alcohol and controlled substances collection process (except calibration of evidential breath testing devices).

(3) **One year.** Records of negative and canceled controlled substances test results (as defined in part 40 of this title) and alcohol test results with a concentration of less than 0.02 shall be maintained for a minimum of one year.

(4) **Indefinite period.** Records related to the education and training of breath alcohol technicians, screening test technicians, supervisors, and drivers shall be maintained by the employer while the individual performs the functions which require the training and for two years after ceasing to perform those functions.

(c) **Types of records.** The following specific types of records shall be maintained. "Documents generated" are documents that may have to be prepared under a requirement of this part. If the record is required to be prepared, it must be maintained.

(1) Records related to the collection process:

(i) Collection logbooks, if used;

(ii) Documents relating to the random selection process;

(iii) Calibration documentation for evidential breath testing devices;

(iv) Documentation of breath alcohol technician training;

(v) Documents generated in connection with decisions to administer reasonable suspicion alcohol or controlled substances tests;

(vi) Documents generated in connection with decisions on post-accident tests;

(vii) Documents verifying existence of a medical explanation of the inability of a driver to provide adequate breath or to provide a urine specimen for testing; and

(viii) Consolidated annual calendar year summaries as required by §382.403.

(2) Records related to a driver's test results:

(i) The employer's copy of the alcohol test form, including the results of the test;

(ii) The employer's copy of the controlled substances test chain of custody and control form;

(iii) Documents sent by the MRO to the employer, including those required by part 40, subpart G, of this title;

(iv) Documents related to the refusal of any driver to submit to an alcohol or controlled substances test required by this part;

(v) Documents presented by a driver to dispute the result of an alcohol or controlled substances test administered under this part; and

(vi) Documents generated in connection with verifications of prior employers' alcohol or controlled substances test results that the employer:

(A) Must obtain in connection with the exception contained in §382.301, and

(B) Must obtain as required by §382.413.

(3) Records related to other violations of this part.

(4) Records related to evaluations:

(i) Records pertaining to a determination by a substance abuse professional concerning a driver's need for assistance; and

(ii) Records concerning a driver's compliance with recommendations of the substance abuse professional.

(5) Records related to education and training:

(i) Materials on alcohol misuse and controlled substance use awareness, including a copy of the employer's policy on alcohol misuse and controlled substance use;

(ii) Documentation of compliance with the requirements of §382.601, including the driver's signed receipt of education materials;

(iii) Documentation of training provided to supervisors for the purpose of qualifying the supervisors to make a determination concerning the need for alcohol and/or controlled substances testing based on reasonable suspicion;

(iv) Documentation of training for breath alcohol technicians as required by §40.213(a) of this title; and

(v) Certification that any training conducted under this part complies with the requirements for such training.

(6) Administrative records related to alcohol and controlled substances testing:

(i) Agreements with collection site facilities, laboratories, breath alcohol technicians, screening test technicians, medical review officers, consortia, and third party service providers;

(ii) Names and positions of officials and their role in the employer's alcohol and controlled substances testing program(s);

(iii) Semi-annual laboratory statistical summaries of urinalysis required by §40.111(a) of this title; and

(iv) The employer's alcohol and controlled substances testing policy and procedures.

(d) **Location of records.** All records required by this part shall be maintained as required by §390.31 of this subchapter and shall be made available for inspection at the employer's principal place of business within two business days after a request has been made by an authorized representative of the Federal Motor Carrier Safety Administration.

(e) **OMB control number.**

(1) The information collection requirements of this part have been reviewed by the Office of Management and Budget pursuant to the Paperwork Reduction Act of 1995 (44 U.S.C. 3501 et seq.) and have been assigned OMB control number 2126-0012.

(2) The information collection requirements of this part are found in the following sections: Sections 382.105, 382.113, 382.301, 382.303, 382.305, 382.307, 382.401, 382.403, 382.405, 382.409, 382.411, 382.601, 382.603.

§382.403 Reporting of results in a management information system.

(a) An employer shall prepare and maintain a summary of the results of its alcohol and controlled substances testing programs performed under this part during the previous calendar year, when requested by the Secretary of Transportation, any DOT agency, or any State or local officials with regulatory authority over the employer or any of its drivers.

(b) If an employer is notified, during the month of January, of a request by the Federal Motor Carrier Safety Administration to report the employer's annual calendar year summary information, the employer shall prepare and submit the report to the FMCSA by March 15 of that year. The employer shall ensure that the annual summary report is accurate and received by March 15 at the location that the FMCSA specifies in its request. The report shall be in the form and manner prescribed by the FMCSA in its request. When the report is submitted to the FMCSA by mail or electronic transmission, the information requested shall be typed, except for the signature of the certifying official. Each employer shall ensure the accuracy and timeliness of each report submitted by the employer or a consortium.

(c) **Detailed summary.** Each annual calendar year summary that contains information on a verified positive controlled substances test result, an alcohol screening test result of 0.02 or greater, or any other violation of the alcohol misuse provisions of subpart B of this part shall include the following informational elements:

(1) Number of drivers subject to this part;

(2) Number of drivers subject to testing under the alcohol misuse or controlled substances use rules of more than one DOT agency, identified by each agency;

(3) Number of urine specimens collected by type of test (e.g., pre-employment, random, reasonable suspicion, post-accident);

(4) Number of positives verified by a MRO by type of test, and type of controlled substance;

(5) Number of negative controlled substance tests verified by a MRO by type of test;

(6) Number of persons denied a position as a driver following a pre-employment verified positive controlled substances test and/or a pre-employment alcohol test that indicates an alcohol concentration of 0.04 or greater;

(7) Number of drivers with tests verified positive by a medical review officer for multiple controlled substances;

(8) Number of drivers who refused to submit to an alcohol or controlled substances test required under this subpart, including those who submitted substituted or adulterated specimens;

(9)(i) Number of supervisors who have received required alcohol training during the reporting period; and

(ii) Number of supervisors who have received required controlled substances training during the reporting period;

(10)(i) Number of screening alcohol tests by type of test; and

(ii) Number of confirmation alcohol tests, by type of test;

(11) Number of confirmation alcohol tests indicating an alcohol concentration of 0.02 or greater but less than 0.04, by type of test;

(12) Number of confirmation alcohol tests indicating an alcohol concentration of 0.04 or greater, by type of test;

(13) Number of drivers who were returned to duty (having complied with the recommendations of a substance abuse professional as described in §382.503 and part 40, subpart O of this title), in this reporting period, who previously:

(i) Had a verified positive controlled substance test result, or

(ii) Engaged in prohibited alcohol misuse under the provisions of this part;

(14) Number of drivers who were administered alcohol and drug tests at the same time, with both a verified positive drug test result and an alcohol test result indicating an alcohol concentration of 0.04 or greater; and

(15) Number of drivers who were found to have violated any non-testing prohibitions of subpart B of this part, and any action taken in response to the violation.

(d) **Short summary.** Each employer's annual calendar year summary that contains only negative controlled substance test results, alcohol screening test results of less than 0.02, and does not contain any other violations of subpart B of this part, may prepare and submit, as required by paragraph (b) of this section, either a standard report form containing all the information elements specified in paragraph (c) of this section, or an "EZ" report form. The "EZ" report shall include the following information elements:

(1) Number of drivers subject to this part;

(2) Number of drivers subject to testing under the alcohol misuse or controlled substance use rules of more than one DOT agency, identified by each agency;

(3) Number of urine specimens collected by type of test (e.g., pre-employment, random, reasonable suspicion, post-accident);

(4) Number of negatives verified by a medical review officer by type of test;

(5) Number of drivers who refused to submit to an alcohol or controlled substances test required under this subpart, including those who submitted substituted or adulterated specimens;

(6)(i) Number of supervisors who have received required alcohol training during the reporting period; and

(ii) Number of supervisors who have received required controlled substances training during the reporting period;

(7) Number of screen alcohol tests by type of test; and

(8) Number of drivers who were returned to duty (having complied with the recommendations of a substance abuse professional as described in §382.503 and part 40, subpart O, of this title), in this reporting period, who previously:

(i) Had a verified positive controlled substance test result, or

(ii) Engaged in prohibited alcohol misuse under the provisions of this part.

(e) Each employer that is subject to more than one DOT agency alcohol or controlled substances rule shall identify each driver covered by the regulations of more than one DOT agency. The identification will be by the total number of covered functions. Prior to conducting any alcohol or controlled substances test on a driver subject to the rules of more than one DOT agency, the employer shall determine which DOT agency rule or rules authorizes or requires the test. The test result information shall be directed to the appropriate DOT agency or agencies.

(f) A C/TPA may prepare annual calendar year summaries and reports on behalf of individual employers for purposes of compliance with this section. However, each employer shall sign and submit such a report and shall remain responsible for ensuring the accuracy and timeliness of each report prepared on its behalf by a C/TPA.

§382.405 Access to facilities and records.

(a) Except as required by law or expressly authorized or required in this section, no employer shall release driver information that is contained in records required to be maintained under §382.401.

(b) A driver is entitled, upon written request, to obtain copies of any records pertaining to the driver's use of alcohol or controlled substances, including any records pertaining to his or her alcohol or controlled substances tests. The employer shall promptly provide the records requested by the driver. Access to a driver's records shall not be contingent upon payment for records other than those specifically requested.

(c) Each employer shall permit access to all facilities utilized in complying with the requirements of this part to the Secretary of Transportation, any DOT agency, or any State or local officials with regulatory authority over the employer or any of its drivers.

(d) Each employer shall make available copies of all results for employer alcohol and/or controlled substances testing conducted under this part and any other information pertaining to the employer's alcohol misuse and/or controlled substances use prevention program, when requested by the Secretary of Transportation, any DOT agency, or any State or local officials with regulatory authority over the employer or any of its drivers.

(e) When requested by the National Transportation Safety Board as part of an accident investigation, employers shall disclose information related to the employer's administration of a post-accident alcohol and/or controlled substance test administered following the accident under investigation.

(f) Records shall be made available to a subsequent employer upon receipt of a written request from a driver. Disclosure by the subsequent employer is permitted only as expressly authorized by the terms of the driver's request.

(g) An employer may disclose information required to be maintained under this part pertaining to a driver to the decision maker in a lawsuit, grievance, or administrative proceeding initiated by or on behalf of the individual, and arising from a positive DOT drug or alcohol test or a refusal to test (including, but not limited to, adulterated or substituted test results) of this part (including, but not limited to, a worker's compensation, unemployment compensation, or other proceeding relating to a benefit sought by the driver). Additionally, an employer may disclose information in criminal or civil actions in accordance with §40.323(a)(2) of this title.

(h) An employer shall release information regarding a driver's records as directed by the specific written consent of the driver authorizing release of the information to an identified person. Release of such information by the person receiving the information is permitted only in accordance with the terms of the employee's specific written consent as outlined in §40.321(b) of this title.

§382.407 Medical review officer notifications to the employer.

Medical review officers shall report the results of controlled substances tests to employers in accordance with the requirements of part 40, Subpart G, of this title.

§382.409 Medical review officer record retention for controlled substances.

(a) A medical review officer or third party administrator shall maintain all dated records and notifications, identified by individual, for a minimum of five years for verified positive controlled substances test results.

(b) A medical review officer or third party administrator shall maintain all dated records and notifications, identified by individual, for a minimum of one year for negative and canceled controlled substances test results.

(c) No person may obtain the individual controlled substances test results retained by a medical review officer or third party administrator, and no medical review officer or third party administrator shall release the individual controlled substances test results of any driver to any person, without first obtaining a specific, written authorization from the tested driver. Nothing in this paragraph (c) shall prohibit a medical review officer or third party administrator from releasing, to the employer or to officials of the Secretary of Transportation, any DOT agency, or any State or local officials with regulatory authority over the controlled substances testing program under this part, the information delineated in part 40, Subpart G, of this title.

§382.411 Employer notifications.

(a) An employer shall notify a driver of the results of a pre-employment controlled substances test conducted under this part, if the driver requests such results within 60 calendar days of being notified of the disposition of the employment application. An employer shall notify a driver of the results of random, reasonable suspicion and post-accident tests for controlled substances conducted under this part if the test results are verified positive. The employer shall also inform the driver which controlled substance or substances were verified as positive.

(b) The designated employer representative shall make reasonable efforts to contact and request each driver who submitted a specimen under the employer's program, regardless of the driver's employment status, to contact and discuss the results of the controlled substances test with a medical review officer who has been unable to contact the driver.

(c) The designated employer representative shall immediately notify the medical review officer that the driver has been notified to contact the medical review officer within 72 hours.

§382.413 Inquiries for alcohol and controlled substances information from previous employers.

Employers shall request alcohol and controlled substances information from previous employers in accordance with the requirements of §40.25 of this title.

Subpart E — Consequences For Drivers Engaging In Substance Use-Related Conduct

§382.501 Removal from safety-sensitive function.

(a) Except as provided in subpart F of this part, no driver shall perform safety-sensitive functions, including driving a commercial motor vehicle, if the driver has engaged in conduct prohibited by subpart B of this part or an alcohol or controlled substances rule of another DOT agency.

(b) No employer shall permit any driver to perform safety-sensitive functions; including driving a commercial motor vehicle, if the employer has determined that the driver has violated this section.

(c) For purposes of this subpart, commercial motor vehicle means a commercial motor vehicle in commerce as defined in §382.107, and a commercial motor vehicle in interstate commerce as defined in Part 390 of this subchapter.

§382.503 Required evaluation and testing.

No driver who has engaged in conduct prohibited by subpart B of this part shall perform safety-sensitive functions, including driving a commercial motor vehicle, unless the driver has met the requirements of part 40, subpart O, of this title. No employer shall permit a driver who has engaged in conduct prohibited by subpart B of this part to perform safety-sensitive functions, including driving a commercial motor vehicle, unless the driver has met the requirements of part 40, subpart O, of this title.

§382.505 Other alcohol-related conduct.

(a) No driver tested under the provisions of subpart C of this part who is found to have an alcohol concentration of 0.02 or greater but less than 0.04 shall perform or continue to perform safety-sensitive functions for an employer, including driving a commercial motor vehicle, nor shall an employer permit the driver to perform or continue to perform safety-sensitive functions, until the start of the driver's next regularly scheduled duty period, but not less than 24 hours following administration of the test.

(b) Except as provided in paragraph (a) of this section, no employer shall take any action under this part against a driver based solely on test results showing an alcohol concentration less than 0.04. This does not prohibit an employer with authority independent of this part from taking any action otherwise consistent with law.

§382.507 Penalties.

Any employer or driver who violates the requirements of this part shall be subject to the civil and/or criminal penalty provisions of 49 U.S.C. 521(b). In addition, any employer or driver who violates the requirements of 49 CFR part 40 shall be subject to the civil and/or criminal penalty provisions of 49 U.S.C. 521(b).

Subpart F — Alcohol Misuse and Controlled Substances Use Information, Training, and Referral

§382.601 Employer obligation to promulgate a policy on the misuse of alcohol and use of controlled substances.

(a) **General requirements.** Each employer shall provide educational materials that explain the requirements of this part and the employer's policies and procedures with respect to meeting these requirements.

(1) The employer shall ensure that a copy of these materials is distributed to each driver prior to the start of alcohol and controlled substances testing under this part and to each driver subsequently hired or transferred into a position requiring driving a commercial motor vehicle.

(2) Each employer shall provide written notice to representatives of employee organizations of the availability of this information.

(b) **Required content.** The materials to be made available to drivers shall include detailed discussion of at least the following:

(1) The identity of the person designated by the employer to answer driver questions about the materials;

(2) The categories of drivers who are subject to the provisions of this part;

(3) Sufficient information about the safety-sensitive functions performed by those drivers to make clear what period of the work day the driver is required to be in compliance with this part;

(4) Specific information concerning driver conduct that is prohibited by this part;

(5) The circumstances under which a driver will be tested for alcohol and/or controlled substances under this part, including post-accident testing under §382.303(d);

(6) The procedures that will be used to test for the presence of alcohol and controlled substances, protect the driver and the integrity of the testing processes, safeguard the validity of the test results, and ensure that those results are attributed to the correct driver, including post-accident information, procedures and instructions required by §382.303(d);

(7) The requirement that a driver submit to alcohol and controlled substances tests administered in accordance with this part;

(8) An explanation of what constitutes a refusal to submit to an alcohol or controlled substances test and the attendant consequences;

(9) The consequences for drivers found to have violated subpart B of this part, including the requirement that the driver be removed immediately from safety-sensitive functions, and the procedures under part 40, subpart O, of this title;

(10) The consequences for drivers found to have an alcohol concentration of 0.02 or greater but less than 0.04;

(11) Information concerning the effects of alcohol and controlled substances use on an individual's health, work, and personal life; signs and symptoms of an alcohol or a controlled substances problem (the driver's or a co-worker's); and available methods of intervening when an alcohol or a controlled substances problem is suspected, including confrontation, referral to any employee assistance program and or referral to management.

(c) **Optional provision.** The materials supplied to drivers may also include information on additional employer policies with respect to the use of alcohol or controlled substances, including any consequences for a driver found to have a specified alcohol or controlled substances level, that are based on the employer's authority independent of this part. Any such additional policies or consequences must be clearly and obviously described as being based on independent authority.

(d) **Certificate of receipt.** Each employer shall ensure that each driver is required to sign a statement certifying that he or she has received a copy of these materials described in this section. Each employer shall maintain the original of the signed certificate and may provide a copy of the certificate to the driver.

§382.603 Training for supervisors.

Each employer shall ensure that all persons designated to supervise drivers receive at least 60 minutes of training on alcohol misuse and receive at least an additional 60 minutes of training on controlled substances use. The training will be used by the supervisors to determine whether reasonable suspicion exists to require a driver to undergo testing under §382.307. The training shall include the physical, behavioral, speech, and performance indicators of probable alcohol misuse and use of controlled substances. Recurrent training for supervisory personnel is not required.

§382.605 Referral, evaluation, and treatment.

The requirements for referral, evaluation, and treatment must be performed in accordance with 49 CFR part 40, Subpart O.

PART 383 — COMMERCIAL DRIVER'S LICENSE STANDARDS; REQUIREMENTS AND PENALTIES

Subpart A — General

AUTHORITY: 49 U.S.C. 521, 31136, 31301 *et seq.,* and 31502; Sec. 214 of Pub. L 106-159, 113 Stat. 1766; Sec. 1012(b) of Pub. L 107.56, 115 Stat. 397; and 49 CFR 1.73.

Subpart A — General

§383.1 Purpose and scope.

(a) The purpose of this part is to help reduce or prevent truck and bus accidents, fatalities, and injuries by requiring drivers to have a single commercial motor vehicle driver's license and by disqualifying drivers who operate commercial motor vehicles in an unsafe manner.

(b) This part:

(1) Prohibits a commercial motor vehicle driver from having more than one commercial motor vehicle driver's license;

(2) Requires a driver to notify the driver's current employer and the driver's State of domicile of certain convictions;

(3) Requires that a driver provide previous employment information when applying for employment as an operator of a commercial motor vehicle;

(4) Prohibits an employer from allowing a person with a suspended license to operate a commercial motor vehicle;

(5) Establishes periods of disqualification and penalties for those persons convicted of certain criminal and other offenses and serious traffic violations, or subject to any suspensions, revocations, or cancellations of certain driving privileges;

(6) Establishes testing and licensing requirements for commercial motor vehicle operators;

(7) Requires States to give knowledge and skills tests to all qualified applicants for commercial drivers' licenses which meet the Federal standard;

(8) Sets forth commercial motor vehicle groups and endorsements;

(9) Sets forth the knowledge and skills test requirements for the motor vehicle groups and endorsements;

(10) Sets forth the Federal standards for procedures, methods, and minimum passing scores for States and others to use in testing and licensing commercial motor vehicle operators; and

(11) Establishes requirements for the State issued commercial license documentation.

§383.3 Applicability.

(a) The rules in this part apply to every person who operates a commercial motor vehicle (CMV) in interstate, foreign, or intrastate commerce, to all employers of such persons, and to all States.

(b) The exceptions contained in §390.3(f) of this subchapter do not apply to this part. The employers and drivers identified in §390.3(f) must comply with the requirements of this part, unless otherwise provided in this section.

(c) **Exception for certain military drivers.** Each State must exempt from the requirements of this part individuals who operate CMVs for military purposes. This exception is applicable to active duty military personnel; members of the military reserves; member of the national guard on active duty, including personnel on full-time national guard duty, personnel on part-time national guard training, and national guard military technicians (civilians who are required to wear military uniforms); and active duty U.S. Coast Guard personnel. This exception is not applicable to U.S. Reserve technicians.

(d) **Exception for farmers, firefighters, emergency response vehicle drivers; and drivers removing snow and ice.** A State may, at its discretion, exempt individuals identified in paragraphs (d)(1), (d)(2), and (d)(3) of this section from the requirements of this part. The use of this waiver is limited to the driver's home State unless there is a reciprocity agreement with adjoining States.

(1) Operators of a farm vehicle which is:

(i) Controlled and operated by a farmer, including operation by employees or family members;

(ii) Used to transport either agricultural products, farm machinery, farm supplies, or both to or from a farm;

(iii) Not used in the operations of a common or contract motor carrier; and

(iv) Used within 241 kilometers (150 miles) of the farmer's farm.

(2) Firefighters and other persons who operate CMVs which are necessary to the preservation of life or property or the execution of emergency governmental functions, are equipped with audible and visual signals and are not subject to normal traffic regulation. These vehicles include fire trucks, hook and ladder trucks, foam or water transport trucks, police SWAT team vehicles, ambulances, or other vehicles that are used in response to emergencies.

(3)(i) A driver, employed by an eligible unit of local government, operating a commercial motor vehicle within the boundaries of that unit for the purpose of removing snow or ice from a roadway by plowing, sanding, or salting, if

(A) The properly licensed employee who ordinarily operates a commercial motor vehicle for these purposes is unable to operate the vehicle; or

(B) The employing governmental entity determines that a snow or ice emergency exists that requires additional assistance.

(ii) This exemption shall not preempt State laws and regulations concerning the safe operation of commercial motor vehicles.

(e) **Restricted commercial drivers license (CDL) for certain drivers in the State of Alaska.** (1) The State of Alaska may, at its discretion, waive only the following requirements of this part and issue a CDL to each driver that meets the conditions set forth in paragraphs (e) (2) and (3) of this section:

(i) The knowledge tests standards for testing procedures and methods of subpart H, but must continue to administer knowledge tests that fulfill the content requirements of subpart G for *all* applicants;

(ii) All the skills test requirements; and

(iii) The requirement under §383.153(a)(4) to have a photograph on the license document.

(2) Drivers of CMVs in the State of Alaska must operate exclusively over roads that meet *both* of the following criteria to

be eligible for the exception in paragraph (e)(1) of this section:

(i) Such roads are not connected by land highway or vehicular way to the land-connected State highway system; and

(ii) Such roads are not connected to any highway or vehicular way with an average daily traffic volume greater than 499.

(3) Any CDL issued under the terms of this paragraph must carry two restrictions:

(i) Holders may not operate CMVs over roads other than those specified in paragraph (e)(2) of this section; and

(ii) The license is not valid for CMV operation outside the State of Alaska.

§383.5 Definitions.

As used in this part:

Administrator means the Federal Motor Carrier Safety Administrator, the chief executive of the Federal Motor Carrier Safety Administration, an agency within the Department of Transportation.

Alcohol or "alcoholic beverage" means: (a) Beer as defined in 26 U.S.C. 5052(a), of the Internal Revenue Code of 1954, (b) wine of not less than one-half of one per centum of alcohol by volume, or (c) distilled spirits as defined in section 5002(a)(8), of such Code.

Alcohol concentration (AC) means the concentration of alcohol in a person's blood or breath. When expressed as a percentage it means grams of alcohol per 100 milliliters of blood or grams of alcohol per 210 liters of breath.

Alien means any person not a citizen or national of the United States.

Commerce means (a) any trade, traffic or transportation within the jurisdiction of the United States between a place in a State and a place outside of such State, including a place outside of the United States and (b) trade, traffic, and transportation in the United States which affects any trade, traffic, and transportation described in paragraph (a) of this definition.

Commercial driver's license (CDL) means a license issued by a State or other jurisdiction, in accordance with the standards contained in 49 CFR Part 383, to an individual which authorizes the individual to operate a class of a commercial motor vehicle.

Commercial driver's license information system (CDLIS) means the CDLIS established by FMCSA pursuant to section 12007 of the Commercial Motor Vehicle Safety Act of 1986.

Commercial motor vehicle (CMV) means a motor vehicle or combination of motor vehicles used in commerce to transport passengers or property if the motor vehicle—

(a) Has a gross combination weight rating of 11,794 kilograms or more (26,001 pounds or more) inclusive of a towed unit(s) with a gross vehicle weight rating of more than 4,536 kilograms (10,000 pounds); or

(b) Has a gross vehicle weight rating of 11,794 or more kilograms (26,001 pounds or more); or

(c) Is designed to transport 16 or more passengers, including the driver; or

(d) Is of any size and is used in the transportation of hazardous materials as defined in this section.

Controlled substance has the meaning such term has under 21 U.S.C. 802(6) and includes all substances listed on schedules I through V of 21 CFR 1308, as they may be amended by the United States Department of Justice.

Conviction means an unvacated adjudication of guilt, or a determination that a person has violated or failed to comply with the law in a court of original jurisdiction or by an authorized administrative tribunal, an unvacated forfeiture of bail or collateral deposited to secure the person's appearance in court, a plea of guilty or nolo contendere accepted by the court, the payment of a fine or court cost, or violation of a condition of release without bail, regardless of whether or not the penalty is rebated, suspended, or probated.

Disqualification means any of the following three actions:

(a) The suspension, revocation, or cancellation of a CDL by the State or jurisdiction of issuance.

(b) Any withdrawal of a person's privileges to drive a CMV by a State or other jurisdiction as the result of a violation of State or local law relating to motor vehicle traffic control (other than parking, vehicle weight or vehicle defect violations).

(c) A determination by the FMCSA that a person is not qualified to operate a commercial motor vehicle under part 391 of this chapter.

Driver applicant means an individual who applies to a State to obtain, transfer, upgrade, or renew a CDL.

Driver's license means a license issued by a State or other jurisdiction, to an individual which authorizes the individual to operate a motor vehicle on the highways.

Driving a commercial motor vehicle while under the influence of alcohol means committing any one or more of the following acts in a CMV—

(a) Driving a CMV while the person's alcohol concentration is 0.04 or more;

(b) Driving under the influence of alcohol, as prescribed by State law; or

(c) Refusal to undergo such testing as is required by any State or jurisdiction in the enforcement of §383.51(b) or §392.5(a)(2) of this subchapter.

Eligible unit of local government means a city, town, borough, county, parish, district, or other public body created by or pursuant to State law which has a total population of 3,000 individuals or less.

Employee means any operator of a commercial motor vehicle, including full time, regularly employed drivers; casual, intermittent or occasional drivers; leased drivers and independent, owner-operator contractors (while in the course of operating a commercial motor vehicle) who are either directly employed by or under lease to an employer.

Employer means any person (including the United States, a State, District of Columbia or a political subdivision of a State) who owns or leases a commercial motor vehicle or assigns employees to operate such a vehicle.

Endorsement means an authorization to an individual's CDL required to permit the individual to operate certain types of commercial motor vehicles.

Fatality means the death of a person as a result of a motor vehicle accident.

Felony means an offense under State or Federal law that is punishable by death or imprisonment for a term exceeding 1 year.

Foreign means outside the fifty United States and the District of Columbia.

Gross combination weight rating (GCWR) means the value specified by the manufacturer as the loaded weight of a combination (articulated) vehicle. In the absence of a value specified by the manufacturer, GCWR will be determined by adding the GVWR of the power unit and the total weight of the towed unit and any load thereon.

Gross vehicle weight rating (GVWR) means the value specified by the manufacturer as the loaded weight of a single vehicle.

Hazardous materials . . .

Imminent hazard means the existence of a condition that presents a substantial likelihood that death, serious illness, severe personal injury, or a substantial endangerment to health, property, or the environment may occur before the reasonably foreseeable completion date of a formal proceeding begun to lessen the risk of that death, illness, injury or endangerment.

Motor vehicle means a vehicle, machine, tractor, trailer, or semitrailer propelled or drawn by mechanical power used on highways, except that such term does not include a vehicle, machine, tractor, trailer, semitrailer operated exclusively on a rail.

Nonresident CDL means a CDL issued by a State under either of the following two conditions:

(a) To an individual domiciled in a foreign country meeting the requirements of §383.23(b)(1).

(b) To an individual domiciled in another State meeting the requirements of §383.23(b)(2).

Non-CMV means a motor vehicle or combination of motor vehicles not defined by the term "commercial motor vehicle (CMV)" in this section.

Out-of-service order means a declaration by an authorized enforcement officer of a Federal, State, Canadian, Mexican, or local jurisdiction that a driver, a commercial motor vehicle, or a motor carrier operation, is out-of-service pursuant to §§386.72, 392.5, 395.13, 396.9, or compatible laws, or the North American Uniform Out-of-Service Criteria.

Representative vehicle means a motor vehicle which represents the type of motor vehicle that a driver applicant operates or expects to operate.

School bus means a CMV used to transport pre-primary, primary, or secondary school students from home to school, from school to home, or to and from school-sponsored events. School bus does not include a bus used as a common carrier.

Serious traffic violation means conviction of any of the following offenses when operating a CMV, except weight, defect and parking violations:

(a) Excessive speeding, involving any single offense for any speed of 15 miles per hour or more above the posted speed limit;

(b) Reckless driving, as defined by State or local law or regulation, including but not limited to offenses of driving a CMV in willful or wanton disregard for the safety of persons or property;

(c) Improper or erratic traffic lane changes;

(d) Following the vehicle ahead too closely;

(e) A violation, arising in connection with a fatal accident, of State or local law relating to motor vehicle traffic control;

(f) Driving a CMV without obtaining a CDL;

(g) Driving a CMV without a CDL in the driver's possession. Any individual who provides proof to the enforcement authority that issued the citation, by the date the individual must appear in court or pay any fine for such a violation, that the individual held a valid CDL on the date the citation was issued, shall not be guilty of this offense; or

(h) Driving a CMV without the proper class of CDL and/or endorsements for the specific vehicle group being operated or for the passengers or type of cargo being transported.

State means a State of the United States and the District of Columbia.

State of domicile means that State where a person has his/her true, fixed, and permanent home and principal residence and to which he/she has the intention of returning whenever he/she is absent.

Tank vehicle . . .

United States the term United States means the 50 States and the District of Columbia.

Vehicle means a motor vehicle unless otherwise specified.

Vehicle group means a class or type of vehicle with certain operating characteristics.

§383.7 Validity of CDL issued by decertified State.

A CDL issued by a State prior to the date the State is notified by the Administrator, in accordance with the provisions of §384.405 of this subchapter, that the State is prohibited from issuing CDLs, will remain valid until its stated expiration date.

Subpart B — Single License Requirement

§383.21 Number of drivers' licenses.

No person who operates a commercial motor vehicle shall at any time have more than one driver's license.

§383.23 Commercial driver's license.

(a) **General rule.** (1) Effective April 1, 1992, no person shall operate a commercial motor vehicle unless such person has taken and passed written and driving tests which meet the Federal standards contained in Subparts F, G, and H of this part for the commercial motor vehicle that person operates or expects to operate.

(2) Except as provided in paragraph (b) of this section, no person may legally operate a CMV unless such person possesses a CDL which meets the standards contained in subpart J of this

part, issued by his/ her State or jurisdiction of domicile.

(b) **Exception**. (1) If a CMV operator is not domiciled in a foreign jurisdiction which the Administrator has determined tests drivers and issues CDLs in accordance with, or under standards similar to, the standards contained in subparts F, G, and H of this part, the person may obtain a Nonresident CDL from a State which does comply with the testing and licensing standards contained in such subparts F, G, and H of this part.[1]

(2) If an individual is domiciled in a State while that State is prohibited from issuing CDLs in accordance with §384.405 of this subchapter, that individual is eligible to obtain a Nonresident CDL from any State that elects to issue a Nonresident CDL and which complies with the testing and licensing standards contained in subparts F, G, and H of this part.

(c) **Learner's permit.** State learners' permits, issued for limited time periods according to State requirements, shall be considered valid commercial drivers' licenses for purposes of behind-the-wheel training on public roads or highways, if the following minimum conditions are met:

(1) The learner's permit holder is at all times accompanied by the holder of a valid CDL;

(2) He/she either holds a valid automobile driver's license, or has passed such vision, sign/symbol, and knowledge tests as the State issuing the learner's permit ordinarily administers to applicants for automotive drivers' licenses; and

(3) He/she does not operate a commercial motor vehicle transporting hazardous materials as defined in §383.5.

---

[1]Effective December 29, 1988, the Administrator determined that commercial drivers' licensees issued by Canadian Provinces and Territories in conformity with the Canadian National Safety Code are in accordance with the standards of this part. Effective November 21, 1991, the Administrator determined that the new Licencias Federales de Conductor issued by the United Mexican States are in accordance with the standards of this part. Therefore, under the single license provision of §383.21, a driver holding a commercial driver's license issued under the Canadian National Safety Code or a new Licencia Federal de Conductor issued by Mexico is prohibited from obtaining nonresident CDL, or any other type of driver's license, from a State or other jurisdiction in the United States.

Subpart C — Notification Requirements and Employer Responsibilities

§383.31 Notification of convictions for driver violations.

(a) Each person who operates a commercial motor vehicle, who has a commercial driver's license issued by a State or jurisdiction, and who is convicted of violating, in any type of motor vehicle, a State or local law relating to motor vehicle traffic control (other than a parking violation) in a State or jurisdiction other than the one which issued his/her license, shall notify an official designated by the State or jurisdiction which issued such license, of such conviction. The notification must be made within 30 days after the date that person has been convicted.

(b) Each person who operates a commercial motor vehicle, who has a commercial driver's license issued by a State or jurisdiction, and who is convicted of violating, in any type of motor vehicle, a State or local law relating to motor vehicle traffic control (other than a parking violation), shall notify his/her current employer of such conviction. The notification must be made within 30 days after the date that the person has been convicted. If the driver is not currently employed, he/she must notify the State or jurisdiction which issued the license according to §383.31(a).

(c) **Notification.** The notification to the State official and employer must be made in writing and contain the following information:

(1) Driver's full name;

(2) Driver's license number;

(3) Date of conviction;

(4) The specific criminal or other offense(s), serious traffic violation(s), and other violation(s) of State or local law relating to motor vehicle traffic control, for which the person was convicted and any suspension, revocation, or cancellation of certain driving privileges which resulted from such conviction(s);

(5) Indication whether the violation was in a commercial motor vehicle;

(6) Location of offense; and

(7) Driver's signature.

§383.33 Notification of driver's license suspensions.

Each employee who has a driver's license suspended, revoked, or canceled by a State or jurisdiction, who loses the right to operate a commercial motor vehicle in a State or jurisdiction for any period, or who is disqualified from operating a commercial motor vehicle for any period, shall notify his/her current employer of such suspension, revocation, cancellation, lost privilege, or disqualification. The notification must be made before the end of the business day following the day the employee received notice of suspension, revocation, cancellation, lost privilege, or disqualification.

§383.35 Notification of previous employment.

(a) Any person applying for employment as an operator of a commercial motor vehicle shall provide at the time of application for employment, the information specified in paragraph (c) of this section.

(b) All employers shall request the information specified in paragraph (c) of this section from all persons applying for employment as a commercial motor vehicle operator. The request shall be made at the time of application for employment.

(c) The following employment history information for the 10 years preceding the date the application is submitted shall be presented to the prospective employer by the applicant:

(1) A list of the names and addresses of the applicant's previous employers for which the applicant was an operator of a commercial motor vehicle;

(2) The dates the applicant was employed by these employers; and

(3) The reason for leaving such employment.

(d) The applicant shall certify that all information furnished is true and complete.

(e) An employer may require an applicant to provide additional information.

(f) Before an application is submitted, the employer shall inform the applicant that the information he/she provides in accordance with paragraph (c) of this section may be used, and the applicant's previous employers may be contacted for the purpose of investigating the applicant's work history.

§383.37 Employer responsibilities.

No employer may knowingly allow, require, permit, or authorize a driver to operate a CMV in the United States:

(a) During any period in which the driver has a CMV driver's license suspended, revoked, or canceled by a State, has lost the right to operate a CMV in a State, or has been disqualified from operating a CMV;

(b) During any period in which the driver has more than one CMV driver's license;

(c) During any period in which the driver, or the CMV he or she is driving, or the motor carrier operation, is subject to an out-of-service order; or

(d) In violation of a Federal, State, or local law or regulation, pertaining to railroad-highway grade crossings.

Subpart D — Driver Disqualifications and Penalties

§383.51 Disqualification of drivers.

(a) **General**. (1) A driver or holder of a CDL who is disqualified must not drive a CMV.

(2) An employer must not knowingly allow, require, permit, or authorize a driver who is disqualified to drive a CMV.

(3) A driver is subject to disqualification sanctions designated in paragraphs (b) and (c) of this section, if the holder of a CDL drives a CMV or non-CMV and is convicted of the violations.

(4) Determining first and subsequent violations. For purposes of determining first and subsequent violations of the offenses specified in this subpart, each conviction for any offense listed in Tables 1 through 4 to this section resulting from a separate incident, whether committed in a CMV or non-CMV, must be counted.

(a)(5) Reinstatement after lifetime disqualification. A State may reinstate any driver disqualified for life for offenses described in paragraphs (1) through (b)(8) of this section (Table 1 to §383.51) after 10 years if that person has voluntarily entered and successfully completed an appropriate rehabilitation program approved by the State. Any person who has been reinstated in accordance with this provision and who is subsequently convicted of a disqualifying offense described in paragraphs (b)(1) through (b)(8) of this section (Table 1 to §383.51) must not be reinstated.

(b) **Disqualification for major offenses**. Table 1 to §383.51 contains a list of the offenses and periods for which a driver must be disqualified, depending upon the type of vehicle the driver is operating at the time of the violation, as follows:

Table 1 to §383.51

If a driver operates a motor vehicle and is convicted of:	For a first conviction or refusal to be tested while operating a CMV, a person required to have a CDL holder must be disqualified from operating a CMV for…	For a first conviction or refusal to be tested while operating a non-CMV, a CDL holder must be disqualified from operating a CMV for…	For a first conviction or refusal to be tested while operating a CMV transporting hazardous materials required to be placarded under the Hazardous Materials Regulations (49 CFR part 172, subpart F), a person required to have a CDL and CDL holder must be disqualified from operating a CMV for…	For a second conviction or refusal to be tested in a separate incident of any combination of offenses in this Table while operating a CMV, a person required to have a CDL and a CDL holder must be disqualified from operating a CMV for…	For a second conviction or refusal to be tested in a separate incident of any combination of offenses in this Table while operating a non-CMV, a CDL holder must be disqualified from operating a CMV for…
(1) Being under the influence of alcohol as prescribed by State law.	1 year	1 year	3 years	Life	Life
(2) Being under the influence of a controlled substance.	1 year	1 year	3 years	Life	Life
(3) Having an alcohol concentration of 0.04 or greater while operating a CMV	1 year	Not applicable	3 years	Life	Not applicable

Table 1 to §383.51, Continued

(4) Refusing to take an alcohol test as required by a State or jurisdiction under its implied consent laws or regulations as defined in §383.72 of this part.	1 year	1 year	3 years	Life	Life
(5) Leaving the scene of an accident.	1 year	1 year	3 years	Life	Life
(6) Using the vehicle to commit a felony other than a felony described in paragraph (b)(9) of this table.	1 year	1 year	3 years	Life	Life
(7) Driving a CMV when, as a result of prior violations committed operating a CMV, the driver's CDL is revoked, suspended, or canceled, or the driver is disqualified from operating a CMV.	1 year	Not applicable	3 years	Life	Not applicable
(8) Causing a fatality through the negligent operation of a CMV, including but not limited to the crimes of motor vehicle manslaughter, homicide by motor vehicle and negligent homicide.	1 year	Not applicable	3 years	Life	Not applicable
(9) Using the vehicle in the commission of a felony involving manufacturing, distributing, or dispensing a controlled substance.	Life-not eligible for 10-year reinstatement.	Life-not eligible for 10-year reinstatement.	Life-not eligible for 10-year reinstatement.	Life-not eligible for 10-year reinstatement.	Life-not eligible for 10-year reinstatement.

(c) **Disqualification for serious traffic violations.** Table 2 to §383.51 contains a list of the offenses and the periods for which a driver must be disqualified, depending upon the type of vehicle the driver is operating at the time of the violation, as follows:

Table 2 to §383.51

If a driver operates a motor vehicle and is convicted of:	For a second conviction of any combination of offenses in this Table in a separate incident within a 3-year period while operating a CMV, a person required to have a CDL and a CDL holder must be disqualified from operating a CMV for...	For a second conviction of any combination of offenses in this Table in a separate incident within a 3-year period while operating a non-CMV, a CDL holder must be disqualified from operating a CMV, if the conviction results in the revocation, cancellation, or suspension of the CDL holder's license or non-CMV driving privileges for...	For a third or subsequent conviction of any combination of offenses in this Table in a separate incident within a 3-year period while operating a CMV, a person required to have a CDL and a CDL holder must be disqualified from operating a CMV for...	For a third or subsequent conviction of any combination of offenses in this Table in a separate incident within a 3-year period while operating a non-CMV, a CDL holder must be disqualified from operating a CMV, if the conviction results in the revocation, cancellation, or suspension of the CDL holder's license or non-CMV driving privileges, for...
(1) Speeding excessively, involving and speed of 24.1 kmph (15 mph) or more above the posted speed limit.	60 days	60 days	120 days	120 days
(2) Driving recklessly, as defined by State or local law or regulation, including but not limited to, offenses of driving a motor vehicle in willful or wanton disregard for the safety of persons or property.	60 days	60 days	120 days	120 days

Table 2 to §383.51, Continued

(3) Making improper or erratic traffic lane changes.	60 days	60 days	120 days	120 days	120 days
(4) Following the vehicle ahead too closely.	60 days	60 days	120 days	120 days	120 days
(5) Violating State or local law relating to motor vehicle traffic control (other than a parking violation) arising in connection with a fatal accident.	60 days	60 days	120 days	120 days	120 days
(6) Driving a CMV without obtaining a CDL.	60 days	Not applicable	120 days	120 days	Not applicable
(7) Driving a CMV without a CDL in the driver's possession.[1]	60 days	Not applicable	120 days	120 days	Not applicable
(8) Driving a CMV without the proper class of CDL and/or endorsements for the specific vehicle group being operated or for the passengers or type of cargo being transported.	60 days	Not applicable	120 days	120 days	Not applicable

[1] Any individual who provides proof to the enforcement authority that issued the citation, by the date the individual must appear in court or pay any fine for such a violation, that the individual held a valid CDL on the date the citation was issued, shall not be guilty of this offense.

(d) **Disqualification for railroad-highway grade crossing offenses.** Table 3 to §383.51 contains a list of the offenses and the periods for which a driver must be disqualified, when the driver is operating a CMV at the time of the violation, as follows:

Table 3 to §383.51

If a driver is convicted of operating a CMV in violation of a Federal, State or local law because...	For a first conviction a person required to have a CDL and a CDL holder must be disqualified from operating a CMV for...	For a second conviction of any combination of offenses in this Table in a separate incident within a 3-year period a person required to have a CDL and a CDL holder must be disqualified from operating a CMV for....	For a third or subsequent conviction of any combination of offenses in this Table in a separate incident within a 3-year period a person required to have a CDL and a CDL holder must be disqualified from operating a CMV for...
(1) The driver is not required to always stop, but fails to slow down and check that tracks are clear of an approaching train.	No less than 60 days	No less than 120 days	No less than 1 year.
(2) The driver is not required to always stop, but fails to stop before reaching the crossing, if the tracks are not clear.	No less than 60 days	No less than 120 days	No less than 1 year.
(3) The driver is always required to stop, but fails to stop before driving onto the crossing.	No less than 60 days	No less than 120 days	No less than 1 year.
(4) The driver fails to have sufficient space to drive completely through the crossing without stopping.	No less than 60 days	No less than 120 days	No less than 1 year.
(5) The driver fails to obey a traffic control device or the directions of an enforcement official at the crossing.	No less than 60 days	No less than 120 days	No less than 1 year.
(6) The driver fails to negotiate a crossing because of insufficient undercarriage clearance.	No less than 60 days	No less than 120 days	No less than 1 year.

(e) **Disqualification for violating out-of-service orders.** Table 4 to §383.51 contains a list of the offenses and periods for which a driver must be disqualified when the driver is operating a CMV at the time of the violation, as follows:

Table 4 to § 383.51

If a driver operates a CMV and is convicted of...	For a first conviction while operating a CMV, a person required to have a CDL and a CDL holder must be disqualified from operating a CMV for...	For a second conviction in a separate incident within a 10-year period while operating a CMV, a person required to have a CDL and a CDL holder must be disqualified from operating a CMV for...	For a third or subsequent conviction in a separate incident within a 10-year period while operating a CMV, a person required to have a CDL and a CDL holder must be disqualified from operating a CMV for...
(1) Violating a driver or vehicle out-of-service order while transporting nonhazardous materials.	No less than 90 days or more than 1 year.	No less than 1 year or more than 5 years.	No less than 3 years or more than 5 years.
(2) Violating a driver or vehicle out-of-service order while transporting hazardous materials required to be placarded under part 172, subpart F of this title, or while operating a vehicle designed to transport 16 or more passengers, including the driver.	No less than 180 days or more than 2 years.	No less than 3 years or more than 5 years.	No less than 3 years or more than 5 years.

§383.52 Disqualification of drivers determined to constitute an imminent hazard.

(a) The Assistant Administrator or his/her designee must disqualify from operating a CMV any driver whose driving is determined to constitute an imminent hazard, as defined in §383.5.

(b) The period of the disqualification may not exceed 30 days unless the FMCSA complies with the provisions of paragraph (c) of this section.

(c) The Assistant Administrator or his/her delegate may provide the driver an opportunity for a hearing after issuing a disqualification for a period of 30 days or less. The Assistant Administrator or his/her delegate must provide the driver notice of a proposed disqualification period of more than 30 days and an opportunity for a hearing to present a defense to the proposed disqualification. A disqualification imposed under this paragraph may not exceed one year in duration. The driver, or a representative on his/her behalf, may file an appeal of the disqualification issued by the Assistant Administrator's delegate with the Assistant Administrator, Adjudications Counsel, Federal Motor Carrier Safety Administration (Room 8217), 400 Seventh Street, SW., Washington, DC 20590.

(d) Any disqualification imposed in accordance with the provisions of this section must be transmitted by the FMCSA to the jurisdiction where the driver is licensed and must become a part of the driver's record maintained by that jurisdiction.

(e) A driver who is simultaneously disqualified under this section and under other provisions of this subpart, or under State law or regulation, shall serve those disqualification periods concurrently.

§383.53 Penalties.

(a) **General rule.** Any person who violates the rules set forth in subparts B and C of this part may be subject to civil or criminal penalties as provided for in 49 U.S.C. 521(b).

(b) **Special penalties pertaining to violation of out of service orders.**—(1) **Driver violations**. A driver who is convicted of violating an out of service order shall be subject to a civil penalty of not less than $1,100 nor more than $2,750, in addition to disqualification under §383.51(e).

(2) **Employer violations.** An employer who is convicted of a violation of §383.37(c) shall be subject to a civil penalty of not

less than $2,750 nor more than $11,000.

(c) **Special penalties pertaining to railroad-highway grade crossing violations.** An employer who is convicted of a violation of §383.37(d) must be subject to a civil penalty of not more than $10,000.

Subpart E — Testing and Licensing Procedures

§383.71 Driver application procedures.

(a) **Initial Commercial Driver's License.** — Prior to obtaining a CDL, a person must meet the following requirements:

(1) A person who operates or expects to operate in interstate or foreign commerce, or is otherwise subject to Part 391 of this title, shall certify that he/she meets the qualification requirements contained in Part 391 of this title. A person who operates or expects to operate entirely in intrastate commerce and is not subject to Part 391, is subject to State driver qualification requirements and must certify that he/she is not subject to Part 391;

(2) Pass a knowledge test in accordance with the standards contained in Subparts G and H of this part for the type of motor vehicle the person operates or expects to operate;

(3) Pass a driving or skills test in accordance with the standards contained in Subparts G and H of this part taken in a motor vehicle which is representative of the type of motor vehicle the person operates or expects to operate; or provide evidence that he/she has successfully passed a driving test administered by an authorized third party;

(4) Certify that the motor vehicle in which the person takes the driving skills test is representative of the type of motor vehicle that person operates or expects to operate;

(5) Provide to the State of issuance the information required to be included on the CDL as specified in Subpart J of this part;

(6) Certify that he/she is not subject to any disqualification under §383.51, or any license suspension, revocation, or cancellation under State law, and that he/she does not have a driver's license from more than one State or jurisdiction;

(7) Surrender the applicant's non-CDL driver's licenses to the State; and

(8) Provide the names of all States where the applicant has previously been licensed to drive any type of motor vehicle during the previous 10 years.

(9) If applying for a hazardous materials endorsement, com-

ply with Transportation Security Administration requirements codified in 49 CFR Part 1572, and provide proof of citizenship or immigration status as specified in Table 1 to this section. A lawful permanent resident of the United States requesting a hazardous materials endorsement must additionally provide his or her Bureau of Citizenship and Immigration Services (BCIS) Alien registration number.

Table 1 to §383.71—List of Acceptable Proofs of Citizenship or Immigration

Status	Proof of status
U.S. Citizen	• U.S. Passport • Certificate of birth that bears an official seal and was issued by a State, county, municipal authority, or outlying possession of the United States • Certification of Birth Abroad issued by the U.S. Department of State (Form FS-545 or DS 1350) • Certificate of Naturalization (Form N-550 or N-570) • Certificate of U.S. Citizenship (Form N-560 or N-561)
Lawful Permanent Resident	• Permanent Resident Card, Alien Registration Receipt Card (Form I-551) • Temporary I-551 stamp in foreign passport • Temporary I-551 stamp on Form I-94, Arrival/Departure Record, with photograph of the bearer • Reentry Permit (Form I-327)

(b) **License transfer.** When applying to transfer a CDL from one State of domicile to a new State domicile, an applicant shall apply for a CDL from the new State of domicile within no more than 30 days after establishing his/her new domicile. The applicant shall:

(1) Provide to the new State of domicile the certifications contained in §383.71(a) (1) and (6);

(2) Provide to the new State of domicile updated information as specified in Subpart J of this part;

(3) If the applicant wishes to retain a hazardous materials endorsement, he/she must comply with the requirements for such endorsement specified in §383.71(a)(9) and State require-

ments as specified in §383.73(b)(4);

(4) Surrender the CDL from the old State of domicile to the new State of domicile; and

(5) Provide the names of all States where the applicant has previously been licensed to drive any type of motor vehicle during the previous 10 years.

(c) **License renewal.** When applying for a renewal of a CDL, all applicants shall:

(1) Provide certification contained in §383.71(a) (1);

(2) Provide updated information as specified in Subpart J of this part; and

(3) If a person wishes to retain a hazardous materials endorsement, he/she must comply with the requirements specified in §383.71(a)(9) and pass the test specified in §383.121 for such endorsement.

(4) Provide the names of all States where the applicant has previously been licensed to drive any type of motor vehicle during the previous 10 years.

(d) **License upgrades.** When applying to operate a commercial motor vehicle in a different group or endorsement from the group or endorsement in which the applicant already has a CDL, all persons shall:

(1) Provide the necessary certifications as specified in §383.71(a)(1) and (a)(4);

(2) Pass all tests specified in §383.71(a)(2) and (a)(3) for the new vehicle group and/or different endorsements; and

(3) To obtain a hazardous materials endorsement, comply with the requirements for such endorsement specified in §383.71(a)(9).

(e) **Nonresident CDL.** When an applicant is domiciled in a foreign jurisdiction, as defined in §383.5, where the commercial motor vehicle operator testing and licensing standards do not meet the standards contained in Subparts G and H of this part, as determined by the Administrator, such applicant shall obtain a Nonresident CDL from a State which meets such standards. Such applicant shall:

(1) Complete the requirements to obtain a CDL contained in §383.71(a); and

(2) After receipt of the CDL, and for as long as it is valid, notify the State which issued the CDL of any adverse action taken by any jurisdiction or governmental agency, foreign or domestic, against his/her driving privileges. Such adverse actions

would include but not be limited to license suspension or revocation, or disqualification from operating a commercial motor vehicle for the convictions described in §383.51. Notifications shall be made within the time periods specified in §383.33.

(f) If a State uses the alternative method described in §383.73(i) to achieve the objectives of the certifications in §383.71(a), then the driver applicant shall satisfy such alternative methods as are applicable to him/her with respect to initial licensing, license transfer, license renewal, and license upgrades.

§383.72 Implied consent to alcohol testing.

Any person who holds a CDL is considered to have consented to such testing as is required by any State or jurisdiction in the enforcement of §§383.51(b)(2)(i) and 392.5(a)(2) of this chapter. Consent is implied by driving a commercial motor vehicle.

§383.73 State procedures.

(a) **Initial licensure.** Prior to issuing a CDL to a person, a State shall:

(1) Require the driver applicant to certify, pass tests, and provide information as described in §§383.71(a)(1) through (6);

(2) Check that the vehicle in which the applicant takes his/her test is representative of the vehicle group the applicant has certified that he/she operates or expects to operate;

(3) Initiate and complete a check of the applicant's driving record to ensure that the person is not subject to any disqualification under §383.51, or any license suspension, revocation, or cancellation under State law, and that the person does not have a driver's license from more than one State or jurisdiction. The record check must include, but is not limited to, the following:

(i) A check of the applicant's driving record as maintained by his/her current State of licensure, if any;

(ii) A check with the CDLIS to determine whether the driver applicant already has been issued a CDL, whether the applicant's license has been suspended, revoked, or canceled, or if the applicant has been disqualified from operating a commercial motor vehicle;

(iii) A check with the National Driver Register (NDR) to determine whether the driver applicant has:

(A) Been disqualified from operating a motor vehicle (other than a commercial motor vehicle);

(B) Had a license (other than CDL) suspended, revoked, or canceled for cause in the 3-year period ending on the date of application; or

(C) Been convicted of any offenses contained in section 205(a)(3) of the National Driver Register Act of 1982 (23 U.S.C. 401 note); and

(iv) A request for the applicant's complete driving record from all States where the applicant was previously licensed over the last 10 years to drive any type of motor vehicle. **Exception:** A State is only required to make the driving record check specified in this paragraph (a)(3) for drivers renewing a CDL for the first time after September 30, 2002, provided a notation is made on the driver's record confirming that the driver record check required by this paragraph (a)(3) has been made and noting the date it was done; and

(4) Require the driver applicant to surrender his/her driver's license issued by another State, if he/she has moved from another State.

(5) For persons applying for a hazardous materials endorsement, require compliance with the standards for such endorsement specified in §383.71(a)(9).

(b) **License transfers.** Prior to issuing a CDL to a person who has a CDL from another State, a State shall:

(1) Require the driver applicant to make the certifications contained in §383.71(a);

(2) Complete a check of the driver applicant's record as contained in §383.73(a) (3);

(3) Request and receive updates of information specified in Subpart J of this part;

(4) . . .

(5) Obtain the CDL issued by the applicant's previous State of domicile.

(c) **License Renewals.** Prior to renewing any CDL, a State shall:

(1) Require the driver applicant to make the certifications contained in §383.71(a);

(2) Complete a check of the driver applicant's record as contained in §383.73(a) (3);

(3) Request and receive updates of information specified in Subpart J of this part; and

(4) . . .

(d) **License upgrades.** Prior to issuing an upgrade of a CDL, a State shall:

(1) Require such driver applicant to provide certifications, pass tests, and meet applicable hazardous materials standards specified in §383.71(d); and

(2) Complete a check of the driver applicant's record as described in §383.73(a) (3).

(e) **Nonresident CDL.** A State may issue a Nonresident CDL to a person domiciled in a foreign country if the Administrator has determined that the commercial motor vehicle testing and licensing standards in the foreign jurisdiction of domicile do not meet the standards contained in this part. State procedures for the issuance of a nonresident CDL, for any modifications thereto, and for notifications to the CDLIS shall at a minimum be identical to those pertaining to any other CDL, with the following exceptions:

(1) If the applicant is requesting a transfer of his/her Nonresident CDL, the State shall obtain the Nonresident CDL currently held by the applicant and issued by another State;

(2) The State shall add the word "Nonresident" to the face of the CDL, in accordance with §383.153(b); and

(3) The State shall have established, prior to issuing any Nonresident CDL, the practical capability of disqualifying the holder of any Nonresident CDL, by withdrawing, suspending, canceling, and revoking his/her Nonresident CDL as if the Nonresident CDL were a CDL issued to a resident of the State.

(f) **License issuance.** After the State has completed the procedures described in §383.73(a), (b), (c), (d), or (e), it may issue a CDL to the driver applicant. The State shall notify the operator of the CDLIS of such issuance, transfer, renewal, or upgrade within the 10-day period beginning on the date of license issuance.

(g) **Penalties for false information.** If a State determines, in its check of an applicant's license status and record prior to issuing a CDL, or at any time after the CDL is issued, that the applicant has falsified information contained in Subpart J of this part or any of the certifications required in §383.71(a), the State shall at a minimum suspend, cancel, or revoke the person's CDL or his/her pending application, or disqualify the person from operating a commercial motor vehicle for a period of at least 60 consecutive days.

(h) **Reciprocity.** A State shall allow any person who has a valid CDL which is not suspended, revoked, or canceled, and who is not disqualified from operating a commercial motor vehicle to operate a commercial motor vehicle in the State.

(i) **Alternative procedures.** A State may implement alternative procedures to the certification requirements of §383.71(a) (1), (4), and (6), provided those procedures ensure that the driver meets the requirements of those paragraphs.

§383.75 Third party testing.

(a) **Third party tests.** A State may authorize a person (including another State, an employer, a private driver training facility or other private institution, or a department, agency or instrumentality of a local government) to administer the skills tests as specified in Subparts G and H of this part, if the following conditions are met:

(1) The tests given by the third party are the same as those which would otherwise by given by the State; and

(2) The third party as an agreement with the State containing, at a minimum, provisions that:

(i) Allow the FMCSA, or its representative, and the State to conduct random examinations, inspections and audits without prior notice;

(ii) Require the State to conduct on-site inspections at least annually;

(iii) Require that all third party examiners meet the same qualification and training standards as State examiners, to the extent necessary to conduct skills tests in compliance with Subparts G and H;

(iv) Require that, at least on an annual basis, State employees take the tests actually administered by the third party as if the State employee were a test applicant, or that States test a sample of drivers who were examined by the third party to compare pass/fail results; and

(v) Reserve unto the State the right to take prompt and appropriate remedial action against the third-party testers in the event that the third-party fails to comply with State or Federal standards for the CDL testing program, or with any other terms of the third-party contract.

(b) **Proof of testing by a third party.** A driver applicant who takes and passes driving tests administered by an authorized third party shall provide evidence to the State licensing agency that he/she has successfully passed the driving tests administered by the third party.

§383.77 Substitute for driving skills tests.

At the discretion of a State, the driving skill test as specified in §383.113 may be waived for a CMV operator who is currently licensed at the time of his/her application for a CDL, and substituted with either an applicant's driving record and previous passage of an acceptable skills test, or an applicant's driving record in combination with certain driving experience. The State shall impose conditions and limitations to restrict the applicants from whom a State may accept alternative requirements for the skills test described in §383.113. Such conditions must require at least the following:

(a) An applicant must certify that, during the two-year period immediately prior to applying for a CDL, he/she:

(1) Has not had more than one license (except in the instances specified in §383.21(b));

(2) Has not had any license suspended, revoked, or canceled;

(3) Has not had any convictions for any type of motor vehicle for the disqualifying offenses contained in §383.51(b);

(4) Has not had more than one conviction for any type of motor vehicle for serious traffic violations; and

(5) Has not had any conviction for a violation of State or local law relating to motor vehicle traffic control (other than a parking violation) arising in connection with any traffic accident, and has no record of an accident in which he/she was at fault; and

(b) An applicant must provide evidence and certify that:

(1) He/she is regularly employed in a job requiring operation of a CMV, and that either:

(2) He/she has previously taken and passed a skills test given by a State with a classified licensing and testing system, and that the test was behind-the-wheel in a representative vehicle for that applicant's driver's license classification; or

(3) He/she has operated, for at least 2 years immediately preceding application for a CDL, a vehicle representative of the commercial motor vehicle the driver applicant operates or expects to operate.

Subpart F — Vehicle Groups and Endorsements

§383.91 Commercial motor vehicle groups.

(a) **Vehicle group descriptions.** Each driver applicant must possess and be tested on his/her knowledge and skills, described in subpart G of this part, for the commercial motor vehicle group(s) for which he/she desires a CDL. The commercial motor vehicle groups are as follows:

(1) Combination vehicle (Group A)—Any combination of vehicles with a gross combination weight rating (GCWR) of 11,794 kilograms or more (26,001 pounds or more) provided the GVWR of the vehicle(s) being towed is in excess of 4,536 kilograms (10,000 pounds).

(2) Heavy Straight Vehicle (Group B)—Any single vehicle with a GVWR of 11,794 kilograms or more (26,001 pounds or more), or any such vehicle towing a vehicle not in excess of 4,536 kilograms (10,000 pounds) GVWR.

(3) Small Vehicle (Group C)—Any single vehicle, or combination of vehicles, that meets neither the definition of Group A nor that of Group B as contained in this section, but that either is designed to transport 16 or more passengers including the driver, or is used in the transportation of materials found to be hazardous for the purposes of the Hazardous Materials Transportation Act and which require the motor vehicle to be placarded under the Hazardous Materials Regulations (49 CFR part 172, subpart F).

(b) **Representative vehicle.** For purposes of taking the driving test in accordance with §383.113, a representative vehicle for a given vehicle group contained in §383.91(a), is any commercial motor vehicle which meets the definition of that vehicle group.

(c) **Relation between vehicle groups.** Each driver applicant who desires to operate in a different commercial motor vehicle group from the one which his/her CDL authorizes shall be required to retake and pass all related tests, except the following:

(1) A driver who has passed the knowledge and skills tests for a combination vehicle (Group A) may operate a heavy straight vehicle (Group B) or a small vehicle (Group C), provided that he/she possesses the requisite endorsement(s); and

(2) A driver who has passed the knowledge and skills tests for a heavy straight vehicle (Group B) may operate any small vehicle (Group C), provided that he/she possesses the requisite endorsement(s).

(d) **Vehicle group illustration.** Figure 1 illustrates typical vehicles within each of the vehicle groups defined in this section.

§383.93 Endorsements.

(a) **General.** In addition to taking and passing the knowledge and skills tests described in Subpart G of this part, all persons who operate or expect to operate the type(s) of motor vehicles described in paragraph (b) of this section shall take and pass specialized tests to obtain each endorsement. The State shall issue CDL endorsements only to drivers who successfully complete the tests.

(b) **Endorsement descriptions.** An operator must obtain State-issued endorsements to his/her CDL to operate commercial motor vehicles which are:

(1) . . .

(2) Passenger vehicles;

(3) . . .

(4) . . .

(5) School buses.

(c) **Endorsement testing requirements.** The following tests are required for the endorsements contained in paragraph (b) of this section:

(1) . . .

(2) **Passenger** — a knowledge and a skills test;

(3) . . .

(4) . . .

(5) **School bus** — a knowledge and a skills test.

§383.93

Figure 1

VEHICLE GROUPS AS ESTABLISHED BY FHWA (SECTION 383.91)

[Note: Certain types of vehicles, such as passenger and doubles/triples, will require an endorsement. Please consult text for particulars.]

Group: *Description:

A Any combination of vehicles with a GCWR of 26,001 or more pounds provided the GVWR of the vehicle(s) being towed is in excess of 10,000 pounds. (Holders of a Group A license may, with any appropriate endorsements, operate all vehicles within Groups B and C.)

Examples include but are not limited to:

B Any single vehicle with a GVWR of 26,001 or more pounds, or any such vehicle towing a vehicle not in excess of 10,000 pounds GVWR (Holders of a Group B license may, with any appropriate endorsements, operate all vehicles within Group C.)

Examples include but are not limited to:

C Any single vehicle, or combination of vehicles, that does not meet the definition of Group A or Group B as contained herein, but that either is designed to transport 16 or more passengers including the driver, or is placarded for hazardous materials.

Examples include but are not limited to:

*The representative vehicle for the skills test must meet the written description for that group. The silhouettes typify, but do not fully cover, the types of vehicles falling within each group.

§383.95 Air brake restrictions.

(a) If an applicant either fails the air brake component of the knowledge test, or performs the skills test in a vehicle not equipped with air brakes, the State shall indicate on the CDL, if issued, that the person is restricted from operating a CMV equipped with air brakes.

(b) For the purposes of the skills test and the restriction, air brakes shall include any braking system operating fully or partially on the air brake principle.

Subpart G — Required Knowledge and Skills

§383.110 General requirement.

All drivers of commercial motor vehicles shall have knowledge and skills necessary to operate a commercial motor vehicle safely as contained in this subpart. A sample of the specific types of items which a State may wish to include in the knowledge and skills tests that it administers to CDL applicants is included in the appendix to this Subpart G.

§383.111 Required knowledge.

All commercial motor vehicle operators must have knowledge of the following general areas:

(a) **Safe operations regulations.** Driver-related elements of the regulations contained in 49 CFR Parts 382, 391, 392, 393, 395, 396, and 397, such as: Motor vehicle inspection, repair, and maintenance requirements; procedures for safe vehicle operations; the effects of fatigue, poor vision, hearing, and general health upon safe commercial motor vehicle operation; the types of motor vehicles and cargoes subject to the requirements; and the effects of alcohol and drug use upon safe commercial motor vehicle operations.

(b) **Commercial motor vehicle safety control systems.** Proper use of the motor vehicle's safety system, including lights, horns, side and rear-view mirrors, proper mirror adjustments, fire extinguishers, symptoms of improper operation revealed through instruments, motor vehicle operation characteristics, and diagnosing malfunctions. Commercial motor vehicle drivers shall have knowledge on the correct procedures needed to use these safety systems in an emergency situation, e.g., skids and loss of brakes.

(c) **Safe vehicle control.** (1) **Control systems** — The purpose and function of the controls and instruments commonly found on commercial motor vehicles.

(2) **Basic control** — The proper procedures for performing various basic maneuvers.

(3) **Shifting** — The basic shifting rules and terms, as well as shift patterns and procedures for common transmissions.

(4) **Backing** — The procedures and rules for various backing maneuvers.

(5) **Visual search** — The importance of proper visual search, and proper visual search methods.

(6) **Communication** — The principles and procedures for proper communications and the hazards of failure to signal properly.

(7) **Speed Management** — The importance of understanding the effects of speed.

(8) **Space management** — The procedures and techniques for controlling the space around the vehicle.

(9) **Night operation** — Preparations and procedures for night driving.

(10) **Extreme driving conditions** — The basic information on operating in extreme driving conditions and the hazards that are encountered in extreme conditions.

(11) **Hazard perceptions** — The basic information on hazard perception and clues for recognition of hazards.

(12) **Emergency maneuvers** — The basic information concerning when and how to make emergency maneuvers.

(13) **Skid control and recovery** — The information on the causes and major types of skids, as well as the procedures for recovering from skids.

(d) **Relationship of cargo to vehicle control.** The principles and procedures for the proper handling of cargo.

(e) **Vehicle inspections:** The objectives and proper procedures for performing vehicle safety inspections, as follows:

(1) The importance of periodic inspection and repair to vehicle safety.

(2) The effect of undiscovered malfunctions upon safety.

(3) What safety-related parts to look for when inspecting vehicles.

(4) Pre-trip/enroute/post-trip inspection procedures.

(5) Reporting findings.

(f) . . .

(g) **Air brake knowledge as follows:**

(1) Air brake system nomenclature;

(2) The dangers of contaminated air supply;

(3) Implications of severed or disconnected air lines between the power unit and the trailer(s);

(4) Implications of low air pressure readings;

(5) Procedures to conduct safe and accurate pre-trip inspections.

(6) Procedures for conducting enroute and post-trip inspections of air actuated brake systems, including ability to detect defects which may cause the system to fail.

(h) **Operators for the combination vehicle group shall also have knowledge of:**

(1) . . .

(2) **Vehicle inspection** — The objectives and proper procedures that are **unique** for performing vehicle safety inspections on combination vehicles.

§383.113 Required skills.

(a) **Basic vehicle control skills.** All applicants for a CDL must possess and demonstrate basic motor vehicle control skills for each vehicle group which the driver operates or expects to operate. These skills should include the ability to start, to stop, and to move the vehicle forward and backward in a safe manner.

(b) **Safe driving skills.** All applicants for a CDL must possess and demonstrate the safe driving skills for their vehicle group. These skills should include proper visual search methods, appropriate use of signals, speed control for weather and traffic conditions, and ability to position the motor vehicle correctly when changing lanes or turning.

(c) **Air brake skills.** Except as provided in §383.95, all applicants shall demonstrate the following skills with respect to inspection and operation of air brakes:

(1) **Pre-trip inspection skills.** Applicants shall demonstrate the skills necessary to conduct a pre-trip inspection which includes the ability to:

(i) Locate and verbally identify air brake operating controls and monitoring devices;

(ii) Determine the motor vehicle's brake system condition for proper adjustments and that air system connections between motor vehicles have been properly made and secured;

(iii) Inspect the low pressure warning device(s) to ensure that they will activate in emergency situations;

(iv) Ascertain, with the engine running, that the system maintains an adequate supply of compressed air;

(v) Determine that required minimum air pressure build up time is within acceptable limits and that required alarms and emergency devices automatically deactivate at the proper pressure level; and

(vi) Operationally check the brake system for proper performance.

(2) **Driving skills.** Applicants shall successfully complete the skills tests contained in §383.113 in a representative vehicle equipped with air brakes.

(d) **Test area.** Skills tests shall be conducted in on-street conditions or under a combination of on-street and off-street conditions.

(e) **Simulation technology.** A State may utilize simulators to perform skills testing, but under no circumstances as a substitute for the required testing in on-street conditions.

§383.115 . . .

§383.117 Requirements for passenger endorsement.

An applicant for the passenger endorsement must satisfy both of the following additional knowledge and skills test requirements.

(a) **Knowledge test.** All applicants for the passenger endorsement must have knowledge covering at least the following topics:

(1) Proper procedures for loading/unloading passengers;

(2) Proper use of emergency exits, including push-out windows;

(3) Proper responses to such emergency situations as fires and unruly passengers;

(4) Proper procedures at railroad crossings and drawbridges; and

(5) Proper braking procedures.

(b) **Skills test.** To obtain a passenger endorsement applicable to a specific vehicle group, an applicant must take his/her skills test in a passenger vehicle satisfying the requirements of that group as defined in §383.91.

§383.119 . . .

§383.121 . . .

Appendix to Subpart G — Required Knowledge and Skills — Sample Guidelines

The following is a sample of the specific types of items which a State may wish to include in the knowledge and skills tests that it administers to CDL applicants. This appendix closely follows the framework of §§383.111 and 383.113. It is intended to provide more specific guidance and suggestion to States. Additional detail in this appendix is not binding and States may depart from it at their discretion provided their CDL program tests for the general areas of knowledge and skill specified in §§383.111 and 383.113.

Examples of specific knowledge elements

(a) **Safe operations regulations.** Driver-related elements of the following regulations:

(1) Motor vehicle inspection, repair, and maintenance requirements as contained in Parts 393 and 396 of this title;

(2) Procedures for safe vehicle operations as contained in Part 392 of this title;

(3) The effects of fatigue, poor vision, hearing, and general health upon safe commercial motor vehicle operation as contained in Parts 391, 392, and 395 of this title;

(4) . . .

(5) The effects of alcohol and drug use upon safe commercial motor vehicle operations as contained in Parts 391 and 395 of this title.

(b) **Commercial motor vehicle safety control systems.** Proper use of the motor vehicle's safety system, including lights, horns, side and rear-view mirrors, proper mirror adjustments, fire extinguishers, symptoms of improper operation revealed through instruments, motor vehicle operation characteristics, and diagnosing malfunctions. Commercial motor vehicle drivers shall have knowledge on the correct procedures needed to use these safety systems in an emergency situation, *e.g.*, skids and loss of brakes.

(c) **Safe vehicle control.** (1) **Control systems** — The purpose and function of the controls and instruments commonly found on commercial motor vehicles.

(2) **Basic control** — The proper procedures for performing various basic maneuvers, including:

(i) Starting, warming up, and shutting down the engine;

(ii) Putting the vehicle in motion and stopping;

(iii) Backing in a straight line; and

(iv) Turning the vehicle, *e.g.*, basic rules, off-tracking, right/left turns and right curves.

(3) **Shifting** — The basic shifting rules and terms, as well as shift patterns and procedures for common transmissions, including:

(i) Key elements of shifting, *e.g.*, controls, when to shift and double clutching;

(ii) Shift patterns and procedures; and

(iii) Consequences of improper shifting.

(4) **Backing** — The procedures and rules for various backing maneuvers, including:

(i) Backing principles and rules; and

(ii) Basic backing maneuvers, e.g., straight-line backing, and backing on a curved path.

(5) **Visual search** — The importance of proper visual search, and proper visual search methods, including:

(i) Seeing ahead and to the sides;

(ii) Use of mirrors; and

(iii) Seeing to the rear.

(6) **Communication** — The principles and procedures for proper communications and the hazards of failure to signal properly, including:

(i) Signaling intent, e.g., signaling when changing speed or direction in traffic;

(ii) Communicating presence, e.g., using horn or lights to signal presence; and

(iii) Misuse of communications.

(7) **Speed Management** — The importance of understanding the effects of speed, including:

(i) Speed and stopping distance;

(ii) Speed and surface conditions;

(iii) Speed and the shape of the road;

(iv) Speed and visibility; and

(v) Speed and traffic flow.

(8) **Space management** — The procedures and techniques for controlling the space around the vehicle, including:

(i) The importance of space management;

(ii) Space cushions, e.g., controlling space ahead/to the rear;

(iii) Space to the sides; and

(iv) Space for traffic gaps.

(9) **Night operation** — Preparations and procedures for night driving, including:

(i) Night driving factors, e.g., driver factors, (vision, glare, fatigue, inexperience), roadway factors, (low illumination, variation in illumination, familiarity with roads, other road users, especially drivers exhibiting erratic or improper driving), vehicle factors (headlights, auxiliary lights, turn signals, windshields and mirrors); and

(ii) Night driving procedures, e.g., preparing to drive at night and driving at night.

(10) **Extreme driving conditions** — The basic information on operating in extreme driving conditions and the hazards that are encountered in extreme conditions, including:

(i) Adverse weather;

(ii) Hot weather; and

(iii) Mountain driving.

(11) **Hazard perceptions** — The basic information on hazard perception and clues for recognition of hazards, including:

(i) Importance of hazards recognition;

(ii) Road characteristics; and

(iii) Road user activities.

(12) **Emergency maneuvers** — The basic information concerning when and how to make emergency maneuvers, including:

(i) Evasive steering;

(ii) Emergency stop;

(iii) Off-road recovery;

(iv) Brake failure; and

(v) Blowouts.

(13) **Skid control and recovery** — The information on the causes and major types of skids, as well as the procedures for recovering from skids.

(d) **Relationship of cargo to vehicle control.** The principles and procedures for the proper handling of cargo, including:

(1) The importance of proper cargo handling, e.g., consequences of improperly secured cargo, drivers' responsibilities, Federal/State and local regulations.

(2) Principles of weight distribution.

(3) Principles and methods of cargo securement.

(e) **Vehicle inspections:** The objectives and proper procedures for performing vehicle safety inspections, as follows:

(1) The importance of periodic inspection and repair to vehicle safety and to prevention of enroute breakdowns.

(2) The effect of undiscovered malfunctions upon safety.

(3) What safety-related parts to look for when inspecting vehicles, e.g., fluid leaks, interference with visibility, bad tires, wheel and rim defects, braking system defects, steering system defects, suspension system defects, exhaust system defects, coupling system defects, and cargo problems.

(4) Pre-trip/enroute/post-trip inspection procedures.

(5) Reporting findings.

(f) . . .

(g) **Air brake knowledge as follows:**

(1) General air brake system nomenclature;

(2) The dangers of contaminated air (dirt, moisture and oil) supply;

(3) Implications of severed or disconnected air lines between the power unit and the trailer(s);

(4) Implications of low air pressure readings;

(5) Procedures to conduct safe and accurate pre-trip inspections, including knowledge about:

(i) Automatic fail-safe devices;

(ii) System monitoring devices; and

(iii) Low pressure warning alarms.

(6) Procedures for conducting enroute and post-trip inspections of air actuated brake systems, including ability to detect defects which may cause the system to fail, including:

(i) Tests which indicate the amount of air loss from the braking system within a specified period, with and without the engine running; and

(ii) Tests which indicate the pressure levels at which the low air pressure warning devices and the tractor protection valve should activate.

(h) **Operators for the combination vehicle group shall also have knowledge of:**

(1) . . .

(2) **Vehicle inspection** — The objectives and proper procedures that are **unique** for performing vehicle safety inspections on combination vehicles.

Examples of Specific Skills Elements

These examples relate to paragraphs (a) and (b) of §383.113 only.

(a) **Basic vehicle control skills.** All applicants for a CDL must possess and demonstrate the following basic motor vehicle control skills for each vehicle group which the driver operates or expects to operate. These skills shall include:

(1) Ability to start, warm-up, and shut down the engine;

(2) Ability to put the motor vehicle in motion and accelerate smoothly, forward and backward;

(3) Ability to bring the motor vehicle to a smooth stop;

(4) Ability to back the motor vehicle in a straight line, and check path and clearance while backing;

(5) Ability to position the motor vehicle to negotiate and then make left and right turns;

(6) Ability to shift as required and select appropriate gear for speed and highway conditions;

(7) Ability to back along a curved path; and

(8) Ability to observe the road and the behavior of other motor vehicles, particularly before changing speed and direction.

(b) **Safe driving skills.** All applicants for a CDL must possess and demonstrate the following safe driving skills for any vehicle group. These skills shall include:

(1) Ability to use proper visual search methods.

(2) Ability to signal appropriately when changing speed or direction in traffic.

(3) Ability to adjust speed to the configuration and condition of the roadway, weather and visibility conditions, traffic conditions, and motor vehicles, cargo and driver conditions;

(4) Ability to choose a safe gap for changing lanes, passing other vehicles, as well as for crossing or entering traffic;

(5) Ability to position the motor vehicle correctly before and during a turn to prevent other vehicles from passing on the wrong side as well as to prevent problems caused by offtracking;

(6) Ability to maintain a safe following distance depending on the condition of the road, on visibility, and on vehicle weight; and

(7) Ability to adjust operation of the motor vehicle to prevailing weather conditions including speed selection, braking, direction changes and following distance to maintain control.

§383.123 Requirements for a school bus endorsement.

(a) **An applicant for a school bus endorsement must satisfy the following three requirements:**

(1) Qualify for passenger vehicle endorsement. Pass the knowledge and skills test for obtaining a passenger vehicle endorsement.

(2) Knowledge test. Must have knowledge covering at least the following three topics:

(i) Loading and unloading children, including the safe operation of stop signal devices, external mirror systems, flashing lights and other warning and passenger safety devices required for school buses by State or Federal law or regulation.

(ii) Emergency exits and procedures for safely evacuating passengers in an emergency.

(iii) State and Federal laws and regulations related to safely traversing highway rail grade crossings.

(3) Skills test. Must take a driving skills test in a school bus of the same vehicle group (see §383.91(a)) as the school bus applicant will drive.

(b) **Substitute for driving skills test.** (1) At the discretion of a State, the driving skills test required in paragraph (a)(3) of this section may be waived for an applicant who is currently licensed, has experience driving a school bus, has a good driving record, and meets the conditions set forth in paragraph (b)(2) of this section.

(2) An applicant must certify and the State must verify that, during the two-year period immediately prior to applying for the school bus endorsement, the applicant:

(i) Held a valid CDL with a passenger vehicle endorsement to operate a school bus representative of the group he or she will be driving;

(ii) Has not had his or her driver's license or CDL suspended, revoked or canceled or been disqualified from operating a CMV;

(iii) Has not been convicted of any of the disqualifying offenses in §383.51(b) while operating a CMV or of any offense in a non-CMV that would be disqualifying under §383.51(b) if committed in a CMV;

(iv) Has not had more than one conviction of any of the serious traffic violations defined in §383.5, while operating any type motor vehicle;

(v) Has not had any conviction for a violation of State or local law relating to motor vehicle traffic control (other than a parking violation) arising in connection with any traffic accident;

(vi) Has not been convicted of any motor vehicle traffic violation that resulted in an accident; and

(vii) Has been regularly employed as a school bus driver, has operated a school bus representative of the group the applicant seeks to drive, and provides evidence of such employment.

(3) After September 30, 2005 the provisions in paragraph (b) of this section do not apply.

Subpart H — Tests

§383.131 Test procedures.

(a) **Driver information manuals.** Information on how to obtain a CDL and endorsements shall be included in manuals and made available by States to CDL applicants. All information provided to the applicant shall include the following:

(1) Information on the requirements described in §383.71, the implied consent to alcohol testing described in §383.72, the procedures and penalties, contained in §383.51(b) to which a CDL holder is exposed for refusal to comply with such alcohol testing, State procedures described in §383.73, and other appropriate driver information contained in Subpart E of this part;

(2) Information on vehicle groups and endorsements as specified in Subpart F of this part;

(3) The substance of the knowledge and skills which drivers shall have as outlined in Subpart G of this part for the different vehicle groups and endorsements;

(4) Details of testing procedures, including the purpose of the tests, how to respond, any time limits for taking the test, and any other special procedures determined by the State of issuance; and

(5) Directions for taking the tests.

(b) **Examiner procedures.** A State shall provide to test examiners details on testing and any other State-imposed requirements in the examiner's manual, and shall ensure that examiners are qualified to administer tests on the basis of training and/or other experience. States shall provide standardized scoring sheets for the skills tests, as well as standardized driving instructions for the applicants. Such examiners' manuals shall contain the following:

(1) Information on driver application procedures contained in §383.71, State procedures described in §383.73, and other appropriate driver information contained in Subpart E of this part;

(2) Details on information which must be given to the applicant;

(3) Details on how to conduct the tests;

(4) Scoring procedures and minimum passing scores;

(5) Information for selecting driving test routes;

(6) List of the skills to be tested;

(7) Instructions on where and how the skills will be tested;

(8) How performance of the skills will be scored; and

(9) Causes for automatic failure of skills tests.

§383.133 Testing methods.

(a) All tests shall be constructed in such a way as to determine if the applicant possesses the required knowledge and skills contained in Subpart G of this part for the type of motor vehicle or endorsement the applicant wishes to obtain.

(b) States shall develop their own specifications for the tests for each vehicle group and endorsement which must be at least as stringent as the Federal standards.

(c) States shall determine specific methods for scoring the knowledge and skills tests.

(d) Passing scores must meet those standards contained in §383.135.

(e) Knowledge and skills tests shall be based solely on the information contained in the driver manuals referred to in §383.131(a).

(f) Each knowledge test shall be valid and reliable so as to assure that driver applicants possess the knowledge required under §383.111.

(g) Each basic knowledge test, i.e., the test covering the areas referred to in §383.111 for the applicable vehicle group, shall contain at least 30 items, exclusive of the number of items testing air brake knowledge. Each endorsement knowledge test, and the air brake component of the basic knowledge test as described in §383.111(g), shall contain a number of questions that is sufficient to test the driver applicant's knowledge of the required subject matter with validity and reliability.

(h) The skills tests shall have administrative procedures, designed to achieve interexaminer reliability, that are sufficient to ensure fairness of pass/fail rates.

§383.135 Minimum passing scores.

(a) The driver applicant must correctly answer at least 80 percent of the questions on each knowledge test in order to achieve a passing score on such knowledge test.

(b) To achieve a passing score on the skills test, the driver applicant must demonstrate that he/she can successfully perform all of the skills listed in §383.113.

(c) If the driver applicant does not obey traffic laws, or causes an accident during the test, he/she shall automatically fail the test.

(d) The scoring of the basic knowledge and skills test shall be adjusted as follows to allow for the air brake restriction (§383.95):

(1) If the applicant scores less than 80 percent on the air

brake component of the basic knowledge test as described in
§383.111 (g), the driver will have failed the air brake component
and, if the driver is issued a CDL, an air brake restriction shall
be indicated on the license; and

(2) If the applicant performs the skills test in a vehicle not
equipped with air brakes, the driver will have omitted the air brake
component as described in §383.113(c) and, if the driver is issued a
CDL, the air brake restriction shall be indicated on the license.

Subpart I — Requirement for Transportation Security Administration Approval of Hazardous Materials Endorsement Issuances

§383.141 General.

(a) **Applicability date.** Beginning on November 3, 2003,
this section applies to State agencies responsible for issuing
hazardous materials endorsements for a CDL, and applicants
for such endorsements.

(b) **Prohibition.** A State may not issue, renew, upgrade, or
transfer a hazardous materials endorsement for a CDL to any
individual authorizing that individual to operate a commercial
motor vehicle transporting a hazardous material in commerce
unless the Transportation Security Administration has determined that the individual does not pose a security risk warrant-
ing denial of the endorsement.

(c) **Individual notification.** At least 180 days prior to the
expiration date of the CDL or hazardous materials endorsement, a State must notify the holder of a hazardous materials
endorsement that the individual must pass a Transportation
Security Administration security screening process as part of
any application for renewal of the hazardous materials endorsement. Before November 3, 2003, a State must give the holder of
a hazardous materials endorsement as much advance notice as
practicable. The notice must advise a driver that, in order to ex-
pedite the security screening process, he or she should file a renewal application as soon as possible, but not later than 90 days
before the date of expiration of the endorsement. An individual
who does not successfully complete the Transportation Security
Administration security screening process referenced in paragraph (b) of this section may not be issued a hazardous materials endorsement.

(d) **Hazardous materials endorsement renewal cycle.** Each State must require that hazardous materials endorsements be renewed every 5 years or less so that individuals are subject to a Transportation Security Administration security screening requirement referenced in paragraph (b) of this section at least every 5 years.

Subpart J — Commercial Driver's License Document

§383.151 General.

The CDL shall be a document that is easy to recognize as a CDL. At a minimum, the document shall contain information specified in §383.153.

§383.153 Information on the document and application.

(a) All CDLs shall contain the following information:

(1) The prominent statement that the license is a "Commercial Driver's License" or "CDL," except as specified in §383.153(b).

(2) The full name, signature, and mailing address of the person to whom such license is issued;

(3) Physical and other information to identify and describe such person including date of birth (month, day, and year), sex, and height;

(4) Color photograph of the driver;

(5) The driver's State license number;

(6) The name of the State which issued the license;

(7) The date of issuance and the date of expiration of the license;

(8) The group or groups of commercial motor vehicle(s) that the driver is authorized to operate, indicated as follows:

(i) A for Combination Vehicle;

(ii) B for Heavy Straight Vehicle; and

(iii) C for Small Vehicle.

(9) The endorsement(s) for which the driver has qualified, if any, indicated as follows:

(i). . .

(ii) P for passenger;

(iii) . . .

(iv) . . .

(v) . . .

(vi) S for school bus; and

(vii) At the discretion of the State, additional codes for additional groupings of endorsements, as long as each such discretionary code is fully explained on the front or back of the CDL document.

(b) If the CDL is a Nonresident CDL, it shall contain the prominent statement that the license is a "Nonresident Commercial Driver's License" or "Nonresident CDL." The word "Nonresident" must be conspicuously and unmistakably displayed, but may be noncontiguous with the words "Commercial Driver's License" or "CDL."

(c) If the State has issued the applicant an air brake restriction as specified in §383.95, that restriction must be indicated on the license.

(d) Except in the case of a Nonresident CDL:

(1) A driver applicant must provide his/her Social Security Number on the application of a CDL; and

(2) The State must provide the Social Security Number to the CDLIS.

§383.155 Tamperproofing requirements.

States shall make the CDL tamperproof to the maximum extent practicable. At a minimum, a State shall use the same tamperproof method used for noncommercial drivers' licenses.

PART 387 — MINIMUM LEVELS OF FINANCIAL RESPONSIBILITY FOR MOTOR CARRIERS

Subpart A — Motor Carriers of Property

-287-

§387.25

AUTHORITY: 49 U.S.C. 13101, 13301, 13906, 14701, 31138 and 31139; and 49 CFR 1.73.

EDITORIAL NOTE: Nomenclature changes to Part 387 appear at 67 FR 61821-61824, Oct. 2, 2002.

Subpart A — Motor Carriers of Property
§§387.1 — 387.17 . . .

Subpart B — Motor Carriers of Passengers

§387.25 Purpose and scope.

This subpart prescribes the minimum levels of financial responsibility required to be maintained by for-hire motor carriers of passengers operating motor vehicles in interstate or foreign commerce. The purpose of these regulations is to create additional incentives to carriers to operate their vehicles in a safe manner and to assure that they maintain adequate levels of financial responsibility.

§387.27 Applicability.

(a) This subpart applies to for-hire motor carriers transporting passengers in interstate or foreign commerce.

(b) **Exception.** The rules in this subpart do not apply to—

(1) A motor vehicle transporting only school children and teachers to or from school;

(2) A motor vehicle providing taxicab service and having a seating capacity of less than 7 passengers and not operated on a regular route or between specified points;

(3) A motor vehicle carrying less than 16 individuals in a single daily round trip to commute to and from work; and

(4) A motor vehicle operated by a motor carrier under contract providing transportation of preprimary, primary, and secondary students for extracurricular trips organized, sponsored, and paid by a school district.

§387.29 Definitions.

As used in this subpart—

Accident — includes continuous or repeated exposure to the same conditions resulting in public liability which the insured neither expected nor intended.

Bodily injury — means injury to the body, sickness, or disease including death resulting from any of these.

Endorsement — an amendment to an insurance policy.

Financial responsibility — the financial reserves (e.g., insurance policies or surety bonds) sufficient to satisfy liability amounts set forth in this subpart covering public liability.

For hire carriage — means the business of transporting, for compensation, passengers and their property, including any compensated transportation of the goods or property or another.

Insured and principal — the motor carrier named in the policy of insurance, surety bond, endorsement, or notice of cancellation, and also the fiduciary of such motor carrier.

Insurance premium — the monetary sum an insured pays an insurer for acceptance of liability for public liability claims made against the insured.

Motor carrier — means a for-hire motor carrier. The term includes, but is not limited to, a motor carrier's agent, officer, or representative; an employee responsible for hiring, supervising, training, assigning, or dispatching a driver; or an employee concerned with the installation, inspection, and maintenance of motor vehicle equipment and/or accessories.

Property damage — means damage to or loss of use of tangible property.

Public liability — liability for bodily injury or property damage.

Seating capacity — any plan view location capable of accommodating a person at least as large as a 5th percentile adult female, if the overall seat configuration and design and vehicle design is such that the position is likely to be used as a seating position while the vehicle is in motion, except for auxiliary seating accommodations such as temporary or folding jump seats. Any bench or split bench seat in a passenger car, truck or multipurpose passenger vehicle with a gross vehicle weight rating less than 10,000 pounds, having greater than 50 inches of hiproom (measured in accordance with SEA Standards J1100(a)) shall have not less than three designated seating positions, unless the seat design or vehicle designis such that the center position cannot be used for seating.

§387.31 Financial responsibility required.

(a) No motor carrier shall operate a motor vehicle transporting passengers until the motor carrier has obtained and has in effect the minimum levels of financial responsibility as set forth in §387.33 of this subpart.

(b) Policies of insurance, surety bonds, and endorsements

required under this section shall remain in effect continuously until terminated.

(1) Cancellation may be effected by the insurer or the insured motor carrier giving 35 days notice in writing to the other. The 35 days notice shall commence to run from the date the notice is mailed. Proof of mailing shall be sufficient proof of notice.

(2) **Exception.** Policies of insurance and surety bonds may be obtained for a finite period of time to cover any lapse in continuous compliance.

(3) **Exception.** Mexican motor carriers may meet the minimum financial responsibility requirements of this subpart by obtaining insurance coverage, in the required amounts, for periods of 24 hours or longer, from insurers that meet the requirements of §387.35 of this subpart. A Mexican motor carrier so insured must have available for inspection in each of its vehicles copies of the following documents:

(i) The required insurance endorsement (Form MCS-90B); and

(ii) An insurance identification card, binder, or other document issued by an authorized insurer which specifies both the effective date and the expiration date of the temporary insurance coverage authorized by this exception.

Mexican motor carriers insured under this exception are also exempt from the notice of cancellation requirements stated on Form MCS-90B.

(c) Policies of insurance and surety bonds required under this section may be replaced by other policies of insurance or surety bonds. The liability of retiring insurer or surety, as to events after the termination date, shall be considered as having terminated on the effective date of the replacement policy of insurance or surety bond or at the end or the 35 day cancellation period required in paragraph (b) of this section, whichever is sooner.

(d) Proof of the required financial responsibility shall be maintained at the motor carrier's principal place of business. The proof shall consist of—

(1) "Endorsement(s) for Motor Carriers of Passengers Policies of Insurance for Public Liability Under Section 18 of theBusRegulatory Reform Act of 1982" (Form MCS-90B) issued by an insurer(s); or

(2) A "Motor Carrier of Passengers Surety Bond for Public Liability Under Section 18 of the Bus Regulatory Reform Act of 1982" (Form MCS-82B) issued by a surety.

(e) The proof of minimum levels of financial responsibility required by this section shall be considered public information and be produced for review upon reasonable request by a member of the public.

(f) All passenger carrying vehicles operated within the United States by motor carriers domiciled in a contiguous foreign country, shall have on board the vehicle a legible copy, in English, of the proof of the required financial responsibility (Forms MCS-90B or MCS-82B) used by the motor carrier to comply with paragraph (d) of this section.

(g) Any motor vehicle in which there is no evidence of financial responsibility required by paragraph (f) of this section shall be denied entry into the United States.

§387.33 Financial responsibility, minimum levels.

The minimum levels of financial responsibility referred to in §387.31 of this subpart are hereby prescribed as follows:

Schedule of Limits

Public Liability

For-hire motor carriers of passengers operating in interstate or foreign commerce.

Vehicle Seating Capacity	Effective Dates	
	Nov. 19, 1983	Nov. 19, 1985
(1) Any vehicle with a seating capacity of 16 passengers or more	$2,500,000	$5,000,000
(2) Any vehicle with a seating capacity of 15 passengers or less[1]	750,000	1,500,000

[1]Except as provided in §387.27(b).

§387.35 State authority and designation of agent.

A policy of insurance or surety bond does not satisfy the financial responsibility requirements of this subpart unless the insurer or surety furnishing the policy or bond is—

(a) Legally authorized to issue such policies or bonds in each State in which the motor carrier operates, or

(b) Legally authorized to issue such policies or bonds in the State in which the motor carrier has its principal place of business or domicile, and is willing to designate a person upon whom process, issued by or under the authority of any court having jurisdiction of the subject matter, may be served in any proceeding at law or equity brought in any State in which the motor carrier operates; or

(c) Legally authorized to issue such policies or bonds in any State of the United States and eligible as an excess or surplus lines insurer in any State in which business is written, and is willing to designate a person upon whom process, issued by or under the authority of any court having jurisdiction of the subject matter, may be served in any proceeding at law or equity brought in any State in which the motor carrier operates.

§387.37 Fiduciaries.

The coverage of fiduciaries shall attach at the moment of succession of such fiduciaries.

§387.39 Forms.

Endorsements for policies of insurance (Illustration I) and surety bonds (Illustration II) must be in the form prescribed by the FMCSA and approved by the OMB. Endorsements to policies of insurance and surety bonds shall specify that coverage thereunder will remain in effect continuously until terminated as required in §387.31 of this subpart. The continuous coverage requirement does not apply to Mexican motor carriers insured under §387.31(b)(3) of this subpart. The endorsement and surety bond shall be issued in the exact name of the motor carrier.

U.S. Department
of Transportation
Federal Motor Carrier
Safety Administration

ENDORSEMENT FOR
MOTOR CARRIER POLICIES OF INSURANCE FOR PUBLIC LIABILITY
UNDER SECTION 18 OF THE BUS REGULATORY REFORM ACT OF 1982

Form Approved:
OMB No: 2126-0008

Issued to _____ of _____
Dated at _____ this _____ day of _____, 20 _____
Amending Policy No. _____ Effective Date _____
Name of Insurance Company _____

Countersigned by _____

Authorized Company Representative

The policy to which this endorsement is attached provides primary or excess insurance, as indicated by "[X]," for the limits shown:

[ ] This insurance is primary and the company shall not be liable for amounts in excess of $_____ for each accident.

[ ] This insurance is excess and the company shall not be liable for amounts in excess of $_____ for each accident in excess of the underlying limit of $_____ for each accident.
Whenever required by the Federal Motor Carrier Safety Administration (FMCSA), the company agrees to furnish to the FMCSA a duplicate of said policy and all its endorsements. The company also agrees, upon telephone request by an authorized representative of the FMCSA, to verify that the policy is in force as of a particular date. The telephone number to call is: _____

Cancellation of this endorsement may be effected by the company of the insured by giving (1) thirty-five (35) days notice in writing to the other party (said 35 days notice to commence from the date the notice is mailed, proof of mailing shall be sufficient proof of notice), and (2) if the insured is subject to the FMCSA's registration requirements, by providing thirty (30) days notice to the FMCSA (said 30 days notice to commence from the date the notice is received by the FMCSA at its office in Washington, D.C.).

DEFINITIONS AS USED IN THIS ENDORSEMENT

Accident includes continuous or repeated exposure to conditions which result in Public Liability which the insured neither expected nor intended. *Bodily Injury* means injury to the body, sickness, or disease to any person, including death resulting from any of these.

The insurance policy to which this endorsement is attached provides automobile liability insurance and is amended to assure compliance by the insured, within the limits stated herein, as a for-hire motor carrier of passengers with Section 18 of the Bus Regulatory Reform Act of 1982 and the rules and regulations of the Federal Motor Carrier Safety Administration.

In consideration of the premium stated in the policy to which this endorsement is attached, the insurer (the company) agrees to pay, within the limits of liability described herein, any final judgment recovered against the insured for public liability resulting from negligence in the operation, maintenance or use of motor vehicles subject to financial responsibility requirements of Section 18 of the Bus Regulatory Reform Act of 1982 regardless of whether or not each motor vehicle is specifically described in the policy and whether or not such negligence occurs on any route or in any territory authorized to be served by the insured or elsewhere. Such insurance as is afforded, for public liability, does not apply to injury to or death of the insured's employees while engaged in the course of their employment, or property transported by the insured, designated as cargo. It is understood and agreed that no condition, provision, stipulation, or limitation contained in the policy, this endorsement, or any other endorsement thereon, or violation thereof, shall relieve the company from liability or from the payment of any final judgment, within the limits of liability herein described, irrespective of the financial condition, insolvency or bankruptcy of the insured.
The Bus Regulatory Reform Act of 1982 requires limits of financial responsibility according to vehicle seating capacity. It is the MOTOR CARRIER'S obligation to obtain the required limits of financial responsibility. THE SCHEDULE OF LIMITS SHOWN ON THE REVERSE SIDE DOES NOT PROVIDE COVERAGE. The limits shown in the schedule are for information purposes only.

Motor Carrier means a for-hire carrier of passengers by motor vehicle. *Property Damage* means damage to or loss of use of tangible property. *Public Liability* means liability for bodily injury or property damage.

However, all terms, conditions, and limitations in the policy to which this endorsement is attached shall remain in full force and effect as binding between the insured and the company. This insured agrees to reimburse the company for any payment made by the company on account of any accident, claim, or suit involving a breach of the terms of the policy, and for any payment that the company would not have been obligated to make under the provisions of the policy except for the agreement contained in this endorsement.

It is further understood and agreed that, upon failure of the company to pay any final judgment recovered against the insured as provided herein, the judgment creditor may maintain an action in any court of competent jurisdiction against the company to compel such payment.

The limits of the company's liability for the amounts prescribed in this endorsement apply separately to each accident and any payment under the policy because of any one accident shall not operate to reduce the liability of the company for the payment of final judgments resulting from any other accident.

SCHEDULE OF LIMITS

PUBLIC LIABILITY
For-hire motor carriers of passengers operating in interstate or foreign commerce

Vehicle Seating Capacity	Effective Dates	
	Nov. 19, 1983	Nov. 19, 1985
(1) Any vehicle with a seating capacity of 16 passengers or more.	$2,500,000	$5,000,000
(2) Any vehicle with a seating capacity of 15 passengers or less.	$ 750,000	$1,500,000

Form MCS-90B
(5/2003)

U.S. Department
of Transportation
Federal Motor Carrier
Safety Administration

Form Approved:
OMB No.: 2126-0008

MOTOR CARRIER PUBLIC LIABILITY SURETY BOND
UNDER SECTION 18 OF THE BUS REGULATORY REFORM ACT OF 1982

PARTIES

Surety Company and Principal
Place of Business Address

Motor Carrier Principal, FMCSA Docket No.
and Principal Place of Business Address

PURPOSE

This is an agreement between the Surety and the Principal under which the Surety, its successors and assignees, agree to be responsible for the payment of any final judgment or judgments against the Principal for public liability and property damage claims in the sums prescribed herein, subject to the governing provisions and following conditions.

GOVERNING PROVISIONS

(1) Section 18 of the Bus Regulatory Reform Act of 1982
(2) Rules and regulations of the Federal Motor Carrier Safety Administration (FMCSA)

CONDITIONS

The Principal is or intends to become a motor carrier of passengers subject to the applicable governing provisions relating to financial responsibility for the protection of the public.

This bond assures ensures compliance by the Principal with the applicable governing provisions, and shall inure to the benefit of any person or persons who shall recover a final judgment or judgments against the Principal for public liability or property damage claims (excluding injury to or death of the Principal's employees while engaged in the course of their employment, and loss of or damage to property of the Principal, and the cargo transported by the Principal). If every final judgment shall be paid for such claims resulting from the negligent operation, maintenance, or use of motor vehicles in transportation subject to the applicable governing provisions, then this obligation shall be void, otherwise it will remain in full effect.

Within the limits described herein, the Surety extends to such losses regardless of whether such motor vehicles are specifically described herein and whether occurring on the route or in the territory authorized to be served by the Principal or elsewhere.

The liability of the Surety for each motor vehicle subject to the applicable governing provisions for each accident shall not exceed $ _____, and shall be a continuing one notwithstanding any recovery thereunder.

The surety agrees, upon telephone request by an authorized representative of the FMCSA, to verify that the surety bond is in force as of a particular date. The telephone number to call is _____.

This bond is effective from _____ (12:01 a.m., standard time, at the address of the Principal as stated herein) and shall continue in force until terminated as described herein. The Principal or the Surety may at any time terminate this bond by giving (1) thirty-five (35) days notice in writing to the other party (said 35 days notice to commence from the date the notice is mailed, proof of mailing shall be sufficient proof of notice), and (2) if the Principal is subject to the FMCSA's registration requirements, by providing thirty (30) days notice to the FMCSA (said 30 days notice to commence from the date notice is received by the FMCSA at its office in Washington, D.C.). The Surety shall not be liable for the payment of any judgment or judgments against the Principal for public liability or property damage claims resulting from accidents which occur after the termination of this bond as described herein, but such termination shall not affect the liability of the Surety from the payment of any such judgment or judgments resulting from accidents which occur during the time the bond is in effect.

(AFFIX CORPORATE SEAL)

_____
Date

_____
Surety

_____   _____
City   State

By _____

ACKNOWLEDGMENT OF SURETY

STATE OF _____   COUNTY OF _____

On this _____ day of _____, 20___, before me personally came _____ who, being by me duly sworn, did depose and say that he resides in _____ that he/she is _____ of the _____ the corporation described in and which executed the foregoing instrument; that he knows the seal of said corporation; that the seal affixed to said instrument is such corporate seal; that it was so affixed by order of the board of directors of said corporation; that he signed his name thereto by like order, and he duly acknowledged to me that he executed the same for and on behalf of said corporation.

_____
Title of official administering oath

(OFFICIAL SEAL)

Surety Company File No. _____
Form MCS-83S
(8/2003)

§387.41 Violation and penalty.

Any person (except an employee who acts without knowledge) who knowingly violates the rules of this subpart shall be liable to the United States for civil penalty of no more than $11,000 for each violation, and if any such violation is a continuing one, each day of violation will constitute a separate offense. The amount of any such penalty shall be assessed by the Administrator or his/her designee, by written notice. In determining the amount of such penalty, the Administrator or his/her designee shall take into account the nature, circumstances, extent, the gravity of the violation committed and, with respect to the person found to have committed such violation, the degree of culpability, any history of prior offenses, ability to pay, effect on ability to continue to do business, and such other matters as justice may require.

Subpart C — Surety Bonds and Policies of Insurance for Motor Carriers and Property Brokers

§387.301 Surety bond, certificate of insurance, or other securities.

(a) **Public liability.** (1) No common or contract carrier or foreign (Mexican) motor private carrier or foreign motor carrier transporting exempt commodities subject to Subtitle IV, part B, chapter 135 of Title 49 of the United States Code shall engage in interstate or foreign commerce, and no certificate or permit shall be issued to such a carrier or remain in force unless and until there shall have been filed with and accepted by the Commission surety bonds, and certificates of insurance, proof of qualifications as self-insurer, or other securities or agreements, in the amounts prescribed in §387.303, conditioned to pay any final judgment recovered against such motor carrier for bodily injuries to or the death of any person resulting from the negligent operation, maintenance or use of motor vehicles in transportation subject to Subtitle IV, part B, chapter 135 of Title 49 of the United States Code, or for loss of or damage to property of others, or, in the case of motor carriers of property operating freight vehicles described in §387.303(b)(2) of this part, for environmental restoration.

(2) Motor Carriers of property which are subject to the conditions set forth in paragraph (a)(1) of this section and transport the commodities described in §387.303(b)(2), are required to obtain security in the minimum limits prescribed in §387.303(b)(2).

(b) **Common carriers—cargo insurance; exempt commodities.....**

(c) **Continuing compliance required.** Such security as is accepted by the FMCSA in accordance with the requirements of Section 13906 of Title 49 of the United States Code shall remain in effect at all times.

§387.303 Security for the protection of the public: Minimum limits.

(a) **Definitions:** (1) "Primary security" means public liability coverage provided by the insurance or surety company responsible for the first dollar of coverage.

(2) "Excess security" means public liability coverage above the primary security, or above any additional underlying security, up to and including the required minimum limits set forth in paragraph (b)(2) of this section.

(b)(1) Motor carriers subject to §387.301(a)(1) are required to have security for the required minimum limits as follows:

(i) **Small Freight Vehicles:...**

(ii) **Passenger Carriers:**

Kind of Equipment		
Vehicle seating capacity	Effective dates	
	Nov. 19, 1983	Nov. 19, 1985
(1) Any vehicle with a seating capacity of 16 passengers or more	$2,500,000	$5,000,000
(2) Any vehicle with a seating capacity of 15 passengers or less	750,000	1,500,000

(2)...

(3) Motor carriers subject to the minimum limits governed by this section, which are also subject to Department of Transportation limits requirements, are at no time required to have security for more than the required minimum limits established by the Secretary of Transportation in the applicable provisions of 49 CFR Part 387— Minimum Levels of Financial Responsibility for Motor Carriers.

(4) **Foreign motor carriers and foreign motor private carriers.** Foreign motor carriers and foreign motor private carriers (Mexican), subject to the requirements of 49 U.S.C. 13902(c) and 49 CFR part 368 regarding obtaining certificates of registration from the FMCSA, must meet our minimum financial responsibility requirements by obtaining insurance coverage, in the required amounts, for periods of 24 hours or longer, from insurance or surety companies, that meet the requirements of 49 CFR 387.315. These carriers must have available for inspection, in each vehicle operating in the United States, copies of the following documents:

(i) The certificate of registration;

(ii) The required insurance endorsement (Form MCS-90); and

(iii) An insurance identification card, binder, or other document issued by an authorized insurer which specifies both the effective date and the expiration date of the insurance coverage.

Notwithstanding the provisions of §387.301(a)(1), the filing of evidence of insurance is not required as a condition to the issuance of a certificate of registration. Further, the reference to continuous coverage at §387.313(a)(6) and the reference to cancellation notice at §387.313(d) are not applicable to these carriers.

(c) **Motor common carriers: Cargo liability....**

§387.305 **Combination vehicles....**

§387.307 **Property broker surety bond or other security....**

(d) **Forms and Procedures —...**

§387.309 **Qualifications as a self-insurer and other securities or agreements.**

(a) **As a self-insurer.** The FMCSA will consider and will approve, subject to appropriate and reasonable conditions, the application of a motor carrier to qualify as a self-insurer, if the carrier furnishes a true and accurate statement of its financial condition and other evidence that establishes to the satisfaction of the FMCSA the ability of the motor carrier to satisfy its obligation for bodily injury liability, property damage liability, or cargo liability. Application Guidelines: In addition to filing Form BMC 40, applicants for authority to self-insure against bodily injury and property damage claims should submit evidence that will allow the FMCSA to determine:

(1) The adequacy of the tangible net worth of the motor carri-

er in relation to the size of operations and the extent of its request for self-insurance authority. Applicant should demonstrate that it will maintain a net worth that will ensure that it will be able to meet its statutory obligations to the public to indemnify all claimants in the event of loss.

(2) The existence of a sound self-insurance program. Applicant should demonstrate that is has established, and will maintain, an insurance program that will protect the public against all claims to the same extent as the minimum security limits applicable to applicant under §387.303 of this part. Such a program may include, but not be limited to, one or more of the following: irrevocable letters of credit; irrevocable trust funds; reserves; sinking funds; third party financial guarantees, parent company or affiliate sureties; excess insurance coverage; or other similar arrangements.

(3) The existence of an adequate safety program. Applicant must submit evidence of a current "satisfactory" safety rating by the United States Department of Transportation. Non-rated carriers need only certify that they have not been rated. Applications by carriers with a less than satisfactory rating will be summarily denied. Any self-insurance authority granted by the FMCSA will automatically expire 30 days after a carrier receives a less than satisfactory rating from DOT.

(4) Additional information. Applicant must submit such additional information to support its application as the FMCSA may require.

(b) **Other securities or agreements.** The ommission also will consider applications for approval of other securities or agreements and will approve any such application if satisfied that the security or agreement offered will afford the security for the protection of the public contemplated by 49 U.S.C. 13906.

§387.311 Bonds and certificates of insurance.

(a) **Public liability.** Each Form BMC 82 surety bond filed with the FMCSA must be for the full limits of liability required under §387.303(b)(1). Form MCS-82 surety bonds and other forms of similar import prescribed by the Department of Transportation, may be aggregated to comply with the minimum security limits required under §387.303(b)(1) or §387.303(b)(2). Each Form BMC 91 certificate of insurance filed with the FMCSA will always represent the full security minimum limits required for the particular carrier, while it remains in force, under §§387.303(b)(1) or 387.303(b)(2), whichever is applicable. Any previously executed Form BMC 91 filed before the current revision which is left on file with the FMCSA after the effective date of this regulation, and not canceled within 30 days of that date will be deemed to certify the same coverage limits as would the filing of a revised Form BMC 91. Each Form BMC 91X certificate of insurance filed with the FMCSA will represent the full security limits under §§387.303(b)(1) or 387.303(b)(2) or the specific security limits of coverage as indicated on the face of the form. If the filing reflects aggregation, the certificate must show clearly whether the insurance is primary or, if excess coverage, the amount of underlying coverage as well as amount of the maximum limits of coverage. *Each Form BMC 91MX certificate of insurance filed with the FMCSA will represent the security limits of coverage as indicated on the face of the form. The Form BMC 91MX must show clearly whether the insurance is primary or, if excess coverage, the amount of underlying coverage as well as amount of the maximum limits of coverage.

(b) **Cargo liability.** Each Form BMC 83 surety bond filed with the FMCSA must be for the full limits of liability required under §387.303(c). Each Form BMC 34 certificate of insurance filed with the FMCSA will represent the full security limits under §387.303(c) or the specific limits of coverage as indicated on the face of the form. If the filing reflects aggregation, the certificate must show clearly whether the insurance is primary or, if excess coverage, the amount of underlying coverage as well as amount of the maximum limits of coverage.

(c) Each policy of insurance in connection with certificate of insurance which is filed with the FMCSA, shall be amended by attachment of the appropriate endorsement prescribed by the FMCSA and the certificate of insurance filed must accurately reflect that endorsement.

*Note: Aggregation to meet the requirement of §387.303(b)(1) will not be allowed until the completion of our rulemaking in Ex Parte No. MC-5 (Sub-No. 2), *Motor Carrier and Freight Forwarder Insurance Procedures and Minimum Amounts of Liability.*

§387.313 Forms and procedure.

(a) **Forms for endorsements, certificates of insurance, and others.**

(1) **In form prescribed.** Endorsements for policies of insurance and surety bonds, certificates of insurance, applications to

qualify as a self-insurer, or for approval of other securities or agreements, and notices of cancellation must be in the form prescribed and approved by FMCSA.

(2) **Aggregation of Insurance.** **When insurance is provided by more than one insurer in order to aggregate security limits for carriers operating only freight vehicles under 10,000 pounds Gross Vehicle Weight Rating, as defined in §387.303(b)(1), a separate Form BMC 90, with the specific amounts of underlying and limits of coverage shown thereon or appended thereto, and Form BMC 91X certificate is required of each insurer.

For aggregation of insurance for all other carriers to cover security limits under §387.303(b)(1) or (b)(2), a separate Department of Transportation prescribed form endorsement and *Form BMC 91X* certificate is required of each insurer.

When insurance is provided by more than one insurer to aggregate coverage for security limits under Section 387.313(c) a separate Form BMC 32 endorsement and Form BMC 34 certificate of insurance is required for each insurer.

For aggregation of insurance for foreign motor private carriers of nonhazardous commodities to cover security limits under §387.303(b)(4), a separate Form BMC 90 with the specific amounts of underlying and limits of coverage shown thereon or appended thereto, or Department of Transportation prescribed form endorsement, and Form BMC 91MX certificate is required for each insurer.

**Note: See NOTE for Rule 387.311. Also, it should be noted that DOT is considering prescribing adaptions of the Form MCS 90 endorsement and the Form MCS 82 surety bond for use by passenger carriers and Rules §§387.311 and 387.313 have been written sufficiently broad to provide for this contingency when new forms are prescribed by that Agency.

(3) **Use of Certificates and Endorsements in BMC Series.—Form BMC 91** certificates of insurance will be filed with the FMCSA for the full security limits under §387.303(b)(1) or (b)(2).

Form BMC 91X certificate of insurance will be filed to represent full coverage or any level of aggregation for the security limits under §387.303(b)(1) or (b)(2).

Form BMC 90 endorsement will be used with each filing of Form BMC 91 or Form BMC 91X certificate with the FMCSA which certifies to coverage not governed by the requirements of the Department of Transportation.

Form BMC 32 endorsement and *Form BMC 34* certificate of insurance and *Form BMC 83* surety bonds are used for the limits of cargo liability under §387.303(c).

Form BMC 91MX certificate of insurance will be filed to represent any level of aggregation for the security limits under §387.303(b)(4).

(4) **Use of Endorsements in MCS Series.** When Security limits certified under §387.303(b)(1) or (b)(2) involves coverage also required by the Department of Transportation a *Form MCS endorsement prescribed by the Department of Transportation such as*, and including, the *Form MCS 90* endorsement is required.

(5) **Surety bonds.** When surety bonds are used rather than certificates of insurance, *Form BMC 82* is required for the security limits under §387.303(b)(1) not subject to regulation by the Department of Transportation, and *Form MCS 82*, or any form of similar import prescribed by the Department of Transportation, is used for the security limits subject also to minimum coverage requirements of the Department of Transportation.

(6) **Surety bonds and certificates in effect continuously.**— Surety bonds and certificates of insurance shall specify that coverage thereunder will remain in effect continuously until terminated as herein provided, except (1) when filed expressly to fill prior gaps or lapses in coverage or to cover grants of emergency temporary authority of unusually short duration and the filing clearly so indicates, or (2) in special or unusual circumstances, when special permission is obtained for filing certificates of insurance or surety bonds on terms meeting other particular needs of the situation.

(b) **Filing and copies.** Certificates of insurance, surety bonds, and notices of cancellation must be filed with the FMCSA in triplicate.

(c) **Name of insured.** Certificates of insurance and surety bonds shall be issued in the full and correct name of the individual, partnership, corporation or other person to whom the certificate, permit, or license is, or is to be, issued. In the case of a partnership all partners shall be named.

(d) **Cancellation notice.** Except as provided in paragraph (e) of this section, surety bonds, certificates of insurance and other securities or agreements shall not be cancelled or withdrawn until 30 days after written notice has been submitted to the FMCSA at its offices in Washington, DC, on the prescribed form (Form BMC-35, Notice of Cancellation Motor Carrier Policies of Insurance under 49 U.S.C. 13906, and BMC-36, Notice of

Cancellation Motor Carrier and Broker Surety Bonds, as appropriate) by the insurance company, surety or sureties, motor carrier, broker or other party thereto, as the case may be, which period of thirty (30) days shall commence to run from the date such notice on the prescribed form is actually received by the FMCSA.

(e) **Termination by replacement.** Certificates of insurance or surety bonds which have been accepted by the FMCSA under these rules may be replaced by other certificates of insurance, surety bonds or other security, and the liability of the retiring insurer or surety under such certificates of insurance or surety bonds shall be considered as having terminated as of the effective date of the replacement certificate of insurance, surety bond or other security, provided the said replacement certificate, bond or other security is acceptable to the FMCSA under the rules and regulations in this part.

§387.315 Insurance and surety companies.

A certificate of insurance or surety bond will not be accepted by the FMCSA unless issued by an insurance or surety company that is authorized (licensed or admitted) to issue bonds or underlying insurance policies:

(a) In each state in which the motor carrier is authorized by the FMCSA to operate, or

(b) In the state in which the motor carrier has its principal place of business or domicile, and will designate in writing upon request by the FMCSA, a person upon whom process, issued by or under the authority of a court of competent jurisdiction, may be served in any proceeding at law or equity brought in any state in which the carrier operates, or

(c) In any state, and is eligible as an excess or surplus lines insurer in any state in which business is written, and will make the designation of process agent described in paragraph (b) of this section.

§387.317 Refusal to accept, or revocation by the FHWA of surety bonds, etc.

The FMCSA may, at any time, refuse to accept or, may revoke its acceptance of any surety bond, certificate of insurance, qualifications as a self-insurer, or other securities or agreements if, in its judgment such security does not comply with these sections or for any reason fails to provide satisfactory or adequate protection for the public. Revocation of acceptance of any certificate of insurance, surety bond or other security shall not relieve the motor carrier from compliance with §387.301(d).

§387.319 Fiduciaries.

(a) **Definitions.** The terms "insured" and "principal" as used in a certificate of insurance, surety bond, and notice of cancellation, filed by or for a motor carrier, include the motor carrier and its fiduciary as the moment of succession. The term "fiduciary" means any person authorized by law to collect and preserve property of incapacitated, financially disabled, bankrupt, or deceased holders of operating rights, and assignees of such holders.

(b) Insurance coverage in behalf of fiduciaries to apply concurrently. The coverage furnished under the provisions of this section on behalf of fiduciaries shall not apply subsequent to the effective date of other insurance, or other security, filed with and approved by the FMCSA in behalf of such fiduciaries. After the coverage provided in this section shall have been in effect thirty (30) days, it may be cancelled or withdrawn within the succeeding period of thirty (30) days by the insurer, the insured, the surety, or the principal upon ten (10) days' notice in writing to the FMCSA at its office in Washington, D.C., which period of ten (10) days shall commence to run from the date such notice is actually received by the FMCSA. After such coverage has been in effect for a total of sixty (60) days, it may be cancelled or withdrawn only in accordance with §1043.7.

§387.321 Operations in foreign commerce.

No motor carrier may operate in the United States in the course of transportation between places in a foreign country or between a place in one foreign country and a place in another foreign country unless and until there shall have been filed with and accepted by the FMCSA a certificate of insurance, surety bond, proof of qualifications as a self-insurer, or other securities or agreements in the amount prescribed in §387.303(b), conditioned to pay any final judgment recovered against such motor carrier for bodily injuries to or the death of any person resulting from the negligent operation, maintenance, or use of motor vehicles in transportation between places in a foreign country or between a place in one foreign country and a place in another foreign country, insofar as such transportation takes place in the United States, or for loss of or damage to property of others. The security for the protection of the public required by this section shall be maintained in effect at all times and shall be subject to the provisions of §§387.309 through 387.319. The requirements of §387.315(a) shall be satisfied if the insurance or surety company, in addition to having been approved by the FMCSA, is legally authorized to issue policies or surety bonds in at least one of the States in the United States, or one of the Provinces in Canada, and has filed with the FMCSA the name and address of a person upon whom legal process may be served in each State in or through which the motor carrier operates. Such designation may from time to time be changed by like designation similarly filed, but shall be maintained during the effectiveness of any certificate of insurance or surety bond issued by the company, and thereafter with respect to any claims arising during the effectiveness of such certificate or bond. The term "motor carrier" as used in this section shall not include private carriers or carriers operating under the partial exemption from regulation in 49 U.S.C. 13503 and 13506.

§387.323 Electronic filing of surety bonds, trust fund agreements, certificates of insurance and cancellations.

(a) Insurers may, at their option and in accordance with the requirements and procedures set forth in paragraphs (a) through (d) of this section, file forms BMC 34, BMC 35, BMC 36, BMC 82, BMC 83, BMC 84 BMC 85, BMC 91, and BMC 91X electronically, in lieu of using the prescribed printed forms.

(b) Each insurer must obtain authorization to file electronically by registering with the FMCSA. An individual account number and password for computer access will be issued to each registered insurer.

(c) Filings may be transmitted online via the Internet at: http://fhwali.volpe.dot.gov or via American Standard Code Information Interchange (ASCII). All ASCII transmission must be in fixed format, i.e., all records must have the same number of fields and same length. The record layouts for ASCII electronic transactions are described in the following table:

ELECTRONIC INSURANCE FILING TRANSACTIONS

Field name	Number of positions	Description	Required F=filing C=cancel B=both	Start field	End field
Record type	1 Numeric .	1 = Filing 2 = Cancellation	B	1	1
Insurer number ..	8 Text	FMCSA Assigned Insurer Number (Home Office) With Suffix (Issuing Office), If Different, e.g. 12345-01.	B	2	9
Filing type .	1 Numeric .	1 = BI & PD 2 = Cargo 3 = Bond 4 = Trust Fund	B	10	10
FMCSA docket number ..	8 Text	FMCSA Assigned MC or FF Number, e.g., MC000045.	B	11	18
Insured legal name	120 Text ..	Legal Name	B	19	138
Insured d/b/a name	60 Text	Doing Business As Name If Different From Legal Name.	B	139	198
Insured address ..	35 Text	Either street or mailing address	B	199	233
Insured city	30 Text	....	B	234	263
Insured state	2 Text	....	B	264	265
Insured zip code	9 Numeric .	(Do not include dash if using 9 digit code) ...	B	266	274
Insured country ..	2 Text	(Will default to US) ...	B	275	276

ELECTRONIC INSURANCE FILING TRANSACTIONS, Continued

Field name	Number of positions	Description	Required F=filing C=cancel B=both	Start field	End field
Form code	10 Text	BMC-91, BMC-91X, BMC-34, BMC-35, ETC	B	277	286
Full, primary or excess coverage .	1 Text	If BMC-91X, P or E = indicator of primary or excess policy; 1 = Full under §387.303(b)(1); 2 = Full under §387.303(b)(2).	F	287	287
Limit of liability ...	5 Numeric .	$ in Thousands	F	288	292
Underlying limit of liability ...	5 Numeric .	$ in Thousands (will default to $000 if Primary).	F	293	297
Effective date	8 Text	MM/DD/YY Format for both Filing or Cancellation.	B	298	305
Policy number ..	25 Text	Surety companies may enter bond number.	B	306	330

(d) All registered insurers agree to furnish upon request to the FMCSA a duplicate original of any policy (or policies) and all endorsements, surety bond, trust fund agreement, or other filing.

Subpart D — Surety Bonds and Policies of Insurance for Freight Forwarders

§§387.401 to 387.419 ...

PART 390 — GENERAL

Subpart A — General Applicability and Definitions

Subpart B — General Requirements and Information

Subpart C — [Removed and reserved]

Subpart D — [Removed and reserved]

AUTHORITY: 49 U.S.C. 13301, 13902, 31132, 31133, 31136, 31502, and 31504; Sec. 204, Pub. L. 104-88, 109 Stat. 803, 941 (49 U.S.C. 701 note); Sec. 212 and 217, Pub. L. 106-159, 113 Stat. 1748, 1766, 1767; and 49 CFR 1.73.

Subpart A — General Applicability and Definitions

§390.1 Purpose.

This part establishes general applicability, definitions, general requirements and information as they pertain to persons subject to this chapter.

§390.3 General applicability.

(a) The rules in Subchapter B of this chapter are applicable to all employers, employees, and commercial motor vehicles, which transport property or passengers in interstate commerce.

(b) The rules in Part 383, Commercial Driver's License Standards; Requirements and Penalties, are applicable to every person who operates a commercial motor vehicle, as defined in §383.5 of this subchapter, in interstate or intrastate commerce and to all employers of such persons.

(c) The rules in Part 387, Minimum levels of financial responsibility for motor carriers, are applicable to motor carriers as provided in §§387.3 or 387.27 of this subchapter.

(d) **Additional requirements.** Nothing in Subchapter B of this chapter shall be construed to prohibit an employer from requiring and enforcing more stringent requirements relating to safety of operation and employee safety and health.

(e) **Knowledge of and compliance with the regulations.**

(1) Every employer shall be knowledgeable of and comply with all regulations contained in this subchapter which are applicable to that motor carrier's operations.

(2) Every driver and employee shall be instructed regarding, and shall comply with, all applicable regulations contained in this subchapter.

(3) All motor vehicle equipment and accessories required by this subchapter shall be maintained in compliance with all applicable performance and design criteria set forth in this subchapter.

(f) **Exceptions.** Unless otherwise specifically provided, the rules in this subchapter do not apply to—

(1) All school bus operations as defined in §390.5;

(2) Transportation performed by the Federal government, a State, or any political subdivision of a State, or an agency established under a compact between States that has been approved by the Congress of the United States;

(3) The occasional transportation of personal property by individuals not for compensation nor in the furtherance of a commercial enterprise;

(4) The transportation of human corpses or sick and injured persons;

(5) . . .

(6)(i) The operation of commercial motor vehicles designed or used to transport between 9 and 15 passengers (including the driver), not for direct compensation, provided the vehicle does not otherwise meet the definition of a commercial motor vehicle, except that motor carriers operating such vehicles are required to comply with §§390.15, 390.19, and 390.21(a) and (b)(2).

(ii) The operation of commercial motor vehicles designed or used to transport between 9 and 15 passengers (including the driver) for direct compensation, provided the vehicle is not being operated beyond a 75 air-mile radius (86.3 statute miles or 138.9 kilometers) from the driver's normal work-reporting location, and provided the vehicle does not otherwise meet the definition of a commercial motor vehicle, except that motor carriers operating such vehicles are required to comply with §§390.15, 390.19, and 390.21(a) and (b)(2).

§390.5 Definitions.

Unless specifically defined elsewhere, in this subchapter:

Accident means—

(1) Except as provided in paragraph (2) of this definition, an occurrence involving a commercial motor vehicle operating on a highway in interstate or intrastate commerce which results in:

(i) A fatality;

(ii) Bodily injury to a person who, as a result of the injury, immediately receives medical treatment away from the scene of the accident; or

(iii) One or more motor vehicles incurring disabling damage as a result of the accident, requiring the motor vehicle(s) to be transported away from the scene by a tow truck or other motor vehicle

(2) The term *accident* does not include:

(i) An occurrence involving only boarding and alighting from a stationary motor vehicle; or

(ii) An occurrence involving only the loading or unloading of cargo.

Alcohol concentration (AC) means the concentration of alcohol in a person's blood or breath. When expressed as a percentage it means grams of alcohol per 100 milliliters of blood or grams of alcohol per 210 liters of breath.

Bus means any motor vehicle designed, constructed, and or used for the transportation of passengers, including taxicabs.

Business district means the territory contiguous to and including a highway when within any 600 feet along such highway there are buildings in use for business or industrial purposes, including but not limited to hotels, banks, or office buildings which

occupy at least 300 feet of frontage on one side or 300 feet collectively on both sides of the highway.

Charter transportation of passengers means transportation, using a bus, of a group of persons who pursuant to a common purpose, under a single contract, at a fixed charge for the motor vehicle, have acquired the exclusive use of the motor vehicle to travel together under an itinerary either specified in advance or modified after having left the place of origin.

Commercial motor vehicle means any self-propelled or towed motor vehicle used on a highway in interstate commerce to transport passengers or property when the vehicle—

(1) Has a gross vehicle weight rating or gross combination weight rating, or gross vehicle weight or gross combination weight, of 4,536 kg (10,001 pounds) or more, whichever is greater; or

(2) Is designed or used to transport more than 8 passengers (including the driver) for compensation; or

(3) Is designed or used to transport more than 15 passengers, including the driver, and is not used to transport passengers for compensation; or

(4) Is used in transporting material found by the Secretary of Transportation to be hazardous under 49 U.S.C. 5103 and transported in a quantity requiring placarding under regulations prescribed by the Secretary under 49 CFR, subtitle B, chapter I, subchapter C.

Conviction means an unvacated adjudication of guilt, or a determination that a person has violated or failed to comply with the law in a court of original jurisdiction or by an authorized administrative tribunal, an unvacated forfeiture of bail or collateral deposited to secure the person's appearance in court, a plea of guilty or nolo contendere accepted by the court, the payment of a fine or court cost, or violation of a condition of release without bail, regardless of whether or not the penalty is rebated, suspended, or probated.

Direct Assistance means transportation and other relief

services provided by a motor carrier or its driver(s) incident to the immediate restoration of essential services (such as, electricity, medical care, sewer, water, telecommunications, and telecommunication transmissions) or essential supplies (such as, food and fuel). It does not include transportation related to long-term rehabilitation of damaged physical infrastructure or routine commercial deliveries after the initial threat to life and property has passed.

Direct compensation means payment made to the motor carrier by the passengers or a person acting on behalf of the passengers for the transportation services provided, and not included in a total package charge or other assessment for highway transportation services.

Disabling damage means damage which precludes departure of a motor vehicle from the scene of the accident in its usual manner in daylight after simple repairs.

(1) *Inclusions*. Damage to motor vehicles that could have been driven, but would have been further damaged if so driven.

(2) *Exclusions*.

(i) Damage which can be remedied temporarily at the scene of the accident without special tools or parts.

(ii) Tire disablement without other damage even if no spare tire is available.

(iii) Headlamp or taillight damage.

(iv) Damage to turn signals, horn, or windshield wipers which makes them inoperative.

Driveaway-towaway operation...

Driver means any person who operates any commercial motor vehicle.

Driving a commercial motor vehicle while under the influence of alcohol means committing any one or more of the following acts in a CMV: Driving a CMV while the person's alcohol concentration is 0.04 or more; driving under the influence of alcohol, as prescribed by State law; or refusal to undergo such testing as is required by any State or jurisdiction in the enforcement of Table 1 to §383.51 or §392.5(a)(2) of this subchapter.

Emergency means any hurricane, tornado, storm (e.g. thunderstorm, snowstorm, icestorm, blizzard, sandstorm, etc.), high water, wind-driven water, tidal wave, tsunami, earthquake, volcanic eruption, mud slide, drought, forest fire, explosion, blackout or other occurrence, natural or man-made, which interrupts the delivery of essential services (such as, electricity, medical care, sewer, water, telecommunications, and telecommunication transmissions) or essential supplies (such as, food and fuel) or otherwise immediately threatens human life or public welfare, provided such hurricane, tornado or other event results in:

(1) A declaration of an emergency by the President of the United States, the Governor of a State, or their authorized representatives having authority to declare emergencies; by the FMCSA Field Administrator for the geographical area in which the occurrence happens; or by other Federal, State or local government officials having authority to declare emergencies; or

(2) ...

Emergency relief means an operation in which a motor carrier or driver of a commercial motor vehicle is providing direct assistance to supplement State and local efforts and capabilities to save lives or property or to protect public health and safety as a result of an emergency as defined in this section.

Employee means any individual, other than an employer, who is employed by an employer and who in the course of his or her employment directly affects commercial motor vehicle safety. Such term includes a driver of a commercial motor vehicle (including an independent contractor while in the course of opeating a commercial motor vehicle), a mechanic, and a freight handler. Such term does not include an employee of the United States, any State, any political subdivision of a State, or any agency established under a compact between States and approved by the Congress of the United States who is acting within the course of such employment.

Employer means any person engaged in a business affecting interstate commerce who owns or leases a commercial motor vehicle in connection with that business, or assigns employees to operate it, but such term does not include the United States, any state, any political subdivision of a State, or an agency established under a compact between States approved by the Congress of the United States.

Exempt intracity zone ...

Exempt motor carrier means a person engaged in transportation exempt from economic regulation by the Federal Motor Carrier Safety Administration (FMCSA) under 49 U.S.G. 13506. "Exempt motor carriers" are subject to the safety regulations set forth in this subchapter.

Farm-to-market agricultural transportation ...

Farm vehicle driver ...

Farmer ...

Fatality means any injury which results in the death of a person at the time of the motor vehicle accident or within 30 days of the accident.

Federal Motor Carrier Safety Administrator means the chief executive of the Federal Motor Carrier Safety Administration, an agency within the Department of Transportation.

For-hire motor carrier means a person engaged in the transportation of goods or passengers for compensation.

Gross combination weight rating (GCWR) means the value specified by the manufacturer as the loaded weight of a combination (articulated) motor vehicle. In the absence of a value specified by the manufacturer, GCWR will be determined by adding the GVWR of the power unit and the total weight of the towed unit and any load thereon.

Gross vehicle weight rating (GVWR) means the value specified by the manufacturer as the loaded weight of a single motor vehicle.

Hazardous material ...

Hazardous substance ...

Hazardous waste ...

Highway means any road, street, or way, whether on public or private property, open to public travel, "Open to public travel" means that the road section is available, except during scheduled periods, extreme weather or emergency conditions, passable by four-wheel standard passenger cars, and open to the general public for use without restrictive gates, prohibitive signs, or regulation other than restrictions based on size, weight, or class of registration. Toll plazas of public toll roads are not considered restrictive gates.

Interstate commerce means trade, traffic, or transportation in the United States—

(1) Between a place in a State and a place outside of such State (including a place outside of the United States);

(2) Between two places in a State through another State or a place outside of the United States; or

(3) Between two places in a State as part of trade, traffic, or transportation originating or terminating outside the State or the United States.

Intrastate commerce means any trade, traffic, or transportation in any State which is not described in the term "interstate commerce."

Medical examiner means a person who is licensed, certified, and/or registered, in accordance with applicable State laws and regulations, to perform physical examinations. The term includes, but is not limited to, doctors of medicine, doctors of osteopathy, physician assistants, advanced practice nurses, and doctors of chiropractic.

Motor carrier means a for-hire motor carrier or a private motor carrier. The term includes a motor carrier's agents, officers and representatives as well as employees responsible for hiring, supervising, training, assigning, or dispatching of drivers and employees concerned with the installation, inspection, and maintenance of motor vehicle equipment and/or accessories. For purposes of subchapter B, this definition includes the terms **employer** and **exempt motor carrier**.

Motor vehicle means any vehicle, machine, tractor, trailer, or semitrailer propelled or drawn by mechanical power and used upon the highways in the transportation of passengers or property, or any combination thereof determined by the Federal Motor Carrier Safety Administration, but does not include any vehicle, locomotive, or car operated exclusively on a rail or rails, or a trolley bus operated by electric power derived from a fixed overhead wire, furnishing local passenger transportation similar to street-railway service.

Multiple-employer driver means a driver, who in any period of 7 consecutive days, is employed or used as a driver by more than one motor carrier.

Operator — See driver.

Other terms — Any other term used in this subchapter is used in its commonly accepted meaning, except where such other term has been defined elsewhere in this subchapter. In that event, the definition therein given shall apply.

Out-of-service order means a declaration by an authorized enforcement officer of a Federal, State, Canadian, Mexican, or local jurisdiction that a driver, a commercial motor vehicle, or a motor carrier operation, is out-of-service pursuant to §§386.72, 392.5, 395.13, 396.9, or compatible laws, or the North American Uniform Out-of-Service Criteria.

Person means any individual, partnership, association, corporation, business trust, or any other organized group of individuals.

Principal place of business means the single location designated by the motor carrier, normally its headquarters, for purposes of identification under this subchapter. The motor carrier must make records required by parts 382, 387, 390, 391, 395, 396, and

397 of this subchapter available for inspection at this location within 48 hours (Saturdays, Sundays, and Federal holidays excluded) after a request has been made by a special agent or authorized representative of the Federal Motor Carrier Safety Administration.

Private motor carrier means a person who provides transportation of property or passengers, by commercial motor vehicle, and is not a for-hire motor carrier.

Private motor carrier of passengers (business) means a private motor carrier engaged in the interstate transportation of passengers which is provided in the furtherance of a commercial enterprise and is not available to the public at large.

Private motor carrier of passengers (nonbusiness) means private motor carrier involved in the interstate transportation of passengers that does not otherwise meet the definition of a private motor carrier of passengers (business).

Radar detector means any device or mechanism to detect the emission of radio microwaves, laser beams or any other future speed measurement technology employed by enforcement personnel to measure the speed of commercial motor vehicles upon public roads and highways for enforcement purposes. Excluded from this definition are radar detection devices that meet both of the following requirements:

(1) Transported outside the driver's compartment of the commercial motor vehicle. For this purpose, the *driver's compartment* of a passenger-carrying CMV shall include all space designed to accommodate both the driver and the passengers; and

(2) Completely inaccessible to, inoperable by, and imperceptible to the driver while operating the commercial motor vehicle.

FMCSA Field Administrator means the Field Administrator, Federal Motor Carrier Safety Administration, for a given geographical area of the United States.

Residential district means the territory adjacent to and including a highway which is not a business district and for a distance of 300 feet or more along the highway is primarily improved with residences.

School bus means a passenger motor vehicle which is designed or used to carry more than 10 passengers in addition to the driver, and which the Secretary determines is likely to be significantly used for the purpose of transporting preprimary, primary, or secondary school students to such schools from home or from such schools to home.

School bus operation means the use of a school bus to

transport only school children and/or school personnel from home to school and from school to home.

Secretary means the Secretary of Transportation.

Single-employer driver means a driver who, in any period of 7 consecutive days, is employed or used as a driver solely by a single motor carrier. This term includes a driver who operates a commercial motor vehicle on an intermittent, casual, or occasional basis.

Special agent See Appendix B to Subchapter B — Special agents.

State means a State of the United States and the District of Columbia and includes a political subdivision of a State.

Trailer . . .

Full trailer . . .

Pole trailer . . .

Semitrailer . . .

Truck . . .

Truck tractor . . .

United States means the 50 States and the District of Columbia.

§390.7 Rules of construction.

(a) In Part 325 of Subchapter A and in this subchapter, unless the context requires otherwise:

(1) Words imparting the singular include the plural;

(2) Words imparting the plural include the singular;

(3) Words imparting the present tense include the future tense.

(b) In this subchapter the word—

(1) **"Officer"** includes any person authorized by law to perform the duties of the office;

(2) **"Writing"** includes printing and typewriting;

(3) **"Shall"** is used in an imperative sense;

(4) **"Must"** is used in an imperative sense;

(5) **"Should"** is used in a recommendatory sense;

(6) **"May"** is used in a permissive sense; and

(7) **"Includes"** is used as a word of inclusion, not limitation.

Subpart B — General Requirements and Information

§390.9 State and local laws, effect on.

Except as otherwise specifically indicated, Subchapter B of

this chapter is not intended to preclude States or subdivisions thereof from establishing or enforcing State or local laws relating to safety, the compliance with which would not prevent full compliance with these regulations by the person subject thereto.

§390.11 Motor carrier to require observance of driver regulations.

Whenever in Part 325 of Subchapter A or in this subchapter a duty is prescribed for a driver or a prohibition is imposed upon the driver, it shall be the duty of the motor carrier to require observance of such duty or prohibition. If the motor carrier is a driver, the driver shall likewise be bound.

§390.13 Aiding or abetting violations.

No person shall aid, abet, encourage, or require a motor carrier or its employees to violate the rules of this chapter.

§390.15 Assistance in investigations and special studies.

(a) A motor carrier shall make all records and information pertaining to an accident available to an authorized representative or special agent of the Federal Motor Carrier Safety Administration upon request or as part of any inquiry within such time as the request or inquiry may specify. A motor carrier shall give an authorized representative of the Federal Motor Carrier Safety Administration all reasonable assistance in the investigation of any accident including providing a full, true and correct answer to any question of the inquiry.

(b) Motor carriers shall maintain for a period of one year after an accident occurs, an accident register containing at least the following information:

(1) A list of accidents containing for each accident:

(i) Date of accident,

(ii) City or town in which or most near where the accident occurred and the State in which the accident occurred,

(iii) Driver name,

(iv) Number of injuries,

(v) Number of fatalities, and

(vi) . . .

(2) Copies of all accident reports required by State or other governmental entities or insurers.

[Approved by the Office of Management and Budget under control number 2125-0526]

§390.16 [Reserved]

§390.17 Additional equipment and accessories.

Nothing in this subchapter shall be construed to prohibit the use of additional equipment and accessories, not inconsistent with or prohibited by this subchapter, provided such equipment and accessories do not decrease the safety of operation of the commercial motor vehicles on which they are used.

§390.19 Motor carrier identification report.

(a) Each motor carrier that conducts operations in interstate commerce must file a Motor Carrier Identification Report, Form MCS-150 at the following times:

(1) Before it begins operations; and

(2) Every 24 months, according to the following schedule:

USDOT Number ending in:	Must file by last day of:
1	January
2	February
3	March
4	April
5	May
6	June
7	July
8	August
9	September
0	October

(3) If the next-to-last digit of its USDOT number is odd, the motor carrier shall file its update in every odd-numbered calendar year. If the next-to-last digit of the USDOT number is even, the motor carrier shall file its update in every even-numbered calendar year.

(b) The Motor Carrier Information Report, Form MCS-150, with complete instructions, is available from the FMCSA's web site at: *http://www.fmcsa.dot.gov* (keyword "MCS-150"), from all FMCSA Service Centers and Division offices nationwide, or by calling 1-800-832-5660.

(c) The completed Motor Carrier Identification Report, Form MCS-150, shall be filed with the FMCSA's Office of Data Analysis and Information Systems.

(1) The form may be filed electronically according to the instructions at the agency's web site, or it may be sent to Federal Motor Carrier Safety Administration, Data Analysis and Information Systems, MC-RIS, 400 Seventh Street, SW, Washington, DC 20590.

(2) A for-hire motor carrier should submit the Form MCS-150 along with its application for operating authority (Form OP-1 or OP-2) to the appropriate address referenced on that form, or may submit it electronically or by mail separately to the address mentioned in this section.

(d) Only the legal name or a single trade name of the motor carrier may be used on the motor carrier identification report (Form MCS-150).

(e) A motor carrier that fails to file a Motor Carrier Identification Report, Form MCS-150, or furnishes misleading information or makes false statements upon form MCS-150, is subject to the penalties prescribed in 49 U.S.C. 521(b)(2)(B).

(f) Upon receipt and processing of the Motor Carrier Identification Report, form MCS-150, the FMCSA will issue the motor carrier an identification number (USDOT number). The motor carrier must display the number on each self-propelled CMV, as defined in §390.5, along with the additional information required by §390.21.

(g) A motor carrier that registers its vehicles in a State that participates in the Performance and Registration Information Systems Management (PRISM) program (authorized under section 4004 of the Transportation Equity Act for the 21st Century [(Public Law 105-178, 112 Stat. 107)] is exempt from the requirements of this section, provided it files all the required information with the appropriate State office.

[Approved by the Office of Management and Budget under control number 2126-0013]

§390.21 Marking of CMVs.

(a) **General.** Every self-propelled CMV, as defined in §390.5, subject to subchapter B of this chapter must be marked as specified in paragraphs (b), (c), and (d) of this section.

(b) **Nature of marking.** The marking must display the following information:

(1) The legal name or a single trade name of the motor carrier operating the self-propelled CMV, as listed on the motor carrier identification report (Form MCS-150) and submitted in accor-

dance with §390.19.

(2) The motor carrier identification number issued by the FMCSA, preceded by the letters "USDOT".

(3) If the name of any person other than the operating carrier appears on the CMV, the name of the operating carrier must be followed by the information required by paragraphs (b)(1), and (2) of this section, and be preceded by the words "operated by."

(4) Other identifying information may be displayed on the vehicle if it is not inconsistent with the information required by this paragraph.

(5) Each motor carrier shall meet the following requirements pertaining to its operation:

(i) All CMVs that are part of a motor carrier's existing fleet on July 3, 2000, and which are marked with an ICCMC number must come into compliance with paragraph (b)(2) of this section by July 3, 2002.

(ii) All CMVs that are part of a motor carrier's existing fleet on July 3, 2000, and which are not marked with the legal name or a single trade name on both sides of their CMVs, as shown on the Motor Carrier Identification Report, Form MCS-150, must come into compliance with paragraph (b)(1) of this section by July 5, 2005.

(iii) All CMVs added to a motor carrier's fleet on or after July 3, 2000, must meet the requirements of this section before being put into service and operating on public ways.

(c) **Size, shape, location, and color of marking.** The marking must—

(1) Appear on both sides of the self-propelled CMV;

(2) Be in letters that contrast sharply in color with the background on which the letters are placed;

(3) Be readily legible, during daylight hours, from a distance of 50 feet (15.24 meters) while the CMV is stationary; and

(4) Be kept and maintained in a manner that retains the legibility required by paragraph (c)(3) of this section.

(d) **Construction and durability.** The marking may be painted on the CMV or may consist of a removable device, if that device meets the identification and legibility requirements of paragraph (c) of this section, and such marking must be maintained as required by paragraph (c)(4) of this section.

(e) **Rented CMVs.** A motor carrier operating a self-propelled CMV under a rental agreement having a term not in excess of 30 calendar days meets the requirements of this section if:

(1) The CMV is marked in accordance with the provisions of paragraphs (b) through (d) of this section; or

(2) The CMV is marked as set forth in paragraph (e)(2)(i) through (iv) of this section:

(i) The legal name or a single trade name of the lessor is displayed in accordance with paragraphs (c) and (d) of this section.

(ii) The lessor's identification number preceded by the letters "USDOT" is displayed in accordance with paragraphs (c) and (d) of this section; and

(iii) The rental agreement entered into by the lessor and the renting motor carrier conspicuously contains the following information:

(A) The name and complete physical address of the principal place of business of the renting motor carrier.

(B) The identification number issued the renting motor carrier by the FMCSA, preceded by the letters "USDOT," if the motor carrier has been issued such a number. In lieu of the identification number required in this paragraph, the following may be shown in the rental agreement:

(1) Information which indicates whether the motor carrier is engaged in "interstate" or "intrastate" commerce; and

(2) Information which indicates whether the renting motor carrier is transporting hazardous materials in the rented CMV;

(C) The sentence: "This lessor cooperates with all Federal, State, and local law enforcement officials nationwide to provide the identity of customers who operate this rental CMV"; and

(iv) The rental agreement entered into by the lessor and the renting motor carrier is carried on the rental CMV during the full term of the rental agreement. See the leasing regulations at 49 CFR 376 for information that should be included in all leasing documents.

(f) **Driveaway services.** In driveaway services, a removable device may be affixed on both sides or at the rear of a single driven vehicle. In a combination driveaway operation, the device may be affixed on both sides of any one unit or at the rear of the last unit. The removable device must display the legal name or a single trade name of the motor carrier and the motor carrier's USDOT number.

§390.23 Relief from regulations.

(a) Parts 390 through 399 of this chapter shall not apply to any motor carrier or driver operating a commercial motor vehicle to provide emergency relief during an emergency, subject to the following time limits:

(1) **Regional emergencies.**

(i) The exemption provided by paragraph (a)(1) of this section is effective only when:

(A) An emergency has been declared by the President of the United States, the Governor of a State, or their authorized representatives having authority to declare emergencies; or

(B) The FMCSA Field Administrator has declared that a regional emergency exists which justifies an exemption from parts 390 through 399 of this chapter.

(ii) Except as provided in §390.25, this exemption shall not exceed the duration of the motor carrier's or driver's direct assistance in providing emergency relief, or 30 days from the date of the initial declaration of the emergency or the exemption from the regulations by the FMCSA Field Administrator, whichever is less.

(2) **Local emergencies.**

(i) The exemption provided by paragraph (a)(2) of this section is effective only when:

(A) An emergency has been declared by a Federal, State, or local government official having authority to declare an emergency; or

(B) The FMCSA Field Administrator has declared that a local emergency exists which justifies an exemption from parts 390 through 399 of this chapter.

(ii) This exemption shall not exceed the duration of the motor carrier's or driver's direct assistance in providing emergency relief, or 5 days from the date of the initial declaration of the emergency or the exemption from the regulations by the FMCSA Field Administrator, whichever is less.

(3) . . .

Editor's Note: Compliance with the following is required as of January 4, 2004.

(b) Upon termination of direct assistance to the regional or local emergency relief effort, the motor carrier or driver is subject to the requirements of parts 390 through 399 of this chapter, with the following exception: A driver may return empty to the motor carrier's terminal or the driver's normal work reporting location without complying with parts 390 through 399 of this chapter. However, a driver who informs the motor carrier that he or she needs immediate rest shall be permitted at least 8 consecutive hours off duty before the driver is required to return to such terminal or location. Having returned to the terminal or other location, the driver must be relieved of all duty and responsibilities. Direct assistance terminates when a driver or commercial motor vehicle is used in interstate commerce to transport cargo not destined for the emergency relief effort, or when the motor carrier dispatches such driver or commercial motor vehicle to another location to begin operations in commerce.

(c) When the driver has been relieved of all duty and responsibilities upon termination of direct assistance to a regional or local emergency relief effort, no motor carrier shall permit or require any driver used by it to drive nor shall any such driver drive in commerce until:

(1) The driver has met the requirements of §395.3(a) and §395.5(a) of this chapter; and

(2) The driver has had at least 34 consecutive hours off-duty when:

(i) The driver has been on duty for more than 60 hours in any 7 consecutive days at the time the driver is relieved of all duty if the employing motor carrier does not operate every day in the week, or

(ii) The driver has been on duty for more than 70 hours in any 8 consecutive days at the time the driver is relieved of all duty if the employing motor carrier operates every day in the week.

Editor's Note: Compliance with the following is required until January 4, 2004.

(b) Upon termination of direct assistance to the regional or local emergency relief effort, the motor carrier or driver is subject to the requirements of parts 390 through 399 of this chapter, with the following exception: A driver may return empty to the motor carrier's terminal or the driver's normal work reporting location without complying with parts 390 through 399 of this chapter. However, a driver who informs the motor carrier that he or she needs immediate rest shall be permitted at least 8 consecutive hours off duty before the driver is required to return to such terminal or location. Having returned to the terminal or other location, the driver must be relieved of all duty and responsibilities. Direct assistance terminates when a driver or commercial motor vehicle is used in interstate commerce to transport cargo not destined for the emergency relief effort, or when the motor carrier dispatches such driver or commercial motor vehicle to another location to begin operations in commerce.

(c) When the driver has been relieved of all duty and responsibilities upon termination of direct assistance to a regional or local emergency relief effort, no motor carrier shall permit or require any driver used by it to drive nor shall any such driver drive in commerce until:

(1) The driver has met the requirements of §395.3(a) of this chapter; and

(2) The driver has had at least 24 consecutive hours off-duty when:

(A) The driver has been on duty for more than 60 hours in any 7 consecutive days at the time the driver is relieved of all duty if the employing motor carrier does not operate every day in the week, or

(B) The driver has been on duty for more than 70 hours in any 8 consecutive days at the time the driver is relieved of all duty if the employing motor carrier operates every day in the week.

§390.25 Extension of relief from regulations—emergencies.

The FMCSA Field Administrator may extend the 30-day time period of the exemption contained in §390.23(a)(1), but not the 5-day time period contained in §390.23(a)(2) or the 24-hour period contained in §390.23(a)(3). Any motor carrier or driver seeking to extend the 30-day limit shall obtain approval from the FMCSA Field Administrator in the region in which the motor carrier's principal place of business is located before the expiration of the 30-day period. The motor carrier or driver shall give full details of the additional relief requested. The FMCSA Field Administrator shall determine if such relief is necessary taking into account both the severity of the ongoing emergency and the nature of the relief services to be provided by the carrier or driver. If the FMCSA Field Administrator approves an extension of the exemption, he or she shall establish a new time limit and place on the motor carrier or driver any other restrictions deemed necessary.

§390.27 Locations of motor carrier safety service centers.

Service center	Territory included	Location of office
Eastern	CT, DC, DE, MA, MD, ME, NJ, NH, NY, PA, PR, RI, VA, VT, WV.	City,Crescent Building, #10 South Howard Street, Suite 4000, Baltimore, MD 21201-2819.
Midwestern ..	IA, IL, IN, KS, MI, MO, MN, NE, OH, WI	19900 Governors Drive, Suie 210, Olympia Fields, IL 60461-1021.
Southern ...	AL, AR, FL, GA, KY, LA, MS, NC, NM, OK, SC, TN, TX.	61 Forsyth Street, SW, Suite 17T75, Atlanta, GA 30303-3104.
Western	American Samoa, AK, AZ, CA, CO, Guam, HI, ID, MarianaIslands, MT, ND, NV, OR, SD, UT, WA, WY.	201 Mission Street, Suite 2100, San Francis-co, CA 94105-1838.

§390.29 Location of records or documents.

(a) A motor carrier with multiple offices or terminals may maintain the records and documents required by this subchapter at its principal place of business, a regional office, or driver work-reporting location unless otherwise specified in this subchapter.

(b) All records and documents required by this subchapter which are maintained at a regional office or driver work-reporting location shall be made available for inspection upon request by a special agent or authorized representative of the Federal Highway Administration at the motor carrier's principal place of business or other location specified by the agent or representative within 48 hours after a request is made. Saturdays, Sundays, and Federal holidays are excluded from the computation of the 48-hour period of time.

§390.31 Copies of records or documents.

(a) All records and documents required to be maintained under this subchapter must be preserved in their original form for the periods specified, unless the records and documents are suitably photographed and the microfilm is retained in lieu of the original record for the required retention period.

(b) To be acceptable in lieu of original records, photographic copies of records must meet the following minimum requirements:

(1) Photographic copies shall be no less readily accessible than the original record or document as normally filed or preserved would be and suitable means or facilities shall be available to locate, identify, read, and reproduce such photographic copies.

(2) Any significant characteristic, feature or other attribute of the original record or document, which photgraphy in black and white will not preserve, shall be clearly indicated before the photograph is made.

(3) The reverse side of printed forms need not be copied if nothing has been added to the printed matter common to all such forms, but an identified specimen of each form shall be on the film for reference.

(4) Film used for photographing copies shall be of permanent record-type meeting in all respects the minimum specifications of the National Bureau of Standards, and all processes recommended by the manufacturer shall be observed to protect it from

deterioration or accidental destruction.

(5) Each roll of film shall include a microfilm of a certificate or certificates stating that the photographs are direct or facsimile reproductions of the original records. Such certificate(s) shall be executed by a person or persons having personal knowledge of the material covered thereby.

(c) All records and documents required to be maintained under this subchapter may be destroyed after they have been suitably photographed for preservation.

(d) **Exception.** All records except those requiring a signature may be maintained through the use of computer technology provided the motor carrier can produce, upon demand, a computer printout of the required data.

§390.33 Commercial motor vehicles used for purposes other than defined.

Whenever a commercial motor vehicle of one type is used to perform the functions normally performed by a commercial motor vehicle of another type, the requirements of this subchapter and Part 325 of Subchapter A shall apply to the commercial motor vehicle and to its operation in the same manner as though the commercial motor vehicle were actually a commercial motor vehicle of the latter type.

Example: If a commercial motor vehicle other than a bus is used to perform the functions normally performed by a bus, the regulations pertaining to buses and to the transportation of passengers shall apply to that commercial motor vehicle.

§390.35 Certificates, reports, and records: falsification, reproduction, or alteration.

No motor carrier, its agents, officers, representatives, or employees shall make or cause to make—

(a) A fraudulent or intentionally false statement on any application, certificate, report, or record required by Part 325 of subchapter A or this subchapter;

(b) A fraudulent or intentionally false entry on any application, certificate, report, or record required to be used, completed, or retained, to comply with any requirement of this subchapter or Part 325 of Subchapter A; or

(c) A reproduction, for fraudulent purposes, of any application, certificate, report, or record required by this subchapter or Part 325 of Subchapter A.

§390.37 Violation and penalty.

Any person who violates the rules set forth in this subchapter or Part 325 of Subchapter A may be subject to civil or criminal penalties.

Subpart C — [Removed and reserved]

Subpart D — [Removed and reserved]

PART 391 — QUALIFICATIONS OF DRIVERS

Subpart A — General

§391.1

AUTHORITY: 49 U.S.C. 322, 504, 31133, 31136, and 31502;
49 CFR 1.73.

Subpart A — General

§391.1 Scope of the rules in this part; additional qualifications; duties of carrier-drivers.

(a) The rules in this part establish minimum qualifications for persons who drive commercial motor vehicles as, for, or on behalf of motor carriers. The rules in this part also establish minimum duties of motor carriers with respect to the qualifications of their drivers.

(b) A motor carrier who employs himself/herself as a driver must comply with both the rules in this part that apply to motor carriers and the rules in this part that apply to drivers.

§391.2 . . .

Subpart B — Qualification and Disqualification of Drivers

§391.11 General qualifications of drivers.

(a) A person shall not drive a commercial motor vehicle unless he/she is qualified to drive a commercial motor vehicle. Except as provided in §391.63, a motor carrier shall not require or permit a person to drive a commercial motor vehicle unless that person is qualified to drive a motor vehicle.

(b) Except as provided in Subpart G of this part, a person is qualified to drive a commercial motor vehicle if he/she—

(1) Is at least 21 years old;

(2) Can read and speak the English language sufficiently to converse with the general public, to understand highway traffic signs and signals in the English language, to respond to official inquiries, and to make entries on reports and records;

(3) Can, by reason of experience, training, or both, safely operate the type of commercial motor vehicle he/she drives;

(4) Is physically qualified to drive a commercial motor vehicle in accordance with Subpart E — Physical Qualifications and Examinations of this part;

(5) Has a currently valid commercial motor vehicle operator's license issued only by one State or jurisdiction.

(6) Has prepared and furnished the motor carrier that employs him/her with the list of violations or the certificate as required by §391.27;

(7) Is not disqualified to drive a commercial motor vehicle under the rules in §391.15;

(8) Has successfully completed a driver's road test and has been issued a certificate of driver's road test in accordance with §391.31, or has presented an operator's license or a certificate of road test which the motor carrier that employs him/her has accepted as equivalent to a road test in accordance with §391.33.

§391.13 Responsibilities of drivers.

In order to comply with the requirements of §392.9(a) and §393.9 of this subchapter, a motor carrier shall not require or permit a person to drive a commercial motor vehicle unless the person—

(a) Can, by reason of experience, training, or both, determine whether the cargo he/she transports (including baggage in a passenger-carrying commercial motor vehicle) has been properly located, distributed, and secured in or on the commercial motor vehicle he/she drives;

(b) Is familiar with methods and procedures for securing cargo in or on the commercial motor vehicle he/she drives.

§391.15 Disqualification of drivers.

(a) **General.** A driver who is disqualified shall not drive a commercial motor vehicle. A motor carrier shall not require or permit a driver who is disqualified to drive a commercial motor vehicle.

(b) **Disqualification for loss of driving privileges.** (1) A driver is disqualified for the duration of the driver's loss of his/her privilege to operate a commercial motor vehicle on public highways, either temporarily or permanently, by reason of the revocation, suspension, withdrawal, or denial of an operator's license, permit, or privilege, until that operator's license, permit, or privilege is restored by the authority that revoked, suspended, withdrew, or denied it.

(2) A driver who receives a notice that his/her license, permit, or privilege to operate a commercial motor vehicle has been revoked, suspended, or withdrawn shall notify the motor carrier that employs him/her of the contents of the notice before the end of the business day following the day the driver received it.

(c) **Disqualification for criminal and other offenses.**

(1) **General rule.** A driver who is convicted of (or forfeits bond or collateral upon a charge of) a disqualifying offense specified in paragraph (c)(2) of this section is disqualified for the period of time specified in paragraph (c)(3) of this section, if—

(i) The offense was committed during on-duty time as defined in §395.2(a) of this subchapter or as otherwise specified; and

(ii) The driver is employed by a motor carrier or is engaged in activities that are in furtherance of a commercial enterprise in interstate, intrastate, or foreign commerce;

(2) **Disqualifying offenses.** The following offenses are disqualifying offenses:

(i) Driving a commercial motor vehicle while under the influence of alcohol. This shall include:

(A) Driving a commercial motor vehicle while the person's alcohol concentration is 0.04 percent or more;

(B) Driving under the influence of alcohol, as prescribed by State law; or

(C) Refusal to undergo such testing as is required by any State or jurisdiction in the enforcement of §391.15(c)(2)(i)(A) or (B), or §392.5(a)(2).

(ii) Driving a commercial motor vehicle under the influence of a 21 CFR 1308.11 *Schedule I* identified controlled substance, an amphetamine, a narcotic drug, a formulation of an amphetamine, a derivative of a narcotic drug;

(iii) Transportation, possession, or unlawful use of, amphetamines, narcotic drugs, formulations of an amphetamine, or derivatives of narcotic drugs while on-duty time the driver is on duty, as the term is defined in §395.2 of this subchapter;

(iv) Leaving the scene of an accident while operating a commercial motor vehicle; or

(v) A felony involving the use of a commercial motor vehicle.

(3) **Duration of disqualification—**(i) **First offenders.** A driver is disqualified for 1 year after the date of conviction or forfeiture of bond or collateral if, during the 3 years preceding that date, the driver was not convicted of, or did not forfeit bond or

collateral upon a charge of an offense that would disqualify the driver under the rules of this section. **Exemption.** The period of disqualification is 6 months if the conviction or forfeiture of bond or collateral solely concerned the transportation or possession of substances named in paragraph (c)(2)(iii) of this section.

(ii) **Subsequent offenders.** A driver is disqualified for 3 years after the date of his/her conviction or forfeiture of bond or collateral if, during the 3 years preceding that date, he/she was convicted of, or forfeited bond or collateral upon a charge of, an offense that would disqualify him/her under the rules in this section.

(d) **Disqualification for violation of out-of-service orders.**

(1) **General rule.** A driver who is convicted of violating an out-of-service order is disqualified for the period of time specified in paragraph (d)(2) of this section.

(2) **Duration of disqualification for violation of out-of-service orders.**

(i) **First violation.** A driver is disqualified for not less than 90 days nor more than one year if the driver is convicted of a first violation of an out-of-service order.

(ii) **Second violation.** A driver is disqualified for not less than one year nor more than five years if, during any 10-year period, the driver is convicted of two violations of out-of-service orders in separate incidents.

(iii) **Third or subsequent violation.** A driver is disqualified for not less than three years nor more than five years if, during any 10-year period, the driver is convicted of three or more violations of out-of-service orders in separate incidents.

(iv) **Special rule for hazardous materials and passenger offenses.** A driver is disqualified for a period of not less than 180 days nor more than two years if the driver is convicted of a first violation of an out-of-service order while transporting hazardous materials required to be placarded under the Hazardous Materials Transportation Act (49 U.S.C. 5101 *et seq.*), or while operating commercial motor vehicles designed to transport more than 15 passengers, including the driver. A driver is disqualified for a period of not less than three years nor more than five years if, during any 10-year period, the driver is convicted of any subsequent violations of out-of-service orders, in separate incidents, while transporting hazardous materials required to be placarded under the Hazardous Materials Transportation Act, or while operating commercial motor vehicles designed to transport more than 15 passengers, including the driver.

Subpart C — Background and Character

§391.21 Application for employment.

(a) Except as provided in Subpart G of this part, a person shall not drive a commercial motor vehicle unless he/she has completed and furnished the motor carrier that employs him/her with an application for employment that meets the requirements of paragraph (b) of this section.

(b) The application for employment shall be made on a form furnished by the motor carrier. Each application form must be completed by the applicant, must be signed by him, and must contain the following information:

(1) The name and address of the employing motor carrier;

(2) The applicant's name, address, date of birth, and social security number;

(3) The addresses at which the applicant has resided during the 3 years preceding the date on which the application is submitted;

(4) The date on which the application is submitted;

(5) The issuing State, number, and expiration date of each unexpired commercial motor vehicle operator's license or permit that has been issued to the applicant;

(6) The nature and extent of the applicant's experience in the operation of motor vehicles, including the type of equipment (such as buses, trucks, truck tractors, semitrailers, full trailers, and pole trailers) which he/she has operated;

(7) A list of all motor vehicle accidents in which the applicant was involved during the 3 years preceding the date the application is submitted, specifying the date and nature of each accident and any fatalities or personal injuries it caused;

(8) A list of all violations of motor vehicle laws or ordinances (other than violations involving only parking) of which the applicant was convicted or forfeited bond or collateral during the 3 years preceding the date the application is submitted;

(9) A statement setting forth in detail the facts and circumstances of any denial, revocation, or suspension of any license, permit, or privilege to operate a motor vehicle that has been issued to the applicant, or a statement that no such denial, revocation, or suspension has occurred;

(10) A list of the names and addresses of the applicant's employers during the 3 years preceding the date the application is submitted, together with the dates he/she was employed by, and

his/her reason for leaving the employ of, each employer;

(11) For those drivers applying to operate a commercial motor vehicle as defined by Part 383 of this subchapter, a list of the names and addresses of the applicant's employers during the 7-year period preceding the 3 years contained in paragraph (b)(10) of this section for which the applicant was an operator of a commercial motor vehicle, together with the dates of employment and the reasons for leaving such employment.

(12) The following certification and signature line, which must appear at the end of the application form and be signed by the applicant:

This certifies that this application was completed by me, and that all entries on it and information in it are true and complete to the best of my knowledge.

_____

(Date)   (Applicant's signature)

(c) A motor carrier may require an applicant to provide information in addition to the information required by paragraph (b) of this section on the application form.

(d) Before an application is submitted, the motor carrier shall inform the applicant that the information he provides in accordance with paragraph (b) (10) of this section may be used, and the applicant's prior employers may be contacted, for the purpose of investigating the applicant's background as required by §391.23.

§391.23 Investigation and inquiries.

(a) Except as provided in Subpart G of this part, each motor carrier shall make the following investigations and inquiries with respect to each driver it employs, other than a person who has been a regularly employed driver of the motor carrier for a continuous period which began before January 1, 1971:

(1) An inquiry into the driver's driving record during the preceding 3 years to the appropriate agency of every State in which the driver held a motor vehicle operator's license or permit during those 3 years; and

(2) An investigation of the driver's employment record during the preceding 3 years.

(b) The inquiry to State agencies required by paragraph (a) (1) of this section must be made within 30 days of the date the driver's employment begins and shall be made in the form and manner those agencies prescribe. A copy of the response by each State agency, showing the driver's driving record or certifying that no driving record exists for that driver, shall be retained in the carrier's files as part of the driver's qualification file.

(c) The investigation of the driver's employment record required by paragraph (a) (2) of this section must be made within 30 days of the date his/her employment begins. The investigation may consist of personal interviews, telephone interviews, letters, or any other method of obtaining information that the carrier deems appropriate. Each motor carrier must make a written record with respect to each past employer who was contacted. The record must include the past employer's name and address, the date he/she was contacted, and his/her comments with respect to the driver. The record shall be retained in the motor carrier's files as part of the driver's qualification file.

§391.25 Annual inquiry and review of driving record.

(a) Except as provided in subpart G of this part, each motor carrier shall, at least once every 12 months, make an inquiry into the driving record of each driver it employs, covering at least the preceding 12 months, to the appropriate agency of every State in which the driver held a commercial motor vehicle operator's license or permit during the time period.

(b) Except as provided in subpart G of this part, each motor carrier shall, at least once every 12 months, review the driving record of each driver it employs to determine whether that driver meets minimum requirements for safe driving or is disqualified to drive a commercial motor vehicle pursuant to §391.15.

(1) The motor carrier must consider any evidence that the driver has violated any applicable Federal Motor Carrier Safety Regulations in this subchapter or Hazardous Materials Regulations (49 CFR chapter I, subchapter C).

(2) The motor carrier must consider the driver's accident record and any evidence that the driver has violated laws governing the operation of motor vehicles, and must give great weight to violations, such as speeding, reckless driving, and operating while under the influence of alcohol or drugs, that indicate that the driver has exhibited a disregard for the safety of the public.

(c) Recordkeeping. (1) A copy of the response from each State agency to the inquiry required by paragraph (a) of this section shall be maintained in the driver's qualification file.

(2) A note, including the name of the person who performed

the review of the driving record required by paragraph (b) of this section and the date of such review, shall be maintained in the driver's qualification file.

§391.27 Record of violations.

(a) Except as provided in Subpart G of this part, each motor carrier shall, at least once every 12 months, require each driver it employs to prepare and furnish it with a list of all violations of motor vehicle traffic laws and ordinances (other than violations involving only parking) of which the driver has been convicted or on account of which he/she has forfeited bond or collateral during the preceding 12 months.

(b) Each driver shall furnish the list required in accordance with paragraph (a) of this section. If the driver has not been convicted of, or forfeited bond or collateral on account of, any violation which must be listed he/she shall so certify.

(c) The form of the driver's list or certification shall be prescribed by the motor carrier. The following form may be used to comply with this section:

Driver's Certification

I certify that the following is a true and complete list of traffic violations (other than parking violations) for which I have been convicted or forfeited bond or collateral during the past 12 months.

Date of
conviction   Offense

_____   _____

_____   _____

_____   _____

_____   _____

Location   Type of motor vehicle operated

_____   _____

_____   _____

_____   _____

If no violations are listed above, I certify that I have not been convicted or forfeited bond or collateral on account of any violation required to be listed during the past 12 months.

_____   _____
(Date of certification)   (Driver's signature)

_____
(Motor carrier's name)

_____
(Motor carrier's address)

_____   _____
(Reviewed by: Signature)   (Title)

(d) The motor carrier shall retain the list or certificate required by this section, or a copy of it, in its files as part of the driver's qualification file.

(e) Drivers who have provided information required by §383.31 of this subchapter need not repeat that information in the annual list of violations required by this section.

Subpart D — Tests

§391.31 Road test.

(a) Except as provided in subpart G, a person shall not drive a commercial motor vehicle unless he/she has first successfully completed a road test and has been issued a certificate of driver's road test in accordance with this section.

(b) The road test shall be given by the motor carrier or a person designated by it. However, a driver who is a motor carrier must be given the test by a person other than himself/herself. The test shall be given by a person who is competent to evaluate and determine whether the person who takes the test has demonstrated that he/she is capable of operating the commercial motor vehicle, and associated equipment, that the motor carrier intends to assign him/her.

(c) The road test must be of sufficient duration to enable the person who gives it to evaluate the skill of the person who takes it at handling the commercial motor vehicle and associated equipment, that the motor carrier intends to assign to him/her. As a minimum, the person who takes the test must be tested, while operating the type of commercial motor vehicle the motor carrier intends to assign him/her, on his/her skill at performing each of the following operations:

(1) The pretrip inspection required by §392.7 of this subchapter;

(2) . . .

(3) Placing the commercial motor vehicle in operation;

(4) Use of the commercial motor vehicle's controls and emergency equipment;

(5) Operating the commercial motor vehicle in traffic and while passing other commercial motor vehicles;

(6) Turning the commercial motor vehicle;

(7) Braking, and slowing the commercial motor vehicle by means other than braking; and

(8) Backing and parking the commercial motor vehicle.

(d) The motor carrier shall provide a road test form on which the person who gives the test shall rate the performance of the person who takes it at each operation or activity which is a part of the test. After he/she completes the form, the person who gave the test shall sign it.

(e) If the road test is successfully completed, the person who gave it shall complete a certificate of driver's road test in substantially the form prescribed in paragraph (f) of this section.

(f) The form for the certificate of driver's road test is substantially as follows:

CERTIFICATION OF ROAD TEST

Driver's name_____

Social Security No._____

Operator's or Chauffeur's License No._____

State_____

Type of power unit_____

Type of trailer(s)_____

If passenger carrier, type of bus_____

This is to certify that the above-named driver was given a road test under my supervision on_____20_____consisting of approximately_____miles of driving.

It is my considered opinion that this driver possesses sufficient driving skill to operate safely the type of commercial motor vehicle listed above.

_____

(Signature of examiner)   (Title)

_____

(Organization and address of examiner)

(g) A copy of the certificate required by paragraph (e) of this section shall be given to the person who was examined. The motor carrier shall retain in the driver qualification file of the person who was examined—

(1) The original of the signed road test form required by paragraph (d) of this section; and

(2) The original, or a copy of, the certificate required by paragraph (e) of this section.

§391.33 Equivalent of road test.

(a) In place of, and as equivalent to, the road test required by §391.31, a person who seeks to drive a commercial motor vehicle may present, and a motor carrier may accept—

(1) A valid Commercial Driver's License as defined in §383.5 of this subchapter, but not including double/triple trailer or tank vehicle endorsements, which has been issued to him/her to operate specific categories of commercial motor vehicles and which, under the laws of that State, licenses him/her after successful completion of a road test in a commercial motor vehicle of the type the motor carrier intends to assign to him/her; or

(2) A copy of a valid certificate of driver's road test issued to him/her pursuant to §391.31 within the preceding 3 years.

(b) If a driver presents, and a motor carrier accepts, a license or certificate as equivalent to the road test, the motor carrier shall retain a legible copy of the license or certificate in its files as part of the driver's qualification file.

(c) A motor carrier may require any person who presents a license or certificate as equivalent to the road test to take a road test or any other test of his/her driving skill as a condition to his/her employment as a driver.

§391.35 [Removed and reserved.]

§391.37 [Removed and reserved.]

Subpart E — Physical Qualifications and Examinations

§391.41 Physical qualifications for drivers.

(a) A person shall not drive a commercial motor vehicle unless he/she is physically qualified to do so and, except as provided in §391.67, has on his/her person the original, or a photographic copy, of a medical examiner's certificate that he/she is physically qualified to drive a commercial motor vehicle.

(b) A person is physically qualified to drive a commercial motor vehicle if that person—

Note: The United States and Canada entered into a Reciprocity Agreement, effective March 30, 1999, recognizing that a Canadian commercial driver's license is proof of medical fitness to drive. Therefore, Canadian commercial motor vehicle (CMV) drivers are no longer required to have in their possession a medical examiner's certificate if the driver has been issued, and possesses, a valid commercial driver's license issued by a Canadian Province or Territory. However, Canadian drivers who are insulin-using diabetics, who have epilepsy, or who are hearing impaired as defined in §391.41(b)(11) are not qualified to drive CMVs in the United States. Furthermore, Canadian drivers who do not meet the medical fitness provisions of the Canadian National Safety Code for Motor Carriers but who have been issued a waiver by one of the Canadian Provinces or Territories are not qualified to drive CMVs in the United States.

(1) Has no loss of a foot, a leg, a hand, or an arm, or has been granted a skill performance evaluation certificate pursuant to §391.49;

(2) Has no impairment of:

(i) A hand or finger which interferes with prehension or power grasping; or

(ii) An arm, foot, or leg which interferes with the ability to perform normal tasks associated with operating a commercial motor vehicle; or any other significant limb defect or limitation which interferes with the ability to perform normal tasks associated with operating a commercial motor vehicle; or has been granted a skill performance evaluation certificate pursuant to §391.49.

(3) Has no established medical history or clinical diagnosis of diabetes mellitus currently requiring insulin for control;

(4) Has no current clinical diagnosis of myocardial infarction, angina pectoris, coronary insufficiency, thrombosis, or any other cardiovascular disease of a variety known to be accompanied by syncope, dyspnea, collapse, or congestive cardiac failure;

(5) Has no established medical history or clinical diagnosis of a respiratory dysfunction likely to interfere with his/her ability to control and drive a commercial motor vehicle safely;

(6) Has no current clinical diagnosis of high blood pressure likely to interfere with his/her ability to operate a commercial motor vehicle safely;

(7) Has no established medical history or clinical diagnosis of rheumatic, arthritic, orthopedic, muscular, neuromuscular, or vascular disease which interferes with his/her ability to control and operate a commercial motor vehicle safely;

(8) Has no established medical history or clinical diagnosis of epilepsy or any other condition which is likely to cause loss of

consciousness or any loss of ability to control a commercial motor vehicle;

(9) Has no mental, nervous, organic, or functional disease or psychiatric disorder likely to interfere with his/her ability to drive a commercial motor vehicle safely;

(10) Has distant visual acuity of at least 20/40 (Snellen) in each eye without corrective lenses or visual acuity separately corrected to 20/40 (Snellen) or better with corrective lenses, distant binocular acuity of at least 20/40 (Snellen) in both eyes with or without corrective lenses, field of vision of at least 70° in the horizontal meridian in each eye, and the ability to recognize the colors of traffic signals and devices showing standard red, green, and amber;

(11) First perceives a forced whispered voice in the better ear at not less than 5 feet with or without the use of a hearing aid or, if tested by use of an audiometric device, does not have an average hearing loss in the better ear greater than 40 decibels at 500 Hz, 1,000 Hz, and 2,000 Hz with or without a hearing aid when the audiometric device is calibrated to American National Standard (formerly ASA Standard) Z24.5-1951;

(12)(i) Does not use a controlled substance identified in 21 CFR 1308.11 *Schedule I,* and amphetamine, a narcotic, or any other habit-forming drug.

(ii) *Exception.* A driver may use such a substance or drug, if the substance or drug is prescribed by a licensed medical practitioner who:

(A) Is familiar with the driver's medical history and assigned duties; and

(B) Has advised the driver that the prescibed substance or drug will not adversely affect the driver's ability to safely operate a commercial motor vehicle; and

(13) Has no current clinical diagnosis of alcoholism.

§391.43 Medical examination; certificate of physical examination.

(a) Except as provided in paragraph (b) of this section, the medical examination shall be performed by a licensed medical examiner as defined in §390.5 of this subchapter.

(b) A licensed optometrist may perform so much of the medical examination as pertains to visual acuity, field of vision, and the ability to recognize colors as specified in paragraph (10) of §391.41 (b).

(c) Medical examiners shall:

(1) Be knowledgeable of the specific physical and mental demands associated with operating a commercial motor vehicle and the requirements of this subpart, including the medical advisory criteria prepared by the FMCSA as guidelines to aid the medical examiner in making the qualification determination; and

(2) Be proficient in the use of and use the medical protocols necessary to adequately perform the medical examination required by this section.

(d) . . .

(e) Any driver operating under a limited exemption authorized by §391.64 shall furnish the medical examiner with a copy of the annual medical findings of the endocrinologist, ophthalmologist or optometrist, as required under that section. If the medical examiner finds the driver qualified under the limited exemption in §391.64, such fact shall be noted on the Medical Examiner's Certificate.

(f) The medical examination shall be performed, and its results shall be recorded, substantially in accordance with the following instructions and examination form. Existing forms may be used until current printed supplies are depleted or until November 6, 2001. Whichever occurs first.

INSTRUCTIONS FOR PERFORMING AND RECORDING PHYSICAL EXAMINATIONS

The medical examiner must be familiar with 49 CFR 391.41, Physical qualifications for drivers, and should review these instructions before performing the physical examination. Answer each question "yes" or "no" and record numerical readings where indicated on the physical examination form.

The medical examiner must be aware of the rigorous physical, mental, and emotional demands placed on the driver of a commercial motor vehicle. In the interest of public safety, the medical examiner is required to certify that the driver does not have any physical, mental, or organic condition that might affect the driver's ability to operate a commercial motor vehicle safely.

General information. The purpose of this history and physical examination is to detect the presence of physical, mental, or organic conditions of such a character and extent as to affect the driver's ability to operate a commercial motor vehicle safely. The examination should be conducted carefully and should at least include all of the information requested in the following form. History of certain conditions may be cause for rejection. Indicate the need for further testing and/or require evaluation by a specialist. Conditions may be recorded which do not, because of their character or degree, indicate that certification of physical fitness should be denied. However, these conditions should be discussed with the driver and he/she should be advised to take the necessary steps to insure correction, particularly of those conditions which, if neglected, might affect the driver's ability to drive safely.

General appearance and development. Note marked overweight. Note any postural defect, perceptible limp, tremor, or other conditions that might be caused by alcoholism, thyroid intoxication or other illnesses.

Head-eyes. When other than the Snellen chart is used, the results of such test must be expressed in values comparable to the standard Snellen test. If the driver wears corrective lenses for driving, these should be worn while driver's visual acuity is being tested. If contact lenses are worn, there should be sufficient evidence of good tolerance of and adaptation to their use. Indicate the driver's need to wear corrective lenses to meet the vision standard on the Medical Examiner's Certificate by checking the box, "Qualified only when wearing corrective lenses." In recording distance vision use 20 feet as normal. Report all vision as a fraction with 20 as the numerator and the smallest type read at 20 feet as the denominator. Monocular drivers are not qualified to operate commercial motor vehicles in interstate commerce.

Ears. Note evidence of any ear disease, symptoms of aural vertigo, or Meniere's Syndrome. When recording hearing, record distance from patient at which a forced whispered voice can first be heard. For the whispered voice test, the individual should be stationed at least 5 feet from the examiner with the ear being tested turned toward the examiner. The other ear is covered. Using the breath which remains after a normal expiration, the examiner whispers words or random numbers such as 66, 18, 23, etc. The examiner should not use only sibilants (s-sounding test materials). The opposite ear should be tested in the same manner. If the individual fails the whispered voice test, the audiometric test should be administered. For the audiometric test, record decibel loss at 500 Hz, 1,000 Hz, and 2,000 Hz. Average the decibel loss at 500 Hz, 1,000 Hz and 2,000 Hz and record as described on the form. If the individual fails the audiometric test and the whispered voice test has not been administered, the whispered voice test should be performed to determine if the standard applicable to that test can be met.

Throat. Note any irremediable deformities likely to interfere with breathing or swallowing.

Heart. Note murmurs and arrhythmias, and any history of an enlarged heart, congestive heart failure, or cardiovascular disease that is accompanied by syncope, dyspnea, or collapse. Indicate onset date, diagnosis, medication, and any current limitation. An electrocardiogram is required when findings so indicate.

Blood pressure (BP). If a driver has hypertension and/or is being medicated for hypertension, he or she should be recertified more frequently. An individual diagnosed with mild hypertension (initial BP is greater than 160/90 but below 181/105) should be certified for one 3-month period and should be recertified on an annual basis thereafter if his or her BP is reduced. An individual diagnosed with moderate to severe hypertension (initial BP is greater than 180/104) should not be certified until the BP has been reduced to the mild range (below 181/105). At that time, a 3-month certification can be issued. Once the driver has reduced his or her BP to below 161/91, he or she should be recertified every 6 months thereafter.

Lungs. Note abnormal chest wall expansion, respiratory rate, breath sounds including wheezes or alveolar rales, impaired respiratory function, dyspnea, or cyanosis. Abnormal finds on physical exam may require further testing such as pulmonary tests and/or x-ray of chest.

Abdomen and Viscera. Note enlarged liver, enlarged spleen, abnormal masses, bruits, hernia, and significant abdominal wall muscle weakness and tenderness. If the diagnosis suggests that the condition might interfere with the control and safe operation of a commercial motor vehicle, further testing and evaluation is required.

Genital-urinary and rectal examination. A urinalysis is required. Protein, blood or sugar in the urine may be an indication for further testing to rule out any underlying medical problems. Note hernias. A condition causing discomfort should be evaluated to determine the extent to which the condition might interfere with the control and safe operation of a commercial motor vehicle.

Neurological. Note impaired equilibrium, coordination, or speech pattern; paresthesia; asymmetric deep tendon reflexes; sensory or positional abnormalities; abnormal patellar and Babinski's reflexes; ataxia. Abnormal neurological responses may be an indication for further testing to rule out an underlying medical condition. Any neurological condition should be evaluated for the nature and severity of the condition, the degree of limitation present, the likelihood of progressive limitation, and the potential for sudden incapacitation. In instances where the medical examiner has determined that more frequent monitoring of a condition is appropriate, a certificate for a shorter period should be issued.

Spine, musculoskeletal. Previous surgery, deformities, limitation of motion, and tenderness should be noted. Findings may indicate additional testing and evaluation should be conducted.

Extremities. Carefully examine upper and lower extremities and note any loss or impairment of leg, foot, toe, arm, hand, or finger. Note any deformities, atrophy, paralysis, partial paralysis, clubbing, edema, or hypotonia. If a hand or finger deformity exists, determine whether prehension and power grasp are sufficient to enable the driver to maintain steering wheel grip and to control other vehicle equipment during routine and emergency driving operations. If a foot or leg deformity exists, determine whether sufficient mobility and strength exist to enable the driver to operate pedals properly. In the case of any loss or impairment to an extremity which may interfere with the driver's ability to operate a commercial motor vehicle safely, the medical examiner should state on the medical certificate "medically unqualified unless accompanied by a Skill Performance Evaluation Certificate." The driver must then apply to the Field Service

Center of the FMCSA, for the State in which the driver has legal residence, for a Skill Performance Evaluation Certificate under §391.49.

Laboratory and Other Testing. Other test(s) may be indicated based upon the medical history or findings of the physical examination.

Diabetes. If insulin is necessary to control a diabetic driver's condition, the driver is not qualified to operate a commercial motor vehicle in interstate commerce. If mild diabetes is present and it is controlled by use of an oral hypoglycemic drug and/or diet and exercise, it should not be considered disqualifying. However, the driver must remain under adequate medical supervision.

Upon completion of the examination, the medical examiner must date and sign the form, provide his/her full name, office address and telephone number. The completed medical examination form shall be retained on file at the office of the medical examiner.

Medical Examination Report

FOR COMMERCIAL DRIVER FITNESS DETERMINATION

1. DRIVER'S INFORMATION   Driver completes this section.

Driver's Name (Last, First, Middle)

Social Security No.

Birthdate M/D/Y

Age

Sex
☐ M
☐ F

New certification
☐ Recertification
☐ Follow Up

Date of Exam

License Class
☐ A ☐ C
☐ B ☐ D
☐ Other

State of Issue

Address

City, State, Zip Code

Work Tel: ( )
Home Tel: ( )

Driver License No.

2. HEALTH HISTORY   Driver completes this section, but medical examiner is encouraged to discuss with driver.

Yes No

☐ ☐ Any illness or injury in last 5 years?
☐ ☐ Head/Brain injuries, disorders or illnesses
☐ ☐ Seizures, epilepsy
    ☐ medication
☐ ☐ Eye disorders or impaired vision (except corrective lenses)
☐ ☐ Ear disorders, loss of hearing or balance
☐ ☐ Heart disease or heart attack; other cardiovascular condition
    ☐ medication
☐ ☐ Heart surgery (valve replacement/bypass, angioplasty, pacemaker)
☐ ☐ High blood pressure ☐ medication
☐ ☐ Muscular disease
☐ ☐ Shortness of breath

☐ ☐ Lung disease, emphysema, asthma, chronic bronchitis
☐ ☐ Kidney disease, dialysis
☐ ☐ Liver disease
☐ ☐ Digestive problems
☐ ☐ Diabetes or elevated blood sugar controlled by:
    ☐ diet
    ☐ pills
    ☐ insulin
☐ ☐ Nervous or psychiatric disorders, e.g., severe depression
☐ ☐ Loss of, or altered consciousness

Yes No

☐ ☐ Fainting, dizziness
☐ ☐ Sleep disorders, pauses in breathing while asleep, daytime sleepiness, loud snoring
☐ ☐ Stroke or paralysis
☐ ☐ Missing or impaired hand, arm, foot, leg, finger, toe
☐ ☐ Spinal injury or disease
☐ ☐ Chronic low back pain
☐ ☐ Regular, frequent alcohol use
☐ ☐ Narcotic or habit forming drug use

For any YES answer, indicate onset date, diagnosis, treating physician's name and address, and any current limitation. List all medications (including over-the-counter medications) used regularly or recently.

I certify that the above information is complete and true. I understand that inaccurate, false or missing information may invalidate the examination and my Medical Examiner's Certificate.

_____
Driver's Signature

_____
Date

Medical Examiners Comments on Health History (The medical examiner must review and discuss with the driver any "yes" answers and potential hazards of medications, including over-the-counter medications, while driving.)

-347-

TESTING (Medical Examiner completes Section 3 through 7)

3. VISION

Standard: At least 20/40 acuity (Snellen) in each eye with or without correction. At least 70° peripheral in horizontal meridian measured in each eye.
The use of corrective lenses should be noted on the Medical Examiner's Certificate.

INSTRUCTIONS: *When other than the Snellen chart is used, give test results in Snellen-comparable values. In recording distance vision, use 20 feet as normal. Report visual acuity as a ratio with 20 as numerator and the smallest type read at 20 feet as denominator. If the applicant wears corrective lenses, these should be worn while visual acuity is being tested. If the driver habitually wears contact lenses, or intends to do so while driving, sufficient evidence of good tolerance and adaptation to their use must be obvious. Monocular drivers are not qualified.*

Numerical readings must be provided.

ACUITY	UNCORRECTED	CORRECTED	HORIZONTAL FIELD OF VISION
Right Eye	20/	20/	Right Eye	°
Left Eye	20/	20/	Left Eye	°
Both Eyes	20/	20/	

Applicant can recognize and distinguish among traffic control signals and devices showing standard red, green, and amber colors?   ☐ Yes   ☐ No

Applicant meets visual acuity requirement only when wearing: ☐ Corrective Lenses

Monocular Vision: ☐ Yes ☐ No

Complete next line only if vision testing is done by an ophthalmologist or optometrist

Date of Examination _____   Name of Ophthalmologist or Optometrist (print) _____   Tel No: _____   License No./State of Issue _____   Signature _____

4. HEARING

Standard: a) Must first perceive forced whispered voice > 5 ft., with or without hearing aid, or **b)** average hearing loss in better ear < 40 dB
☐ Check if hearing aid used for tests.   ☐ Check if hearing aid required to meet standard.

INSTRUCTIONS: *To convert audiometric test results from ISO to ANSI, -14 dB from ISO for 500 Hz, -10 dB for 1,000 Hz, -8.5 dB for 2,000 Hz. To average, add the readings for 3 frequencies tested and divide by 3.*

Numerical readings must be recorded.

a) Record distance from individual at which forced whispered voice can first be heard.

	Right Ear	Left Ear	Feet

b) If audiometer is used, record hearing loss in decibels. (acc. to ANSI Z24.5-1951)

	Right Ear			Left Ear		
	500 Hz	1000 Hz	2000 Hz	500 Hz	1000 Hz	2000 Hz
			Average:			Average:

5. BLOOD PRESSURE / PULSE RATE

Numerical readings must be recorded.

Blood Pressure	Systolic	Diastolic
Pulse Rate	☐ Regular ☐ Irregular	

Driver qualified if ≤ 160/90 on initial exam.

GUIDELINES FOR BLOOD PRESSURE EVALUATION

On initial exam	Within 3 months	Certify
If 161-180 and/or 91-104, Qualify 3 mos. only	≤ 160 and/or 90, Qualify for 1 yr. Document Rx & control the 3rd month	Annually if acceptable BP is maintained
If > 180 and/or 104, not qualified until reduced to ≤ 181/105. Then qualify for 3 mos. only.	If < 160 and/or 90, qualify for 6 mos. Document Rx & control the 3rd month	Biannually

Medical examiner should take at least 2 readings to confirm blood pressure.

6. LABORATORY AND OTHER TEST FINDINGS

Numerical readings must be recorded.

Urinalysis is required. Protein, blood or sugar in the urine may be an indication for further testing to rule out any underlying medical problem.

URINE SPECIMEN	Sp. GR.	PROTEIN	BLOOD	SUGAR

Other Testing (Describe and record)

7. PHYSICAL EXAMINATION

Height: _____ (in.) Weight: _____ (lbs)

The presence of a certain condition may not necessarily disqualify a driver, particularly if the condition is controlled adequately, is not likely to worsen or is readily amenable to treatment. Even if a condition does not disqualify a driver, the medical examiner may consider defining the driver temporarily. Also, the driver should be advised to take the necessary steps to correct the condition as soon as possible particularly if the condition, if neglected, could result in more serious illness that might affect driving.

Check YES if there are any abnormalities. Check NO if the body system is normal. Discuss any YES answers in detail in the space below, and indicate what it would affect the driver's ability to operate a commercial motor vehicle safely. Enter applicable item number before each comment. If organic disease is present, note that it has been compensated for.

See Instructions To The Medical Examiner for guidance.

BODY SYSTEM	CHECK FOR:	YES*	NO	BODY SYSTEM	CHECK FOR:	YES*	NO
1. General Appearance	Marked overweight, tremor, signs of alcoholism, problem drinking, or drug abuse.			7. Abdomen and Viscera	Enlarged liver, enlarged spleen, masses, bruits, hernia, significant abdominal wall muscle weakness.		
2. Eyes	Pupillary equality, reaction to light, accommodation, ocular motility, ocular muscle imbalance, extraocular movement, nystagmus, exophthalmos, strabismus uncorrected by corrective lenses, retinopathy, cataracts, aphakia, glaucoma, macular degeneration.			8. Vascular system	Abnormal pulse and amplitude, carotid or arterial bruits, varicose veins.		
				9. Genito-urinary system.	Hernias.		
3. Ears	Middle ear disease, occlusion of external canal, perforated eardrums.			10. Extremities - Limb impaired. Driver may be subject to SPE certificate if otherwise qualified.	Loss or impairment of leg, foot, toe, arm, hand, finger. Perceptible limp, deformities, atrophy, weakness, paralysis, clubbing, edema, hypotonia. Insufficient grasp and prehension in upper limb to maintain steering wheel grip. Insufficient mobility and strength in lower limb to operate pedals properly.		
4. Mouth and Throat	Irremediable deformities likely to interfere with breathing or swallowing.						
5. Heart	Murmurs, extra sounds, enlarged heart, pacemaker			11. Spine, other musculoskeletal	Previous surgery, deformities, limitation of motion, tenderness		
6. Lungs and chest, not including breast examination.	Abnormal chest wall expansion, abnormal respiratory rate, abnormal breath sounds including wheezes or alveolar rales, impaired respiratory function, dyspnea, cyanosis. Abnormal findings on physical exam may require further testing such as pulmonary tests and/or x-ray of chest.			12. Neurological	Impaired equilibrium, coordination or speech pattern; paresthesias, asymmetric deep tendon reflexes, sensory or positional abnormalities, abnormal patellar and Babinski's reflexes, ataxia.		

* COMMENTS: _____

_____

Meets certification status here. See Instructions to the Medical Examiner for guidance.

☐ Meets standards in 49 CFR 391.41; qualifies for 2 year certificate

☐ Does not meet standards

☐ Meets standards, but periodic evaluation required.
    Due to _____ driver qualified only for:
    ☐ 3 months   ☐ 1 year
    ☐ 6 months   ☐ Other

☐ ↑ Temporarily disqualified due to (condition or medication): _____

Return to medical examiner's office for follow up on _____

☐ Wearing corrective lenses
☐ Wearing hearing aid
☐ Accompanied by a _____ waiver/exemption
☐ Skill Performance Evaluation (SPE) Certificate
☐ Driving within an exempt intracity zone.
☐ Qualified by operation of 49 CFR 391.64

Medical Examiner's Signature

Medical Examiner's Name (print)

Address _____

Telephone Number _____

If meets standards, complete a Medical Examiner's Certificate according to 49 CFR 391.43(h). (Driver must carry certificate when operating a commercial vehicle.)

49 CFR 391.41 Physical Qualifications for Drivers

THE DRIVER'S ROLE

Responsibilities, work schedules, physical and emotional demands, and lifestyles among commercial drivers vary by the type of driving that they do. Some of the main types of drivers include the following: turn around or short relay (drivers return to their home base each evening), long relay (drivers drive 8-10 hours and then have an 8-hour off-duty period), straight through haul (cross country drivers), and team drivers (drivers share the driving by alternating their driving and rest periods).

The following factors may be involved in a driver's performance of duties, abrupt schedule changes and rotating work schedules, which may result in irregular sleep patterns and a driver beginning a trip in a fatigued condition, long hours, much physical and mental exertion, irregularity in work, rest, and eating patterns, adverse road, weather and traffic conditions, which may cause delays and lead to hurriedly loading or unloading cargo in order to compensate for the lost time, and environmental conditions such as excessive vibration, noise, and extremes in temperature. Transporting passengers or hazardous materials may add to the demands on the commercial driver.

There may be duties in addition to the driving task for which a driver is responsible and much to be fit. Some of these responsibilities are: coupling and uncoupling trailer(s) from the tractor, loading and unloading trailer(s) (sometimes a driver may lift a heavy load or unload as much as 50,000 lbs. of freight after sitting for a long period of time without any stretching period), inspecting the operating condition of tractor and trailer(s) before, during, and after delivery of cargo, lifting, installing, and removing heavy tire chains, and, lifting heavy tarpaulins to cover open top trailers. The above tasks demand agility, the ability to bend and stoop, the ability to maintain a crouching position to inspect the underside of the vehicle, frequent entering and exiting of the cab, and the ability to climb ladders on the tractor and/or trailer(s).

In addition, a driver must have the perceptual skills to monitor a sometimes complex driving situation, the judgment skills to make quick decisions, when necessary, and the manipulative skills to control an oversize steering wheel, shift gears using a manual transmission, and maneuver a vehicle in crowded areas.

§ 391.41 PHYSICAL QUALIFICATIONS FOR DRIVERS

(a) A person shall not drive a commercial motor vehicle unless he is physically qualified to do so and, except as provided in §391.67, has on his person the original, or a photographic copy, of a medical examiner's certificate that he is physically qualified to drive a commercial motor vehicle.

(b) A person is physically qualified to drive a motor vehicle if that person -

(1) Has no loss of a foot, a leg, a hand, or an arm, or has been granted a Skill Performance Evaluation (SPE) Certificate (formerly Limb Waiver Program) pursuant to §391.49.

(2) Has no impairment of: (i) A hand or finger which interferes with prehension or power grasping; or (ii) An arm, foot, or leg which interferes with the ability to perform normal tasks associated with operating a commercial motor vehicle; or any other significant limb defect or limitation which interferes with the ability to perform normal tasks associated with operating a commercial motor vehicle; or has been granted a SPE Certificate pursuant to §391.49.

(3) Has no current clinical diagnosis of diabetes mellitus currently requiring insulin for control;

(4) Has no current clinical diagnosis of myocardial infarction, angina pectoris, coronary insufficiency, thrombosis, or any other cardiovascular disease of a variety known to be accompanied by syncope, dyspnea, collapse, or congestive cardiac failure.

(5) Has no current clinical diagnosis of a respiratory dysfunction likely to interfere with his ability to control and drive a commercial motor vehicle safely;

(6) Has no current clinical diagnosis of high blood pressure likely to interfere with his ability to operate a commercial motor vehicle safely.

(7) Has no established medical history or clinical diagnosis of rheumatic, arthritic, orthopedic, muscular, neuromuscular, or vascular disease which interferes with his ability to control and operate a commercial motor vehicle safely;

(8) Has no established medical history or clinical diagnosis of epilepsy or any other condition which is likely to cause loss of consciousness or any loss of ability to control a commercial motor vehicle;

(9) Has no mental, nervous, organic, or functional disease or psychiatric disorder likely to interfere with his ability to drive a commercial motor vehicle safely;

(10) Has distant visual acuity of at least 20/40 (Snellen) in each eye without corrective lenses or visual acuity separately corrected to 20/40 (Snellen) or better with corrective lenses, distant binocular acuity of at least 20/40 (Snellen) in both eyes with or without corrective lenses, field of vision of at least 70 degrees in the horizontal meridian in each eye, and the ability to recognize the colors of traffic signals and devices showing standard red, green and amber;

(11) First perceives a forced whispered voice in the better ear at not less than 5 feet with or without the use of a hearing aid, or, if tested by use of an audiometric device, does not have an average hearing loss in the better ear greater than 40 decibels at 500 Hz, 1,000 Hz and 2,000 Hz with or without a hearing aid when the audiometric device is calibrated to American National Standard (formerly ASA Standard) Z24.5-1951;

(12)(i) Does not use a controlled substance identified in 21 CFR 1308.11 Schedule 1, an amphetamine, a narcotic, or any other habit-forming drug, (ii) Exception: A driver may use such a substance or drug, if the substance or drug is prescribed by a licensed medical practitioner who: (A) Is familiar with the driver's medical history and assigned duties; and (B) Has advised the driver that the prescribed substance or drug will not adversely affect the driver's ability to safely operate a commercial motor vehicle; and

(13) Has no current clinical diagnosis of alcoholism.

INSTRUCTIONS TO THE MEDICAL EXAMINER

Federal Motor Carrier Safety Regulations
Advisory Criteria -

General Information

The purpose of this examination is to determine a driver's physical qualification to operate a commercial motor vehicle (CMV) in interstate commerce according to the requirements in 49 CFR 391.41-49. Therefore, the medical examiner must be knowledgeable of these requirements and guidelines developed by the FMCSA to assist the medical examiner in making a determination. Not only should the medical examiner be familiar with these driver's responsibilities and work environment and as referred to the section on the form. The Driver's Role.

In addition to reviewing the Health History section with the driver and conducting the physical examination, the medical examiner should discuss common precautions and over-the-counter medications relative to the side effects and hazards of their medications while driving. Educate the driver to most warning signs or indicators of certain conditions may be the cause for rejection, particularly if required by regulation, or may indicate the need for additional laboratory tests or more attention or examination by a medical specialist. These decisions are usually made by the medical examiner in light of the driver's job responsibilities, work schedule and potential for the condition to render the driver unsafe.

Medical conditions should be recorded even if they are not cause for denial, and they should be discussed with the driver to ensure awareness of the condition. These matters may especially needed when a condition, if neglected, could develop into a serious illness that could affect driving.

Since the medical examiner determines that the driver is fit to drive and or also able to perform non-driving responsibilities as may be required, the medical examiner signs the medical certificate must be dated. Under current regulations, the certificate is valid for two years, unless there has a medical condition that does not warrant certification for the longer period. More frequent monitoring. In such situations, the medical certificate should be issued for a shorter length of time. The physical examination form provided here is recommended for use as included by the attached form. Contact the FMCSA at (202) 366-1790 for further information (a vision exemption, qualifying drivers under 49 CFR 391.64, etc.).

Interpretation of Medical Standards

Since the issuance of the regulations for physical qualifications of commercial drivers, the Federal Motor Carrier Safety Administration (FMCSA) has published recommendations called advisory criteria to help medical examiners in determining whether a driver meets the physical qualifications for commercial driving. These recommendations have been condensed and incorporated into the physical qualification. It is directly relevant to the physical examination and (2) is not already included in the medical examination form. These specific regulations is printed in italics and the reference by section is highlighted.

Loss of Limb:
§391.41(b)(1)

A person is physically qualified to drive a commercial motor vehicle if that person:

Has no loss of a foot, leg, hand or an arm, or has been granted a Skill Performance Evaluation (SPE) Certificate pursuant to Section 391.49

Limb Impairment:
§391.41(b)(2)

A person is physically qualified to drive a commercial motor vehicle if that person:

Has no impairment of: (i) A hand or finger which interferes with prehension or power grasping; or (ii) An arm, foot, or leg which interferes with the ability to perform normal tasks associated with operating a commercial motor vehicle; or (iii) Any other significant limb defect or limitation which interferes with the ability to perform normal tasks associated with operating a commercial motor vehicle; or (iv) Has been granted a Skill Performance Evaluation Certificate pursuant to Section 391.49.

A person who suffers loss of a foot, leg, hand or arm or whose limb impairment in any way interferes with the safe performance of normal tasks associated with operating a commercial motor vehicle is subject to the Skill Performance Evaluation (SPE) Certification Program pursuant to section 391.49, assuming the person is otherwise qualified.

With the advancement of technology, medical aids and equipment modifications have been developed to compensate for certain disabilities. The SPE Certification Program (formerly the Limb Waiver Program) was designed to allow persons with the loss of a foot or arm or with functional impairment to qualify under the Federal Motor Carrier Safety Regulations (FMCSR) by use of prosthetic devices or equipment modifications which enable them to safely operate a commercial motor vehicle. Since there are no medical aids equivalent to the original body or limb, certain devices are present, and thus restrictions may be included on individual SPE certificates when a State Director for the FMCSA determines they are necessary to be consistent with safety and public welfare.

If the driver is otherwise medically qualified (391.41(b)(3) through (13)), the medical examiner must check on the medical certificate that the driver is qualified only if accompanied by a SPE certificate. The driver and the employing motor carrier are subject to appropriate penalty if the driver operates a motor vehicle in interstate commerce without a current SPE certificate for further physical disability.

Diabetes
§391.41(b)(3)

A person is physically qualified to drive a commercial motor vehicle if that person:

Has no established medical history or clinical diagnosis of diabetes mellitus currently requiring insulin for control

Diabetes mellitus is a disease which, on occasion, can result in a loss of consciousness or disorientation in time and space. Individuals who require insulin for control have conditions which can get out of control by the use of too much or too little insulin, or food intake not consistent with the insulin dosage. Incapacitation may occur from symptoms of hypoglycemic or hyperglycemic reactions (drowsiness, semiconsciousness, diabetic coma or insulin shock).

The administration of insulin is, within itself, a complicated process requiring insulin, syringe, needle, alcohol sponge and a sterile technique. Factors related to long-haul commercial motor vehicle operations, such as fatigue, lack of sleep, poor diet, emotional conditions, stress, and concomitant illness, compound the diabetic problem. Thus, because of these inherent dangers, the FMCSA has consistently held that a diabetic who uses insulin for control does not meet the minimum physical requirements of the FMCSRs.

Hypoglycemic drugs, taken orally, are sometimes prescribed for diabetic individuals to help stimulate natural body production of insulin. If the condition can be controlled by the use of oral medication and diet, then an individual may be qualified under the present rule.

(See Conference Report on Diabetes Disorders and Commercial Drivers and Insulin-Using Commercial Motor Vehicle Drivers at

http://www.fmcsa.dot.gov/rulesregs/medreports.htm)

Cardiovascular Condition
§391.41(b)(4)

A person is physically qualified to drive a commercial motor vehicle if that person:

Has no current clinical diagnosis of myocardial infarction, angina pectoris, coronary insufficiency, thrombosis or any other cardiovascular disease of a variety known to be accompanied by syncope, dyspnea, collapse or congestive cardiac failure.

The term "has no current clinical diagnosis of" is specifically designed to encompass "a clinical diagnosis of" (1) a current cardiovascular condition, or (2) a cardiovascular condition which has not fully stabilized regardless of the time limit. The term "known to be accompanied by" is defined to include: a clinical diagnosis of a cardiovascular disease (1) which is accompanied by symptoms of syncope, dyspnea, collapse or congestive cardiac failure; and/or (2) which is likely to cause vehicle or cardiovascular syncope.

It is the intent of the FMCSRs to render unqualified a driver who has a current cardiovascular disease which is accompanied by above indications or episodes of syncope, dyspnea, collapse or congestive cardiac failure. The cardiovascular examination should assess the nature and severity of an individual's condition will likely cause symptoms of cardiovascular insufficiency, is an individual hazard and qualification rests with the medical examiner and the motor carrier. In those cases where there is an occurrence of cardiovascular insufficiency myocardial infarction, angina pectoris, etc., it is suggested before a driver is certified that he or she have a normal resting and stress electrocardiogram (ECG), no residual complications and no physical limitations, and is taking no medication likely to interfere with safe driving.

Coronary artery bypass surgery and pacemaker implantation are remedial procedures and thus, not unqualifying. Coumadin is a medical treatment which can improve the health and safety of the driver and should not, by its use, medically disqualify the commercial driver. The emphasis should be on the underlying medical condition(s) which require treatment and the general health of the driver. The FMCSA should be contacted at (202) 366-1790 for additional recommendations regarding the physical qualification of drivers on coumadin.

(See Conference on Cardiac Disorders and Commercial Drivers at http://www.fmcsa.dot.gov/rulesregs/medreports.htm)

Respiratory Dysfunction
§ 391.41(b)(5)

A person is physically qualified to drive a commercial motor vehicle if that person:

Has no established medical history or clinical diagnosis of a respiratory dysfunction likely to interfere with ability to control and drive a commercial motor vehicle safely.

Since a driver must be alert at all times, any change in his or her mental state is in direct conflict with highway safety. Even the slightest impairment in respiratory function under emergency conditions (when greater oxygen supply is necessary) may result in incapacitation, including a serious degree of mental confusion or collapse while driving.

There are many conditions that interfere with oxygen exchange and may result in incapacitation, including emphysema, chronic asthma, carcinoma, tuberculosis, chronic bronchitis and sleep apnea. If the medical examiner detects a respiratory dysfunction, that in any way is likely to interfere with the driver's ability to safely control and drive a commercial motor vehicle, the driver must be referred to a specialist for further evaluation and therapy. Anticoagulation therapy for deep venous thrombosis and/or pulmonary thromboembolism is not unqualifying once optimum dose is achieved, provided lower extremity venous examinations remain normal and the treating physician gives a favorable recommendation.

(See Conference on Pulmonary/Respiratory Disorders and Commercial Drivers at http://www.fmcsa.dot.gov/rulesregs/medreports.htm)

Hypertension
§ 391.41(b)(6)

A person is physically qualified to drive a commercial motor vehicle if that person:

Has no current clinical diagnosis of high blood pressure likely to interfere with ability to operate a commercial motor vehicle safely.

Hypertension alone is unlikely to cause sudden collapse; however, the likelihood increases when target organ damage, particularly coronary vascular disease, is present. This regulatory criteria is based on FMCSA's Cardiac Conference recommendations, which used the report of the 1994 Joint National Committee on Detection, Evaluation, and Treatment of High Blood Pressure.

A blood pressure of 161-180 diastolic is considered mild hypertension, and the driver is not unqualified while being treated. If the driver is given a 3-month certificate and at the time of renewal has a blood pressure of less than or equal to 140/90, he or she may be recertified for one year thereafter. The driver with a blood pressure of 161-180/101-104 diastolic is considered to have stage 2 hypertension and is likely to qualify unqualified. The driver should be given a one-time certificate of 3-month duration to reduce his or her blood pressure to less than or equal to 140/90. At this time the physician may issue a one-year certificate if it is only valid for that 3-month period. If the driver is subsequently found qualified with a blood pressure less than or equal to 140/90, the certifying physician may issue certificate for a 1-year period, but should confirm blood pressure control in the third month of that 1-year period. The individual should be certified annually thereafter. The expiration date must be stated on the medical certificate.

A blood pressure of greater than 180 systolic and/or greater than 104 diastolic is considered unfit to work. The driver may not be qualified, even temporarily, until his or her blood pressure has been reduced to less than 181/105. The examining physician may temporarily certify the individual once the individual should be certified for only one 3-month period. For blood pressure greater than 180 and/or 104, documentation of continued control should be made every 6 months. The individual should be certified biannually if his or her blood pressure is reduced to less than 181/105. The expiration date must be stated on the medical certificate.

Commercial drivers who present for certification with normal blood pressures but who are taking medications for hypertension should be certified on the same basis as individuals who present with blood pressures in the mild or moderate to severe range. Annual recertification is recommended if the medical examiner is unable to establish that the blood pressure at the time of diagnosis.

As elevated blood pressure finding should be confirmed by at least two subsequent measurements on different days. Inquiry should be completed of the past use of alcohol, the use of drugs, and overweight, use of alcohol. An electrocardiogram (ECG) lipid profile, serum glucose, cholesterol, HDL cholesterol, creatinine and potassium, should be made. An echocardiogram and chest x-ray are desirable in subjects with moderate or severe hypertension.

Since the presence of target damage increases the risk of sudden collapse, group 3 or 4 hypertensive retinopathy, left ventricular or hypertrophy by echocardiography or ECG (echocardiography or ECG by Estes criteria, evidence of greater than 2.5 warrants the driver being found unqualified to operate a commercial motor vehicle as the diagnosis constitutes serious hazard.

Treatment includes nonpharmacologic and pharmacologic modalities as well as correcting to reduce other risk factors. Most antihypertensive medications also have side effects, the importance of which must be judged on an individual basis. Individuals must be alerted to the hazards of these medications while driving. Side effects of somnolence or syncope are particularly undesirable in commercial drivers.

A commercial driver who has normal blood pressure 3 or more months after a successful operation for pheochromocytoma, primary aldosteronism (unless bilateral adrenalectomy has been performed), renovascular disease, or unilateral renal parenchymal disease, and who shows no evidence of target organ may be qualified. Hypertension that persists despite surgical intervention with no target organ disease should be evaluated and treated following the guidelines set forth above.

(See Conference on Cardiac Disorders and Commercial Drivers at http://www.fmcsa.dot.gov/rulesregs/medreports.htm)

Rheumatic, Arthritic, Orthopedic, Muscular, Neuromuscular or Vascular Disease
§ 391.41(b)(7)

A person is physically qualified to drive a commercial motor vehicle if that person:

Has no established medical history or clinical diagnosis of rheumatic, arthritic, orthopedic, muscular, neuromuscular or vascular disease which interferes with ability to control and operate a commercial motor vehicle safely.

Certain diseases are known to have acute episodes of transient muscle weakness, poor muscular coordination (ataxia), abnormal sensations (paresthesia), decreased muscular tone (hypotonia), visual disturbances and pain which may be suddenly incapacitating. With each recurring episode, these symptoms may become more pronounced and remain for longer periods of time. Other diseases have more insidious onsets and display symptoms of muscle wasting (atrophy), swelling and paralysis which may eventually incapacitate a person but may restrict his/her movements and eventually interfere with the ability to operate a motor vehicle. In many instances these diseases are degenerative in nature or may result in deterioration of the involved area.

Once the individual has been diagnosed as having a rheumatic, arthritic, orthopedic, muscular, neuromuscular or vascular

vascular disease, also he/she has an established history of that disease. They are rare, when examining an individual should consider the following: (1) the nature and severity of the individual's condition (such as sensory loss or loss of strength); (2) the degree of limitation present (such as range of motion); (3) the likelihood of progressive limitation; and (4) the likelihood of sudden incapacitation. If severe functional impairments exist, the driver does not qualify. In cases where more frequent monitoring is required, a certificate for a shorter time period may be issued.
(See Conference on Neurological Disorders and Commercial Drivers at
http://www.fmcsa.dot.gov/rulesregs/medreports.htm)

Epilepsy
§391.41(b)(8)
A person is physically qualified to drive a commercial motor vehicle if that person:
Has an established medical history or clinical diagnosis of epilepsy or any other condition which is likely to cause loss of consciousness or any loss of ability to control a motor vehicle

Epilepsy is a chronic functional disease characterized by seizures or episodes that occur without warning, resulting in loss of voluntary control which may lead to loss of consciousness and/or seizures. Therefore, the following individuals cannot be qualified: (1) a driver who has a medical history of epilepsy; (2) a driver who has a current clinical diagnosis of epilepsy; or (3) a driver who is taking antiseizure medications.

In those individual cases where a driver has had a sudden episode of a nonepileptic seizure or loss of consciousness of unknown cause which did not require antiseizure medication, the decision as to whether that person's condition will likely cause loss of consciousness or loss of ability to control a motor vehicle is made on an individual basis by the medical examiner in consultation with the treating physician. Before certification is considered, it is suggested that a 6-month waiting period, then the time of the episode. Following the waiting period, it is suggested that the individual have a complete neurological examination. If the results of the examination are negative and antiseizure medication is not required, then the driver may be qualified.

In those individual cases where a driver had a single unprovoked seizure (e.g., drug reaction, high temperature, acute infectious disease, dehydration or acute metabolic disturbance), certification should be deferred until the driver has fully recovered from that condition and has no existing neurological and any medication is not existing for seizures.
(See Conference on Neurological Disorders and Commercial Drivers at
http://www.fmcsa.dot.gov/rulesregs/medreports.htm)

Mental Disorders
§391.41(b)(9)
A person is physically qualified to drive a commercial motor vehicle if that person:
Has no mental, nervous, organic or functional disease or psychiatric disorder likely to interfere with ability to drive a motor vehicle safely

Emotional or adjustment problems contribute directly to an individual's level of memory, reasoning, attention, and judgment. These problems often underlie physical disorders. A variety of functional disorders can cause dizziness, confusion, weakness or paralysis that may lead to inconsistency, inattention, loss of functional control and susceptibility to accidents while driving. Physical fatigue, headache, impaired coordination, recurring physical ailments and chronic "nagging" pain may be present to such a degree that certification for commercial driving is inadvisable. Somatic and psychosomatic complaints should be thoroughly examined when determining an individual's overall fitness to drive. Disorders of a periodically incapacitating nature, even in the early stages of development, may warrant disqualification.

All such tend track drivers have demonstrated that "nervous trouble" related to neurotic, personality, emotional or adjustment problems is responsible, for a significant fraction of their preventable accidents. The degree to which an individual is able to appreciate, evaluate and adequately respond to environmental strain and emotional stress is critical when assessing an individual's mental alertness and flexibility to cope with the stresses of commercial motor vehicle driving.

When examining the driver, it should be kept in mind that individuals who live under chronic conditions such as deeply ingrained maladaptive or erratic behavior patterns. Excessively antagonistic, instinctive, impulsive, overtly aggressive, paranoid or severely depressed behavior greatly interfere with the driver's ability to drive safely. Those individuals who are highly susceptible to frequent states of emotional instability (schizophrenia, affective psychosis, paranoia, anxiety or depressive neuroses) may warrant disqualification. Careful consideration should be given to the side effects and interactions of medications in the overall qualification determination. See Psychiatric Conference Report for specific recommendations on the use of these medications and potential hazards for driving.
(See Conference on Psychiatric Disorders and Commercial Drivers at
http://www.fmcsa.dot.gov/rulesregs/medreports.htm)

Vision
§391.41(b)(10)
A person is physically qualified to drive a commercial motor vehicle if that person:
Has distant visual acuity of at least 20/40 (Snellen) in each eye with or without corrective lenses or visual acuity separately corrected to 20/40 (Snellen) or better with corrective lenses, distant binocular acuity of at least 20/40 (Snellen) in both eyes with or without corrective lenses, field of vision of at least 70 degrees in the horizontal meridian in each eye, and the ability to recognize the colors of traffic signals and devices showing standard red, green, and amber.

The term "ability to recognize the colors of" is interpreted to mean if a person can recognize and distinguish among traffic control signals and devices showing standard red, green and amber, he or she also meets the minimum standard, even though he or she may have some type of color perception deficiency. If certain color perception tests are administered (such as Ishihara, Pseudoisochromatic, Yarn) and doubtful findings are discovered, additional tests may be employed. Signal red, green and amber may be employed to determine the driver's ability to recognize these colors.

Contact lenses are permissible if there is sufficient evidence to indicate that the driver has good tolerance and is well adapted to their use. Use of a contact lens in one eye for distance visual acuity and another lens in the other eye for near vision is not acceptable, nor telescopic lenses acceptable for the driving of commercial motor vehicles.

If an individual meets the criteria by the use of glasses or contact lenses, the following statement shall appear on his Medical Examiner's Certificate: 'Qualified only if wearing corrective lenses'
(See Visual Disorders and Commercial Drivers at
http://www.fmcsa.dot.gov/rulesregs/medreports.htm)

Hearing
§391.41(b)(11)
A person is physically qualified to drive a commercial motor vehicle if that person:
First perceives a forced whispered voice in the better ear at not less than 5 feet with or without the use of a hearing aid, or, if tested by use of an audiometric device, does not have an average hearing loss in the better ear greater than 40 decibels at 500 Hz, 1,000 Hz, and 2,000 Hz with or without a hearing aid when the audiometric device is calibrated to American National Standard (formerly ASA Standard) Z24.5-1951.

Since the prescribed standard under the FMCSRs is the American Intersociety (ANSI), it may be necessary to convert the audiometric results from the ISO standard to the ANSI standard. Instructions are included on the Medical Examination report form.

If an individual meets the criteria by using a hearing aid, the driver must wear that hearing aid and have it in operation at all times while driving. Also, the driver must be in possession of a spare power source for the hearing aid.

For the whispered voice test, the individual should be stationed at least 5 feet from the examiner with the ear being tested turned toward the examiner and the other ear covered. Using the breath which remains after a normal expiration, the examiner whispers words or random numbers such as 66, 18, 23, and 5. The examiner should not use only sibilants (s-sounding test materials). The opposite ear should be tested in the same manner. If the individual fails the whispered voice test, the individual should be administered an audiometric test.

If an individual meets the criteria by the use of a hearing aid, the following statement must appear on the Medical Examiner's Certificate "Qualified only when wearing a hearing aid."

(See Hearing Disorders and Commercial Motor Vehicle Drivers at
http://www.fmcsa.dot.gov/rulesregs/medreports.htm)

Drug Use
§391.41(b)(12)
A person is physically qualified to drive a commercial motor vehicle if that person:

Does not use any drug or substance identified in 21 CFR 1308.11 Schedule I, an amphetamine, a narcotic, or any other habit-forming drug. Exception: A driver may use such a substance or drug, if the substance or drug is prescribed by a licensed medical practitioner who is familiar with the driver's medical history and assigned duties; and has advised the driver that the prescribed substance or drug will not adversely affect the driver's ability to safely operate a commercial motor vehicle.

This exception does not apply to methadone. The intent of the medical certification process is to medically evaluate a driver to ensure that the driver has no medical condition which interferes with the safe performance of driving tasks on a public road. If a driver uses a Schedule I drug or other substance, an amphetamine, a narcotic, or any other habit-forming drug, it may be cause for the driver to be found medically unqualified. Motor carriers are encouraged to obtain a practitioner's written statement about the effects on transportation safety of the use of a particular drug.

A test for controlled substances is not part of this biennial certification process. The FMCSA, or the driver's employer should be contacted directly for information on controlled substances and alcohol testing under Part 382 of the FMCSRs.

The term "uses" is designed to encompass instances of prohibited drug use determined by a physician through established medical means. This may or may not involve body fluid testing. If body fluid testing takes place, positive test results should be confirmed by a second test of greater specificity. The term "habit-forming" is intended to include any drug or medication generally recognized as capable of becoming habitual, and which may impair the user's ability to operate a commercial motor vehicle safely.

The driver is medically unqualified for the duration of the prohibited drug(s) use and until a second examination shows the driver is free from the prohibited drug(s) use. Recertification may involve a substance abuse evaluation, the successful completion of a drug rehabilitation program, and a negative drug test result. Additionally, given that the certification period is normally two years, the examiner has the discretion to certify for a period of less than 2 years if this examiner determines more frequent monitoring is required. (See Conference on Neurological Disorders and Commercial Drivers and Conference on Psychiatric Disorders and Commercial Drivers at
http://www.fmcsa.dot.gov/rulesregs/medreports.htm)

Alcoholism
§391.41(b)(13)
A person is physically qualified to drive a commercial motor vehicle if that person:

Has no current clinical diagnosis of alcoholism.

The term "current clinical diagnosis of" is specifically designed to encompass a current alcoholic illness or those instances where the individual's physical condition has not fully stabilized, regardless of the time element. If an individual shows signs of having an alcohol-use problem, he or she should be referred to a specialist. After counseling and/or treatment, he or she may be considered for certification.

(g) If the medical examiner finds that the person he/she examined is physically qualified to drive a commercial motor vehicle in accordance with §391.41(b), the medical examiner shall complete a certificate in the form prescribed in paragraph (h) of this section and furnish one copy to the person who was examined and one copy to the motor carrier that employs him/her.

(h) The medical examiner's certificate shall be substantially in accordance with the following form. Existing forms may be used until current printed supplies are depleted or until November 6, 2001, whichever occurs first.

MEDICAL EXAMINER'S CERTIFICATE

I certify that I have examined _____ in accordance with the Federal Motor Carrier Safety Regulations (49 CFR 391.41-391.49) and with knowledge of the driving duties, I find this person is qualified; and, if applicable, only when:

☐ wearing corrective lenses   driving within an exempt intracity zone (49 CFR 391.62)

☐ wearing hearing aid   accompanied by a Skill Performance Evaluation Certificate (SPE)

☐ accompanied by a _____ waiver/exemption   ☐ Qualified by operation of 49 CFR 391.64

The information I have provided regarding this physical examination is true and complete. A complete examination form with any attachment embodies my findings completely and correctly, and is on file in my office.

SIGNATURE OF MEDICAL EXAMINER	TELEPHONE	DATE

MEDICAL EXAMINER'S NAME (PRINT)	☐ MD ☐ DO	☐ Chiropractor
	☐ Physician Assistant	☐ Advanced Practice Nurse

MEDICAL EXAMINER'S LICENSE OR CERTIFICATE NO. / ISSUING STATE

SIGNATURE OF DRIVER	DRIVER'S LICENSE NO.	STATE

ADDRESS OF DRIVER

MEDICAL CERTIFICATE EXPIRATION DATE

§391.45 Persons who must be medically examined and certified.

Except as provided in §391.67, the following persons must be medically examined and certified in accordance with §391.43 as physically qualified to operate a commercial motor vehicle:

(a) Any person who has not been medically examined and certified as physically qualified to operate a commercial motor vehicle;

(b)(1) Any driver who has not been medically examined and certified as qualified to operate a commercial motor vehicle during the preceding 24 months; or

(2) . . .

(c) Any driver whose ability to perform his/her normal duties has been impaired by a physical or mental injury or disease.

§391.47 Resolution of conflicts of medical evaluation.

(a) **Applications.** Applications for determination of a driver's medical qualifications under standards in this part will only be accepted if they conform to the requirements of this section.

(b) **Content.** Applications will be accepted for consideration only if the following conditions are met.

(1) The application must contain the name and address of the driver, motor carrier, and all physicians involved in the proceeding.

(2) The applicant must submit proof that there is a disagreement between the physician for the driver and the physician for the motor carrier concerning the driver's qualifications.

(3) The applicant must submit a copy of an opinion and report including results of all tests of an impartial medical specialist in the field in which the medical conflict arose. The specialist should be one agreed to by the motor carrier and the driver.

(i) In cases where the driver refuses to agree on a specialist and the applicant is the motor carrier the applicant must submit a statement of his/her agreement to submit the matter to an impartial medical specialist in the field, proof that he/she has requested the driver to submit to the medical specialist, and the response, if any, of the driver to his/her request.

(ii) In cases where the motor carrier refuses to agree on a medical specialist, the driver must submit an opinion and test results of an impartial medical specialist, proof that he/she has requested the motor carrier to agree to submit the matter to the medical specialist and the response, if any, of the motor carrier to his/her request.

(4) The applicant must include a statement explaining in detail why the decision of the medical specialist identified in paragraph (b)(3) of this section is unacceptable.

(5) The applicant must submit proof that the medical specialist mentioned in paragraph (b)(3) of this section was provided, prior to his/her determination, the medical history of the driver and an agreed-upon statement of the work the driver performs.

(6) The applicant must submit the medical history and statement of work provided to the medical specialist under paragraph (b)(5) of this section.

(7) The applicant must submit all medical records and statements of the physicians who have given opinions on the driver's qualifications.

(8) The applicant must submit a description and a copy of all written and documentary evidence upon which the party making application relies in the form set out in 49 CFR §386.37.

(9) . . .

(10) The applicant must submit three copies of the application and all records.

(c) **Information.** The Director, Office of Bus and Truck Standards and Operations (MC PSD) may request further information from the applicant if he/she determines that a decision cannot be made on the evidence submitted. If the applicant fails to submit the information requested, the Director, Office of Bus and Truck Standards and Operations (MC PSD) may refuse to issue a determination.

(d)(1) **Action.** Upon receiving a satisfactory application the Director, Office of Bus and Truck Standards and Operations (MC PSD) shall notify the parties (the driver, motor carrier, or any other interested party) that the application has been accepted and that a determination will be made. A copy of all evidence received shall be attached to the notice.

(2) **Reply.** Any party may submit a reply to the notification within 15 days after service. Such reply must be accompanied by all evidence the party wants the Director, Office of Bus and Truck Standards and Operations (MC PSD) to consider in making his/her determination. Evidence submitted should include all medical records and test results upon which the party relies.

(3) **Parties.** A party for the purposes of this section includes the motor carrier and the driver, or anyone else submitting an application.

(e) **Petitions to review, burden of proof.** The driver or motor carrier may petition to review the Director's determination. Such petition must be submitted in accordance with §386.13(a) of this chapter. The burden of proof in such a proceeding is on the petitioner.

(f) **Status of driver.** Once an application is submitted to the Director, Office of Bus and Truck Standards and Operations (MC PSD), the driver shall be deemed disqualified until such time as the Director, Office of Motor Carrier Research and Standards makes a determination, or until the Director, Office of Motor Carrier Research and Standards orders otherwise.

§391.49 Alternative physical qualification standards for the loss or impairment of limbs.

(a) A person who is not physically qualified to drive under §391.41(b)(1) or (b)(2) and who is otherwise qualified to drive a commercial motor vehicle, may drive a commercial motor vehicle, if the Division Administrator, FMCSA, has granted a Skill Performance Evaluation (SPE) Certificate to that person.

(b) *SPE certificate.*—(1) *Application.* A letter of application for an SPE certificate may be submitted jointly by the person (driver applicant) who seeks an SPE certificate and by the motor carrier that will employ the driver applicant, if the application is accepted.

(2) *Application address.* The application must be addressed to the applicable field service center, FMCSA, for the State in which the co-applicant motor carrier's principal place of business is located. The address of each, and the States serviced, are listed in §390.27 of this chapter.

(3) *Exception.* A letter of application for an SPE certificate may be submitted unilaterally by a driver applicant. The application must be addressed to the field service center, FMCSA, for the State in which the driver has legal residence. The driver applicant must comply with all the requirements of paragraph (c) of this section except those in (c)(1)(i) and (iii). The driver applicant shall respond to the requirements of paragraphs (c)(2)(i) to (v) of this section, if the information is known.

(c) A letter of application for an SPE certificate shall contain:

(1) Identification of the applicant(s):

(i) Name and complete address of the motor carrier coapplicant;

(ii) Name and complete address of the driver applicant;

(iii) The U.S. DOT Motor Carrier Identification Number, if known; and

(iv) A description of the driver applicant's limb impairment for which SPE certificate is requested.

(2) Description of the type of operation the driver will be employed to perform:

(i) State(s) in which the driver will operate for the motor carrier coapplicant (if more than 10 States, designate general geographic area only);

(ii) Average period of time the driver will be driving and/or on duty, per day;

(iii) Type of commodities or cargo to be transported;

(iv) Type of driver operation (*i.e.*, sleeper team, relay, owner operator, etc.); and

(v) Number of years experience operating the type of commercial motor vehicle(s) requested in the letter of application and total years of experience operating all types of commercial motor vehicles.

(3) Description of the commercial motor vehicle(s) the driver applicant intends to drive:

(i) Truck, truck tractor, or bus make, model, and year (if known);

(ii) Drive train;

(A) Transmission type (automatic or manual—if manual, designate number of forward speeds);

(B) Auxiliary transmission (if any) and number of forward speeds; and

(C) Rear axle (designate single speed, 2 speed, or 3 speed).

(iii) Type of brake system;

(iv) Steering, manual or power assisted;

(v) Description of type of trailer(s) (i.e., van, flatbed, cargo tank, drop frame, lowboy, or pole);

(vi) Number of semitrailers or full trailers to be towed at one time;

(vii) For commercial motor vehicles designed to transport passengers, indicate the seating capacity of commercial motor vehicle; and

(viii) Description of any modification(s) made to the commercial motor vehicle for the driver applicant; attach photograph(s) where applicable.

(4) Otherwise qualified:

(i) The coapplicant motor carrier must certify that the driver applicant is otherwise qualified under the regulations of this part;

(ii) In the case of a unilateral application, the driver applicant must certify that he/she is otherwise qualified under the regulations of this part.

(5) Signature of applicant(s):

(i) Driver applicant's signature and date signed;

(ii) Motor carrier official's signature (if application has a coapplicant), title, and date signed. Depending upon the motor carrier's organizational structure (corporation, partnership, or proprietorship), the signer of the application shall be an officer, partner, or the proprietor.

(d) The letter of application for an SPE certificate shall be accompanied by:

(1) A copy of the results of the medical examination performed pursuant to §391.43;

(2) A copy of the medical certificate completed pursuant to §391.43(h);

(3) A medical evaluation summary completed by either a board qualified or board certified physiatrist (doctor of physical medicine) or orthopedic surgeon. The coapplicant motor carrier or the driver applicant shall provide the physiatrist or orthopedic surgeon with a description of the job-related tasks the driver applicant will be required to perform;

(i) The medical evaluation summary for a driver applicant disqualified under §391.41(b)(1) shall include:

(A) An assessment of the functional capabilities of the driver as they relate to the ability of the driver to perform normal tasks associated with operating a commercial motor vehicle; and

(B) A statement by the examiner that the applicant is capable of demonstrating precision prehension (*e.g.*, manipulating knobs and switches) and power grasp prehension (*e.g.*, holding and maneuvering the steering wheel) with each upper limb separately. This requirement does not apply to an individual who was granted a waiver, absent a prosthetic device, prior to the publication of this amendment.

(ii) The medical evaluation summary for a driver applicant disqualified under §391.41(b)(2) shall include:

(A) An explanation as to how and why the impairment interferes with the ability of the applicant to perform normal tasks associated with operating a commercial motor vehicle;

(B) An assessment and medical opinion of whether the condition will likely remain medically stable over the lifetime of the driver applicant; and

(C) A statement by the examiner that the applicant is capable of demonstrating precision prehension (*e.g.*, manipulating knobs and switches) and power grasp prehension (*e.g.*, holding and maneuvering the steering wheel) with each upper limb separately. This requirement does not apply to an individual who was granted an SPE certificate, absent an orthotic device, prior to the publication of this amendment.

(4) A description of the driver applicant's prosthetic or orthotic device worn, if any;

(5) Road test:

(i) A copy of the driver applicant's road test administered by the motor carrier coapplicant and the certificate issued pursuant to §391.31(b) through (g); or

(ii) A unilateral applicant shall be responsible for having a road test administered by a motor carrier or a person who is competent to administer the test and evaluate its results.

(6) Application for employment:

(i) A copy of the driver applicant's application for employment completed pursuant to §391.21; or

(ii) A unilateral applicant shall be responsible for submitting a copy of the last commercial driving position's employment application he/she held. If not previously employed as a commercial driver, so state.

(7) A copy of the driver applicant's SPE certificate of certain physical defects issued by the individual State(s), where applicable; and

(8) A copy of the driver applicant's State Motor Vehicle Driving Record for the past 3 years from each State in which a motor vehicle driver's license or permit has been obtained.

(e) *Agreement.* A motor carrier that employs a driver with an SPE certificate agrees to:

(1) File promptly (within 30 days of the involved incident) with the Medical Program Specialist, FMCSA service center, such documents and information as may be required about driv-

ing activities, accidents, arrests, license suspensions, revocations, or withdrawals, and convictions which involve the driver applicant. This applies whether the driver's SPE certificate is a unilateral one or has a coapplicant motor carrier;

(i) A motor carrier who is a coapplicant must file the required documents with the Medical Program Specialist, FMCSA for the State in which the carrier's principal place of business is located; or

(ii) A motor carrier who employs a driver who has been issued a unilateral SPE certificate must file the required documents with the Medical Program Specialist, FMCSA service center, for the State in which the driver has legal residence.

(2) Evaluate the driver with a road test using the trailer the motor carrier intends the driver to transport or, in lieu of, accept a certificate of a trailer road test from another motor carrier if the trailer type(s) is similar, or accept the trailer road test done during the Skill Performance Evaluation if it is a similar trailer type(s) to that of the prospective motor carrier. Job tasks, as stated in paragraph (e)(3) of this section, are notevaluated in the Skill Performance Evaluation;

(3) Evaluate the driver for those nondriving safety related job tasks associated with whatever type of trailer(s) will be used and any other nondriving safety related or job related tasks unique to the operations of the employing motor carrier; and

(4) Use the driver to operate the type of commercial motor vehicle defined in the SPE certificate only when the driver is in compliance with the conditions and limitations of the SPE certificate.

(f) The driver shall supply each employing motor carrier with a copy of the SPE certificate.

(g) The State Director, FMCSA, may require the driver applicant to demonstrate his or her ability to safely operate the commercial motor vehicle(s) the driver intends to drive to an agent of the State Director, FMCSA. The SPE certificate form will identify the power unit (bus, truck, truck tractor) for which the SPE certificate has been granted. The SPE certificate forms will also identify the trailer type used in the Skill Performance Evaluation; however, the SPE certificate is not limited to that specific trailer type. A driver may use the SPE certificate with other trailer types if a successful trailer road test is completed in accordance with paragraph (e)(2) of this section. Job tasks, as stated in paragraph (e)(3) of this section, are not evaluated during the Skill Performance Evaluation.

(h) The State Director, FMCSA, may deny the application for SPE certificate or may grant it totally or in part and issue the SPE certificate subject to such terms, conditions, and limitations as deemed consistent with the public interest. The SPE certificate is valid for a period not to exceed 2 years from date of issue, and may be renewed 30 days prior to the expiration date.

(i) The SPE certificate renewal application shall be submitted to the Medical Program Specialist, FMCSA service center, for the State in which the driver has legal residence, if the SPE certificate was issued unilaterally. If the SPE certificate has a coapplicant, then the renewal application is submitted to the Medical Program Specialist, FMCSA field service center, for the State in which the coapplicant motor carrier's principal place of business is located. The SPE certificate renewal application shall contain the following:

(1) Name and complete address of motor carrier currently employing the applicant;

(2) Name and complete address of the driver;

(3) Effective date of the current SPE certificate;

(4) Expiration date of the current SPE certificate;

(5) Total miles driven under the current SPE certificate;

(6) Number of accidents incurred while driving under the current SPE certificate, including date of the accident(s), number of fatalities, number of injuries, and the estimated dollar amount of property damage;

(7) A current medical examination report;

(8) A medical evaluation summary pursuant to paragraph (d)(3) of this section, if an unstable medical condition exists. All handicapped conditions classified under §391.41(b)(1) are considered unstable. Refer to paragraph (d)(3)(ii) of this section for the condition under §391.41(b)(2) which may be considered medically stable.

(9) A copy of driver's current State motor vehicle driving record for the period of time the current SPE certificate has been in effect;

(10) Notification of any change in the type of tractor the driver will operate;

(11) Driver's signature and date signed; and

(12) Motor carrier coapplicant's signature and date signed.

(j)(1) Upon granting an SPE certificate, the State Director, FMCSA, will notify the driver applicant and co-applicant motor carrier (if applicable) by letter. The terms, conditions, and limitations of the SPE certificate will be set forth. A motor carrier shall maintain a copy of the SPE certificate in its driver qualification file. A copy of the SPE certificate shall be retained in the motor carrier's file for a period of 3 years after the driver's employment is terminated. The driver applicant shall have the SPE certificate (or a legible copy) in his/her possession whenever on duty.

(2) Upon successful completion of the skill performance evaluation, the State Director, FMCSA, for the State where the driver applicant has legal residence, must notify the driver by letter and enclose an SPE certificate substantially in the following form:

Skill Performance Evaluation Certificate

Name of Issuing Agency:_____

Agency Address:_____

Telephone Number: (   )_____

Issued Under 49 CFR 391.49, subchapter B of the Federal Motor Carrier Safety Regulations

Driver's Name:_____

Effective Date:_____

SSN:_____

DOB:_____

Expiration Date:_____

Address:_____

_____

_____

Driver Disability:_____

Check One:__New__Renewal

Driver's License:_____
                    (State)   (Number)

In accordance with 49 CFR 391.49, subchapter B of the Federal Motor Carrier Safety Regulations (FMCSRs), the driver application for a skill performance evaluation (SPE) certificate is hereby granted authorizing the above-named driver to operate in interstate or foreign commerce under the provisions set forth below. This certificate is granted for the period shown above, not to exceed 2 years, subject to periodic review as may be found necessary. This certificate may be renewed upon sumission of a renewal application. Continuation of this certificate is dependent upon strict adherence by the above-named driver to the provisions set forth below and compliance with the FMCSRs. Any failure to comply with provisions herein may be cause for cancellation.

CONDITIONS: As a condition of this certificate, reports of all accidents, arrests, suspensions, revocations, withdrawals of driver licenses or permits, and convictions involving the above-named driver shall be reported in writing to the Issuing Agency by the EMPLOYING MOTOR CARRIER within 30 days after occurrence.

LIMITATIONS:

1. Vehicle Type (power unit):*_____

2. Vehicle modification(s): _____

_____

3. Prosthetic or Orthotic device(s) (Required to be Worn While Driving):_____

4. Additional Provision(s):_____

_____

NOTICE: To all MOTOR CARRIERS employing a driver with an SPE certificate. This certificate is granted for the operation of the *power unit only*. It is the responsibility of the employing motor carrier to evaluate the driver with a road test using the trailer type(s) the motor carrier intends the driver to transport, or in lieu of, accept the trailer road test done during the SPE if it is a similar trailer type(s) to that of the prospective motor carrier. Also, it is the responsibility of the employing motor carrier to evaluate the driver for those non-driving safety-related job tasks associated with the type of trailer(s) utilized, as well as, any other non-driving safety-related or job-related tasks unique to the operations of the employing motor carrier.

The SPE of the above named driver was given by a Skill Performance Evaluation Program Specialist. It was successfully completed utilizing the above named power unit and _____(trailer, if applicable)

The tractor or truck had a _____ transmission.

Please read the *NOTICE* paragraph above.

Name:_____
Signature:_____
Title:_____
Date:_____

(k) The State Director, FMCSA, may revoke an SPE certificate after the person to whom it was issued is given notice of the proposed revocation and has been allowed a reasonable opportunity to appeal.

(l) Falsifying information in the letter of application, the renewal application, or falsifying information required by this section by either the applicant or motor carrier is prohibited.

Subpart F — Files and Records

§391.51 General requirements for driver qualification files.

(a) Each motor carrier shall maintain a driver qualification file for each driver it employs. A driver's qualification file may be combined with his/her personnel file.

(b) The qualification file for a driver must include:

(1) The driver's application for employment completed in accordance with §391.21;

(2) A written record with respect to each past employer who was contacted and a copy of the response by each State agency, pursuant to §391.23 involving investigation and inquiries;

(3) The certificate of driver's road test issued to the driver pursuant to §391.31(e), or a copy of the license or certificate which the motor carrier accepted as equivalent to the driver's road test pursuant to §391.33;

(4) The response of each State agency to the annual driver record inquiry required by §391.25(a);

(5) A note relating to the annual review of the driver's driving record as required by §391.25(c)(2);

(6) A list or certificate relating to violations of motor vehicle laws and ordinances required by §391.27;

(7) The medical examiner's certificate of his/her physical qualification to drive a commercial motor vehicle as required by §391.43(f) or a legible photographic copy of the certificate; and

(8) A letter from the Field Administrator, Division Administrator, or State Director granting a waiver of a physical disqualification, if a waiver was issued under §391.49.

(c) Except as provided in paragraph (d) of this section, each driver's qualification file shall be retained for as long as a driver is employed by that motor carrier and for three years thereafter.

(d) The following records may be removed from a driver's qualification file three years after the date of execution:

(1) The response of each State agency to the annual driver record inquiry required by §391.25(a);

(2) The note relating to the annual review of the driver's driving record as required by §391.25(c)(2);

(3) The list or certificate relating to violations of motor vehicle laws and ordinances required by §391.27;

(4) The medical examiner's certificate of the driver's physical

qualification to drive a commercial motor vehicle or the photographic copy of the certificate as required by §391.43(f); and

(5) The letter issued under §391.49 granting a waiver of a physical disqualification.

(Approved by the Office of management and Budget under control number 2125-0065)

Subpart G — Limited Exemptions

§391.61 Drivers who were regularly employed before January 1, 1971.

The provisions of §391.21 (relating to applications for employment), §391.23 (relating to investigations and inquiries), and §391.31 (relating to road tests) do not apply to a driver who has been a single-employer driver (as defined in §390.5 of this subchapter) of a motor carrier for a continuous period which began before January 1, 1971, as long as he/she continues to be a single-employer driver of that motor carrier.

§391.62 Limited exemptions for intra-city zone drivers.

The provisions of §§391.11(b)(1) and 391.41(b)(1) through (b)(11) do not apply to a person who:

(a) Was otherwise qualified to operate and operated a commercial motor vehicle in a municipality or exempt intracity zone thereof throughout the one-year period ending November 18, 1988;

(b) Meets all the other requirements of this section;

(c) Operates wholly within the exempt intracity zone (as defined in 49 CFR 390.5);

(d) Does not operate a vehicle used in the transportation of hazardous materials in a quantity requiring placarding under regulations issued by the Secretary under 49 U.S.C. chapter 51.; and

(e) Has a medical or physical condition which:

(1) Would have prevented such person from operating a commercial motor vehicle under the Federal Motor Carrier Safety Regulations contained in this subchapter;

(2) Existed on July 1, 1988, or at the time of the first required physical examination after that date; and

(3) The examining physician has determined this condition has not substantially worsened since July 1, 1988, or at the time of the first required physical examination after that date.

§391.63 Multiple-employer drivers.

(a) If a motor carrier employs a person as a multiple-employer driver (as defined in §390.5 of this subchapter) the motor carrier shall comply with all requirements of this part, except that the motor carrier need not —

(1) Require the person to furnish an application for employment in accordance with §391.21;

(2) Make the investigations and inquiries specified in §391.23 with respect to that person;

(3) Perform the annual driving record inquiry required by §391.25(a);

(4) Perform the annual review of the person's driving record required by §391.25(b); or

(5) Require the person to furnish a record of violations or a certificate in accordance with §391.27.

(b) Before a motor carrier permits a multiple-employer driver to drive a commercial motor vehicle, the motor carrier must obtain his/her name, his/her social security number, and the identification number, type and issuing State of his/her commercial motor vehicle operator's license. The motor carrier must maintain this information for 3 years after employment of the multiple-employer driver ceases.

(Approved by the Office of Management and Budget under control number 2125-0081)

§391.64 Grandfathering for certain drivers participating in vision and diabetes waiver study programs.

(a) The provisions of §391.41(b)(3) do not apply to a driver who was a participant in good standing on March 31, 1996, in a waiver study program concerning the operation of commercial motor vehicles by insulin-controlled diabetic drivers; provided:

(1) The driver is physically examined every year, including an examination by a board-certified/eligible endocrinologist attesting to the fact that the driver is:

(i) Otherwise qualified under §391.41;

(ii) Free of insulin reactions (an individual is free of insulin reactions if that individual does not have severe hypoglycemia or hypoglycemia unawareness, and has less than one documented, symptomatic hypoglycemic reaction per month);

(iii) Able to and has demonstrated willingness to properly monitor and manage his/her diabetes; and

(iv) Not likely to suffer any diminution in driving ability due to his/her diabetic condition.

(2) The driver agrees to and complies with the following conditions:

(i) A source of rapidly absorbable glucose shall be carried at all times while driving;

(ii) Blood glucose levels shall be self-monitored one hour prior to driving and at least once every four hours while driving or on duty prior to driving using a portable glucose monitoring device equipped with a computerized memory;

(iii) Submit blood glucose logs to the endocrinologist or medical examiner at the annual examination or when otherwise directed by an authorized agent of the FMCSA;

(iv) Provide a copy of the endocrinologist's report to the medical examiner at the time of the annual medical examination; and

(v) Provide a copy of the annual medical certification to the employer for retention in the driver's qualification file and retain a copy of the certification on his/her person while driving for presentation to a duly authorized Federal, State or local enforcement official.

(b) The provisions of §391.41(b)(10) do not apply to a driver who was a participant in good standing on March 31, 1996, in a waiver study program concerning the operation of commercial motor vehicles by drivers with visual impairment in one eye; provided:

(1) The driver is physically examined every year, including an examination by an ophthalmologist or optometrist attesting to the fact that the driver:

(i) Is otherwise qualified under §391.41; and

(ii) Continues to measure at least 20/40 (Snellen) in the better eye.

(2) The driver provides a copy of the ophthalmologist or optometrist report to the medical examiner at the time of the annual medical examination.

(3) The driver provides a copy of the annual medical certification to the employer for retention in the driver's qualification file and retains a copy of the certification on his/her person while driving for presentation to a duly authorized federal, state or local enforcement official.

§391.65 Drivers furnished by other motor carriers.

(a) A motor carrier may employ a driver who is not a regularly employed driver of that motor carrier without complying with the generally applicable driver qualification file requirements in this part, if —

(1) The driver is regularly employed by another motor carrier; and

(2) The motor carrier which regularly employs the driver certifies that the driver is fully qualified to drive a commercial motor vehicle in a written statement which—

(i) Is signed and dated by an officer or authorized employee of the regularly employing carrier;

(ii) Contains the driver's name and signature;

(iii) Certifies that the driver has been regularly employed as defined in §390.5;

(iv) Certifies that the driver is fully qualified to drive a commercial motor vehicle under the rules in Part 391 of the Federal Motor Carrier Safety Regulations;

(v) States the expiration date of the driver's medical examiner's certificate;

(vi) Specifies an expiration date for the certificate, which shall be not longer that 2 years or, if earlier, the expiration date of the driver's current medical examiner's certificate; and

(vii) After April 1, 1977, is substantially in accordance with the following form:

(Name of driver)   (SS No.)

(Signature of driver)

I certify that the above named driver, as defined in §390.5 is regularly driving a commercial motor vehicle operated by the below named carrier and is fully qualified under Part 391, Federal Motor Carrier Safety Regulations. His current medical examiner's certificate expires on _____

(Date)

This certificate expires: _____
        (Date not later than expiration date of medical certificate)

Issued on _____

(Date)

Issued by _____

(Name of carrier)

_____
(Address)

_____
(Signature)   (Title)

(b) A motor carrier that obtains a certificate in accordance with paragraph (a)(2) of this section shall:

(1) Contact the motor carrier which certified the driver's qualifications under this section to verify the validity of the certificate. This contact may be made in person, by telephone, or by letter.

(2) Retain a copy of that certificate in its files for three years.

(c) A motor carrier which certifies a driver's qualifications under this section shall be responsible for the accuracy of the certificate. The certificate is no longer valid if the driver leaves the employment of the motor carrier which issued the certificate or is no longer qualified under the rules in this part.

§391.67 . . .

§391.68 Private motor carrier of passengers (nonbusiness).

The following rules in this part do not apply to a private motor carrier of passengers (nonbusiness) and its drivers:

(a) Section 391.11(b)(1), (b)(6), and (b)(8), (relating to general qualifications of drivers);

(b) Subpart C (relating to disclosure of, investigation into, and inquiries about the background, character, and driving record of, drivers);

(c) So much of §§391.41 and 391.45 as require a driver to be medically examined and to have a medical examiner's certificate on his/her person; and

(d) Subpart F (relating to maintenance of files and records).

§391.69 Private motor carrier of passengers (business).

The provisions of §391.21 (relating to applications for employment), §391.23 (relating to investigations and inquiries), and §391.31 (relating to road tests) do not apply to a driver who was a single-employer driver (as defined in §390.5 of this subchapter) of a private motor carrier of passengers (business) as of July 1, 1994, so long as the driver continues to be a single-employer driver of that motor carrier.

§391.71 [Removed and reserved.]

PART 392 — DRIVING OF COMMERCIAL MOTOR VEHICLES

Subpart A — General

392.41   [Removed and reserved.]
392.42   [Removed]

Subpart F — Fueling Precautions

392.50   Ignition of fuel; prevention.
392.51   Reserve fuel, materials of trade.
392.52   [Removed and reserved.]

Subpart G — Prohibited Practices

392.60   Unauthorized persons not to be transported.
392.61   [Removed and reserved.]
392.62   Safe operations, buses.
392.63   Towing or pushing loaded buses.
392.64   Riding within closed commercial motor vehicles without proper exits.
392.65   [Removed and reserved.]
392.66   Carbon monoxide; use of commercial motor vehicle when detected.
392.67   Heater, flame-producing; on commercial motor vehicle in motion.
392.68   [Removed and reserved.]
392.69   [Removed and reserved.]
392.71   Radar detectors; use and/or possession.

AUTHORITY: 49 U.S.C. 13902, 31136, 31502; and 49 CFR 1.73.

Subpart A — General

§392.1 Scope of the rules in this part.

Every motor carrier, its officers, agents, representatives, and employees responsible for the management, maintenance, operation, or driving of commercial motor vehicles, or the hiring, supervising, training, assigning, or dispatching of drivers, shall be instructed in and comply with the rules in this part.

§392.2 Applicable operating rules.

Every commercial motor vehicle must be operated in accordance with the laws, ordinances, and regulations of the jurisdiction in which it is being operated. However, if a regulation of the Federal Highway Administration imposes a higher standard of care than that law, ordinance or regulation, the Federal Motor Carrier Safety Administration regulation must be complied with.

§392.3 Ill or fatigued operator.

No driver shall operate a commercial motor vehicle, and a

motor carrier shall not require or permit a driver to operate a commercial motor vehicle, while the driver's ability or alertness is so impaired, or so likely to become impaired, through fatigue, illness, or any other cause, as to make it unsafe for him/her to begin or continue to operate the commercial motor vehicle. However, in a case of grave emergency where the hazard to occupants of the commercial motor vehicle or other users of the highway would be increased by compliance with this section, the driver may continue to operate the commercial motor vehicle to the nearest place at which that hazard is removed.

§392.4 Drugs and other substances.

(a) No driver shall be on duty and possess, be under the influence of, or use, any of the following drugs or other substances:

(1) Any 21 CFR 1308.11 *Schedule I* substance;

(2) An amphetamine or any formulation thereof (including, but not limited, to "pep pills," and "bennies");

(3) A narcotic drug or any derivative thereof; or

(4) Any other substance, to a degree which renders the driver incapable of safely operating a motor vehicle.

(b) No motor carrier shall require or permit a driver to violate paragraph (a) of this section.

(c) Paragraphs (a) (2), (3), and (4) do not apply to the possession or use of a substance administered to a driver by or under the instructions of a licensed medical practitioner, as defined in §382.107 of this subchapter, who has advised the driver that the substance will not affect the driver's ability to safely operate a motor vehicle.

(d) As used in this section, "possession" does not include possession of a substance which is manifested and transported as part of a shipment.

§392.5 Alcohol prohibition.

(a) No driver shall—

(1) Use alcohol, as defined in §382.107 of this subchapter, or be under the influence of alcohol, within 4 hours before going on duty or operating, or having physical control of, a commercial motor vehicle; or

(2) Use alcohol, be under the influence of alcohol, or have any measured alcohol concentration or detected presence of alcohol, while on duty, or operating, or in physical control of a commercial motor vehicle; or

(3) Be on duty or operate a commercial motor vehicle while the driver possesses wine of not less than one-half of one per centum of

alcohol by volume, beer *as defined in 26 U.S.C. 5052(a), of the Internal Revenue Code of 1954,* and distilled spirits *as defined in section 5002(a)(8), of such Code.* However, this does not apply to possession of wine, beer, or distilled spirits which are:

(i) Manifested and transported as part of a shipment; or

(ii) Possessed or used by bus passengers.

(b) No motor carrier shall require or permit a driver to—

(1) Violate any provision of paragraph (a) of this section; or

(2) Be on duty or operate a commercial motor vehicle if, by the driver's general appearance or conduct or by other substantiating evidence, the driver appears to have used alcohol within the preceding 4 hours.

(c) Any driver who is found to be in violation of the provisions of paragraph (a) or (b) of this section shall be placed out-of-service immediately for a period of 24 hours.

(1) The 24-hour out-of-service period will commence upon issuance of an out-of-service order.

(2) No driver shall violate the terms of an out-of-service order issued under this section.

(d) Any driver who is issued an out-of-service order under this section shall:

(1) Report such issuance to his/her employer within 24 hours; and

(2) Report such issuance to a State official, designated by the State which issued his/her driver's license, within 30 days unless the driver chooses to request a review of the order. In this case, the driver shall report the order to the State official within 30 days of an affirmation of the order by either the Division Administrator or State Director for the geographical area or the Administrator.

(e) Any driver who is subject to an out-of-service order under this section may petition for review of that order by submitting a petition for review in writing within 10 days of the issuance of the order to the Division Administrator or State Director for the geographical area in which the order was issued. The Division Administrator or State Director may affirm or reverse the order. Any driver adversely affected by such order of the Division Administrator or State Director may petition the Administrator for review in accordance with 49 CFR 386.13.

§392.6 Schedules to conform with speed limits.

No motor carrier shall schedule a run nor permit nor require the operation of any commercial motor vehicle between points in such period of time as would necessitate the commercial motor vehicle being operated at speeds greater than those prescribed by the jurisdictions in or through which the commercial motor vehicle is being operated.

§392.7 Equipment, inspection and use.

No commercial motor vehicle shall be driven unless the driver is satisfied that the following parts and accessories are in good working order, nor shall any driver fail to use or make use of such parts and accessories when and as needed:

Service brakes, including trailer brake connections.
Parking (hand) brake.
Steering mechanism.
Lighting devices and reflectors.
Tires.
Horn.
Windshield wiper or wipers.
Rear-vision mirror or mirrors.

§392.8 Emergency equipment, inspection, and use.

No commercial motor vehicle shall be driven unless the driver thereof is satisfied that the emergency equipment required by §393.95 of this subchapter is in place and ready for use; nor shall any driver fail to use or make use of such equipment when and as needed.

§392.9 Inspection of cargo, cargo securement devices and systems.

(a) **General.** A driver may not operate a commercial motor vehicle and a motor carrier may not require or permit a driver to operate a commercial motor vehicle unless—

(1) The commercial motor vehicle's cargo is properly distributed and adequately secured as specified in §§393.100 through 393.142 of this subchapter.

(2) The commercial motor vehicle's tailgate, tailboard, doors, tarpaulins, spare tire and other equipment used in its operation, and the means of fastening the commercial motor vehicle's cargo, are secured; and

(3) The commercial motor vehicle's cargo or any other object does not obscure the driver's view ahead or to the right or left sides (except for drivers of self-steer dollies), interfere with the free movement of his/her arms or legs, prevent his/her free and ready access to accessories required for emergencies, or prevent

the free and ready exit of any person from the commercial motor vehicle's cab or driver's compartment.

(b) **Drivers of trucks and truck tractors.** Except as provided in paragraph (b)(4) of this section, the driver of a truck or truck tractor must—

(1) Assure himself/herself that the provisions of paragraph (a) of this section have been complied with before he/she drives that commercial motor vehicle;

(2) Inspect the cargo and the devices used to secure the cargo within the first 50 miles after beginning a trip and cause any adjustments to be made to the cargo or load securement devices as necessary, including adding more securement devices, to ensure that cargo cannot shift on or within, or fall from the commercial motor vehicle; and

(3) Reexamine the commercial motor vehicle's cargo and its load securement devices during the course of transportation and make any necessary adjustment to the cargo or load securement devices, including adding more securement devices, to ensure that cargo cannot shift on or within, or fall from, the commercial motor vehicle. Reexamination and any necessary adjustments must be made whenever—

(i) The driver makes a change of his/her duty status; or

(ii) The commercial motor vehicle has been driven for 3 hours; or

(iii) The commercial motor vehicle has been driven for 150 miles, whichever occurs first.

(4) The rules in this paragraph (b) do not apply to the driver of a sealed commercial motor vehicle who has been ordered not to open it to inspect its cargo or to the driver of a commercial motor vehicle that has been loaded in a manner that makes inspection of its cargo impracticable.

(b) . . .

§392.9a Operating authority.

(a) **Registration required.** A motor vehicle providing transportation requiring registration under 49 U.S.C. 13902 may not be operated without the required registration or operated beyond the scope of its registration.

(b) **Penalties.** Every motor vehicle providing transportation requiring registration under 49 U.S.C. 13902 shall be ordered out-of-service if determined to be operating without registration or beyond the scope of its registration. In addition, the motor carrier may be subject to penalties in accordance with 49 U.S.C. 14901.

(c) **Administrative Review.** Upon the issuance of the out-of-service order under paragraph (b) of this section, the driver shall comply immediately with such order. Opportunity for review shall be provided in accordance with section 554 of title 5, United States Code not later than 10 days after issuance of such order.

§392.9b [Removed and reserved.]

Subpart B — Driving of Vehicles

§392.10 Railroad grade crossings; stopping required.

(a) Except as provided in paragraph (b) of this section, the driver of a commercial motor vehicle specified in paragraphs (1) through (6) of this section shall not cross a railroad track or tracks at grade unless he/she first: Stops the commercial motor vehicle within 50 feet of, and not closer than 15 feet to, the tracks; thereafter listens and looks in each direction along the tracks for an approaching train; and ascertains that no train is approaching. When it is safe to do so, the driver may drive the commercial motor vehicle across the tracks in a gear that permits the commercial motor vehicle to complete the crossing without a change of gears. The driver must not shift gears while crossing the tracks.

(1) Every bus transporting passengers,

(2) . . .

(3) . . .

(4) . . .

(5) . .

(6) . . .

(b) A stop need not be made at:

(1) A streetcar crossing, or railroad tracks used exclusively for industrial switching purposes, within a business district, as defined in §390.5 of this chapter,

(2) A railroad grade crossing when a police officer or crossing flagman directs traffic to proceed,

(3) A railroad grade crossing controlled by a functioning highway traffic signal transmitting a green indication which, under local law, permits the commercial motor vehicle to proceed across the railroad tracks without slowing or stopping.

(4) An abandoned railroad grade crossing which is marked with a sign indicating that the rail line is abandoned,

(5) An industrial or spur line railroad grade crossing

marked with a sign reading "Exempt." Such "Exempt" signs shall be erected only by or with the consent of the appropriate State or local authority.

§392.11 . . .

§392.12 [Removed and reserved.]

§392.13 [Removed and reserved.]

§392.14 Hazardous conditions; extreme caution.

Extreme caution in the operation of a commercial motor vehicle shall be exercised when hazardous conditions, such as those caused by snow, ice, sleet, fog, mist, rain, dust, or smoke, adversely affect visibility or traction. Speed shall be reduced when such conditions exist. If conditions become sufficiently dangerous, the operation of the commercial motor vehicle shall be discontinued and shall not be resumed until the commercial motor vehicle can be safely operated. Whenever compliance with the foregoing provisions of this rule increases hazard to passengers, the commercial motor vehicle may be operated to the nearest point at which the safety of passengers is assured.

§392.15 [Removed and reserved.]

§392.16 Use of seat belts.

A commercial motor vehicle which has a seat belt assembly installed at the driver's seat shall not be driven unless the driver has properly restrained himself/herself with the seat belt assembly.

§392.18 [Removed and reserved.]

Subpart C — Stopped Vehicles

§392.20 [Removed and reserved.]

§392.21 [Removed and reserved.]

§392.22 Emergency signals; stopped commercial motor vehicles.

(a) **Hazard warning signal flashers.** Whenever a commercial motor vehicle is stopped upon the traveled portion of a highway or the shoulder of a highway for any cause other than necessary traffic stops, the driver of the stopped commercial motor vehicle shall immediately activate the vehicular hazard warning signal flashers and continue the flashing until the driver places the warning devices required by paragraph (b) of this section. The flashing signals shall be used during the time the warning devices are picked up for storage before movement of the commercial motor vehicle. The flashing lights may be used at other times while a commercial motor vehicle is stopped in addition to, but not in lieu of, the warning devices required by paragraph (b) of this section.

(b) **Placement of warning devices—**

(1) **General rule.** Except as provided in paragraph (b)(2) of this section, whenever a commercial motor vehicle is stopped upon the traveled portion or the shoulder of a highway for any cause other than necessary traffic stops, the driver shall, as soon as possible, but in any event within 10 minutes, place the warning devices required by §393.95 of this subchapter, in the following manner:

(i) One on the traffic side of and 4 paces (approximately 3 meters or 10 feet) from the stopped commercial motor vehicle in the direction of approaching traffic;

(ii) One at 40 paces (approximately 30 meters or 100 feet) from the stopped commercial motor vehicle in the center of the traffic lane or shoulder occupied by the commercial motor vehicle and in the direction of approaching traffic; and

(iii) One at 40 paces (approximately 30 meters or 100 feet) from the stopped commercial motor vehicle in the center of the traffic lane or shoulder occupied by the commercial motor vehicle and in the direction away from approaching traffic.

(2) **Special rules—(i) Fusees and liquid-burning flares.** The driver of a commercial motor vehicle equipped with only fusees or liquid-burning flares shall place a lighted fusee or liquid-burning flare at each of the locations specified in paragraph (b)(1) of this section. There shall be at least one lighted fusee or liquid-burning flare at each of the prescribed locations, as long as the commercial motor vehicle is stopped. Before the stopped vehicle is moved, the driver shall extinguish and remove each fusee or liquid-burning flare.

(ii) **Daylight hours.** Except as provided in paragraph (b)(2)(iii) of this section, during the period lighted lamps are not required, three bidirectional reflective triangles, or three lighted fusees or liquid-burning flares shall be placed as specified in paragraph (b)(1) of this section within a time of 10 minutes. In the event the driver elects to use only fusees or liquid-burning flares in lieu of bidirectional reflective triangles or red flags, the driver must ensure that at least one fusee or liquid-burning flare remains lighted at each of the prescribed locations as long as the commercial motor vehicle is stopped or parked.

(iii) **Business or residential districts.** The placement of warning devices is not required within the business or residential district of a municipality, except during the time lighted lamps are required and when street or highway lighting is insufficient to make a commercial motor vehicle clearly discernable at a distance of 500 feet to persons on the highway.

(iv) **Hills, curves, and obstructions.** If a commercial motor vehicle is stopped within 500 feet of a curve, crest of a hill, or other obstruction to view, the driver shall place the warning signal required by paragraph (b)(1) of this section in the direction of the obstruction to view a distance of 100 feet to 500 feet from the stopped commercial motor vehicle so as to afford ample warning to other users of the highway.

(v) **Divided or one-way roads.** If a commercial motor vehicle is stopped upon the traveled portion or the shoulder of a divided or one-way highway, the driver shall place the warning devices required by paragraph (b)(1) of this section, one warning device at a distance of 200 feet and one warning device at a distance of 100 feet in a direction toward approaching traffic in the center of the lane or shoulder occupied by the commercial motor vehicle. He/she shall place one warning device at the traffic side of the commercial motor vehicle within 10 feet of the rear of the vehicle.

(vi) **Leaking, flammable material.** If gasoline or any other flammable liquid, or combustible liquid or gas seeps or leaks from a fuel container or a commercial motor vehicle stopped upon a highway, no emergency warning signal producing a flame shall be lighted or placed except at such a distance from any such liquid or gas as will assure the prevention of a fire or explosion.

§392.24 Emergency signals; flame-producing.

No driver shall attach or permit any person to attach a lighted fusee or other flame-producing emergency signal to any part of a commercial motor vehicle.

§392.25 ...

Subpart D — Use of Lighted Lamps and Reflectors

§392.30 [Removed and reserved.]

§392.31 [Removed and reserved.]

§392.32 [Removed and reserved.]

§392.33 Obscured lamps or reflectors.

No commercial motor vehicle shall be driven when any of the required lamps or reflectors are obscured by the tailboard, by any part of the load, by dirt, or otherwise.

Subpart E — License Revocation: Duties of Driver

§392.40 [Removed and reserved.]

§392.41 [Removed and reserved.]

§392.42 [Removed.]

Subpart F — Fueling Precautions

§392.50 Ignition of fuel; prevention.

No driver or any employee of a motor carrier shall:

(a) Fuel a commercial motor vehicle with the engine running, except when it is necessary to run the engine to fuel the commercial motor vehicle;

(b) Smoke or expose any open flame in the vicinity of a commercial motor vehicle being fueled;

(c) Fuel a commercial motor vehicle unless the nozzle of the fuel hose is continuously in contact with the intake pipe of the fuel tank;

(d) Permit, insofar as practicable, any other person to engage in such activities as would be likely to result in fire or explosion.

§392.51 Reserve fuel; materials of trade.

Small amounts of fuel for the operation or maintenance of a commercial motor vehicle (including its auxiliary equipment) may be designated as materials of trade (see 49 CFR 171.8).

(a) The aggregate gross weight of all materials of trade on a motor vehicle may not exceed 200 kg (440 pounds).

(b) Packaging for gasoline must be made of metal or plastic and conform to requirements of 49 CFR Parts 171, 172, 173, and 178 or requirements of the Occupational Safety and Health Administration contained in 29 CFR 1910.106.

(c) For Packing Group II (including gasoline), Packing Group III (including aviation fuel and fuel oil), or ORM-D, the material is limited to 30 kg (66 pounds) or 30 L (8 gallons).

(d) For diesel fuel, the capacity of the package is limited to 450 L (119 gallons).

(e) A Division 2.1 material in a cylinder is limited to a gross weight of 100 kg (220 pounds). (A Division 2.1 material is a flammable gas, including liquefied petroleum gas, butane, propane, liquefied natural gas, and methane).

§392.52 [Removed and reserved.]

Subpart G — Prohibited Practices

§392.60 Unauthorized persons not to be transported.

Unless specifically authorized in writing to do so by the motor carrier under whose authority the commercial motor vehicle is being operated, no driver shall transport any person or permit any person to be transported on any commercial motor vehicle other than a bus.

§392.61 [Removed and reserved.]

§392.62 Safe operation, buses.

No person shall drive a bus and a motor carrier shall not require or permit a person to drive a bus unless—

(a) All standees on the bus are rearward of the standee line or other means prescribed in §393.90 of this subchapter;

(b) All aisle seats in the bus conform to the requirements of §393.91 of this subchapter; and

(c) Baggage or freight on the bus is stowed and secured in a manner which assures—

(1) Unrestricted freedom of movement to the driver and his proper operation of the bus;

(2) Unobstructed access to all exits by any occupant of the bus; and

(3) Protection of occupants of the bus against injury resulting from the falling or displacement of articles transported in the bus.

§392.63 Towing or pushing loaded buses.

No disabled bus with passengers aboard shall be towed or pushed; nor shall any person use or permit to be used a bus with passengers aboard for the purpose of towing or pushing any disabled motor vehicle, except in such circumstances where the hazard to passengers would be increased by observance of the foregoing provisions of this section, and then only in traveling to the nearest point where the safety of the passengers is assured.

§392.64 Riding within closed commercial motor vehicles without proper exits.

No person shall ride within the closed body of any commercial motor vehicle unless there are means on the inside thereof of obtaining exit. Said means shall be in such condition as to permit ready operation by the occupant.

§392.65 [Removed and reserved.]

§392.66 Carbon monoxide; use of commercial motor vehicle when detected.

(a) No person shall dispatch or drive any commercial motor vehicle or permit any passengers thereon, when the following conditions are known to exist, until such conditions have been remedied or repaired:

(1) Where an occupant has been affected by carbon monoxide;

(2) Where carbon monoxide has been detected in the interior of the commercial motor vehicle;

(3) When a mechanical condition of the commercial motor vehicle is discovered which would be likely to produce a hazard to the occupants by reason of carbon monoxide.

(b) [Reserved]

§392.67 Heater, flame-producing; on commercial motor vehicle in motion.

No open flame heater used in the loading or unloading of the commodity transported shall be in operation while the commercial motor vehicle is in motion.

§392.68 [Removed and reserved.]

§392.69 [Removed and reserved.]

§392.71 Radar detectors; use and/or possession.

(a) No driver shall use a radar detector in a commercial motor vehicle, or operate a commercial motor vehicle that is equipped with or contains any radar detector.

(b) No motor carrier shall require or permit a driver to violate paragraph (a) of this section.

PART 393 — PARTS AND ACCESSORIES NECESSARY FOR SAFE OPERATION

Subpart A — General

Subpart B — Lighting Devices, Reflectors, and Electrical Equipment

Subpart C — Brakes

AUTHORITY: Section 1041(b) of Pub. L. 102-240, 105 Stat. 1914; 49 U.S.C. 31136 and 31502; 49 CFR 1.73.

Subpart A — General

§393.1 Scope of the rules in this part.

Every employer and employee shall comply and be conversant with the requirements and specifications of this part. No employer shall operate a commercial motor vehicle, or cause or permit it to be operated, unless it is equipped in accordance with the requirements and specifications of this part.

§393.3 Additional equipment and accessories.

Nothing contained in this subchapter shall be construed to prohibit the use of additional equipment and accessories, not inconsistent with or prohibited by this subchapter, provided such equipment and accessories do not decrease the safety of operation of the motor vehicles on which they are used.

§393.5 Definitions.

As used in this part, the following words and terms are construed to mean:

*Aggregate working load limit. The summation of the working load limits or restraining capacity of all devices used to secure an article of cargo on a vehicle.

Agricultural Commodity Trailer....

*Anchor point. Part of the structure, fitting or attachment on a vehicle or article of cargo to which a tiedown is attached.

Antilock Brake System or ABS means a portion of a service brake system that automatically controls the degree of rotational wheel slip during braking by:

(1) Sensing the rate of angular rotation of the wheels;

(2) Transmitting signals regarding the rate of wheel angular rotation to one or more controlling devices which interpret those signals and generate responsive controlling output signals; and

(3) Transmitting those controlling signals to one or more modulators which adjust brake actuating forces in response to those signals.

*Article of cargo. A unit of cargo, other than a liquid, gas, or aggregate that lacks physical structure (e.g., grain, gravel, etc.) including articles grouped together so that they can be handled as a single unit or unitized by wrapping, strapping, banding or edge protection device(s).

*Bell pipe concrete. Pipe whose flanged end is of larger diameter than its barrel.

*Blocking. A structure, device or another substantial article placed against or around an article of cargo to prevent horizontal movement of the article of cargo.

*Bracing. A structure, device, or another substantial article placed against an article of cargo to prevent it from tipping, that may also prevent it from shifting.

Brake. An energy conversion mechanism used to stop, or hold a vehicle stationary.

Brake tubing/hose. Metallic brake tubing, nonmetallic brake tubing and brake hose are conduits or lines used in a brake system to transmit or contain the medium (fluid or vacuum) used to apply the motor vehicle's brakes.

Bus. A vehicle designed to carry more than 15 passengers, including the driver.

Chassis....

Clearance Lamp. A lamp used on the front and the rear of a motor vehicle to indicate its overall width and height.

Container Chassis....

Curb Weight. The weight of a motor vehicle with standard equipment, maximum capacity of fuel, oil, and coolant; and, if so equipped, air conditioning and additional weight of optional engine. Curb weight does not include the driver.

Dunnage....

Dunnage bag....

Edge protector....

Emergency Brake System. A mechanism designed to stop a vehicle after a single failure occurs in the service brake system of a part designed to contain compressed air or brake fluid or vacuum (except failure of a common valve, manifold brake fluid housing or brake chamber housing).

Fifth Wheel....

Frame vehicle....

Friction mat....

Fuel Tank Fitting. Any removable device affixed to an opening in the fuel tank with the exception of the filler cap.

Grommet. A device that serves as a support and protection to that which passes through it.

Hazard Warning Signal. Lamps that flash simultaneously to the front and rear, on both the right and left sides of a commercial motor vehicle, to indicate to an approaching driver the presence of a vehicular hazard.

Head Lamps. Lamps used to provide general illumination ahead of a motor vehicle.

Heater. Any device or assembly of devices or appliances used to heat the interior of any motor vehicle. This includes a catalytic heater which must meet the requirements of §177.834(1) of this title when flammable liquid or gas is transported.

Heavy Hauler Trailer....

Hook-lift container....

Identification Lamps. Lamps used to identify certain types of commercial motor vehicles.

Integral securement system....

Lamp. A device used to produce artificial light.

Length of a manufactured home....

License Plate Lamp. A lamp used to illuminate the license plate on the rear of a motor vehicle.

Low chassis vehicle. (1) A trailer or semitrailer manufactured on or after January 26, 1998, having a chassis which extends behind the rearmost point of the rearmost tires and which has a lower rear surface that meets the guard width, height, and rear surface requirements of §571.224 in effect on the date of manufacture, or a subsequent edition.

(2) A motor vehicle, not described by paragraph (1) of this definition, having a chassis which extends behind the rearmost point of the rearmost tires and which has a lower rear surface that meets the guard configuration requirements of §393.86(b)(1).

Manufactured home...

Parking Brake System. A brake system used to hold a vehicle stationary.

Play. Any free movement of components.

Pulpwood Trailer....

Rear Extremity. The rearmost point on a motor vehicle that falls above a horizontal plane located 560 mm (22 inches) above the ground and below a horizontal plane located 1,900 mm (75 inches) above the ground when the motor vehicle is stopped on level ground; unloaded; its fuel tanks are full; the tires (and air suspension, if so equipped) are inflated in accordance with the manufacturer's recommendations; and the motor vehicle's cargo doors, tailgate, or other permanent structures are positioned as they normally are when the vehicle is in motion. Nonstructural protrusions such as taillamps, rubber bumpers, hinges and latches are excluded from the determination of the rearmost point.

Reflective Material. A material conforming to Federal Specification L-S-300, "Sheeting and Tape, Reflective; Non-exposed Lens, Adhesive Backing," (September 7, 1965) meeting the performance standard in either Table 1 or Table 1A of SAE Standard J594f, "Reflex Reflectors" (January, 1977).

Reflex Reflector. A device which is used on a vehicle to give an indication to an approaching driver by reflected light from the lamps on the approaching vehicle.

Saddle-mount....

Service Brake System. A primary brake system used for slowing and stopping a vehicle.

Side Extremity. The outermost point on a side of the motor vehicle that is above a horizontal plane located 560 mm (22 inches) above the ground, below a horizontal plane located 1,900 mm (75 inches) above the ground, and between a transverse vertical plane tangent to the rear extremity of the vehicle and a transverse vertical plane located 305 mm (12 inches) forward of that plane when the vehicle is unloaded; its fuel tanks are full; and the tires (and air suspension, if so equipped) are inflated in accordance with the manufacturer's recommendations. Non-structural protrusions such as taillights, hinges and latches are excluded from the determination of the outermost point.

Side Marker Lamp (Intermediate)....

Side Marker Lamps....

*Steering Wheel Lash. The condition in which the steering wheel may be turned through some part of a revolution without associated movement of the front wheels.

Stop Lamps. Lamps shown to the rear of a motor vehicle to indicate that the service brake system is engaged.

Tail Lamps. Lamps used to designate the rear of a motor vehicle.

Turn Signals. Lamps used to indicate a change in direction by emitting a flashing light on the side of a motor vehicle towards which a turn will be made.

Wheels Back Vehicle. (1) A trailer or semitrailer manufactured on or after January 26, 1998, whose rearmost axle is permanently fixed and is located such that the rearmost surface of the tires (of the size recommended by the vehicle manufacturer for the rear axle) is not more than 305 mm (12 inches) forward of the transverse vertical plane tangent to the rear extremity of the vehicle.

(2) A motor vehicle, not described by paragraph (1) of this definition, whose rearmost axle is permanently fixed and is located such that the rearmost surface of the tires (of the size recommended by the vehicle manufacturer for the rear axle) is not more than 610 mm (24 inches) forward of the transverse vertical plane tangent to the rear extremity of the vehicle.

§393.7 Matter incorporated by reference.

(a) **Incorporation by reference.** Part 393 includes references to certain matter or materials, as listed in paragraph (b) of this section. The text of the materials is not included in the regulations contained in part 393. The materials are hereby made a part of the regulations in part 393. The Director of the Federal Register has approved the materials incorporated by reference in accordance with 5 U.S.C. 552(a) and 1 CFR part 51. For materials subject to change, only the specific version approved by the Director of the Federal Register and specified in the regulation are incorporated. Material is incorporated as it exists on the date of the approval and a notice of any change in these materials will be published in the Federal Register.

(b) **Matter or materials referenced in part 393.** The matter or materials listed in this paragraph are incorporated by reference in the corresponding sections noted.

(1) Highway Emergency Signals, Fourth Edition, Underwriters Laboratories, Inc., UL No. 912, July 30, 1979, (with an amendment dated November 9, 1981), incorporation by reference approved for §393.95(j).

(2) . . .

(3) . . .

(4) .

(5) . . .

(6) . . .

(7)-(9) [Reserved].

(10) All of the materials incorporated by reference are available for inspection at:

(i) The Federal Motor Carrier Safety Administration, Office of Bus and Truck Standards and Operations, 400 Seventh Street, SW., Washington, DC 20590; and

(ii) The Office of the Federal Register, 800 North Capitol Street, NW, Suite 700, Washington, DC.

Subpart B — Lighting Devices, Reflectors, and Electrical Equipment

§393.9 Lamps operable.

All lamps required by this subpart shall be capable of being operated at all times.

§393.11 Lighting devices and reflectors.

The following Table 1 sets forth the required color, position, and required lighting devices by type of commercial motor vehicle. Diagrams illustrating the locations of lighting devices and reflectors, by type and size of commercial motor vehicle, are shown immediately following Table 1. All lighting devices on motor vehicles placed in operation after March 7, 1989, must meet the requirements of 49 CFR 571.108 in effect at the time of manufacture of the vehicle. Motor vehicles placed in operation on or before March 7, 1989 must meet either the requirements of this Subchapter or Part 571 of this title in effect at the time of manufacture.

TABLE 1—REQUIRED COMMERCIAL VEHICLE LIGHTING EQUIPMENT

Item on the vehicle	Quantity	Color	Location	Position	Height above road surface in inches measured from the center of the lamp at the top of curb weight	Required lighting devices/ vehicles
Headlamps	2 At Least	White	Front	On the front at the same height, an equal number at each side of the vertical centerline as far apart as practicable.	Not less than 22 nor more than 54.	A,B,C
Turn Signal (Front) See Footnotes #2 & 12	2	Amber	At or Near Front	On each side of the vertical centerline at the same height and as far apart as practicable.	Not Less Than 15 nor more than 83.	A,B,C,
Identification Lamp (Front) Footnote #1	3	Amber	Front	Mounted on the vertical centerline of the vehicle or the vertical centerline of the cab where different from the centerline of the vehicle.	All three on same level as close as practicable to the top of the vehicle with lamp centers spaced not less than 6 inches or more than 12 inches apart.	B,C
Tail Lamp See Footnotes #5 & 11	2	Red	Rear	One lamp each side of the vertical centerline at the same height and as far apart as practicable.	Both on the same level between 15 and 72.	A,B,C,D, E,F,G,H
Stop Lamp See Footnotes #5 & 13	2	Red	Rear	One lamp each side of the vertical centerline at the same height and as far apart as practicable.	Both on the same level between 15 and 72.	A,B,C,D, E,F,G
Clearance Lamps See Footnotes #9, 10 & 15	2	Amber	One on each side of front.	One on each side of the vertical centerline to indicate width.	Both on same level as high as practicable.	B,C,D,G, H
	2	Red	One on each side of rear.	One on each side of the vertical centerline to indicate overall width.	Both on same level as high as practicable.	B,D,G,H
Side Marker Lamp Intermediate	2	Amber	One on each side	At or near midpoint between front and rear side marker lamps. If over 30' in length.	Not less than 15	A,B,D,F, G
Reflex Reflector Intermediate (Side).	2	Amber	One on each side	At or near midpoint between front and rear side reflectors if over 30' in length.	Between 15 and 60.	A,B,D,F, G
Reflex Reflector (Rear) See Footnotes #5, 6 & 8	2	Red	Rear	One on each side of vertical centerline as far apart as practicable	Both on same level, between 15 and 60.	A,B,C,D, E,F,G
Reflex Reflector (Rear Side) Footnote #4	2	Red	One on each side (rear)	As far to the rear as practicable	Both on same level, between 15 and 60	A,B,D,F, G

TABLE 1—REQUIRED COMMERCIAL VEHICLE LIGHTING EQUIPMENT, Continued

Item on the vehicle	Quantity	Color	Location	Position	Height above road surface in inches measured from the center of the lamp at curb weight	Required lighting devices/ vehicles
Reflex Reflector (Front Side)	2	Amber	One on each side (front).	As far to the front as practicable	Between 15 and 60.	A,B,C,D, F,G
License Plate lamp rear See Footnote #11	1	White	At rear license plate	To illuminate the license plate from the top or sides.	No requirements.	A,B,C,D, F,G
Side Marker Lamp (Front)	2	Amber	One on each side	As far to the front as practicable.	Not less than 15.	A,B,C,D, F
Side Marker Lamp (Rear) See Footnotes #4 & 8 ...	2	Red	One on each side	As far to the rear as practicable	Not less than 15 and on the rear of trailer, not more than 60.	A,B,D,F, G
Turn Signal (Rear) See Footnotes #5 & 12	2	Amber or Red	Rear	One lamp on each side of the vertical centerline as far apart as practicable.	Both on the same level, between 15 and 83.	A,B,C,D, E,F,G
Identification Lamp (Rear) See Footnotes #3, 7 & 15	3	Red	Rear	One as close as practicable to vertical centerline. One on each side with lamp centers spaced not less than 6" or more than 12" apart.	All three on same level as close as practicable to the top of the vehicle.	B,D,G
Vehicular Hazard Warning Flashing Lamps See Footnote #12	2	Amber	Front	One lamp on each side of vertical centerline as far apart as practicable.	Both on same level, between 15 and 83.	A,B,C,D, E,F,G
	2	Amber or Red	Rear	....	....	
Backup Lamp See Footnote #14	1	White	Rear	Rear	No requirement	A,B,C
Parking Lamp	2	Amber or white	Front	One lamp on each side of vertical centerline as far apart as practicable.	Both on same level, between 15 and 72.	A

*Lighting Required per Type of Commercial Vehicle as Shown Last Column of Table.
A. Small buses and trucks less than 80 inches in overall width.
B. Buses and trucks 80 inches or more in overall width.
C. Truck Tractors.
D. Large semitrailers and full trailers 80 inches or more in overall width except converter dollies.
E. Converter dolly.
F. Small semitrailers and full trailers less than 80 inches in overall width.
G. Pole Trailers.
H. Projecting loads.
Lamps and reflectors may be combined as permitted by Paragraphs 393.22 and S4.4 of 49 CFR 571.106. Equipment combinations.

Footnote — 1
Identification lamps may be mounted on the vertical centerline of the cab where different from the centerline of the vehicle, except where the cab is not more than 42 inches wide at the front roofline, then a single lamp at the center of the cab shall be deemed to comply with the requirements for identification lamps. No part of the identification lamps or their mountings may extend below the top of the vehicle windshield.

Footnote — 2 ...

Footnote — 3
The identification lamps need not be visible or lighted if obscured by a vehicle in the same combination.

Footnote — 4 ...

Footnote — 5 ...

Footnote — 6 ...

Footnote — 7 ...

Footnote — 8 ...

Footnote — 9 ...

Footnote — 10 ...

Footnote — 11 ...

Footnote — 12
Every bus, truck, and truck tractor shall be equipped with a signaling system that, in addition to signaling turning movements, shall have a switch or combination of switches that will cause the two front turn signals and the two rear signals to flash simultaneously as a vehicular traffic signal warning, required by §392.22(a). The system shall be capable of flashing simultaneously with the ignition of the vehicle on or off.

Footnote — 13
To be actuated upon application of service brakes.

Footnote — 14
Backup lamp required to operate when bus, truck, or truck tractor is in reverse.

Footnote — 15
When the rear identification lamps are mounted at the extreme height of a vehicle, rear clearance lamps need not meet the requirement that they be located as close as practicable to the top of the vehicle.

Large Bus

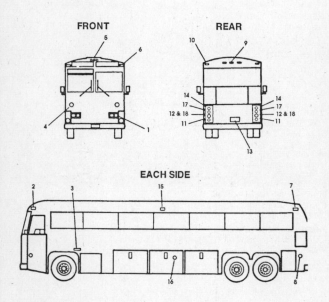

FRONT

REAR

EACH SIDE

Legend (Used in illustrations)

1. Headlamps (2)-White (4 optional)
2. Side-marker lamps. Front (2)-Amber
3. Side-reflectors. Front (2)-Amber
4. Turn-signal lamps. Front (2)-Amber
4a. Turn-signal lamps. Front (2)-Amber (Optional location)
5. Identification lamps. Front (3)-Amber
5a. Identification lamps. Front (3)-Amber (Optional location)
6. Clearance lamps. Front (2)-Amber
7. Side-marker lamps. Rear (2)-Red
8. Side-reflectors. Rear (2)-Red
9. Identification lamps. Rear (3)-Red
10. Clearance lamps. Rear (2)-Red
11. Reflectors Rear (2)-Red
12. Stop lamps. Rear (2)-Red
13. License plate lamp. Rear (1)-White
14. Backup lamp. Rear (1)-White (location optional provided optional requirements are met)
15. Side-marker lamps. Intermediate (2)-Amber (if vehicle is 30' or more overall length)
16. Side reflectors. Intermediate (2)-Amber (if vehicle is 30' or more overall length)
17. Turn signal lamps. Rear (2)-Amber or Red
18. Tail lamps. Rear (2)-Red
19. Parking lamps. Front (2)-Amber or White

§393.13 . . .

§393.17 . . .

§393.19 Requirements for turn signaling systems.

(a) Every bus, truck, or truck tractor shall be equipped with a signaling system that in addition to signaling turning movements shall have a switch or combination of switches that will cause the two front turn signals and the two rear turn signals to flash simultaneously as a vehicular traffic hazard warning as required by §392.22 with the ignition on or off.

(b) . . .

§393.20 Clearance lamps to indicate extreme width and height.

Clearance lamps shall be mounted so as to indicate the extreme width of the motor vehicle (not including mirrors) and as near the top thereof as practicable: **Provided**, that when rear identification lamps are mounted at the extreme height of the vehicle, rear clearance lamps may be mounted at optional height.

§393.22 Combination of lighting devices and reflectors.

(a) **Permitted combinations.** Except as provided in paragraph (b) of this section, two or more lighting devices and reflectors (whether or not required by the rules in this part) may be combined optically if —

(1) Each required lighting device and reflector conforms to the applicable rules in this Part; and

(2) Neither the mounting nor the use of a nonrequired lighting device or reflector impairs the effectiveness of a required lighting device or reflector or causes that device or reflector to be inconsistent with the applicable rules in this Part.

(b) **Prohibited combinations.** (1) A turn signal lamp must not be combined optically with either a head lamp or other lighting device or combination of lighting devices that produces a greater intensity of light than the turn signal lamp;

(2) A turn signal lamp must not be combined optically with a stop lamp unless the stop lamp function is always deactivated when the turn signal function is activated;

(3) A clearance lamp must not be combined optically with a tail lamp or identification lamp.

§393.23 Lighting devices to be electric.

Lighting devices shall be electric.

§393.24 Requirements for head lamps and auxiliary road lighting lamps.

(a) **Mounting.** Head lamps and auxiliary road lighting lamps shall be mounted so that the beams are readily adjustable, both vertically and horizontally, and the mounting shall be such that the aim is not readily disturbed by ordinary conditions or service.

(b) **Head lamps required.** Every bus, truck, and truck tractor shall be equipped with a headlighting system composed of at least two head lamps, not including fog or other auxiliary lamps, with an equal number on each side of the vehicle. The headlighting system shall provide an upper and lower distribution of light, selectable at the driver's will.

(c) **Fog, adverse-weather, and auxiliary road-lighting lamps.** For the purposes of this section, fog, adverse-weather, auxiliary road lighting lamps, when installed, are considered to be a part of the headlighting system. Such lamps may be used in lieu of head lamps under conditions making their use advisable if there be at least one such lamp conforming to the appropriate SAE Standard[1] for such lamps on each side of the vehicle.

(d) **Aiming and intensity.** Head lamps shall be constructed and installed so as to provide adequate and reliable illumination and shall conform to the appropriate specification set forth in the SAE Standards[1] for "Electric Head Lamps for Motor Vehicles" or "Sealed-Beam Head Lamp Units for Motor Vehicles."

§393.25 Requirements for lamps other than head lamps.

(a) **Mounting.** All lamps shall be permanently and securely mounted in workmanlike manner on a permanent part of the motor vehicle. The requirement for three identification lamps on the centerline of a vehicle will be met as to location by one lamp on the centerline, with the other two at right and left. All temporary lamps must be firmly attached.

(b) **Visibility.** All required exterior lamps shall be so mounted as to be capable of being seen at all distances between 500 feet and 50 feet under clear atmospheric conditions during the time lamps are required to be lighted. The light from front clearance and front identification lamps shall be visible to the front, that from sidemarker lamps to the side, that from rear clearance, rear identification, and tail lamps to the rear.

(c) **Specifications.** All required lamps shall conform to appropriate requirements of the SAE Standards and/or Recom-

---

[1] Wherever reference is made in these regulations to SAE Standards or SAE Recommended Practices, they shall be:
(a) As found in the 1985 edition of the SAE Handbook with respect to parts and accessories other than lighting devices and reflectors.
(b) When reference is made in these regulations to SAE Standards or SAE Recommended Practices, they shall be as found in the 1985 edition of the SAE Handbook:
(1) With respect to parts and accessories other than lighting devices and reflectors:
(2) Lighting devices and reflectors on motor vehicles manufactured on and after March 7, 1990, shall conform to FMVSS 571.108 (49 CFR 571.108) in effect at the time of manufacture of the vehicle. Should a conflict arise between FMVSS 571.108 and a SAE Standard, FMVSS 571.108 will prevail.
The "SAE Handbook" and Pamphlet No. TR-34 are published by the SAE, Inc., 400 Commonwealth Drive, Warrendale, Pennsylvania 15096.

mended Practices[1] as indicated below, except that the minimum required marking of lamps conforming to the 1985 requirements shall be as specified in paragraph (d) of this section. Turn signals shall conform to the requirements for Class A, Type I turn signals, provided:

(1) Lamps on vehicles made before July 1, 1961, excepting replacement lamps as specified in paragraph (c)(2) of this section, shall conform to the 1952 requirements.

(2) Lamps on vehicles made on and after July 1, 1961, and replacement lamps installed on and after December 31, 1961, shall conform to the 1985 requirements.

(3) . . .

(d) **Certification and markings.** All lamps required to conform to the requirements of the SAE Standards shall be certified by the manufacturer or supplier that they do so conform, by markings indicated below. The markings in each case shall be visible when the lamp is in place on the vehicle:

(1) Stop lamps shall be marked with the manufacturer's or supplier's name or trade name and shall be marked "SAE-S".

(2) Turn signal units shall be marked with the manufacturer's or supplier's name or trade name and shall be marked "SAE-AI" or "SAE-I".

(3) Tail lamps shall be marked with the manufacturer's or supplier's name or trade name and shall be marked "SAE-T".

(4) Clearance, side marker, identification, and projecting load-marker lamps, except combination lamps, shall be marked with the manufacturer's or supplier's name or trade name and shall be marked "SAE" or "SAE-P".

(5) Combination lamps shall be marked with the manufacturer's or supplier's name or trade name and shall be marked "SAE" followed by the appropriate letters indicating the individual lamps combined. The letter "A", as specified in §393.26 (c), may be included to certify that a reflector in the combination conforms to the requirements appropriate to such marking. If the letter "I" follows a letter "A" immediately, the two letters shall be deemed to refer to a turn signal unit, as specified in paragraph (d)(2) of this section. Combination clearance and side marker lamps may be marked "SAE-PC".

(e) **Lighting devices to be steady-burning.** All exterior lighting devices shall be of the steady-burning type except turn

---

[1]See footnote 1 to Sec. 393.24(c)

signals on any vehicle, stop lamps when used as turn signals, warning lamps on school buses when operating as such, and warning lamps on emergency and service vehicles authorized by State or local authorities, and except that lamps combined into the same shell or housing with any turn signal may be turned off by the same switch that turns the signal on for flashing and turned on again when the turn signal as such is turned off. This paragraph shall not be construed to prohibit the use of vehicular hazard warning signal flashers as required by §392.22 or permitted by §392.18.

(f) **Stop lamp operation.** All stop lamps on each motor vehicle shall be actuated upon application of any of the service brakes, except that no stop lamp need be actuated as such when it is in use as a turn signal or when it is turned off by the turn signal switch as provided in paragraph (e) of this section.

§393.26 Requirements for reflectors.

(a) **Mounting.** All required reflectors shall be mounted upon the motor vehicle at a height not less than 15 inches nor more than 60 inches above the ground on which the motor vehicle stands, except that reflectors shall be mounted as high as practicable on motor vehicles which are so constructed as to make compliance with the 15-inch requirement impractical. They shall be so installed as to perform their function adequately and reliably, and all reflectors shall be permanently and securely mounted in workmanlike manner so as to provide the maximum of stability and the minimum likelihood of damage. Required reflectors otherwise properly mounted may be securely installed on flexible strapping or belting provided that under conditions of normal operation they reflect light in the required directions.

(b) **Specifications.** All required reflectors shall comply with FMVSS 571.108 (49 CFR 571.108) in effect at the time the vehicle was manufactured or the current FMVSS 571.108 requirements.

(c) **Certification and markings.** All reflectors required to conform to the specifications in paragraph (b) shall be certifed by the manufacturer or supplier that they do so conform, by marking with the manufacturer's or supplier's name or trade name and the letters "SAE-A". The marking in each case shall be visible when the reflector is in place on the vehicle.

(d) **Retroreflective surfaces.** Retroreflective surfaces

other than required reflectors may be used, provided:

(1) Designs do not resemble traffic control signs, lights, or devices, except that straight edge striping resembling a barricade pattern may be used.

(2) Designs do not tend to distort the length and/or width of the motor vehicle.

(3) Such surfaces shall be at least 3 inches from any required lamp or reflector unless of the same color as such lamp or reflector.

(4) No red color shall be used on the front of any motor vehicle.

(5) Retroreflective license plates required by State or local authorities may be used.

§393.27 Wiring specifications.

(a) Wiring for both low voltage (tension) and high voltage (tension) circuits shall be constructed and installed so as to meet design requirements. Wiring shall meet or exceed, both mechanically and electrically, the following SAE Standards as found in the 1985 edition of the SAE Handbook:

(1) Commercial vehicle engine ignition systems—SAE J557—High Tension Ignition Cable.

(2) Commercial vehicle battery cable—SAE J1127—Jan 80—Battery Cable.

(3) Other commercial vehicle wiring—SAE J1128—Low Tension Primary Cable.

(b) The source of power and the electrical wiring shall be of such size and characteristics as to provide the necessary voltage as the design requires to comply with FMVSS 571.108.

(c) Lamps shall be properly grounded.

Note: This shall not prohibit the use of the frame or other metal parts of a motor vehicle as a return ground system provided truck-tractor semitrailer/full trailer combinations are electrically connected.

§393.28 Wiring to be protected.

(a) The wiring shall—

(1) Be so installed that connections are protected from weather, abrasion, road splash, grease, oil, fuel and chafing;

(2) Be grouped together, when possible, and protected by nonconductive tape, braid, or other covering capable of withstanding severe abrasion or shall be protected by being enclosed in a sheath or tube;

(3) Be properly supported in a manner to prevent chafing;

(4) Not be so located as to be likely to be charred, overheated, or enmeshed in moving parts;

(5) Not have terminals or splices located above the fuel tank except for the fuel sender wiring and terminal; and

(6) Be protected when passing through holes in metal by a grommet, or other means, or the wiring shall be encased in a protective covering.

(b) The complete wiring system including lamps, junction boxes, receptacle boxes, conduit and fittings must be weather resistant.

(c) Harness connections shall be accomplished by a mechanical means.

§393.29 Grounds.

The battery ground and trailer return ground connections on a grounded system shall be readily accessible. The contact surfaces of electrical connections shall be clean and free of oxide, paint, or other nonconductive coating.

§393.30 Battery installation.

Every storage battery on every vehicle, unless located in the engine compartment, shall be covered by a fixed part of the motor vehicle or protected by a removable cover or enclosure. Removable covers, or enclosures shall be substantial and shall be securely latched or fastened. The storage battery compartment and adjacent metal parts which might corrode by reason of battery leakage shall be painted or coated with an acidresisting paint or coating and shall have openings to provide ample battery ventilation and drainage. Whenever the cable to the starting motor passes through a metal compartment, the cable shall be protected against grounding by an acid and waterproof insulating bushing. Wherever a battery and a fuel tank are both placed under the driver's seat, they shall be partitioned from each other, and each compartment shall be provided with an independent cover, ventilation, and drainage.

§393.31 Overload protective devices.

(a) The current to all low tension circuits shall pass through overload protective devices except that this requirement shall not be applicable to battery-to-starting motor or battery-to-generator circuits, ignition and engine control circuits, horn circuits, electrically-operated fuel pump circuits, or electric brake circuits.

(b) Buses meeting the definition of a commercial motor vehicle and manufactured after June 30, 1953 shall have protective devices for electrical circuits arranged so that:

(i) The headlamp circuit or circuits shall not be affected by a short circuit in any other lighting circuits on the motor vehicle; or

(ii) The protective device shall be an automatic reset overload circuit breaker if the headlight circuit is protected in common with other circuits.

§393.32 . . .

§393.33 Wiring, installation.

Electrical wiring shall be systematically arranged and installed in a workmanlike manner. All detachable wiring, shall be attached to posts or terminals by means of suitable cable terminals which conform to the SAE Standard[1] for "Cable Terminals" or by cable terminals which are mechanically and electrically at least equal to such terminals. The number of wires attached to any post shall be limited to the number which such post was designed to accommodate. The presence of bare, loose, dangling, chafing, or poorly connected wires is prohibited.

Subpart C — Brakes

§393.40 Required brake systems.

(a) **General.** A bus must have brakes adequate to control the movement of, and to stop and hold, the vehicle or combination of vehicles.

(b) **Specific systems required.** (1) A bus must have —

(i) A service brake system that conforms to the requirements of §393.52; and

(ii) A parking brake system that conforms to the requirements of §393.41.

(2) A bus manufactured on or after July 1, 1973, must have an emergency brake system that conforms to the requirements of §393.52(b) and consists of either—

(i) Emergency features of the service brake system; or

(ii) A system separate from the service brake system.

A control by which the driver applies the emergency brake system must be located so that the driver can readily operate it

---

[1]See footnote 1 to 393.24(c).

when he/she is properly restrained by any seat belt assembly provided for his/her use. The control for applying the emergency brake system may be combined with either the control for applying the service brake system or the control for applying the parking brake system. However, all three controls may not be combined.

(c) **Interconnected systems.** (1) If the brake systems specified in paragraph (b) of this section are interconnected in any way, they must be designed, constructed, and maintained so that, upon the failure of any part of the operating mechanism of one or more of the systems (except the service brake actuation pedal or valve)—

(i) The vehicle will have operative brakes; and

(ii) In the case of a vehicle manufactured on or after July 1, 1973, the vehicle will have operative brakes capable of performing as specified in §393.52(b).

(2) A motor vehicle to which the emergency brake system requirements of Federal Motor Vehicle Safety Standard No. 105 (§571.105 of this title) applied at the time of its manufacture conforms to the requirements of paragraph (c)(1) of this section if—

(i) It is maintained in conformity with the emergency brake requirements of Standard No. 105 in effect on the date of its manufacture; and

(ii) It is capable of performing as specified in §393.52(b), except upon structural failure of its brake master cylinder body or effectiveness indicator body.

(3) A bus conforms to the requirements of paragraph (c)(1) of this section if it meets the requirements of §393.44 and is capable of performing as specified in §393.52(b).

§393.41 Parking brake system.

(a) Every commercial motor vehicle manufactured on and after one year after March 7, 1989, shall at all times be equipped with a parking brake system adequate to hold the vehicle under any condition of loading as required by FMVSS 571.121.

(b) The parking brake system shall at all times be capable of being applied in conformance with the requirements of paragraph (a) of this section by either the driver's muscular effort, or by spring action, or by other energy, provided, that if such other energy is depended on for application of the parking brake, then an accumulation of such energy shall be isolated from any common source and used exclusively for the operation of the parking brake.

(c) The parking brake system shall be held in the applied position by energy other than fluid pressure, air pressure, or electric energy. The parking brake system shall be such that it cannot be released unless adequate energy is available upon release of the parking brake to make immediate further application with the required effectiveness.

§393.42 Brakes required on all wheels.

(a) Every commercial motor vehicle shall be equipped with brakes acting on all wheels.

(b) . . .

§393.43 . . .

§393.44 Front brake lines, protection.

On every bus, if equipped with air brakes, the braking system shall be so constructed that in the event any brake line to any of the front wheels is broken, the driver can apply the brakes on the rear wheels despite such breakage. The means used to apply the brakes may be located forward of the driver's seat as long as it can be operated manually by the driver when the driver is properly restrained by any seat belt assembly provided for use. Every bus shall meet this requirement or comply with the regulations in effect at the time of its manufacture.

§393.45 Brake tubing and hose, adequacy.

(a) **General requirements.** Brake tubing and brake hose must—

(1) Be designed and constructed in a manner that insures proper, adequate, and continued functioning of the tubing or hose;

(2) Be installed in a manner that insures proper continued functioning of the tubing or hose;

(3) Be long and flexible enough to accommodate without damage all normal motions of the parts to which it is attached;

(4) Be suitably secured against chafing, kinking, or other mechanical damage;

(5) Be installed in a manner that prevents it from contacting the vehicle's exhaust system or any other source of high temperatures; and

(6) Conform to the applicable requirements of paragraph (b) or (c) of this section. In addition, all hose installed on and after

January 1, 1981, must conform to those applicable subsections of FMVSS 106 (49 CFR 571.106).

(b) **Special requirements for metallic brake tubing, nonmetallic brake tubing, coiled nonmetallic brake tubing and brake hose.**

(1) Metallic brake tubing, nonmetallic brake tubing, coiled nonmetallic brake tubing, and brake hose installed on a commercial motor vehicle on and after March 7, 1989, must meet or exceed one of the following specifications set forth in the SAE Handbook 1985 edition:

(i) Metallic Air Brake Tubing—SAE Recommended Practice J1149—Metallic Air Brake System Tubing and Pipe—July 76.

(ii) Nonmetallic Air Brake Tubing—SAE Recommended Practice J844—Nonmetallic Air Brake System Type B—OCT 80.

(iii) Air Brake Hose—SAE Recommended Practice J1402-Automotive Air Brake Hose and Hose Assemblies—JUN 85.

(iv) Hydraulic Brake Hose—SAE Recommended Practice J1401 Road Vehicle-Hydraulic Brake Hose Assemblies for Use with Non-Petroleum Base Hydraulic Fluid JUN 85.

(v) Vacuum Brake Hose—SAE Recommended Practice J1403 Vacuum Brake Hose JUN 85.

(2) Except as provided in paragraph (c) of this section, brake hose and brake tubing installed on a motor vehicle before March 7, 1989, must conform to 49 CFR 393.45 effective October 31, 1983.

(c) . . .

(d) **Brake tubing and brake hose, uses.** Metallic and nonmetallic brake tubing is intended for use in areas of the brake system where relative movement in the line is not anticipated. Brake hose and coiled nonmetallic brake tubing is intended for use in the brake system where substantial relative movement in the line is anticipated or the hose/coiled nonmetallic brake tubing is exposed to potential tension or impact such as between the frame and axle in a conventional type suspension system (axle attached to frame by suspension system). Nonmetallic brake tubing may be used through an articulation point provided movement is less than 4.5 degrees in a vertical plane, and 7.4 degrees in a transverse horizontal plane.

§393.46 Brake tubing and hose connections.

All connections for air, vacuum, or hydraulic braking

§393.47

systems shall:

(a) Be adequate in material and construction to insure proper continued functioning;

(b) Be designed, constructed, and installed so as to insure, when properly connected, an attachment free of leaks, constrictions, or other defects;

(c) Have suitable provision in every detachable connection to afford reasonable assurance against accidental disconnection;

(d) Have the vacuum brake engine manifold connection at least $3/8$ inch in diameter.

(e) If installed on a vehicle on or after January 1, 1981, meet requirements under applicable subsections of FMVSS 106 (49 CFR 571.106).

(f) Splices in tubing if installed on a vehicle after March 7, 1989, must use fittings that meet the requirements of SAE Standard J512-OCT 80 Automotive Tube Fittings or for air brake systems SAE J246—March 81 Spherical and Flanged Sleeve (Compression) Tube Fittings as found in the SAE Handbook 1985 edition.

§393.47 Brake lining.

The brake lining on every motor vehicle shall be so constructed and installed as not to be subject to excessive fading and grabbing and shall be adequate in thickness, means of attachment, and physical characteristics to provide for safe and reliable stopping of the motor vehicle.

§393.48 Brakes to be operative.

(a) **General rule.** Except as provided in paragraphs (b) and (c) of this section, all brakes with which a motor vehicle is equipped must at all times be capable of operating.

(b) **Devices to reduce or remove front-wheel braking effort.** A motor vehicle may be equipped with a device to reduce the braking effort upon its front wheels or, in the case of a three-axle truck or truck tractor manufactured before March 1, 1975, to remove the braking effort upon its front wheels, if that device conforms to, and is used in compliance with, the rules in paragraph (b)(1) or (2) of this section.

(1) **Manually operated devices.** A manually operated device to reduce or remove the front-wheel braking effort must not be—

(i) Installed in a motor vehicle other than a bus

(ii) Installed in a bus, manufactured after February 28, 1975;

or

(iii) Used in the reduced mode except when the vehicle is operating under adverse conditions such as wet, snowy, or icy roads.

(2) **Automatic Devices.** An automatic device to reduce the front-wheel braking effort by up to 50 percent of the normal braking force, regardless of whether or not antilock system failure has occurred on any axle, must not—

(i) Be operable by the driver except upon application of the control that activates the braking system; and

(ii) Be operable when the pressure that transmits brake control application force exceeds—

(A) 85 psig on air-mechanical braking systems; or

(B) 85 percent of the maximum system pressure in the case of vehicles utilizing other than compressed air.

(c) **Towed vehicle.** Paragraph (a) of this section does not apply to—

(1) A disabled vehicle being towed; or

(2) . . .

§393.49 Single valve to operate all brakes.

Every motor vehicle, the date of manufacture of which is subsequent to June 30, 1953, which is equipped with power brakes, shall have the braking system so arranged that one application valve shall when applied operate all the service brakes on the motor vehicle.

§393.50 Reservoirs required.

(a) **General.** Every commercial motor vehicle using air or vacuum for braking shall be equipped with reserve capacity or a reservoir sufficient to ensure a full service brake application with the engine stopped without depleting the air pressure or vacuum below 70 percent of that pressure or degree of vacuum indicated by the gauge immediately before the brake application is made. For purposes of this section, a full service brake application is considered to be made when the service brake pedal is pushed to the limit of its travel.

(b) **Safeguarding of air and vacuum.** (1) Every bus, when equipped with air or vacuum reservoirs and regardless of date of manufacture, shall have such reservoirs so safeguarded by a check valve or equivalent device that in the event of failure or leakage in its connection to the source of compressed air or vacuum the air or vacuum supply in the reservoir shall not be depleted by the leak or failure.

(2) Means shall be provided to establish the check valve to be in working order. On and after May 1, 1966, means other than loosening or disconnection of any connection between the source of compressed air or vacuum and the check valve, and necessary tools for operation of such means, shall be provided to prove that the check valve is in working order. The means shall be readily accessible either from the front, side, or rear of the vehicle, or from the driver's compartment.

(i) In air brake systems with one reservoir, the means shall be a cock, valve, plug, or equivalent device arranged to vent a cavity having free communication with the connection between the check valve and the source of compressed air or vacuum.

(ii) Where air is delivered by a compressor into one tank or compartment (wet tank), and air for braking is taken directly from another tank or compartment (dry tank) only, with the required check valve between the tanks or compartments, a manually operated drain cock on the first (wet) tank or compartment will serve as a means herein required if it conforms to the requirements herein.

(iii) In vacuum systems stopping the engine will serve as the required means, the system remaining evacuated as indicated by the vacuum gauge.

§393.51 Warning devices and gauges.

(a) **General.** In the manner and to the extent specified in paragraphs (b), (c), (d), and (e) of this section, a bus must be equipped with a signal that provides a warning to the driver when a failure occurs in the vehicle's service brake system.

(b) **Hydraulic brakes.** A vehicle manufactured on or after July 1, 1973, and having service brakes activated by hydraulic fluid must be equipped with a warning signal that performs as follows:

(1) If Federal Motor Vehicle Safety Standard No. 105 (§571.105 of this title) was applicable to the vehicle at the time it was manufactured, the warning signal must conform to the requirements of that standard.

(2) If Federal Motor Vehicle Safety Standard No. 105 (§571.105) was not applicable to the vehicle at the time it was manufactured, the warning signal must become operative, before or upon application of the brakes in the event of a hydraulic-type complete failure of a partial system. The signal

must be readily audible or visible to the driver.

(c) **Air brakes.** A vehicle (regardless of the date it was manufactured) having service brakes activated by compressed air (air-mechanical brakes) or a vehicle towing a vehicle having service brakes activated by compressed air (air-mechanical brakes) must be equipped, and perform, as follows:

(1) The vehicle must have a low air pressure warning device that conforms to the requirements of either paragraph (c)(1)(i) or (ii) of this section.

(i) If Federal Motor Vehicle Safety Standard No. 121 (§571.121 of this title) was applicable to the vehicle at the time it was manufactured, the warning device must conform to the requirements of that standard.

(ii) If Federal Motor Vehicle Safety Standard No. 121 (§571.121) was not applicable to the vehicle at the time it was manufactured, the vehicle must have a device that provides a readily audible or visible continuous warning to the driver whenever the pressure of the compressed air in the braking system is below a specified pressure, which must be at least one-half of the compressor governor cutout pressure.

(2) The vehicle must have a pressure gauge which indicates to the driver the pressure in pounds per square inch available for braking.

(d) **Vacuum brakes.** A vehicle (regardless of the date it was manufactured) having service brakes activated by vacuum or a vehicle towing a vehicle having service brakes activated by vacuum must be equipped with—

(1) A device that provides a readily audible or visible continuous warning to the driver whenever the vacuum in the vehicle's supply reservoir is less than 8 inches of mercury; and

(2) A vacuum gauge which indicates to the driver the vacuum in inches of mercury available for braking.

(e) **Hydraulic brakes applied or assisted by air or vacuum.** A vehicle having a braking system in which hydraulically activated service brakes are applied or assisted by compressed air or vacuum must be equipped with both a warning signal that conforms to the requirements of paragraph (b) of this section and a warning device that conforms to the requirements of either paragraph (c) or paragraph (d) of this section.

(f) **Maintenance.** The warning signals, devices, and gauges required by this section must be maintained in operative condition.

§393.52 Brake performance.

(a) Upon application of its service brakes, a motor vehicle or combination of motor vehicles must under any condition of loading in which it is found on a public highway, be capable of—

(1) Developing a braking force at least equal to the percentage of its gross weight specified in the table in paragraph (d) of this section;

(2) Decelerating to a stop from 20 miles per hour at not less than the rate specified in the table in paragraph (d) of this section; and

(3) Stopping from 20 miles per hour in a distance, measured from the point at which movement of the service brake pedal or control begins, that is not greater than the distance specified in the table in paragraph (d) of this section; or, for motor vehicles or motor vehicle combinations that have a GVWR or GVW greater than 4,536 kg (10,000 pounds),

(4) Developing only the braking force specified in paragraph (a)(1) of this section and the stopping distance specified in paragraph (a)(3) of this section, if braking force is measured by a performance-based brake tester which meets the requirements of functional specifications for performance-based brake testers for commercial motor vehicles, where braking force is the sum of the braking force at each wheel of the vehicle or vehicle combination as a percentage of gross vehicle or combination weight.

(b) Upon application of its emergency brake system and with no other brake system applied, a motor vehicle or combination of motor vehicles must, under any condition of loading in which it is found on a public highway, be capable of stopping from 20 miles per hour in a distance, measured from the point at which movement of the emergency brake control begins, that is not greater than the distance specified in the table in paragraph (d) of this section.

(c) Conformity to the stopping-distance requirements of paragraphs (a) and (b) of this section shall be determined under the following conditions:

(1) Any test must be made with the vehicle on a hard surface that is substantially level, dry, smooth, and free of loose material.

(2) The vehicle must be in the center of a 12-foot-wide lane when the test begins and must not deviate from that lane during the test.

(d) Vehicle brake performance table:

Type of motor vehicle	Service brake systems			Emergency brake systems
	Braking force as a percentage of gross vehicle or combination weight	Deceleration in feet per second per second	Application and braking distance in feet from initial speed of 20 m.p.h.	Application and braking distance in feet from initial speed of 20 m.p.h.
A. Passenger-carrying vehicles.				
(1) Vehicles with a seating capacity of 10 persons or less, including driver, and built on a passenger car chassis	65.2	21	20	54
(2) Vehicles with a seating capacity of more than 10 persons, including driver, and built on a passenger car chassis; vehicles built on a truck or bus chassis and having a manufacturer's GVWR of 10,000 pounds or less	52.8	17	25	66
(3) All other passenger-carrying vehicles	43.5	14	35	85
B. Property-carrying vehicles.				
(1) Single unit vehicles having a manufacturer's GVWR of 10,000 pounds or less	52.8	17	25	66
(2) Single unit vehicles having a manufacturer's GVWR of more than 10,000 pounds, except truck tractors. Combinations of a 2-axle towing vehicle and trailer having a GVWR of 3,000 pounds or less. All combinations of 2 or less vehicles in driveway or towaway operation	53.5	14	35	85
(3) All other property-carrying vehicles and combinations of property-carrying vehicles	43.5	14	40	90

(see note on following page)

§393.53

Notes: (a) There is a definite mathematical relationship between the figures in columns 2 and 3. If the decelerations set forth in column 3 are divided by 32.2 feet per-second per-second, the figures in column 2 will be obtained. (For example, 21 divided by 32.2 equals 65.2 percent.) Column 2 is included in the tabulation because certain brake testing devices utilize this factor.

(b) The decelerations specified in column 3 are an indication of the effectiveness of the basic brakes, and as measured in practical brake testing are the maximum decelerations attained at some time during the stop. These decelerations as measured in brake tests cannot be used to compute the values in column 4 because the deceleration is not sustained at the same rate over the entire period of the stop. The deceleration increases from zero to a maximum during a period of brake system application and brake-force build-up. Also, other factors may cause the deceleration to decrease after reaching a maximum. The added distance that results because maximum deceleration is not sustained is included in the figures in column 4 but is not indicated by the usual brake-testing devices for checking deceleration.

(c) The distances in column 4 and the decelerations in column 3 are not directly related. "Brake-system application and braking distance in feet" (column 4) is a definite measure of the overall effectiveness of the braking system, being the distance traveled between the point at which the driver starts to move the braking controls and the point at which the vehicle comes to rest. It includes distance traveled while the brakes are being applied and distance traveled while the brakes are retarding the vehicle.

(d) The distance traveled during the period of brake-system application and brake-force buildup varies with vehicle type, being negligible for many passenger cars and greatest for combinations of commercial vehicles. This fact accounts for the variation from 20 to 40 feet in the values in column 4 for the various classes of vehicles.

(e) The terms "GVWR" and "GVW" refer to the manufacturer's gross vehicle weight rating and the actual gross vehicle weight, respectively.

§393.53 Automatic brake adjusters and brake adjustment indicators.

(a) **Automatic brake adjusters (hydraulic brake systems).** Each commercial motor vehicle manufactured on or after October 20, 1993, and equipped with a hydraulic brake system, shall meet the automatic brake adjustment system requirements of Federal Motor Vehicle Safety Standard No. 105 (49 CFR 571.105, S5.1) applicable to the vehicle at the time it was manufactured.

(b) **Automatic brake adjusters (air brake systems).** Each commercial motor vehicle manufactured on or after October 20, 1994, and equipped with an air brake system, shall meet the automatic brake adjustment system requirements of Federal Motor Vehicle Safety Standard No. 121 (49 CFR 571.121, S5.1.8) applicable to the vehicle at the time it was manufactured.

(c) **Brake adjustment indicator (air brake systems).** On each commercial motor vehicle manufactured on or after October 20, 1994, and equipped with an air brake system which contains an external automatic adjustment mechanism and an exposed pushrod, the condition of service brake under-adjustment shall be displayed by a brake adjustment indicator conforming to the requirements of Federal Motor Vehicle Safety Standard No. 121 (49 CFR 571.121, S5.1.8) applicable to the vehicle at the time it was manufactured.

Sec. 393.55 Antilock brake systems.

(a) **Hydraulic brake systems.** Each truck and bus manufactured on or after March 1, 1999 (except trucks and buses engaged in driveaway-towaway operations), and equipped with a hydraulic brake system, shall be equipped with an antilock brake system that meets the requirements of Federal Motor Vehicle Safety Standard (FMVSS) No. 105 (49 CFR 571.105, S5.5).

(b) **ABS malfunction indicators for hydraulic braked vehicles.** Each hydraulic braked vehicle subject to the requirements of paragraph (a) of this section shall be equipped with an ABS malfunction indicator system that meets the requirements of FMVSS No. 105 (49 CFR 571.105, S5.3).

(c) **Air brake systems.** (1) Each truck tractor manufactured on or after March 1, 1997 (except truck tractors engaged in driveaway-towaway operations), shall be equipped with an antilock brake system that meets the requirements of FMVSS No. 121 (49 CFR 571.121, S5.1.6.1(b)).

(2) Each air braked commercial motor vehicle other than a truck tractor, manufactured on or after March 1, 1998 (except commercial motor vehicles engaged in driveaway-towaway operations), shall be equipped with an antilock brake system that meets the requirements of FMVSS No. 121 (49 CFR 571.121, S5.1.6.1(a) for trucks and buses, S5.2.3 for semitrailers, converter dollies and full trailers).

(d) **ABS malfunction circuits and signals for air braked vehicles.** (1) Each truck tractor manufactured on or after March 1, 1997, and each single-unit air braked vehicle manufactured on or after March 1, 1998, subject to the requirements of paragraph (c) of this section, shall be equipped with an electrical circuit that is capable of signaling a malfunction that affects the generation or transmission of response or control signals to the vehicle's antilock brake system (49 CFR 571.121, S5.1.6.2(a)).

(2) Each truck tractor manufactured on or after March 1, 2001, and each single-unit vehicle that is equipped to tow another air-braked vehicle, subject to the requirements of paragraph (c) of this section, shall be equipped with an electrical circuit that is capable of transmitting a malfunction signal from the antilock brake system(s) on the towed vehicle(s) to the trailer ABS malfunction lamp in the cab of the towing vehicle, and shall have the means for connection of the electrical circuit to the towed vehicle. The ABS malfunction circuit and signal shall meet the requirements of FMVSS No. 121 (49 CFR 571.121, S5.1.6.2(b)).

(3) Each semitrailer, trailer converter dolly, and full trailer manufactured on or after March 1, 2001, and subject to the requirements of paragraph (c)(2) of this section, shall be equipped with an electrical circuit that is capable of signaling a malfunction in the trailer's antilock brake system, and shall have the means for connection of this ABS malfunction circuit to the towing vehicle. In addition, each trailer manufactured on or after March 1, 2001, subject to the requirements of paragraph (c)(2) of this section, that is designed to tow another air-brake equipped trailer shall be capable of transmitting a malfunction signal from the antilock brake system(s) of the trailer(s) it tows to the vehicle in front of the trailer. The ABS malfunction circuit and signal shall meet the requirements of FMVSS No. 121 (49 CFR 571.121, S5.2.3.2).

(e) **Exterior ABS malfunction indicator lamps for trailers.** Each trailer (including a trailer converter dolly) manufactured on or after March 1, 1998 and before March 1, 2009, and subject to the requirements of paragraph (c)(2) of this section, shall be equipped with an ABS malfunction indicator lamp which meets the requirements of FMVSS No. 121 (49 CFR 571.121, S5.2.3.3).

Subpart D — Glazing and Window Construction

§393.60 Glazing in specified openings.

(a) **Glazing material.** Glazing material used in windshields, windows, and doors on a motor vehicle manufactured on or after December 25, 1968, shall at a minimum meet the requirements of Federal Motor Vehicle Safety Standard (FMVSS) No. 205 in effect on the date of manufacture of the motor vehicle. The glazing material shall be marked in accordance with FMVSS No. 205 (49 CFR 571.205, S6).

(b) **Windshields required.** Each bus, truck and truck-tractor shall be equipped with a windshield. Each windshield or portion of a multi-piece windshield shall be mounted using the full periphery of the glazing material.

(c) **Windshield condition.** With the exception of the conditions listed in paragraphs (c)(1), (c)(2), and (c)(3) of this section, each windshield shall be free of discoloration or damage in the area extending upward from the height of the top of the steering wheel (excluding a 51 mm (2 inch) border at the top of the windshield) and extending from a 25 mm (1 inch) border at each side of the windshield or windshield panel. **Exceptions:**

(1) Coloring or tinting which meets the requirements of paragraph (d) of this section;

(2) Any crack that is not intersected by any other cracks;

(3) Any damaged area which can be covered by a disc 19 mm (¾ inch) in diameter if not closer than 76 mm (3 inches) to any other similarly damaged area.

(d) **Coloring or tinting of windshields and windows.** Coloring or tinting of windshields and the windows to the immediate right and left of the driver is allowed, provided the parallel luminous transmittance through the colored or tinted glazing is not less than 70 percent of the light at normal incidence in those portions of the windshield or windows which are marked as having a parallel luminous transmittance of not less than 70 percent. The transmittance restriction does not apply to other windows on the commercial motor vehicle.

(e) **Prohibition on obstructions to the driver's field of view**—(1) **Devices mounted at the top of the windshield.** Antennas, transponders, and similar devices must not be mounted more than 152 mm (6 inches) below the upper edge of the windshield. These devices must be located outside the area swept by the windshield wipers, and outside the driver's sight lines to the road and highway signs and signals.

(2) **Decals and stickers mounted on the windshield.** Commercial Vehicle Safety Alliance (CVSA) inspection decals, and stickers and/or decals required under Federal or State laws may be placed at the bottom or sides of the windshield provided such decals or stickers do not extend more than 115 mm (4½ inches) from the bottom of the windshield and are located outside the area swept by the windshield wipers, and outside the driver's sight lines to the road and highway signs or signals.

§393.61 Window construction.

(a) . . .

(b) **Bus windows.** (1) Except as provided in paragraph (b)(3) of this section a bus manufactured before September 1, 1973, having a seating capacity of more than eight persons shall have, in addition to the area provided by the windshield, adequate means of escape for passengers through windows. The adequacy of such means shall be determined in accordance with the following standards: For each seated passenger space provided, inclusive of the driver there shall be at least 67 square inches of glazing if such glazing is not contained in a push-out window; or at least 67 square inches of free opening resulting from opening of a push-out type window. No area shall be included in this minimum prescribed area unless it will provide an unobstructed opening sufficient to contain an ellipse having a major axis of 18 inches and a minor axis of 13 inches or an opening containing 200 square inches formed by a rectangle 13 inches by 17-3/4 inches with corner arcs of 6-inch maximum radius. The major axis of the ellipse and the long axis of the rectangle shall make an angle of not more than 45° with the surface on which the unladen vehicle stands. The area shall be measured either by removal of the glazing if not of the pushout type or of the movable sash if of the push-out type, and it shall be either glazed with laminated safety glass or comply with paragraph (c) of this section. No less than 40 percent of such prescribed glazing or opening shall be on one side of any bus.

(2) A bus, including a school bus, manufactured on and after September 1, 1973, having a seating capacity of more than 10 persons shall have emergency exits in conformity with Federal Motor Vehicle Safety Standard No. 217, Part 571 of this title.

(3) A bus manufactured before September 1, 1973, may

conform to Federal Motor Vehicle Safety Standard No. 217, Part 571 of this title, in lieu of conforming to paragraph (b)(1) of this section.

(c) **Push-out window requirements.** (1) Except as provided in paragraph (c)(3) of this section, every glazed opening in a bus manufactured before September 1, 1973, and having a seating capacity of more than eight persons, used to satisfy the requirements of paragraph (b)(1) of this section, if not glazed with laminated safety glass, shall have a frame or sash so designed, constructed, and maintained that it will yield outwardly to provide the required free opening when subjected to the drop test specified in Test 25 of the American Standard Safety Code referred to in §393.60. The height of drop required to open such push-out windows shall not exceed the height of drop required to break the glass in the same window when glazed with the type of laminated glass specified in Test 25 of the Code. The sash for such windows shall be constructed of such material and be of such design and construction as to be continuously capable of complying with the above requirement.

(2) On a bus manufactured on and after September 1, 1973, having a seating capacity of more than 10 persons, each push-out window shall conform to Federal Motor Vehicle Safety Standard No. 217, (§571.217) of this title.

(3) A bus manufactured before September 1, 1973, may conform to Federal Motor Vehicle Safety Standard No. 217, (§571.217) of this title, in lieu of conforming to paragraph (c)(1) of this section.

§393.62 Window obstructions.

Windows, if otherwise capable of complying with §393.61 (a) and (b), shall not be obstructed by bars or other such means located either inside or outside such windows such as would hinder the escape of occupants unless such bars or other such means are so constructed as to provide a clear opening, at least equal to the opening provided by the window to which it is adjacent when subjected to the same test specified in §393.61(c). The point of application of such test force shall be such as will be most likely to result in the removal of the obstruction.

§393.63 Windows, markings.

(a) On a bus manufactured before September 1, 1973, each bus push-out window and any other bus escape window glazed with laminated safety glass required in §393.61 shall be identified as such by clearly legible and visible signs, lettering, or decalcomania. Such marking shall include appropriate wording to indicate that it is an escape window and also the method to be used for obtaining emergency exit.

(b) On a bus manufactured on and after September 1, 1973, emergency exits required in §393.61 shall be marked to conform to Federal Motor Vehicle Safety Standard No. 217, (§571.217) of this title.

(c) A bus manufactured before September 1, 1973, may mark emergency exits to conform to Federal Motor Vehicle Safety Standard No. 217, (§571.217) of this title in lieu of conforming to paragraph (a) of this section.

Subpart E — Fuel Systems

§393.65 All fuel systems.

(a) **Application of the rules in this section.** The rules in this section apply to systems for containing and supplying fuel for the operation of motor vehicles or for the operation of auxiliary equipment installed on, or used in connection with, motor vehicles.

(b) **Location.** Each fuel system must be located on the motor vehicle so that—

(1) No part of the system extends beyond the widest part of the vehicle;

(2) No part of a fuel tank is forward of the front axle of a power unit;

(3) Fuel spilled vertically from a fuel tank while it is being filled will not contact any part of the exhaust or electrical systems of the vehicle, except the fuel level indicator assembly;

(4) Fill pipe openings are located outside the vehicle's passenger compartment and its cargo compartment;

(5) . . .

(6) No part of the fuel system of a bus manufactured on or after January 1, 1973, is located within or above the passenger compartment.

(c) **Fuel tank installation.** Each fuel tank must be securely attached to the motor vehicle in a workmanlike manner.

(d) **Gravity or syphon feed prohibited.** A fuel system must not supply fuel by gravity or syphon feed directly to the carburetor or injector.

(e) **Selection control valve location.** If a fuel system includes a selection control valve which is operable by the driver to regulate the flow of fuel from two or more fuel tanks, the valve must be installed so that either—

(1) The driver may operate it while watching the roadway and without leaving his/her driving position; or

(2) The driver must stop the vehicle and leave his/her seat in order to operate the valve.

(f) **Fuel lines.** A fuel line which is not completely enclosed in a protective housing must not extend more than 2 inches below the fuel tank or its sump. Diesel fuel crossover, return, and withdrawal lines which extend below the bottom of the tank or sump must be protected against damage from impact. Every fuel line must be—

(1) Long enough and flexible enough to accommodate normal movements of the parts to which it is attached without incurring damage; and

(2) Secured against chafing, kinking, or other causes of mechanical damage.

(g) **Excess flow valve.** When pressure devices are used to force fuel from a fuel tank, a device which prevents the flow of fuel from the fuel tank if the fuel feed line is broken must be installed in the fuel system.

§393.67 Liquid fuel tanks.

(a) **Application of the rules in this section.** (1) A liquid fuel tank manufactured on or after January 1, 1973, and a side-mounted gasoline tank must conform to all the rules in this section.

(2) A diesel fuel tank manufactured before January 1, 1973, and mounted on a bus must conform to the rules in paragraphs (c)(7)(iii) and (d)(2) of this section.

(3) . . .

(4) A gasoline tank, other than a side-mounted gasoline tank, manufactured before January 1, 1973, and mounted on a bus must conform to the rules in paragraphs (c)(1) through (10) and (d)(2) of this section.

(5) . . .

(6) **Private motor carrier of passengers.** Motor carriers engaged in the private transportation of passengers may continue to operate a commercial motor vehicle which was not subject to this section or 49 CFR 571.301 at the time of its manufacture, provided the fuel tank of such vehicle is maintained to the original manufacturer's standards.

(b) **Definitions.** As used in this section—

(1) The term "liquid fuel tank" means a fuel tank designed to contain a fuel that is liquid at normal atmospheric pressures and temperatures.

(2) . . .

(c) **Construction of liquid fuel tanks—**

(1) **Joints.** Joints of a fuel tank body must be closed by arc-, gas-, seam-, or spot-welding, by brazing, by silver soldering, or by techniques which provide heat resistance and mechanical securement at least equal to those specifically named. Joints must not be closed solely by crimping or by soldering with a lead-based or other soft solder.

(2) **Fittings.** The fuel tank body must have flanges or spuds suitable for the installation of all fittings.

(3) **Threads.** The threads of all fittings must be Dryseal American Standard Taper Pipe Thread or Dryseal SAE Short Taper Pipe Thread, specified in Society of Automotive Engineers Standard J476, as contained in the 1971 edition of the "SAE Handbook", except that straight (non-tapered) threads may be used on fittings having integral flanges and using gaskets for sealing. At least four full threads must be in engagement in each fitting.

(4) **Drains and bottom fittings.**

(i) Drains or other bottom fittings must not extend more than $3/4$ of an inch below the lowest part of the fuel tank or sump.

(ii) Drains or other bottom fittings must be protected against damage from impact.

(iii) If a fuel tank has drains the drain fittings must permit substantially complete drainage of the tank.

(iv) Drains or other bottom fittings must be installed in a flange or spud designed to accommodate it.

(5) **Fuel withdrawal fittings.** Except for diesel fuel tanks, the fittings through which fuel is withdrawn from a fuel tank must be located above the normal level of fuel in the tank when the tank is full.

(6) [Reserved]

(7) **Fill pipe.**

(i) Each fill pipe must be designed and constructed to minimize the risk of fuel spillage during fueling operations and when the vehicle is involved in a crash.

(ii) The fill pipe and vents of a fuel tank having a capacity of more than 25 gallons of fuel must permit filling the tank with fuel at a rate of at least 20 gallons per minute without fuel spillage.

(iii) Each fill pipe must be fitted with a cap that can be fastened securely over the opening in the fill pipe. Screw threads or a bayonet-type joint are methods of conforming to the requirements of this subdivision.

(8) **Safety venting system.** A liquid fuel tank with a capacity of more than 25 gallons of fuel must have a venting system which, in the event the tank is subjected to fire, will prevent internal tank pressure from rupturing the tank's body, seams, or bottom opening (if any).

(9) **Pressure resistance.** The body and fittings of a liquid fuel tank with a capacity of more than 25 gallons of fuel must be capable of withstanding an internal hydrostatic pressure equal to 150 percent of the maximum internal pressure reached in the tank during the safety venting systems test specified in paragraph (d)(1) of this section.

(10) **Air vent.** Each fuel tank must be equipped with a non-spill air vent (such as a ball check). The air vent may be combined with the fill-pipe cap or safety vent, or it may be a separate unit installed on the fuel tank.

(11) **Markings.** If the body of the fuel tank is readily visible when the tank is installed on the vehicle, the tank must be plainly marked with its liquid capacity. The tank must also be plainly marked with a warning against filling it to more than 95 percent of its liquid capacity.

(12) **Overfill restriction.** A liquid fuel tank manufactured on or after January 1, 1973, must be designed and constructed so that—

(i) The tank cannot be filled, in a normal filling operation, with a quantity of fuel that exceeds 95 percent of the tank's liquid capacity; and

(ii) When the tank is filled, normal expansion of the fuel will not cause fuel spillage.

(d) **Liquid fuel tank tests.** Each liquid fuel tank must be capable of passing the tests specified in paragraphs (d)(1) and

(2) of this section.[1]

(1) **Safety venting system test—**

(i) **Procedure.** Fill the tank three-fourths full with fuel, seal the fuel feed outlet, and invert the tank. When the fuel temperature is between 50°F. and 80°F., apply an enveloping flame to the tank so that the temperature of the fuel rises at a rate of not less than 6°F. and not more than 8°F. per minute.

(ii) **Required performance.** The safety venting system required by paragraph (c)(8) of this section must activate before the internal pressure in the tank exceeds 50 pounds per square inch, gauge, and the internal pressure must not thereafter exceed the pressure at which the system activated by more than five pounds per square inch despite any further increase in the temperature of the fuel.

(2) **Leakage test—**

(i) **Procedure.** Fill the tank to capacity with fuel having a temperature between 50 °F. and 80 °F. With the fill-pipe cap installed, turn the tank through an angle of 150° in any direction about any axis from its normal position.

(ii) **Required performance.** Neither the tank nor any fitting may leak more than a total of one ounce by weight of fuel per minute in any position the tank assumes during the test.

(e) . . .

(f) **Certification and markings.** Each liquid fuel tank shall be legibly and permanently marked by the manufacturer with the following minimum information:

(1) The month and year of manufacture.

(2) The manufacturer's name on tanks manufactured on and after July 1, 1988, and means of identifying the facility at which the tank was manfactured, and

(3) A certificate that it conforms to the rules in this section applicable to the tank. The certificate must be in the form set forth in either of the following:

(i) . . .

(ii) If a tank conforms to all rules in this section pertaining to tanks which are not side-mounted fuel tanks: "Meets all FMCSA requirements for non-side-mounted fuel tanks."

(iii) The form of certificate specified in paragraph (f)(3) (i) or

---

[1]The specified tests are a measure of performance only. Manufacturers and carriers may use any alternative procedures which assure that their equipment meets the required performance criteria.

(ii) of this section may be used on a liquid fuel tank manufactured before July 11, 1973, but it is not mandatory for liquid fuel tanks manufactured before March 7, 1989. The form of certification manufactured on or before March 7, 1989, must meet the requirements in effect at the time of manufacture.

§393.69 Liquefied petroleum gas systems.

(a) A fuel system that uses liquefied petroleum gas as a fuel for the operation of a motor vehicle or for the operation of auxiliary equipment installed on, or used in connection with, a motor vehicle must conform to the "Standards for the Storage and Handling of Liquefied Petroleum Gases" of the National Fire Protection Association, Battery March Park, Quincy, MA 02269, as follows:

(1) A fuel system installed before December 31, 1962, must conform to the 1951 edition of the Standards.

(2) A fuel system installed on or after December 31, 1962, and before January 1, 1973, must conform to Division IV of the June 1959 edition of the Standards.

(3) A fuel system installed on or after January 1, 1973, and providing fuel for propulsion of the motor vehicle must conform to Division IV of the 1969 edition of the Standards.

(4) A fuel system installed on or after January 1, 1973, and providing fuel for the operation of auxiliary equipment must conform to Division VII of the 1969 edition of the Standards.

(b) When the rules in this section require a fuel system to conform to a specific edition of the Standards, the fuel system may conform to the applicable provisions in a later edition of the Standards specified in this section.

(c) The tank of a fuel system must be marked to indicate that the system conforms to the Standards.

Subpart F — Coupling Devices and Towing Methods

§§393.70 — 393.71 . . .

Subpart G — Miscellaneous Parts and Accessories

§393.75 Tires.

(a) No motor vehicle shall be operated on any tire that (1) has body ply or belt material exposed through the tread or sidewall,

(2) has any tread or sidewall separation, (3) is flat or has an audible leak, or (4) has a cut to the extent that the ply or belt material is exposed.

(b) Any tire on the front wheels of a bus shall have a tread groove pattern depth of at least $4/32$ of an inch when measured at any point on a major tread groove. The measurements shall not be made where tie bars, humps, or fillets are located.

(c) Except as provided in paragraph (b) of this section, tires shall have a tread groove pattern depth of at least $2/32$ of an inch when measured in a major tread groove. The measurement shall not be made where tie bars, humps or fillets are located.

(d) No bus shall be operated with regrooved, recapped or retreaded tires on the front wheels.

(e) . . .

(f) **Tire loading restrictions (except on manufactured homes).** No motor vehicle (except manufactured homes, which are governed by paragraph (g) of this section) shall be operated with tires that carry a weight greater than that marked on the sidewall of the tire or, in the absence of such a marking, a weight greater than that specified for the tires in any of the publications of any of the organizations listed in Federal Motor Vehicle Safety Standard No. 119 (49 CFR 571.119, S5.1(b)) unless:

(1) The vehicle is being operated under the terms of a special permit issued by the State; and

(2) The vehicle is being operated at a reduced speed to compensate for the tire loading in excess of the manufacturer's rated capacity for the tire. In no case shall the speed exceed 80 km/hr (50 mph).

(g) **Tire loading restrictions for manufactured homes. . . .**

(h) **Tire inflation pressure.** (1) No motor vehicle shall be operated on a tire which has a cold inflation pressure less than that specified for the load being carried.

(2) If the inflation pressure of the tire has been increased by heat because of the recent operation of the vehicle, the cold inflation pressure shall be estimated by subtracting the inflation buildup factor shown in Table 1 from the measured inflation pressure.

TABLE 1 — INFLATION PRESSURE MEASUREMENT CORRECTION FOR HEAT

Average speed of vehicle in the previous hour	Minimum inflation pressure buildup	
	Tires with 1,814 kg (4,000 lbs.) maximum load rating or less	Tires with over 1,814 kg (4,000 lbs.) load rating
66-88.5 km/hr (41-55 mph)	34.5 kPa (5 psi)	103.4 kPa (15 psi).

§393.76 Sleeper berths.

(a) **Dimensions** — (1) **Size.** A sleeper berth must be at least the following size:

Date of installation on motor vehicle	Length measured on centerline of longitudinal axis (inches)	Width measured on centerline of transverse axis (inches)	Height measured from highest point of top of mattress (inches)[1]
Before January 1, 1953	72	18	18
After December 31, 1952 and before October 1, 1975	75	21	21
After September 30, 1975	75	24	24

[1]In the case of a sleeper berth which utilizes an adjustable mechanical suspension system, the required clearance can be measured when the suspension system is adjusted to the height to which it would settle when occupied by a driver.

(2) **Shape.** A sleeper berth installed on a motor vehicle on or after January 1, 1953 must be of generally rectangular shape, except that the horizontal corners and the roof corners may be rounded to radii not exceeding 10-1/2 inches.

(3) **Access.** A sleeper berth must be constructed so that an occupant's ready entrance to, and exit from, the sleeper berth is not unduly hindered.

(b) **Location.** (1) A sleeper berth must not be installed in or on a semitrailer or a full trailer other than a house trailer.

(2) A sleeper berth located within the cargo space of a motor vehicle must be securely compartmentalized from the remainder of the cargo space. A sleeper berth installed on or after January 1, 1953 must be located in the cab or immediately adjacent to the cab and must be securely fixed with relation to the cab.

(c) **Exit from the berth.** (1) Except as provided in paragraph (c)(2) of this section, there must be a direct and ready means of exit from a sleeper berth into the driver's seat or compartment. If the sleeper berth was installed on or after January 1, 1963, the exit must be a doorway or opening at least 18 inches high and 36 inches wide. If the sleeper berth was installed before January 1, 1963, the exit must have sufficient area to contain an ellipse having a major axis of 24 inches and a minor axis of 16 inches.

(2) A sleeper berth installed before January 1, 1953 must either:

(i) Conform to the requirements of paragraph (c)(1) of this section; or

(ii) Have at least two exits, each of which is at least 18 inches high and 21 inches wide, located at opposite ends of the vehicle and useable by the occupant without the assistance of any other person.

(d) **Communication with the driver.** A sleeper berth which is not located within the driver's compartment and has no direct entrance into the driver's compartment must be equipped with a means of communication between the occupant and the driver. The means of communication may consist of a telephone, speaker tube, buzzer, pull cord, or other mechanical or electrical device.

(e) **Equipment.** A sleeper berth must be properly equipped for sleeping. Its equipment must include:

(1) Adequate bedclothing and blankets; and

(2) Either:

(i) Springs and a mattress; or

(ii) An innerspring mattress; or

(iii) A cellular rubber or flexible foam mattress at least four inches thick; or

(iv) A mattress filled with a fluid and of sufficient thickness when filled to prevent "bottoming-out" when occupied while the vehicle is in motion.

(f) **Ventilation.** A sleeper berth must have louvers or other means of providing adequate ventilation. A sleeper berth must be reasonably tight against dust and rain.

(g) **Protection against exhaust and fuel leaks and exhaust heat.** A sleeper berth must be located so that leaks in the vehicle's exhaust system or fuel system do not permit fuel, fuel system gases, or exhaust gases to enter the sleeper berth. A sleeper berth must be located so that it will not be overheated or damaged by reason of its proximity to the vehicle's exhaust system.

(h) **Occupant restraint.** A motor vehicle manufactured on or after July 1, 1971, and equipped with a sleeper berth must be equipped with a means of preventing ejection of the occupant of the sleeper berth during deceleration of the vehicle. The restraint system must be designed, installed, and maintained to withstand a minimum total force of 6,000 pounds applied toward the front of the vehicle and parallel to the longitudinal axis of the vehicle.

§393.77 Heaters.

On every motor vehicle, every heater shall comply with the following requirements:

(a) **Prohibited types of heaters.** The installation or use of the following types of heaters is prohibited:

(1) **Exhaust heaters.** Any type of exhaust heater in which the engine exhaust gases are conducted into or through any space occupied by persons or any heater which conducts engine compartment air into any such space.

(2) **Unenclosed flame heaters.** Any type of heater employing a flame which is not fully enclosed, except that such heaters are not prohibited when used for heating the cargo of tank motor vehicles.

(3) **Heaters permitting fuel leakage.** Any type of heater from the burner of which there could be spillage or leakage of fuel upon the tilting or overturning of the vehicle in which it is mounted.

(4) **Heaters permitting air contamination.** Any heater taking air, heated or to be heated, from the engine compartment or from direct contact with any portion of the exhaust system; or any heater taking air in ducts from the outside atmosphere to be conveyed through the engine compartment, unless said ducts are so constructed and installed as to prevent contamination of the air so conveyed by exhaust or engine compartment gases.

(5) **Solid fuel heaters except wood charcoal.** Any stove or other heater employing solid fuel except wood charcoal.

(6) **Portable heaters.** Portable heaters shall not be used in any space occupied by persons except the cargo space of motor vehicles which are being loaded or unloaded.

(b) **Heater specifications.** All heaters shall comply with the following specifications:

(1) **Heating elements, protection.** Every heater shall be so located or protected as to prevent contact therewith by occupants, unless the surface temperature of the protecting grilles or of any exposed portions of the heaters, inclusive of exhaust stacks, pipes, or conduits shall be lower than would cause contact burns. Adequate protection shall be afforded against igniting parts of the vehicle or burning occupants by direct radiation. Wood charcoal heaters shall be enclosed within a metal barrel, drum, or similar protective enclosure which enclosure shall be provided with a securely fastened cover.

(2) **Moving parts, guards.** Effective guards shall be provided for the protection of passengers or occupants against injury by fans, belts, or any other moving parts.

(3) **Heaters, secured.** Every heater and every heater enclosure shall be securely fastened to the vehicle in a substantial manner so as to provide against relative motion within the vehicle during normal usage or in the event the vehicle overturns. Every heater shall be so designed, constructed, and mounted as to minimize the likelihood of disassembly of any of its parts, including exhaust stacks, pipes, or conduits, upon overturn of the vehicle in or on which it is mounted. Wood charcoal heaters shall be secured against relative motion within the enclosure required by paragraph (c)(1) of this section, and the enclosure shall be securely fastened to the motor vehicle.

(4) **Relative motion between fuel tank and heater.** When either in normal operation or in the event of overturn, there is or is likely to be relative motion between the fuel tank for a heater and the heater, or between either of such units and the fuel lines between them, a suitable means shall be provided at the point of greatest relative motion so as to allow this motion without causing failure of the fuel lines.

(5) **Operating controls to be protected.** On every bus designed to transport more than 15 passengers, including the driver, means shall be provided to prevent unauthorized persons from tampering with the operating controls. Such means may include remote control by the driver; installation of controls at inaccessible places; control of adjustments by key or keys; enclosure of controls in a locked space, locking of controls, or other means of accomplishing this purpose.

(6) **Heater, hoses.** Hoses for all hot water and steam heater systems shall be specifically designed and constructed for that purpose.

(7) **Electrical apparatus.** Every heater employing any electrical apparatus shall be equipped with electrical conductors, switches, connectors, and other electrical parts of ample current-carrying capacity to provide against overheating; any electric motor employed in any heater shall be of adequate size and so located that it will not be overheated; electrical circuits shall be provided with fuses and/or circuit breakers to provide against electrical overloading; and all electrical conductors employed in or leading to any heater shall be secured against dangling, chafing, and rubbing and shall have suitable protection against any other condition likely to produce short or open circuits.

Note: Electrical parts certified as proper for use by Underwriters' Laboratories, Inc., shall be deemed to comply with the foregoing requirements.

(8) **Storage battery caps.** If a separate storage battery is located within the personnel or cargo space, such battery shall be securely mounted and equipped with nonspill filler caps.

(9) **Combustion heater exhaust construction.** Every heater employing the combustion of oil, gas, liquefied petroleum gas, or any other combustible material shall be provided with substantial means of conducting the products of combustion to the outside of the vehicle: Provided, however, That this requirement shall not apply to heaters used solely to heat the cargo space of motor vehicles where such motor vehicles or heaters are equipped with means specifically designed and maintained so that the carbon monoxide concentration will never exceed 0.2 percent in the cargo space. The exhaust pipe, stack, or conduit if required shall be sufficiently substantial and so secured as to provide reasonable assurance against leakage or discharge of products of combustion within the vehicle and, if necessary, shall be so insulated as to make unlikely the burning or charring of parts of the vehicle by radiation or by direct contact. The place of discharge of the products of combustion to the atmosphere and the means of discharge of such products shall be such as to minimize the likelihood of their reentry into the vehicle under all operating conditions.

(10) **Combustion chamber construction.** The design and construction of any combustion-type heater except cargo space heaters permitted by the proviso of paragraph (c)(9) of this section and unenclosed flame heaters used for heating cargo of tank motor vehicles shall be such as to provide against the leakage of products of combustion into air to be heated and circu-

lated. The material employed in combustion chambers shall be such as to provide against leakage because of corrosion, oxidation or other deterioration. Joints between combustion chambers and the air chambers with which they are in thermal and mechanical contact shall be so designed and constructed as to prevent leakage between the chambers and the materials employed in such joints shall have melting points substantially higher than the maximum temperatures likely to be attained at the points of jointure.

(11) **Heater fuel tank location.** Every bus designed to transport more than 15 passengers, including the driver, with heaters of the combustion type shall have fuel tanks therefor located outside of and lower than the passenger space. When necessary, suitable protection shall be afforded by shielding or other means against the puncturing of any such tank or its connections by flying stones or other objects.

(12) **Heater, automatic fuel control.** Gravity or siphon feed shall not be permitted for heaters using liquid fuels. Heaters using liquid fuels shall be equipped with automatic means for shutting off the fuel or for reducing such flow of fuel to the smallest practicable magnitude, in the event of overturn of the vehicle. Heaters using liquefied petroleum gas as fuel shall have the fuel line equipped with automatic means at the source of supply for shutting off the fuel in the event of separation, breakage, or disconnection of any of the fuel lines between the supply source and the heater.

(13) **"Tell-tale" indicators.** Heaters subject to paragraph (c)(14) of this section and not provided with automatic controls shall be provided with "tell-tale" means to indicate to the driver that the heater is properly functioning. The requirement shall not apply to heaters used solely for the cargo space in semitrailers or full trailers.

(14) **Shut-off control.** Automatic means, or manual means if the control is readily accessible to the driver without moving from the driver's seat, shall be provided to shut off the fuel and electrical supply in case of failure of the heater to function for any reason, or in case the heater should function improperly or overheat. This requirement shall not apply to wood charcoal heaters or to heaters used solely to heat the contents of cargo tank motor vehicles, but wood charcoal heaters must be provided with a controlled method of regulating the flow of combustion air.

(15) **Certification required.** Every combustion-type heater, except wood charcoal heaters, the date of manufacture of which is subsequent to December 31, 1952, and every wood charcoal heater, the date of manufacture of which is subsequent to September 1, 1953, shall be marked plainly to indicate the type of service for which such heater is designed and with a certification by the manufacturer that the heater meets the applicable requirements for such use. For example, "Meets I.C.C. Bus Heater Requirements," "Meets I.C.C. Flue-Vented Cargo Space Heater Requirements," and after December 31, 1967, such certification shall read "Meets FMCSA Bus Heater Requirements," "Meets FMCSA Flue-Vented Cargo Space Heater Requirements," etc.

(i) . . .

§393.78 Windshield wipers.

(a) Every bus having a windshield, shall be equipped with at least two automatically-operating windshield wiper blades, one on each side of the centerline of the windshield, for cleaning rain, snow, or other moisture from the windshield and which shall be in such condition as to provide clear vision for the driver, unless one such blade be so arranged as to clean an area of the windshield extending to within 1 inch of the limit of vision through the windshield at each side.

(b) Every bus, truck, and truck tractor, the date of manufacture of which is subsequent to June 30, 1953, which depends upon vacuum to operate the windshield wipers, shall be so constructed that the operation of the wipers will not be materially impaired by change in the intake manifold pressure.

§393.79 Defrosting device.

Every bus having a windshield, when operating under conditions such that ice, snow, or frost would be likely to collect on the outside of the windshield or condensation on the inside of the windshield, shall be equipped with a device or other means, not manually operated, for preventing or removing such obstructions to the driver's view.

§393.80 Rear-vision mirrors.

(a) Every bus shall be equipped with two rear-vision mirrors, one at each side, firmly attached to the outside of the motor vehicle, and so located as to reflect to the driver a view of the highway to the rear, along both sides of the vehicle. All such regulated rear-vision mirrors and their replacements shall meet, as a minimum, the requirements of FMVSS No. 111 (49 CFR 571.111) in force at the time the vehicle was manufactured.

(b) **Exceptions.** (1) Mirrors installed on a vehicle manufactured prior to January 1, 1981, may be continued in service, provided that if the mirrors are replaced they shall be replaced with mirrors meeting, as a minimum, the requirements of FMVSS No. 111 (49 CFR 571.111) in force at the time the vehicle was manufactured.

(2) Only one outside mirror shall be required, which shall be on the driver's side, on trucks which are so constructed that the driver has a view to the rear by means of an interior mirror.

(3) . . .

§393.81 Horn.

Every bus shall be equipped with a horn and actuating elements which shall be in such condition as to give an adequate and reliable warning signal.

§393.82 Speedometer.

Every bus shall be equipped with a speedometer indicating vehicle speed in miles per hour, which shall be operative with reasonable accuracy.

§393.83 Exhaust systems.

(a) Every motor vehicle having a device (other than as part of its cargo) capable of expelling harmful combustion fumes shall have a system to direct the discharge of such fumes. No part shall be located where its location would likely result in burning, charring, or damaging the electrical wiring, the fuel supply, or any combustible part of the motor vehicle.

(b) No exhaust system shall discharge to the atmosphere at a location immediately below the fuel tank or the fuel tank filler pipe.

(c) The exhaust system of a bus powered by a gasoline engine shall discharge to the atmosphere at or within 6 inches forward of the rearmost part of the bus.

(d) The exhaust system of a bus using fuels other than gasoline shall discharge to the atmosphere either:

(1) At or within 15 inches forward of the rearmost part of the vehicle; or

(2) To the rear of all doors or windows designed to be open, except windows designed to be opened solely as emergency exits.

(e) . . .

(f) No part of the exhaust system shall be temporarily repaired with wrap or patches.

(g) No part of the exhaust system shall leak or discharge at a point forward of or directly below the driver/sleeper compartment. The exhaust outlet may discharge above the cab/sleeper roofline.

(h) The exhaust system must be securely fastened to th vehicle.

(i) Exhaust systems may use hangers which permit required movement due to expansion and contraction caused by heat of the exhaust and relative motion between engine and chassis of a vehicle.

§393.84 Floors.

The flooring in all motor vehicles shall be substantially constructed, free of unnecessary holes and openings, and shall be maintained so as to minimize the entrance of fumes, exhaust gases, or fire. Floors shall not be permeated with oil or other substances likely to cause injury to persons using the floor as a traction surface.

§393.85 (Reserved)

§393.86 Rear impact guards and rear end protection.

(a) ...

(b)(1) **Requirements for motor vehicles manufactured after December 31, 1952 (except trailers or semitrailers manufactured on or after January 26, 1998).** Each motor vehicle manufactured after December 31, 1952, (except truck tractors, pole trailers, pulpwood trailers, or vehicles in drive-away-towaway operations) in which the vertical distance between the rear bottom edge of the body (or the chassis assembly if the chassis is the rearmost part of the vehicle) and the ground is greater than 76.2 cm (30 inches) when the motor vehicle is empty, shall be equipped with a rear impact guard(s). The rear impact guard(s) must be installed and maintained in such a manner that:

(i) The vertical distance between the bottom of the guard(s) and the ground does not exceed 76.2 cm (30 inches) when the motor vehicle is empty;

(ii) The maximum lateral distance between the closest points between guards, if more than one is used, does not exceed 61 cm (24 inches);

(iii) The outermost surfaces of the horizontal member of the guard are no more than 45.7 cm (18 inches) from each side extremity of the motor vehicle;

(iv) The impact guard(s) are no more than 61 cm (24 inches) forward of the rear extremity of the motor vehicle.

(2) **Construction and Attachment.** The rear impact guard(s) must be substantially constructed and attached by means of bolts, welding, or other comparable means.

(3) **Vehicle Components and Structures that may be used to satisfy the requirements of paragraph (b) of this section.** Low chassis vehicles, special purpose vehicles, or wheels back vehicles constructed and maintained so that the body, chassis, or other parts of the vehicle provide the rear end protection comparable to impact guard(s) conforming to the requirements of paragraph (b)(1) of this section shall be considered to be in compliance with those requirements.

§393.87 . . .

§393.88 Television receivers.

Any motor vehicle equipped with a television viewer, screen or other means of visually receiving a television broadcast shall have the viewer or screen located in the motor vehicle at a point to the rear of the back of the driver's seat if such viewer or screen is in the same compartment as the driver and the viewer or screen shall be so located as not to be visible to the driver, while he/she is driving the motor vehicle. The operating controls for the television receiver shall be so located that the driver cannot operate them without leaving the driver's seat.

§393.89 Buses, driveshaft protection.

Any driveshaft extending lengthways under the floor of the passenger compartment of a bus, shall be protected by means of at least one guard or bracket at that end of the shaft which is provided with a sliding connection (spline or other such device) to prevent the whipping of the shaft in the event of failure thereof or of any of its component parts. A shaft contained within a torque tube shall not require any such device.

§393.90 Buses, standee line or bar.

Except as provided below, every bus which is designed and constructed so as to allow standees, shall be plainly marked with a line of contrasting color at least 2 inches wide or equipped with some other means so as to indicate to any person that he/she is prohibited from occupying a space forward of a perpendicular plane drawn through the rear of the driver's seat and perpendicular to the longitudinal axis of the bus. Every bus shall have clearly posted at or near the front, a sign with letters at least one-half inch high stating that it is a violation of the Federal Motor Carrier Safety Administration's regulations for a bus to be operated with persons occupying the prohibited area. The requirements of this section shall not apply to any bus being transported in driveaway-towaway operation or to any level of the bus other than that level in which the driver is located nor shall they be construed to prohibit any seated person from occupying permanent seats located in the prohibited area provided such seats are so located that persons sitting therein will not interfere with the driver's safe operation of the bus.

§393.91 Buses, aisle seats prohibited.

No bus shall be equipped with aisle seats unless such seats are so designed and installed as to automatically fold and leave a clear aisle when they are unoccupied. No bus shall be operated if any seat therein is not securely fastened to the vehicle.

§393.92 Buses, marking emergency doors.

Any bus equipped with an emergency door shall have such door clearly marked in letters at least 1 inch in height with the words "Emergency Door" or "Emergency Exit." Emergency doors shall also be identified by a red electric lamp readily visible to passengers which lamp shall be lighted at all times when lamps are required to be lighted by §392.30.

§393.93 Seats, seat belt assemblies, and seat belt assembly anchorages.

(a) **Buses**—(1) **Buses manufactured on or after January 1, 1965, and before July 1, 1971.** After June 30, 1972, every bus manufactured on or after January 1, 1965, and before July 1, 1971, must be equipped with a Type 1 or Type 2 seat belt assembly that conforms to Federal Motor Vehicle Safety Standard No. 209[1] (§571.209) installed at the driver's seat and seat belt assembly anchorages that conform to the location and geometric requirements of Federal Motor Vehicle Safety Standard No. 210[1] (§571.210) for that seat belt assembly.

---

[1]Individual copies of Federal Motor Vehicle Safety Standards may be obtained from the National Highway Traffic Safety Administration, Nassif Building, 400 Seventh Street SW, Washington, D.C. 20590.

(2) **Buses manufactured on or after July 1, 1971.** Every bus manufactured on or after July 1, 1971, must conform to the requirements of Federal Motor Vehicle Safety Standard No. 208[1] (§571.208) (relating to installation of seat belt assemblies) and Federal Motor Vehicle Safety Standard No. 210[1] (§571.210) (relating to installation of seat belt assembly anchorages).

(3) **Buses manufactured on or after January 1, 1972.** Every bus manufactured on or after January 1, 1972, must conform to the requirements of Federal Motor Vehicle Safety Standard No. 207[1] (§571.207) (relating to seating systems).

(b) . . .

(c) **Effective date of standards.** Whenever paragraph (a) or (b) of this section requires conformity to a Federal Motor Vehicle Safety Standard, the vehicle or equipment must conform to the version of the Standard that is in effect on the date the vehicle is manufactured or on the date the vehicle is modified to conform to the requirements of paragraph (a) or (b) of this section, whichever is later.

(d) . . .

§393.94 Vehicle interior noise levels.

(a) **Application of the rule in this section.** Except as provided in paragraph (d) of this section, this section applies to all motor vehicles manufactured on and after October 1, 1974. On and after April 1, 1975, this section applies to all motor vehicles manufactured before October 1, 1974.

(b) **General rule.** The interior sound level at the driver's seating position of a motor vehicle must not exceed 90 dB(A) when measured in accordance with paragraph (c) of this section.

(c) **Test procedure.**[1] (1) Park the vehicle at a location so that no large reflecting surfaces, such as other vehicles, signboards, buildings, or hills, are within 50 feet of the driver's seating position.

(2) Close all vehicle doors, windows, and vents. Turn off all power-operated accessories.

(3) Place the driver in his/her normal seated position at the vehicle's controls. Evacuate all occupants except the driver and

---

[1]Standards of the American National Standards Institute are published by the American National Standards Institute. Information and copies may be obtained by writing to the Institute at 1430 Broadway, New York, N.Y.10018.

the person conducting the test.

(4) Use a sound level meter which meets the requirements of the American National Standards Institute Standard ANSI S1.4-1971 Specification for Sound Level Meters, for Type 2 Meters. Set the meter to the A-weighting network, "fast" meter response.

(5) Locate the microphone, oriented vertically upward, 6 inches to the right of, in the same plane as, and directly in line with, the driver's right ear.

(6) With the vehicle's transmission in neutral gear, accelerate its engine to either its maximum governed engine speed, if it is equipped with an engine governor, or its speed at its maximum rated horsepower, if it is not equipped with an engine governor. Stabilize the engine at that speed.

(7) Observe the A-weighted sound level reading on the meter for the stabilized engine speed condition. Record that reading, if the reading has not been influenced by extraneous noise sources such as motor vehicles operating on adjacent roadways.

(8) Return the vehicle's engine speed to idle and repeat the procedure specified in paragraphs (c)(6) and (7) of this section until two maximum sound levels within 2 dB of each other are recorded. Numerically average those two maximum sound level readings.

(9) The average obtained in accordance with paragraph (c)(8) of this section is the vehicle's interior sound level at the driver's seating position for the purpose of determining whether the vehicle conforms to the rule in paragraph (b) of this section. However, a 2dB tolerance over the sound level limitation specified in that paragraph is permitted to allow for variations in test conditions and variations in the capabilities of meters.

(10) If the motor vehicle's engine radiator fan drive is equipped with a clutch or similar device that automatically either reduces the rotational speed of the fan or completely disengages the fan from its power source in response to reduced engine cooling loads the vehicle may be parked before testing with its engine running at high idle or any other speed the operator may choose, for sufficient time but not more than 10 minutes, to permit the engine radiator fan to automatically disengage.

(d) Vehicles manufactured before October 1, 1974, and operated wholly within the State of Hawaii, need not comply with this section until April 1, 1976.

Subpart H — Emergency Equipment

§393.95 Emergency equipment on all power units.

Except for a lightweight vehicle, every bus, truck, truck-tractor, and every driven vehicle in driveaway-towaway operation must be equipped as follows:

(a) **Fire extinguisher.** (1) Except as provided in paragraph (a)(4) of this section, every power unit must be equipped with a fire extinguisher that is properly filled and located so that it is readily accessible for use. The fire extinguisher must be securely mounted on the vehicle. The fire extinguisher must be designed, constructed, and maintained to permit visual determination of whether it is fully charged. The fire extinguisher must have an extinguishing agent that does not need protection from freezing. The fire extinguisher must not use a vaporizing liquid that gives off vapors more toxic than those produced by the substances shown as having a toxicity rating of 5 or 6 in the Underwriters' Laboratories "Classification of Comparative Life Hazard of Gases and Vapors."[1]

(2)(i) . . .

(ii) Before January 1, 1973, a power unit that is not used to transport hazardous materials must be equipped with a fire extinguisher having an Underwriters' Laboratories rating[2] of 4 B:C or more. On and after January 1, 1973, a power unit that is not used to transport hazardous materials must be equipped with either—

(A) A fire extinguisher having an Underwriters' Laboratories rating[2] of 5 B:C or more; or

(B) Two fire extinguishers, each of which has an Underwriters' Laboratories rating[2] of 4 B:C or more.

(iii) Each fire extinguisher required by this subparagraph must be labeled or marked with its Underwriters' Laboratories rating[2] and must meet the requirements of paragraph (a)(1) of this section.

(3) For purposes of this paragraph a power unit is used to transport hazardous materials only if the power unit or a motor

---

[1] Copies of the Classification can be obtained by writing to Underwriters' Laboratories, Inc., 205 East Ohio Street, Chicago, Ill. 60611.

[2] Underwriters' Laboratories ratings are given to fire extinguishers under the standards of Underwriters' Laboratories, Inc., 205 East Ohio Street, Chicago, Ill. 60611. Extinguishers must conform to the standards in effect on the date of manufacture or on Jan. 1, 1969, whichever is earlier.

vehicle towed by the power unit must be marked or placarded in accordance with §177.823 of this title.

(4) . . .

(b) [Reserved]

(c) **Spare fuses.** At least one spare fuse or other overload protective device, if the devices used are not of a reset type for each kind and size used. In driveaway-towaway operations, spares located on any one of the vehicles will be deemed adequate.

(d) [Reserved]

(e) [Reserved]

(f) **Warning devices for stopped vehicles.** Except as provided in paragraph (g) of this section, one of the following combinations of warning devices:

(1) **Vehicles equipped with warning devices before January 1, 1974.** Warning devices specified below may be used until replacements are necessary:

(i) Three liquid-burning emergency flares which satisfy the requirements of SAE Standard J597, "Liquid Burning Emergency Flares," and three fusees and two red flags; or

(ii) Three electric emergency lanterns which satisfy the requirements of SAE Standard J596, "Electric Emergency Lanterns," and two red flags; or

(iii) Three red emergency reflectors which satisfy the requirements of paragraph (i) of this section, and two red flags; or

(iv) Three red emergency reflective triangles which satisfy the requirements of paragraph (h) of this section; or

(v) Three bidirectional emergency reflective triangles that conform to the requirements of Federal Motor Vehicle Safety Standard No. 125, §571.125 of this title.

(2) **Vehicles equipped with warning devices on and after January 1, 1974.**

(i) Three bidirectional emergency reflective triangles that conform to the requirements of Federal Motor Vehicle Safety Standard No. 125, §571.125 of this title; or

(ii) At least 6 fusees or 3 liquid-burning flares. The vehicle must have as many additional fusees or liquid-burning flares as are necessary to satisfy the requirements of §392.22.

(3) **Supplemental warning devices.** Other warning devices may be used in addition to, but not in lieu of, the required warning devices, provided those warning devices do not decrease the effectiveness of the required warning devices.

(g) . . .

(h) **Requirements for emergency reflective triangles manufactured before January 1, 1974.** (1) Each reflector shall be a collapsible equilateral triangle, with legs not less than 17 inches long and not less than 2 inches wide. The front and back of the exposed leg surfaces shall be covered with red reflective material not less than one half inch in width. The reflective surface, front and back, shall be approximately parallel. When placed in position, one point of the triangle shall be upward. The area within the sides of the triangle shall be open.

(2) **Reflective material:** The reflecting material covering the leg of the equilateral triangle shall comply either with:

(i) The requirements for reflex-reflector elements made of red methyl-methacrylate plastic material, meeting the color, sealing, minimum candlepower, wind test, vibration test, and corrosion resistance test of section 3 and 4 of Federal Specification RR-R-1185, dated November 17, 1966, or

(ii) The requirements for red reflective sheeting of Federal Specification L-S-300, dated September 7, 1965, except that the aggregate candlepower of the assembled triangle, in one direction, shall be not less than eight when measured at 0.2° divergence angle and -4° incidence angle, and not less than 80 percent of the candlepower specified for 1 square foot of material at all other angles shown in Table II, reflective Intensity Values, of L-S-300.

(3) **Reflective surfaces alignment:** Every reflective triangle shall be so constructed that, when the triangle is properly placed, the reflective surfaces shall be in a plane perpendicular to the plane of the roadway surface with a permissible tolerance of ± 10°. Reflective triangles which are collapsible shall be provided with means for holding the reflective surfaces within the required tolerance. Such holding means shall be readily capable of adjustment without the use of tools or special equipment.

(4) **Reflectors mechanical adequacy:** Every reflective triangle shall be of such weight and dimensions as to remain stationary when subjected to a 40 mile per hour wind when properly placed on any clean, dry paved road surface. The reflective triangle shall be so constructed as to withstand reasonable shocks without breakage.

(5) **Reflectors, incorporation in holding device:** Each set of reflective triangles shall be adequately protected by enclo-

sure in a box, rack, or other adequate container specially designed and constructed so that the reflectors may be readily extracted for use.

(6) **Certification:** Every red emergency reflective triangle designed and constructed to comply with these requirements shall be plainly marked with the certification of the manufacturer that it complies therewith.

(i) **Requirements for red emergency reflectors.** Each red emergency reflector shall conform in all respects to the following requirements:

(1) **Reflecting elements required.** Each reflector shall be composed of at least two reflecting elements or surfaces on each side, front and back. The reflecting elements, front and back, shall be approximately parallel.

(2) **Reflecting elements to be Class A.** Each reflecting element or surface shall meet the requirement for a red Class A reflector contained in the SAE Recommended Practice[1] "Reflex Reflectors." The aggregate candlepower output of all the reflecting elements or surface in one direction shall not be less than 12 when tested in a perpendicular position with observation at one-third degree as specified in the Photometric Test contained in the abovementioned Recommended Practice.

(3) **Reflecting surfaces, protection.** If the reflector or the reflecting elements are so designed or constructed that the reflecting surfaces would be adversely affected by dust, soot, or other foreign matter or contacts with other parts of the reflector or its container, then such reflecting surfaces shall be adequately sealed within the body of the reflector.

(4) **Reflecting surfaces to be perpendicular.** Every reflector shall be so constructed that, when the reflector is properly placed, every reflecting element or surface is in a plane perpendicular to the plane of the roadway surface. Reflectors which are collapsible shall be provided with means for locking the reflector elements or surfaces in the required position; such locking means shall be readily capable of adjustment without the use of tools or special equipment.

(5) **Reflectors, mechanical adequacy.** Every reflector shall be of such weight and dimensions as to remain stationary when subjected to a 40 mile per hour wind when properly placed on any clean, dry, paved road surface. The reflector shall

---

[1] See footnote 1 to §393.24(c).

be so constructed as to withstand reasonable shocks without breakage.

(6) **Reflectors, incorporation on holding device.** Each set of reflectors and the reflecting elements or surfaces incorporated therein shall be adequately protected by enclosure in a box, rack, or other adequate container specially designed and constructed so that the reflectors may be readily extracted for use.

(7) **Certification.** Every red emergency reflector designed and constructed to comply with these requirements shall be plainly marked with the certification of the manufacturer that it complies therewith.

(j) **Requirements for fusees and liquid-burning flares.** Each fusee shall be capable of burning for 30 minutes, and each liquid-burning flare shall contain enough fuel to burn continuously for at least 60 minutes. Fuseès and liquid-burning flares shall conform to the requirements of Underwriters Laboratories, Inc., UL No. 912, Highway Emergency Signals, Fourth Edition, July 30, 1979, (with an amendment dated November 9, 1981). (See §393.7(b) for information on the incorporation by reference and availability of this document.) Each fusee and liquid-burning flare shall be marked with the UL symbol in accordance with the requirements of UL 912.

(k) **Requirements for red flags.** Red flags shall be not less than 12 inches square, with standards adequate to maintain the flags in an upright position.

Subpart I — Protection Against Shifting or Falling Cargo

§§393.100 to 393.106 . . .

Subpart J — Frames, Cab and Body Components, Wheels, Steering, and Suspension Systems

§393.201 Frames.

(a) The frame of every bus shall not be cracked, loose, sagging or broken.

(b) Bolts or brackets securing the cab or the body of the vehicle to the frame must not be loose, broken, or missing.

(c) The frame rail flanges between the axles shall not be bent, cut or notched, except as specified by the manufacturer.

(d) . . .

(e) No holes shall be drilled in the top or bottom rail flanges, except as specified by the manufacturer.

(f) Field repairs are allowed.

§393.203 Cab and body components.

(a) The cab compartment doors or door parts used as an entrance or exit shall not be missing or broken. Doors shall not sag so that they cannot be properly opened or closed. No door shall be wired shut or otherwise secured in the closed position so that it cannot be readily opened. **Exception:** When the vehicle is loaded with pipe or bar stock that blocks the door and the cab has a roof exit.

(b) Bolts or brackets securing the cab or the body of the vehicle to the frame shall not be loose, broken, or missing.

(c) The hood must be securely fastened.

(d) All seats must be securely mounted.

(e) The front bumper must not be missing, loosely attached, or protruding beyond the confines of the vehicle so as to create a hazard.

§393.205 Wheels.

(a) Wheels and rims shall not be cracked or broken.

(b) Stud or bolt holes on the wheels shall not be elongated (out of round).

(c) Nuts or bolts shall not be missing or loose.

§393.207 Suspension systems.

(a) **Axles.** No axle positioning part shall be cracked, broken, loose or missing. All axles must be in proper alignment.

(b) **Adjustable axles.** Adjustable axle assemblies shall not have locking pins missing or disengaged.

(c) **Leaf springs.** No leaf spring shall be cracked, broken, or missing nor shifted out of position.

(d) **Coil springs.** No coil spring shall be cracked or broken.

(e) **Torsion bar.** No torsion bar or torsion bar suspension shall be cracked or broken.

(f) **Air Suspensions.** The air pressure regulator valve shall not allow air into the suspension system until at least 55 psi is in the braking system. The vehicle shall be level (not tilting to the left or right). Air leakage shall not be greater than 3 psi in a 5-minute time period when the vehicle's air pressure gauge shows normal operating pressure.

§393.209 Steering wheel systems.

(a) The steering wheel shall be secured and must not have any spokes cracked through or missing.

(b) The steering wheel lash shall not exceed the following parameters:

Steering wheel diameter	Manual steering system	Power steering system
16″ or less	2″+	4 $1/2$″+
18″	2 $1/4$″+	4 $3/4$″+
20″	2 $1/2$″+	5 $1/4$″+
22″	2 $3/4$″+	5 $3/4$″+

(c) **Steering column.** The steering column must be securely fastened.

(d) **Steering system.** Universal joints shall not be worn, faulty or repaired by welding. The steering gear box shall not have loose or missing mounting bolts or cracks in the gear box or mounting brackets. The pitman arm on the steering gear output shaft shall not be loose. Steering wheels shall turn freely through the limit of travel in both directions.

(e) **Power steering systems.** All components of the power system must be in operating condition. No parts shall be loose or broken. Belts shall not be frayed, cracked or slipping. The system shall not leak. The power steering system shall have sufficient fluid in the reservoir.

PART 394

[REMOVED AND RESERVED]

Editor's Note: Effective March 4, 1993, the Accident Reporting Requirements were deleted. An accident register is now required to be maintained in accordance with Sec. 390.15(b). DOT's definition of an "Accident" is contained in Sec. 390.5.

PART 395 — HOURS OF SERVICE OF DRIVERS

AUTHORITY: 49 U.S.C. 504, 14122, 31133, 31136, and 31502; sec. 113, Pub.L. 103-311, 108 Stat. 1673, 1676; and 49 CFR 1.73.

Editor's Note: §395.0 is effective from June 27, 2003, through June 30, 2004.

§395.0 Compliance date for certain requirements for hours of service of drivers.

(a) Motor carriers and drivers must comply with the following requirements of this chapter through January 3, 2004, that were in effect on or before June 27, 2003 and are contained in 49 CFR Chapter III revised as of October 1, 2002:

(1) §§395.1(b), (e)(3), (e)(4), (g), (h), and (j) of this part;

(2) §395.3 of this part;

(3) §390.23(b) and (c) of this subchapter; and

(4) The citations and text for §§395.1(h)(1)(i) through 395.3(b)(2) in section VII. List of Acute and Critical Regulations in Appendix B to Part 385 of this subchapter.

(b) Motor carriers and drivers must comply beginning on January 4, 2004 with the amendments made to the following sections that took effect on June 27, 2003 and are contained in 49 CFR Chapter III revised as of October 1, 2003:

(1) §§395.1(b), (e)(3), (e)(4), (g), (h), (j), and (o) of this part;

(2) §395.3 of this part;

(3) §395.5 of this part;

(4) §§390.23(b) and (c) of this subchapter; and

(5) The citations and text for §§395.1(h)(1)(i) through 395.5(b)(2) in section VII. List of Acute and Critical Regulations in Appendix B to Part 385 of this subchapter.

§395.1 Scope of rules in this part.

(a) **General.** (1) The rules in this part apply to all motor carriers and drivers, except as provided in paragraphs (b) through (n) of this section.

(2) The exceptions from Federal requirements contained in paragraphs (l) through (n) do not preempt State laws and regulations governing the safe operation of commercial motor vehicles.

Editor's Note: Compliance with the following is required as of January 4, 2004.

(b) **Adverse driving conditions.** (1) Except as provided in paragraph (h)(2) of this section, a driver who encounters adverse driving conditions, as defined in §395.2, and cannot, because of those conditions, safely complete the run within the maximum driving time permitted by §§395.3(a) or 395.5(a) may drive and be permitted or required to drive a commercial motor vehicle for not more than 2 additional hours in order to complete that run or to reach a place offering safety for the occupants of the commercial motor vehicle and security for the commercial motor vehicle and its cargo. However, that driver may not drive or be permitted to drive—

(i) . . .

(ii) . . .

(iii) For more than 12 hours in the aggregate following 8 consecutive hours off duty for drivers of passenger-carrying commercial motor vehicles; or

(iv) After he/she has been on duty 15 hours following 8 consecutive hours off duty for drivers of passenger-carrying commercial motor vehicles.

Editor's Note: All motor carriers and drivers are required to comply with §395.1(b)(1) listed below until January 4, 2004.

(b) **Adverse driving conditions.** (1) Except as provided in paragraph (i)(2) of this section, a driver who encounters adverse driving conditions, as defined in §395.2, and cannot, because of those conditions, safely complete the run within the 10-hour maximum driving time permitted by §395.3(a) may drive and be permitted or required to drive a commercial motor vehicle for not more than 2 additional hours in order to complete that run or to reach a place offering safety for the occupants of the commercial motor vehicle and security for the commercial motor vehicle and its cargo. However, that driver may not drive or be permitted to drive—

(i) For more than 12 hours in the aggregate following 8 consecutive hours off duty; or

(ii) After he/she has been on duty 15 hours following 8 consecutive hours off duty.

(2) **Emergency conditions.** In case of any emergency, a driver may complete his/her run without being in violation of the provisions of the regulations in this part, if such run reasonably could have been completed absent the emergency.

(c) . . .

(d) . . .

(e) **100 air-mile radius driver.** A driver is exempt from the requirements of Section 395.8 if:

(1) The driver operates within a 100 air-mile radius of the normal work reporting location;

(2) The driver, except a driver salesperson, returns to the work reporting location and is released from work within 12 consecutive hours;

Editor's Note: Compliance with the following is required as of January 4, 2004.

(3)(i) . . .

(ii) A passenger-carrying commercial motor vehicle driver has at least 8 consecutive hours off duty separating each 12 hours on duty;

(4)(i) . . .

(ii) A passenger-carrying commercial motor vehicle driver does not exceed 10 hours maximum driving time following 8 consecutive hours off duty; and

Editor's Note: All motor carriers and drivers are required to comply with 395.1(e)(3), (4) listed below until January 4, 2004.

(3) At least 8 consecutive hours off duty separate each 12 hours on duty;

(4) The driver does not exceed 10 hours maximum driving time following 8 consecutive hours off duty; and

(5) The motor carrier that employs the driver maintains and retains for a period of 6 months accurate and true time records showing:

(i) The time the driver reports for duty each day;

(ii) The total number of hours the driver is on duty each day;

(iii) The time the driver is released from duty each day; and

(iv) The total time for the preceding 7 days in accordance with §395.8(j)(2) for drivers used for the first time or intermittently.

(f) . . .

Editor's Note: Compliance with the following is required as of January 4, 2004.

(g) **Sleeper berths.** (1) .

(2) . . .

(3) **Passenger-carrying commercial motor vehicles.** A driver who is driving a passenger-carrying commercial motor vehicle that is equipped with a sleeper berth, as defined in §§395.2 and 393.76 of this subchapter, may accumulate the equivalent of 8 consecutive hours of off-duty time by taking two periods of rest in the sleeper berth, providing:

(i) Neither rest period is shorter than two hours;

(ii) The driving time in the period immediately before and after each rest period, when added together, does not exceed 10 hours;

(iii) The on-duty time in the period immediately before and after each rest period, when added together, does not include any driving time after the 15th hour; and

(iv) The driver may not return to driving subject to the normal limits under §395.5 without taking at least 8 consecutive hours off duty, at least 8 consecutive hours in the sleeper berth, or a combination of at least 8 consecutive hours off duty and sleeper berth time.

Editor's Note: All motor carriers and drivers are required to comply with 395.1(g) listed below until January 4, 2004.

(g) **Sleeper berths.** Drivers using sleeper berth equipment as defined in §395.2 or who are off duty at a natural gas or oil well location, may cumulate the required 8 consecutive hours off duty, as required by §395.3, resting in a sleeper berth in two separate periods totaling 8 hours, neither period to be less than 2 hours, or resting while off duty in other sleeping accommodations at a natural gas or oil well location.

Editor's Note: Compliance with the following is required as of January 4, 2004.

(h) **State of Alaska.** (1) . . .

(2) **Passenger-carrying commercial motor vehicle.** The

provisions of §395.5 do not apply to any driver who is driving a passenger-carrying commercial motor vehicle in the State of Alaska. A driver who is driving a passenger-carrying commercial motor vehicle in the State of Alaska must not drive or be required or permitted to drive ☐

(i) More than 15 hours following 8 consecutive hours off duty;

(ii) After being on duty for 20 hours or more following 8 consecutive hours off duty;

(iii) After having been on duty for 70 hours in any period of 7 consecutive days, if the motor carrier for which the driver drives does not operate every day in the week; or

(iv) After having been on duty for 80 hours in any period of 8 consecutive days, if the motor carrier for which the driver drives operates every day in the week.

(3) A driver who is driving a commercial motor vehicle in the State of Alaska and who encounters adverse driving conditions (as defined in §395.2) may drive and be permitted or required to drive a commercial motor vehicle for the period of time needed to complete the run.

(i) . . .

(ii) After a passenger-carrying commercial motor vehicle driver completes the run, that driver must be off duty for at least 8 consecutive hours before he/she drives again.

Editor's Note: All motor carriers and drivers are required to comply with 395.1(h) listed below until January 4, 2004.

(h) **State of Alaska.** (1) The provisions of §395.3 shall not apply to any driver who is driving a commercial motor vehicle in the State of Alaska. A driver who is driving a commercial motor vehicle in the State of Alaska must not drive or be required or permitted to drive—

(i) More than 15 hours following 8 consecutive hours off duty;

(ii) After being on duty for 20 hours or more following 8 consecutive hours off duty;

(iii) After having been on duty for 70 hours in any period of 7 consecutive days, if the motor carrier for which the driver drives does not operate every day in the week; or

(iv) After having been on duty for 80 hours in any period of 8 consecutive days, if the motor carrier for which the driver drives operates every day in the week.

(2) A driver who is driving a commercial motor vehicle in the State of Alaska and who encounters adverse driving conditions (as defined in §395.2) may drive and be permitted or required to

drive a commercial motor vehicle for the period of time needed to complete the run. After he/she completes the run, that driver must be off duty for 8 consecutive hours before he/she drives again.

(i) **State of Hawaii.** The rules in §395.8 do not apply to a driver who drives a commercial motor vehicle in the State of Hawaii, if the motor carrier who employs the driver maintains and retains for a period of 6 months accurate and true records showing—

(1) The total number of hours the driver is on duty each day; and

(2) The time at which the driver reports for, and is released from, duty each day.

Editor's Note: Compliance with the following is required as of January 4, 2004.

(j) **Travel time.** (1) . . .

(2) When a passenger-carrying commercial motor vehicle driver at the direction of the motor carrier is traveling, but not driving or assuming any other responsibility to the carrier, such time must be counted as on-duty time unless the driver is afforded at least 8 consecutive hours off duty when arriving at destination, in which case he/she must be considered off duty for the entire period.

Editor's Note: All motor carriers and drivers are required to comply with 395.1(j) listed below until January 4, 2004.

(j) **Travel time.** When a driver at the direction of the motor carrier is traveling, but not driving or assuming any other responsibility to the carrier, such time shall be counted as on-duty time unless the driver is afforded at least 8 consecutive hours off duty when arriving at destination, in which case he/she shall be considered off duty for the entire period.

Editor's Note: Compliance date for paragraph (o) is January 4, 2004.

(o) **Property-carrying driver.** A property-carrying driver is exempt from the requirements of §395.3(a)(2) if:

(1) The driver has returned to the driver's normal work reporting location and the carrier released the driver from duty at that location for the previous five duty tours the driver has worked;

(2) The driver has returned to the normal work reporting location and the carrier releases the driver from duty within 16 hours after coming on duty following 10 consecutive hours off

duty; and

(3) The driver has not taken this exemption within the previous 7 consecutive days, except when the driver has begun a new 7- or 8-consecutive day period with the beginning of any off duty period of 34 or more consecutive hours as allowed by §395.3(c).

(k) ..

(l) ...

(m) .

(n) ...

§395.2 Definitions.

As used in this part, the following words and terms are construed to mean:

Adverse driving conditions means snow, sleet, fog, other adverse weather conditions, a highway covered with snow or ice, or unusual road and traffic conditions, none of which were apparent on the basis of information known to the person dispatching the run at the time it was begun.

Automatic on-board recording device means an electric, electronic, electromechanical, or mechanical device capable of recording driver's duty status information accurately and automatically as required by §395.15. The device must be integrally synchronized with specific operations of the commercial motor vehicle in which it is installed. At a minimum, the device must record engine use, road speed, miles driven, the date, and time of day.

Driver-salesperson ...

Driving time means all time spent at the driving controls of a commercial motor vehicle in operation.

Eight consecutive days means the period of 8 consecutive days beginning on any day at the time designated by the motor carrier for a 24-hour period.

Ground water drilling rig ...

Multiple stops means all stops made in any one village, town, or city may be computed as one.

On duty time means all time from the time a driver begins to work or is required to be in readiness to work until the time the driver is relieved from work and all responsibility for performing work. **On-duty time** shall include:

(1) All time at a plant, terminal, facility, or other property of a motor carrier or shipper, or on any public property, waiting to

be dispatched, unless the driver has been relieved from duty by the motor carrier;

(2) All time inspecting, servicing, or conditioning any commercial motor vehicle at any time;

(3) All driving time as defined in the term **driving time**;

(4) All time, other than driving time, in or upon any commercial motor vehicle except time spent resting in a sleeper berth;

(5) All time loading or unloading a commercial motor vehicle, supervising, or assisting in the loading or unloading, attending a commercial motor vehicle being loaded or unloaded, remaining in readiness to operate the commercial motor vehicle, or in giving or receiving receipts for shipments loaded or unloaded;

(6) All time repairing, obtaining assistance, or remaining in attendance upon a disabled commercial motor vehicle;

(7) All time spent providing a breath sample or urine specimen, including travel time to and from the collection site, in order to comply with the random, reasonable suspicion, post-accident, or follow-up testing required by part 382, of this subchapter, when directed by a motor carrier.

(8) Performing any other work in the capacity, employ, or service of a motor carrier; and

(9) Performing any compensated work for a person who is not a motor carrier.

Seven consecutive days means the period of 7 consecutive days beginning on any day at the time designated by the motor carrier for a 24-hour period.

Sleeper berth means a berth conforming to the requirements of §393.76 of this chapter.

Transportation of construction materials and equipment . . .

Twenty-four-hour period means any 24-consecutive-hour period beginning at the time designated by the motor carrier for the terminal from which the driver is normally dispatched.

Utility service vehicle . . .

Editor's Note: All motor carriers and drivers are required to comply with the requirements listed below until January 4, 2004.

§395.3 Maximum driving time.

(a) Except as provided in §§395.1(b)(1), 395.1(f), and 395.1(h), no motor carrier shall permit or require any driver used by it to drive nor shall any such driver drive:

(1) More than 10 hours following 8 consecutive hours off duty; or

(2) For any period after having been on duty 15 hours following 8 consecutive hours off duty.

(b) No motor carrier shall permit or require a driver of a commercial motor vehicle to drive, nor shall any driver drive, regardless of the number of motor carriers using the driver's services, for any period after—

(1) Having been on duty 60 hours in any 7 consecutive days if the employing motor carrier does not operate commercial motor vehicles every day of the week; or

(2) Having been on duty 70 hours in any period of 8 consecutive days if the employing motor carrier operates commercial motor vehicles every day of the week.

Editor's Note: Compliance with the following is required for carriers and drivers of property-carrying commercial motor vehicles as of January 4, 2004.

§395.3 . . .

Editor's Note: Beginning on January 4, 2004, carriers and drivers of passenger-carrying commercial motor vehicles will be required to comply with the requirements listed below.

§395.5 Maximum driving time for passenger-carrying vehicles.

Subject to the exceptions and exemptions in §395.1:

(a) No motor carrier shall permit or require any driver used by it to drive a passenger-carrying commercial motor vehicle, nor shall any such driver drive a passenger-carrying commercial motor vehicle:

(1) More than 10 hours following 8 consecutive hours off duty; or

(2) For any period after having been on duty 15 hours following 8 consecutive hours off duty.

(b) No motor carrier shall permit or require a driver of a passenger-carrying commercial motor vehicle to drive, nor shall any driver drive a passenger-carrying commercial motor vehicle, regardless of the number of motor carriers using the driver's services, for any period after—

(1) Having been on duty 60 hours in any 7 consecutive days if the employing motor carrier does not operate commercial motor vehicles every day of the week; or

(2) Having been on duty 70 hours in any period of 8 consecu-

tive days if the employing motor carrier operates commercial motor vehicles every day of the week.

§395.7 [Removed and reserved.]

§395.8 Driver's record of duty status.

(a) Except for a private motor carrier of passengers (nonbusiness), every motor carrier shall require every driver used by the motor carrier to record his/her duty status for each 24 hour period using the methods prescribed in either paragraphs (a)(1) or (2) of this section.

(1) Every driver who operates a commercial motor vehicle shall record his/her duty status, in duplicate, for each 24-hour period. The duty status time shall be recorded on a specified grid, as shown in paragraph (g) of this section. The grid and the requirements of paragraph (d) of this section may be combined with any company forms. The previously approved format of the Daily Log, Form MCS-59 or the Multi-day Log, MCS-139 and 139A, which meets the requirements of this section, may continue to be used.

(2) Every driver who operates a commercial motor vehicle shall record his/her duty status by using an automatic on-board recording device that meets the requirements of §395.15 of this part. The requirements of §395.8 shall not apply, except paragraphs (e) and (k)(1) and (2) of this section.

(b) The duty status shall be recorded as follows:

(1) "Off duty" or "OFF."

(2) "Sleeper berth" or "SB" (only if a sleeper berth used).

(3) "Driving" or "D."

(4) "On-duty not driving" or "ON."

(c) For each change of duty status (e.g., the place of reporting for work, starting to drive, on-duty not driving and where released from work), the name of the city, town or village, with State abbreviation, shall be recorded.

Note: If a change of duty status occurs at a location other than a city, town, or village, show one of the following: (1) the highway number and nearest milepost followed by the name of the nearest city, town, or village and State abbreviation, (2) the highway number and the name of the service plaza followed by the name of the nearest city, town, or village and State abbreviation, or (3) the highway numbers of the nearest two intersecting roadways followed by the name of the nearest city, town, or village and State abbreviation.

(d) The following information must be included on the form

in addition to the grid:

(1) Date;

(2) Total miles driving today;

(3) Truck or tractor and trailer number;

(4) Name of carrier;

(5) Driver's signature/certification;

(6) 24-hour period starting time (e.g., midnight, 9:00 a.m., noon, 3:00 p.m.);

(7) Main office address;

(8) Remarks;

(9) Name of co-driver;

(10) Total hours (far right edge of grid); and

(11) Shipping document number(s), or name of shipper and commodity.

(e) Failure to complete the record of duty activities of this section or §395.15, failure to preserve a record of such duty activities, or making of false reports in connection with such duty activities shall make the driver and/or the carrier liable to prosecution.

(f) The driver's activities shall be recorded in accordance with the following provisions:

(1) **Entries to be current.** Drivers shall keep their record of duty status current to the time shown for the last change of duty status.

(2) **Entries made by driver only.** All entries relating to driver's duty status must be legible and in the driver's own handwriting.

(3) **Date.** The month, day and year for the beginning of each 24-hour period shall be shown on the form containing the driver's duty status record.

(4) **Total miles driving today.** Total mileage driven during the 24-hour period shall be recorded on the form containing the driver's duty status record.

(5) **Commercial motor vehicle identification.** The driver shall show the number assigned by the motor carrier, or the license number and licensing state of each commercial motor vehicle operated during each 24-hour period on his/her record of duty status. The driver of an articulated (combination) commercial motor vehicle shall show the number assigned by the motor carrier, or the license number and licensing state of each motor vehicle used in each commercial motor vehicle combination operated during that 24-hour period on his/her record of duty status.

(6) **Name of motor carrier.** The name(s) of the motor carrier(s) for which work is performed shall be shown on the form containing the driver's record of duty status. When work is performed for more than one motor carrier during the same 24-hour period, the beginning and finishing time, showing a.m. or p.m., worked for each motor carrier shall be shown after each motor carrier's name. Drivers of leased commercial motor vehicles shall show the name of the motor carrier performing the transportation.

(7) **Signature/certification.** The driver shall certify to the correctness of all entries by signing the form containing the driver's duty status record with his/her legal name or name of record. The driver's signature certifies that all entries required by this section made by the driver are true and correct.

(8) **Time base to be used.**

(i) The driver's duty status record shall be prepared, maintained, and submitted using the time standard in effect at the driver's home terminal, for a 24-hour period beginning with the time specified by the motor carrier for that driver's home terminal.

(ii) The term "7 or 8 consecutive days" means the 7 or 8 consecutive 24-hour periods as designated by the carrier for the driver's home terminal.

(iii) The 24-hour period starting time must be identified on the driver's duty status record. One-hour increments must appear on the graph, be identified, and preprinted. The words "Midnight" and "Noon" must appear above or beside the appropriate one-hour increment.

(9) **Main office address.** The motor carrier's main office address shall be shown on the form containing the driver's duty status record.

(10) Recording days off duty. Two or more consecutive 24-hour periods off duty may be recorded on one duty status record.

(11) **Total hours.** The total hours in each duty status: off duty other than in a sleeper berth; off duty in a sleeper berth; driving, and on duty not driving, shall be entered to the right of the grid, the total of such entries shall equal 24 hours.

(12) . . .

(g) **Graph grid.** The following graph grid must be incorporated into a motor carrier recordkeeping system which must also contain the information required in paragraph (d) of this section.

Graph Grid—Vertically

1: OFF DUTY
2: SLEEPER BERTH
3: DRIVING
4: ON DUTY (NOT DRIVING)

REMARKS

Graph Grid—Horizontally

1: OFF DUTY

2: SLEEPER BERTH

3: DRIVING

4: ON DUTY (NOT DRIVING)

REMARKS

(h) **Graph Grid Preparation.** The graph grid may be used horizontally or vertically and shall be completed as follows:

(1) **Off-duty.** Except for time spent resting in a sleeper berth, a continuous line shall be drawn between the appropriate time markers to record the period(s) of time when the driver is not on duty, is not required to be in readiness to work, or is not under any responsibility for performing work.

(2) **Sleeper berth.** A continuous line shall be drawn between the appropriate time markers to record the period(s) of time off duty resting in a sleeper berth, as defined in §395.2. (If a non-sleeper berth operation, sleeper berth need not be shown on the grid.)

(3) **Driving.** A continuous line shall be drawn between the appropriate time markers to record the period(s) of driving time, as defined in §395.2.

(4) **On duty not driving.** A continuous line shall be drawn between the appropriate time markers to record the period(s) of time on duty not driving specified in §395.2.

(5) **Location - Remarks.** The name of the city, town, or village, with State abbreviation where each change of duty status occurs shall be recorded.

Note: If a change of duty status occurs at a location other than a city, town, or village, show one of the following: (1) the highway number and nearest milepost followed by the name of the nearest city, town, or village and State abbreviation, (2) the highway number and the name of the service plaza followed by the name of the nearest city, town, or village and State abbreviation, or (3) the highway numbers of the nearest two intersecting roadways followed by the name of the nearest city, town, or village and State abbreviation.

(i) **Filing driver's record of duty status.** The driver shall submit or forward by mail the original driver's record of duty status to the regular employing motor carrier within 13 days following the completion of the form.

(j) **Drivers used by more than one motor carrier.** (1) When the services of a driver are used by more than one motor carrier during any 24-hour period in effect at the driver's home terminal, the driver shall submit a copy of the record of duty status to each motor carrier. The record shall include:

(i) All duty time for the entire 24-hour period;

(ii) The name of each motor carrier served by the driver during that period; and

(iii) The beginning and finishing time, including a.m. or p.m., worked for each carrier.

(2) Motor carriers, when using a driver for the first time or intermittently, shall obtain from the driver a signed statement giving the total time on duty during the immediately preceding 7 days and the time at which the driver was last relieved from duty prior to beginning work for the motor carriers.

(k) **Retention of driver's record of duty status.** (1) Each motor carrier shall maintain records of duty status and all supporting documents for each driver it employs for a period of six months from the date of receipt.

(2) The driver shall retain a copy of each record of duty status for the previous 7 consecutive days which shall be in his/her possession and available for inspection while on duty.

Note: Driver's record of duty status. The graph grid, when incorporated as part of any form used by a motor carrier, must be of sufficient size to be legible.

The following executed specimen grid illustrates how a driver's duty status should be recorded for a trip from Richmond, Virginia, to Newark, New Jersey. The grid reflects the midnight to midnight 24 hour period.

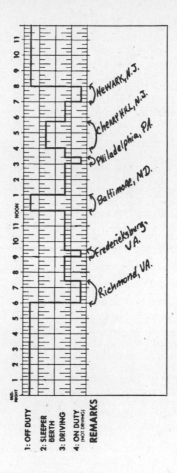

Graph Grid (midnight to midnight operation).
The driver in this instance reported for duty at the motor carrier's terminal. The driver reported for work at 6 a.m., helped load, checked with dispatch, made a pretrip inspection, and performed other duties until 7:30 a.m. when the driver began driving. At 9 a.m. the driver had a minor accident in Fredericksburg, Virginia, and spent one half hour handling details with the local police. The driver arrived at the company's Baltimore, Maryland, terminal at noon and went to lunch while minor repairs were made to the tractor. At 1 p.m. the driver resumed the trip and made a delivery in Philadelphia, Pennsylvania, between 3 p.m. and 3:30 p.m. at which time the driver started driving again. Upon arrival at Cherry Hill, New Jersey, at 4 p.m., the driver entered the sleeper berth for a rest break until 5:45 p.m. at which time the driver resumed driving again. At 7 p.m. the driver arrived at the company's terminal in Newark, New Jersey. Between 7 p.m. and 8 p.m. the driver prepared the required paperwork including completing the driver's record of duty status, driver vehicle inspection report, insurance report for the Fredericksburg, Virginia accident, checked for the next day's dispatch, etc. At 8 p.m., the driver went off duty.

§395.10 [Removed and reserved.]

§395.11 [Removed and reserved.]

§395.12 [Removed and reserved.]

§395.13 Drivers declared out of service.

(a) **Authority to declare drivers Out of Service.** Every special agent of the Federal Motor Carrier Safety Administration (as defined in Appendix B to this subchapter) is authorized to declare a driver out of service and to notify the motor carrier of that declaration, upon finding at the time and place of examination that the driver has violated the out of service criteria as set forth in paragraph (b) of this section.

(b) **Out of Service criteria.** (1) No driver shall drive after being on duty in excess of the maximum periods permitted by this part.

(2) No driver required to maintain a record of duty status under §395.8 or §395.15 of this part shall fail to have a record of duty status current on the day of examination and for the prior 7 consecutive days.

(3) **Exception.** A driver failing only to have possession of a record of duty status current on the day of examination and the prior day, but has completed records of duty status up to that time (previous 6 days), will be given the opportunity to make the duty status record current.

(c) **Responsibilities of motor carriers.** (1) No motor carrier shall:

(i) Require or permit a driver who has been declared out of service to operate a commercial motor vehicle until that driver may lawfully do so under the rules in this part.

(ii) Require a driver who has been declared out of service for failure to prepare a record of duty status to operate a commercial motor vehicle until that driver has been off duty for the appropriate number of consecutive hours required by this part and is in compliance with this section. The appropriate consecutive hours off-duty period may include sleeper berth time.

(2) A motor carrier shall complete the "Motor Carrier Certification of Action Taken" portion of the form MCS-63 (Driver-Vehicle Examination Report) and deliver the copy of the form either personally or by mail to the Division Administrator or State Director, Federal Motor Carrier Safety Administration, at the address specified upon the form within 15 days following the date of examination. If the motor carrier mails the form, delivery is made on the date it is postmarked.

(d) **Responsibilities of the driver.** (1) No driver who has been declared out of service shall operate a commercial motor vehicle until that driver may lawfully do so under the rules of this Part.

(2) No driver who has been declared out of service, for failing to prepare a record of duty status, shall operate a commercial motor vehicle until the driver has been off duty for the appropriate number of consecutive hours required by this part and is in compliance with this section.

(3) A driver to whom a form has been tendered declaring the driver out of service shall within 24 hours thereafter deliver or mail the copy to a person or place designated by motor carrier to receive it.

(4) . . .

§395.15 Automatic on-board recording devices.

(a) **Authority to use automatic on-board recording device.**

(1) A motor carrier may require a driver to use an automatic on-board recording device to record the driver's hours of service in lieu of complying with the requirements of §395.8 of this part.

(2) Every driver required by a motor carrier to use an automatic on-board recording device shall use such device to record the driver's hours of service.

(b) **Information requirements.**

(1) Automatic on-board recording devices shall produce, upon demand, a driver's hours of service chart, electronic display, or printout showing the time and sequence of duty status changes including the drivers' starting time at the beginning of each day.

(2) The device shall provide a means whereby authorized Federal, State, or local officials can immediately check the status of a driver's hours of service. This information may be used in conjunction with handwritten or printed records of duty status, for the previous 7 days.

(3) Support systems used in conjunction with on-board recorders at a driver's home terminal or the motor carrier's principal place of business must be capable of providing authorized Federal, State or local officials with summaries of an individual driver's hours of service records, including the information specified in §395.8(d) of this part. The support systems must also provide information concerning on-board system sensor failures and identification of edited data. Such support systems should meet the information interchange requirements of the American National Standard Code for Information Interchange (ANSCII) (EIARS-232/CCITT V.24 port (National Bureau of Standards "Code for Information Interchange," FIPS PUB 1-1)).

(4) The driver shall have in his/her possession records of duty status for the previous 7 consecutive days available for inspection while on duty. These records shall consist of information stored in and retrievable from the automatic on-board recording device, handwritten records, computer generated records, or any combination thereof.

(5) All hard copies of the driver's record of duty status must be signed by the driver. The driver's signature certifies that the information contained thereon is true and correct.

(c) **The duty status and additional information shall be recorded as follows:**

(1) "Off duty" or "OFF", or by an identifiable code or character;

(2) "Sleeper berth" or "SB" or by an identifiable code or character (only if the sleeper berth is used);

(3) "Driving" or "D", or by an identifiable code or character; and

(4) "On-duty not driving" or "ON", or by an identifiable code or character.

(5) Date;

(6) Total miles driving today;

(7) Truck or tractor and trailer number;

(8) Name of carrier;

(9) Main office address;

(10) 24-hour period starting time (e.g., midnight, 9:00 a.m., noon, 3:00 p.m.);

(11) Name of co-driver;

(12) Total hours; and

(13) . . .

(d) **Location of duty status change.**

(1) For each change of duty status (e.g., the place and time of reporting for work, starting to drive, on-duty not driving and where released from work), the name of the city, town, or village, with State abbreviation, shall be recorded.

(2) Motor carriers are permitted to use location codes in lieu of the requirements of paragraph (d)(1) of this section. A list of such codes showing all possible location identifiers shall be carried in the cab of the commercial motor vehicle and available at the motor carrier's principal place of business. Such lists shall be made available to an enforcement official on request.

(e) **Entries made by driver only.** If a driver is required to make written entries relating to the driver's duty status, such entries must be legible and in the driver's own handwriting.

(f) **Reconstruction of records of duty status.** Drivers are required to note any failure of automatic on-board recording devices, and to reconstruct the driver's record of duty status for the current day, and the past 7 days, less any days for which the drivers have records, and to continue to prepare a handwritten record of all subsequent duty status until the device is again operational.

(g) **On-board information.** Each commercial motor vehicle must have on-board the commercial motor vehicle an information packet containing the following items:

(1) An instruction sheet describing in detail how data may be stored and retrieved from an automatic on-board recording system; and

(2) A supply of blank driver's records of duty status graph-grids sufficient to record the driver's duty status and other related information for the duration of the current trip.

(h) **Submission of driver's record of duty status.**

(1) The driver shall submit, electronically or by mail, to the employing motor carrier, each record of the driver's duty status within 13 days following the completion of each record;

(2) The driver shall review and verify that all entries are accurate prior to submission to the employing motor carrier; and

(3) The submission of the record of duty status certifies that all entries made by the driver are true and correct.

(i) **Performance of recorders.** Motor carriers that use automatic on-board recording devices for recording their drivers' records of duty status in lieu of the handwritten record shall ensure that:

(1) A certificate is obtained from the manufacturer certifying that the design of the automatic on-board recorder has been sufficiently tested to meet the requirements of this section and under the conditions it will be used;

(2) The automatic on-board recording device permits duty status to be updated only when the commercial motor vehicle is at rest, except when registering the time a commercial motor vehicle crosses a State boundary;

(3) The automatic on-board recording device and associated support systems are, to the maximum extent practicable, tamperproof and do not permit altering of the information collected concerning the driver's hours of service;

(4) The automatic on-board recording device warns the driver visually and/or audibly that the device has ceased to function. Devices installed and operational as of October 31, 1988 and authorized to be used in lieu of the handwritten record of duty status by the FMCSA are exempted from this requirement.

(5) Automatic on-board recording devices with electronic displays shall have the capability of displaying the following:

(i) Driver's total hours of driving today;

(ii) The total hours on duty today;

(iii) Total miles driving today;

(iv) Total hours on duty for the 7 consecutive day period, including today;

(v) Total hours on duty for the prior 8 consecutive day period, including the present day; and

(vi) the sequential changes in duty status and the times the changes occurred for each driver using the device.

(6) The on-board recorder is capable of recording separately each driver's duty status when there is a multiple-driver operation;

(7) The on-board recording device/system identifies sensor failures and edited data when reproduced in printed form. Devices installed and operational as of October 31, 1988 and authorized to be used in lieu of the handwritten record of duty status by the FMCSA are exempted from this requirement.

(8) The on-board recording device is maintained and recalibrated in accordance with the manufacturer's specifications;

(9) The motor carrier's drivers are adequately trained regarding the proper operation of the device; and

(10) The motor carrier must maintain a second copy (back-up copy) of the electronic hours-of-service files, by month, in a different physical location than where the original data is stored.

(j) **Rescission of authority.**

(1) The FMCSA may, after notice and opportunity to reply, order any motor carrier or driver to comply with the requirements of §395.8 of this part.

(2) The FMCSA may issue such an order if the FMCSA has determined that—

(i) The motor carrier has been issued conditional or unsatisfactory safety rating by the FMCSA;

(ii) The motor carrier has required or permitted a driver to establish, or the driver has established, a pattern of exceeding the hours of service limitations of this part;

(iii) The motor carrier has required or permitted a driver to fail, or the driver has failed, to accurately and completely record the driver's hours of service as required in this section; or

(iv) The motor carrier or driver has tampered with or otherwise abused the automatic on-board recording device on any commercial motor vehicle.

PART 396 — INSPECTION, REPAIR, AND MAINTENANCE

AUTHORITY: 49 U.S.C. 31133, 31136, and 31502; 49 CFR 1.73.

§396.1 Scope.

General — Every motor carrier, its officers, drivers, agents, representatives, and employees directly concerned with the inspection or maintenance of motor vehicles shall comply and be conversant with the rules of this part.

§396.3 Inspection, repair and maintenance.

(a) **General** — Every motor carrier shall systematically inspect, repair, and maintain, or cause to be systematically inspected, repaired, and maintained, all motor vehicles subject to its control.

(1) Parts and accessories shall be in safe and proper operating condition at all times. These include those specified in Part 393 of this subchapter and any additional parts and accessories which may affect safety of operation, including but not limited to, frame and frame assemblies, suspension systems, axles and attaching parts, wheels and rims, and steering systems.

(2) Pushout windows, emergency doors, and emergency door marking lights in buses shall be inspected at least every 90 days.

(b) **Required records** — For vehicles controlled for 30 consecutive days or more, except for a private motor carrier of passengers (nonbusiness), the motor carriers shall maintain, or cause to be maintained, the following record for each vehicle:

(1) An identification of the vehicle including company number, if so marked, make, serial number, year, and tire size. In addition, if the motor vehicle is not owned by the motor carrier, the record shall identify the name of the person furnishing the vehicle;

(2) A means to indicate the nature and due date of the various inspection and maintenance operations to be performed;

(3) A record of inspection, repairs and maintenance indicating their date and nature; and

(4) A record of tests conducted on pushout windows, emergency doors, and emergency door marking lights on buses.

(c) **Record retention** — The records required by this section shall be retained where the vehicle is either housed or maintained for a period of 1 year and for 6 months after the motor vehicle leaves the motor carrier's control.

§396.5 Lubrication.

Every motor carrier shall ensure that each motor vehicle subject to its control is—

(a) Properly lubricated; and

(b) Free of oil and grease leaks.

§396.7 Unsafe operations forbidden.

(a) **General** — A motor vehicle shall not be operated in such a condition as to likely cause an accident or a breakdown of the vehicle.

(b) **Exemption** — Any motor vehicle discovered to be in an unsafe condition while being operated on the highway may be continued in operation only to the nearest place where repairs can safely be effected. Such operation shall be conducted only if it is less hazardous to the public than to permit the vehicle to remain on the highway.

§396.9 Inspection of motor vehicles in operation.

(a) **Personnel authorized to perform inspections** — Every special agent of the FMCSA (as defined in Appendix B to this subchapter) is authorized to enter upon and perform inspections of motor carrier's vehicles in operation.

(b) **Prescribed inspection report** — The Driver-Equipment Compliance Check shall be used to record results of motor vehicle inspections conducted by authorized FMCSA personnel.

(c) **Motor vehicles declared "out of service".**

(1) Authorized personnel shall declare and mark "out of service" any motor vehicle which by reason of its mechanical condition or loading would likely cause an accident or a breakdown. An "Out of Service Vehicle" sticker shall be used to mark vehicles "out of service".

(2) No motor carrier shall require or permit any person to operate nor shall any person operate any motor vehicle declared and marked "out of service" until all repairs required by the "out of service notice" have been satisfactorily completed. The term "operate" as used in this section shall include towing the vehicle, except that vehicles marked "out of service" may be towed away by means of a vehicle using a crane or hoist.

(3) No person shall remove the "Out of Service Vehicle" sticker from any motor vehicle prior to completion of all repairs, required by the "out of service notice".

(d) **Motor carrier disposition.**

(1) The driver of any motor vehicle receiving an inspection report shall deliver it to the motor carrier operating the vehicle upon his/her arrival at the next terminal or facility. If the driver is not scheduled to arrive at a terminal or facility of the motor carrier operating the vehicle within 24 hours, the driver shall immediately mail the report to the motor carrier.

(2) Motor carriers shall examine the report. Violations or defects noted thereon shall be corrected.

(3) Within 15 days following the date of the inspection, the motor carrier shall —

(i) Certify that all violations noted have been corrected by completing the "Signature of Carrier Official, Title, and Date Signed" portions of the form; and

(ii) Return the completed roadside inspection form to the issuing agency at the address indicated on the form and retain a copy at the motor carrier's principal place of business or where the vehicle is housed for 12 months from the date of the inspection.

§396.11 Driver vehicle inspection report(s).

(a) **Report required.** Every motor carrier shall require its drivers to report, and every driver shall prepare a report in writing at the completion of each day's work on each vehicle operated and the report shall cover at least the following parts and accessories:

-Service brakes
-Parking (hand) brake
-Steering mechanism
-Lighting devices and reflectors
-Tires
-Horn
-Windshield wipers
-Rear vision mirrors
- . . .
-Wheels and rims
-Emergency equipment

(b) **Report content.** The report shall identify the vehicle and list any defect or deficiency discovered by or reported to the driver which would affect the safety of operation of the vehicle or result in its mechanical breakdown. If no defect or deficiency is discovered by or reported to the driver, the report shall so indicate. In all instances, the driver shall sign the report. On two-driver operations, only one driver needs to sign the driver vehicle inspection report, provided both drivers agree as to the defects or deficiencies identified. If a driver operates more than one vehicle during the day, a report shall be prepared for each vehicle operated.

(c) **Corrective action.** Prior to requiring or permitting a driver to operate a vehicle, every motor carrier or its agent shall repair any defect or deficiency listed on the driver vehicle inspection report which would be likely to affect the safety of operation of the vehicle.

(1) Every motor carrier or its agent shall certify on the original driver vehicle inspection report which lists any defect or deficiency that the defect or deficiency has been repaired or that repair is unnecessary before the vehicle is operated again.

(2) Every motor carrier shall maintain the original driver vehicle inspection report, the certification of repairs, and the certification of the driver's review for three months from the date the written report was prepared.

(d) **Exceptions.** The rules in this section shall not apply to a private motor carrier of passengers (nonbusiness), a driveaway-towaway operation, or any motor carrier operating only one commercial motor vehicle.

§396.13 Driver inspection.

Before driving a motor vehicle, the driver shall:

(a) Be satisfied that the motor vehicle is in safe operating condition;

(b) Review the last driver vehicle inspection report; and

(c) Sign the report, only if defects or deficiencies were noted by the driver who prepared the report, to acknowledge that the driver has reviewed it and that there is a certification that the required repairs have been performed.

§396.15 ...

§396.17 Periodic inspection.

(a) Every commercial motor vehicle shall be inspected as required by this section. The inspection shall include, at a minimum, the parts and accessories set forth in Appendix G of this subchapter.[1]

(b) Except as provided in §396.23, a motor carrier shall inspect or cause to be inspected all motor vehicles subject to its control.

(c) A motor carrier shall not use a commercial motor vehicle unless each component identified in Appendix G has passed an inspection in accordance with the terms of this section at least once during the preceding 12 months and documentation of such inspection is on the vehicle. The documentation may be:

(1) The inspection report prepared in accordance with paragraph 396.21(a), or

(2) Other forms of documentation, based on the inspection report (*e.g.*, sticker or decal), which contains the following information:

(i) The date of inspection;

(ii) Name and address of the motor carrier or other entity where the inspection report is maintained;

(iii) Information uniquely identifying the vehicle inspected if not clearly marked on the motor vehicle; and

(iv) A certification that the vehicle has passed an inspection in accordance with §396.17.

(d) A motor carrier may perform the required annual inspection for vehicles under the carrier's control which are not subject to an inspection under §396.23(b)(1).

---

[1] EDITOR'S NOTE: Appendix G begins on page 480 in this Pocketbook.

(e) In lieu of the self inspection provided for in paragraph (d) of this section, a motor carrier may choose to have a commercial garage, fleet leasing company, truck stop, or other similar commercial business perform the inspection as its agent, provided that business operates and maintains facilities appropriate for commercial vehicle inspections and it employs qualified inspectors, as required by §396.19.

(f) Vehicles passing roadside or periodic inspections performed under the auspices of any State government or equivalent jurisdiction or the FMCSA, meeting the minimum standards contained in Appendix G of this subchapter, will be considered to have met the requirements of an annual inspection for a period of 12 months commencing from the last day of the month in which the inspection was performed, except as provided in §396.23(b)(1).

(g) It shall be the responsibility of the motor carrier to ensure that all parts and accessories not meeting the minimum standards set forth in Appendix G to this subchapter are repaired promptly.

(h) Failure to perform properly the annual inspection set forth in this section shall cause the motor carrier to be subject to the penalty provisions provided by 49 U.S.C.521(b).

§396.19 Inspector qualifications.

(a) It shall be the motor carrier's responsibility to ensure that the individual(s) performing an annual inspection under §396.17(d) or (e) is qualified as follows:

(1) Understands the inspection criteria set forth in 49 CFR Part 393 and Appendix G of this subchapter and can identify defective components;

(2) Is knowledgeable of and has mastered the methods, procedures, tools and equipment used when performing an inspection; and

(3) Is capable of performing an inspection by reason of experience, training, or both as follows:

(i) Successfully completed a State or Federal-sponsored training program or has a certificate from a State or Canadian Province which qualifies the person to perform commercial motor vehicle safety inspections, or

(ii) Have a combination of training and/or experience totaling at least 1 year. Such training and/or experience may consist of:

(A) Participation in a truck manufacturer-sponsored training program or similar commercial training program designed to train students in truck operation and maintenance;

(B) Experience as a mechanic or inspector in a motor carrier maintenance program;

(C) Experience as a mechanic or inspector in truck maintenance at a commercial garage, fleet leasing company, or similar facility; or

(D) Experience as a commercial vehicle inspector for a State, Provincial or Federal Government.

(b) Evidence of that individual's qualifications under this section shall be retained by the motor carrier for the period during which that individual is performing annual motor vehicle inspections for the motor carrier, and for one year thereafter. However, motor carriers do not have to maintain documentation of inspector qualifications for those inspections performed either as part of a State periodic inspection program or at the roadside as part of a random roadside inspection program.

§396.21 Periodic inspection recordkeeping requirements.

(a) The qualified inspector performing the inspection shall prepare a report which:

(1) Identifies the individual performing the inspection;

(2) Identifies the motor carrier operating the vehicle;

(3) Identifies the date of the inspection;

(4) Identifies the vehicle inspected;

(5) Identifies the vehicle components inspected and describes the results of the inspection, including the identification of those components not meeting the minimum standards set forth in Appendix G to this subchapter; and

(6) Certifies the accuracy and completeness of the inspection as complying with all the requirements of this section.

(b)(1) The original or a copy of the inspection report shall be retained by the motor carrier or other entity who is responsible for the inspection for a period of fourteen months from the date of the inspection report. The original or a copy of the inspection report shall be retained where the vehicle is either housed or maintained.

(2) The original or a copy of the inspection report shall be available for inspection upon demand of an authorized Federal, State or local official.

(3) **Exception.** Where the motor carrier operating the commercial motor vehicles did not perform the commercial motor vehicle's last annual inspection, the motor carrier shall be responsible for obtaining the original or a copy of the last annual inspection report upon demand of an authorized Federal, State, or local official.

§396.23 Equivalent to periodic inspection.

(a) The motor carrier may meet the requirements of §396.17 through a State or other jurisdiction's roadside inspection program. The inspection must have been performed during the preceding 12 months. In using the roadside inspection, the motor carrier would need to retain a copy of an annual inspection report showing that the inspection was performed in accordance with the minimum periodic inspection standards set forth in appendix G to this subchapter. When accepting such an inspection report, the motor carrier must ensure that the report complies with the requirements of §396.21(a).

(b)(1) If a commercial motor vehicle is subject to a mandatory State inspection program which is determined by the Administrator to be as effective as §396.17, the motor carrier shall meet the requirement of §396.17 through that State's inspection program. Commercial motor vehicle inspections may be conducted by State personnel, at State authorized commercial facilities, or by the motor carrier under the auspices of a State authorized self-inspection program.

(2) Should the FMCSA determine that a State inspection program, in whole or in part, is not as effective as §396.17, the motor carrier must ensure that the periodic inspection required by §396.17 is performed on all commercial motor vehicles under its control in a manner specified in §396.17.

Editor's Note: A vehicle will meet the Federal requirements if inspected under a state mandatory inspection program in Alabama, California, Connecticut, Hawaii, Louisiana, Maine, Maryland, Michigan, Minnesota, New Hampshire, New Jersey, New York, Ohio, Pennsylvania, Rhode Island, Texas, Utah, Vermont, Virginia, West Virginia, Wisconsin, and the District of Columbia. Of the above states, Alabama, California, Connecticut, Michigan, Minnesota, New Jersey, New York, Ohio, and Wisconsin have inspection programs that do not cover all commercial motor vehicles. There are three other states — Arkansas, Illinois, and Oklahoma — where the inspection is not mandatory but where the inspection will satisfy Federal requirements. The

Federal Highway Administration has also determined that all of the Canadian Provinces and the Yukon Territory have periodic inspection programs that are as effective as the Federal requirements.

§396.25 Qualifications of brake inspectors.

(a) The motor carrier shall ensure that all inspections, maintenance, repairs or service to the brakes of its commercial motor vehicles, are performed in compliance with the requirements of this section.

(b) For purposes of this section, "brake inspector" means any employee of a motor carrier who is responsible for ensuring all brake inspections, maintenance, service, or repairs to any commercial motor vehicle, subject to the motor carrier's control, meet the applicable Federal standards.

(c) No motor carrier shall require or permit any employee who does not meet the minimum brake inspector qualifications of §396.25(d) to be responsible for the inspection, maintenance, service or repairs of any brakes on its commercial motor vehicles.

(d) The motor carrier shall ensure that each brake inspector is qualified as follows:

(1) Understands the brake service or inspection task to be accomplished and can perform that task; and

(2) Is knowledgeable of and has mastered the methods, procedures, tools and equipment used when performing an assigned brake service or inspection task; and

(3) Is capable of performing the assigned brake service or inspection by reason of experience, training or both as follows:

(i) Has successfully completed an apprenticeship program sponsored by a State, a Canadian Province, a Federal agency or a labor union, or a training program approved by a State, Provincial or Federal agency, or has a certificate from a State or Canadian Province which qualifies the person to perform the assigned brake service or inspection task (including passage of Commercial Driver's License air brake tests in the case of a brake inspection); or

(ii) Has brake-related training or experience or a combination thereof totaling at least one year. Such training or experience may consist of:

(A) Participation in a training program sponsored by a brake or vehicle manufacturer or similar commercial training program designed to train students in brake maintenance or inspection similar to the assigned brake service or inspection tasks; or

(B) Experience performing brake maintenance or inspection similar to the assigned brake service or inspection task in a motor carrier maintenance program; or

(C) Experience performing brake maintenance or inspection similar to the assigned brake service or inspection task at a commercial garage, fleet leasing company, or similar facility.

(e) No motor carrier shall employ any person as a brake inspector unless the evidence of the inspector's qualifications, required under this section is maintained by the motor carrier at its principal place of business, or at the location at which the brake inspector is employed. The evidence must be maintained for the period during which the brake inspector is employed in that capacity and for one year thereafter. However, motor carriers do not have to maintain evidence of qualifications to inspect air brake systems for such inspections performed by persons who have passed the air brake knowledge and skills test for a Commercial Driver's License.

Appendix G to Subchapter B — Minimum Periodic Inspection Standards

A vehicle does not pass an inspection if it has one of the following defects or deficiencies:

1. **Brake System.**
   a. **Service Brakes.**
      (1) Absence of braking action on any axle required to have brakes upon application of the service brakes (such as missing brakes or brake shoe(s) failing to move upon application of a wedge. S-cam, cam, or disc brake).
      (2) Missing or broken mechanical components including: shoes, lining pads, springs, anchor pins, spiders, cam rollers, push-rods, and air chamber mounting bolts.
      (3) Loose brake components including air chambers, spiders, and cam shaft support brackets.
      (4) Audible air leak at brake chamber (Example-ruptured diaphragm, loose chamber clamp, etc.).
      (5) **Readjustment limits.** The maximum stroke at which brakes should be readjusted is given below. Any brake $1/4''$ or more past the readjustment limit or any two brakes less than $1/4''$ beyond the readjustment limit shall be cause for rejection. Stroke shall be measured with engine off and reservoir pressure of 80 to 90 psi with brakes fully applied.

BOLT TYPE BRAKE CHAMBER DATA

Type	Effective area (sq. in.)	Outside dia. (in.)	Maximum stroke at which brakes should be readjusted
A	12	$6\,^{15}/_{16}$	$1\,^3/_8$
B	24	$9\,^3/_{16}$	$1\,^3/_4$
C	16	$8\,^1/_{16}$	$1\,^3/_4$
D	6	$5\,^1/_4$	$1\,^1/_4$
E	9	$6\,^3/_{16}$	$1\,^3/_8$
F	36	11	$2\,^1/_4$
G	30	$9\,^7/_8$	2

ROTOCHAMBER DATA

Type	Effective area (sq. in.)	Outside dia. (in.)	Maximum stroke at which brakes should be readjusted
9	9	$4\,^9/_{32}$	$1\,^1/_2$
12	12	$4\,^{13}/_{16}$	$1\,^1/_2$
16	16	$5\,^{13}/_{32}$	2
20	20	$5\,^{15}/_{16}$	2
24	24	$6\,^{13}/_{32}$	2
30	30	$7\,^1/_{16}$	$2\,^1/_4$
36	36	$7\,^5/_8$	$2\,^3/_4$
50	50	$8\,^7/_8$	3

CLAMP TYPE BRAKE CHAMBER DATA

Type	Effective area (sq. in.)	Outside dia. (in.)	Maximum stroke at which brakes should be readjusted
6	6	$4\,^1/_2$	$1\,^1/_4$
9	9	$5\,^1/_4$	$1\,^3/_8$
12	12	$5\,^{11}/_{16}$	$1\,^3/_8$
16	16	$6\,^3/_8$	$1\,^3/_4$
20	20	$6\,^{25}/_{32}$	$1\,^3/_4$
24	24	$7\,^7/_{32}$	$1\,^3/_4$[1]
30	30	$8\,^3/_{32}$	2
36	36	9	$2\,^1/_4$

$^1/_2''$ for long stroke design).

WEDGE BRAKE DATA.—Movement of the scribe mark on the lining shall not exceed $^1/_{16}$ inch.

(6) Brake linings or pads.

   (a) Lining or pad is not firmly attached to the shoe;

   (b) Saturated with oil, grease, or brake fluid; or

   (c) Non-steering axles: Lining with a thickness less than $^1/_4$ inch at the shoe center for air drum brakes, $^1/_{16}$ inch or less at the shoe center for hydraulic and electric drum brakes, and less than $^1/_8$ inch for air disc brakes.

   (d) Steering axles: Lining with a thickness less than $^1/_4$ inch at the shoe center for drum brakes, less than $^1/_8$ inch for air disc brakes and $^1/_{16}$ inch or less for hydraulic disc and electric brakes.

    (7) Missing brake on any axle required to have brakes.

    (8) Mismatch across any power unit steering axle of:

      (a) Air chamber sizes.

      (b) Slack adjuster length.

b. **Parking Brake System.** No brakes on the vehicle or combination are applied upon actuation of the parking brake control, including driveline hand controlled parking brakes.

c. **Brake Drum or Rotors.**

    (1) With any external crack or cracks that open upon brake application (do not confuse short hairline heat check cracks with flexural cracks).

    (2) Any portion of the drum or rotor missing or in danger of falling away.

d. **Brake Hose.**

    (1) Hose with any damage extending through the outer reinforcement ply. (Rubber impregnated fabric cover is not a reinforcement ply). (Thermoplastic nylon may have braid reinforcement or color difference between cover and inner tube. Exposure of second color is cause for rejection.

    (2) Bulge or swelling when air pressure is applied.

    (3) Any audible leaks.

    (4) Two hoses improperly joined (such as a splice made by sliding the hose ends over a piece of tubing and clamping the hose to the tube).

    (5) Air hose cracked, broken or crimped.

e. **Brake Tubing.**

    (1) Any audible leak.

    (2) Tubing cracked, damaged by heat, broken or crimped.

f. **Low Pressure Warning Device** missing, inoperative, or does not operate at 55 psi and below, or $1/2$ the governor cut-out pressure, whichever is less.

g. **Tractor Protection Valve.** Inoperable or missing tractor protection valve(s) on power unit.

h. **Air Compressor.**

    (1) Compressor drive belts in condition of impending or probable failure.

    (2) Loose compressor mounting bolts.

(3) Cracked, broken or loose pulley.

(4) Cracked or broken mounting brackets, braces or adapters.

i. **Electric Brakes.**

(1) Absence of braking action on any wheel required to have brakes.

(2) Missing or inoperable breakaway braking device.

j. **Hydraulic Brakes. (Including Power Assist Over Hydraulic and Engine Drive Hydraulic Booster).**

(1) Master cylinder less than $1/4$ full.

(2) No pedal reserve with engine running except by pumping pedal.

(3) Power assist unit fails to operate.

(4) Seeping or swelling brake hose(s) under application of pressure.

(5) Missing or inoperative check valve.

(6) Has any visually observed leaking hydraulic fluid in the brake system.

(7) Has hydraulic hose(s) abraded (chafed) through outer cover-to-fabric layer.

(8) Fluid lines or connections leaking restricted, crimped, cracked or broken.

(9) Brake failure or low fluid warning light on and/or inoperative.

k. **Vacuum Systems.** Any vacuum system which:

(1) Has insufficient vacuum reserve to permit one full brake application after engine is shut off.

(2) Has vacuum hose(s) or line(s) restricted, abraded (chafed) through outer cover to cord ply, crimped, cracked, broken or has collapse of vacuum hose(s) when vacuum is applied.

(3) Lacks an operative low-vacuum warning device as required.

2. **Coupling Devices.**

a. **Fifth Wheels.**

(1) Mounting to frame.

(a) Any fasteners missing or ineffective.

(b) Any movement between mounting components.

(c) Any mounting angle iron cracked or broken.

(2) Mounting plates and pivot brackets.
  (a) Any fasteners missing or ineffective.
  (b) Any welds or parent metal cracked.
  (c) More than $3/8$ inch horizontal movement between pivot bracket pin and bracket.
  (d) Pivot bracket pin missing or not secured.
(3) Sliders.
  (a) Any latching fasteners missing or ineffective.
  (b) Any fore or aft stop missing or not securely attached.
  (c) Movement more than $3/8$ inch between slider bracket and slider base.
  (d) Any slider component cracked in parent metal or weld.
(4) Lower coupler.
  (a) Horizontal movement between the upper and lower fifth wheel halves exceeds $1/2$ inch.
  (b) Operating handle not in closed or locked position.
  (c) Kingpin not properly engaged.
  (d) Separation between upper and lower coupler allowing light to show through from side to side.
  (e) Cracks in the fifth wheel plate.
    Exceptions: Cracks in fifth wheel approach ramps and casting shrinkage cracks in the ribs of the body of a cast fifth wheel.
  (f) Locking mechanism parts missing, broken, or deformed to the extent the kingpin is not securely held.

b. **Pintle Hooks.**
  (1) Mounting to frame.
    (a) Any missing or ineffective fasteners (a fastener is not considered missing if there is an empty hole in the device but no corresponding hole in the frame or vise versa).
    (b) Mounting surface cracks extending from point of attachment (*e.g.*, cracks in the frame at mounting bolt holes).
    (c) Loose mounting.
    (d) Frame crossmember providing pintle hook attachment cracked.

(2) Integrity.
- (a) Cracks anywhere in pintle hook assembly.
- (b) Any welded repairs to the pintle hook.
- (c) Any part of the horn section reduced by more than 20%.
- (d) Latch insecure.

c. **Drawbar/Towbar Eye.**
(1) Mounting.
- (a) Any cracks in attachment welds.
- (b) Any missing or ineffective fasteners.

(2) Integrity.
- (a) Any cracks.
- (b) Any part of the eye reduced by more than 20%.

d. **Drawbar/Towbar Tongue.**
(1) Slider (power or manual).
- (a) Ineffective latching mechanism.
- (b) Missing or ineffective stop.
- (c) Movement of more than $1/4$ inch between slider and housing.
- (d) Any leaking, air or hydraulic cylinders, hoses, or chambers (other than slight oil weeping normal with hydraulic seals).

(2) Integrity.
- (a) Any cracks.
- (b) Movement of $1/4$ inch between subframe and drawbar at point of attachment.

e. **Safety Devices.**
(1) Safety devices missing.
(2) Unattached or incapable of secure attachment.
(3) Chains and hooks.
- (a) Worn to the extent of a measurable reduction in link cross section.
- (b) Improper repairs including welding, wire, small bolts, rope and tape.

(4) Cable.
- (a) Kinked or broken cable strands.
- (b) Improper clamps or clamping.

f. **Saddle-Mounts.**
  (1) Method of attachment.
    (a) Any missing or ineffective fasteners.
    (b) Loose mountings.
    (c) Any cracks or breaks in a stress or load bearing member.
    (d) Horizontal movement between upper and lower saddle-mount halves exceeds $1/4$ inch.

3. **Exhaust System.**
  a. Any exhaust system determined to be leaking at a point forward of or directly below the driver/sleeper compartment.
  b. A bus exhaust system leaking or discharging to the atmosphere:
    (1) **Gasoline powered** — excess of 6 inches forward of the rearmost part of the bus.
    (2) **Other than gasoline powered** — in excess of 15 inches forward of the rearmost part of the bus.
    (3) **Other than gasoline powered** — forward of a door or window designed to be opened. (**Exception:** emergency exits).
  c. No part of the exhaust system of any motor vehicle shall be so located as would be likely to result in burning, charring, or damaging the electrical wiring, the fuel supply, or any combustible part of the motor vehicle.

4. **Fuel System.**
  a. A fuel system with a visible leak at any point.
  b. A fuel tank filler cap missing.
  c. A fuel tank not securely attached to the motor vehicle by reason of loose, broken or missing mounting bolts or brackets (some fuel tanks use springs or rubber bushings to permit movement).

5. **Lighting Devices.**
All lighting devices and reflectors required by Section 393 shall be operable.

6. **Safe loading.**
  a. Part(s) of vehicle or condition of loading such that the spare tire or any part of the load or dunnage can fall onto the roadway.

b. Protection Against Shifting Cargo—Any vehicle without a front-end structure or equivalent device as required.

7. **Steering Mechanism.**

a. **Steering Wheel Free Play** (on vehicles equipped with power steering the engine must be running).

Steering wheel diameter	Manual steering system	Power steering system
16″	2″	4 $1/2$″
18″	2 $1/4$″	4 $3/4$″
20″	2 $1/2$″	5 $1/4$″
22″	2 $3/4$″	5 $3/4$″

b. **Steering Column.**
   (1) Any absence or looseness of U-bolt(s) or positioning part(s).
   (2) Worn, faulty or obviously repair welded universal joint(s).
   (3) Steering wheel not properly secured.

c. **Front Axle Beam and All Steering Components Other Than Steering Column.**
   (1) Any crack(s).
   (2) Any obvious welded repair(s).

d. **Steering Gear Box.**
   (1) Any mounting bolt(s) loose or missing.
   (2) Any crack(s) in gear box or mounting brackets.

e. **Pitman Arm.** Any looseness of the pitman arm on the steering gear output shaft.

f. **Power Steering.** Auxiliary power assist cylinder loose.

g. **Ball and Socket Joints.**
   (1) Any movement under steering load of a stud nut.
   (2) Any motion, other than rotational, between any linkage member and it's attachment point of more than $1/4$ inch.

h. **Tie Rods and Drag Links.**
   (1) Loose clamp(s) or clamp bolt(s) on tie rods or drag links.
   (2) Any looseness in any threaded joint.

i. **Nuts.** Nut(s) loose or missing on tie rods pitman arm, drag link, steering arm or tie rod arm.

j. **Steering System.** Any modification or other condition that interferes with free movement of any steering component.

8. **Suspension.**
   a. Any U-bolt(s), spring hanger(s), or other axle positioning part(s) cracked, broken, loose or missing resulting in shifting of an axle from its normal position. (After a turn, lateral axle displacement is normal with some suspensions. Forward or rearward operation in a straight line will cause the axle to return to alignment).
   b. **Spring Assembly.**
      (1) Any leaves in a leaf spring assembly broken or missing.
      (2) Any broken main leaf in a leaf spring assembly. (Includes assembly with more than one main spring).
      (3) Coil spring broken.
      (4) Rubber spring missing.
      (5) One or more leaves displaced in a manner that could result in contact with a tire, rim, brake drum or frame.
      (6) Broken torsion bar spring in a torsion bar suspension.
      (7) Deflated air suspension, *i.e.*, system failure, leak, etc.
   c. **Torque, Radius or Tracking Components.**
      Any part of a torque, radius or tracking component assembly or any part used for attaching the same to the vehicle frame or axle that is cracked, loose, broken or missing. (Does not apply to loose bushings in torque or track rods.)

9. **Frame.**
   a. **Frame Members.**
      (1) Any cracked, broken, loose, or sagging frame member.
      (2) Any loose or missing fasteners including fasteners attaching functional component such as engine, transmission, steering gear, suspension, body parts, and fifth wheel.
   b. **Tire and Wheel Clearance.** Any condition, including loading, that causes the body or frame to be in contact with a tire or any part of the wheel assemblies.
   c. (1) **Adjustable Axle Assemblies (Sliding Subframes).** Adjustable axle assembly with locking pins missing or not engaged.

10. **Tires.**
   a. **Any tire on any steering axle of a power unit.**
      (1) With less than $^4/_{32}$ inch tread when measured at any point on a major tread groove.
      (2) Has body ply or belt material exposed through the tread or sidewall.
      (3) Has any tread or sidewall separation.
      (4) Has a cut where the ply or belt material is exposed.
      (5) Labeled "Not for Highway Use" or displaying other marking which would exclude use on steering axle.
      (6) A tube-type radial tire without radial tube stem markings. These markings include a red band around the tube stem, the word "radial" embossed in metal stems, or the word "radial" molded in rubber stems.
      (7) Mixing bias and radial tires on the same axle.
      (8) Tire flap protrudes through valve slot in rim and touches stem.
      (9) Regrooved tire except motor vehicles used solely in urban or suburban service (see exception in 393.75(e).
      (10) Boot, blowout patch or other ply repair.
      (11) Weight carried exceeds tire load limit. This includes overloaded tire resulting from low air pressure.
      (12) Tire is flat or has noticeable (*e.g.*, can be heard or felt) leak.
      (13) Any bus equipped with recapped or retreaded tire(s).
      (14) So mounted or inflated that it comes in contact with any part of the vehicle.
   b. **All tires other than those found on the steering axle of a power unit:**
      (1) Weight carried exceeds tire load limit. This includes overloaded tire resulting from low air pressure.
      (2) Tire is flat or has noticeable (*e.g.*, can be heard or felt) leak.
      (3) Has body ply or belt material exposed through the tread or sidewall.
      (4) Has any tread or sidewall separation.
      (5) Has a cut where ply or belt material is exposed.

(6) So mounted or inflated that it comes in contact with any part of the vehicle. (This includes a tire that contacts its mate.)

(7) Is marked "Not for highway use" or otherwise marked and having like meaning.

(8) With less than $2/32$ inch tread when measured at any point on a major tread groove.

11. Wheels and Rims.

a. **Lock or Side Ring.** Bent, broken, cracked, improperly seated, sprung or mismatched ring(s).

b. **Wheels and Rims.** Cracked or broken or has elongated bolt holes.

c. **Fasteners (both spoke and disc wheels).** Any loose, missing, broken, cracked, stripped or otherwise ineffective fasteners.

d. **Welds.**

(1) Any cracks in welds attaching disc wheel disc to rim.

(2) Any crack in welds attaching tubeless demountable rim to adapter.

(3) Any welded repair on aluminum wheel(s) on a steering axle.

(4) Any welded repair other than disc to rim attachment on steel disc wheel(s) mounted on the steering axle.

12. Windshield Glazing.

(Not including a 2 inch border at the top, a 1 inch border at each side and the area below the topmost portion of the steering wheel.) Any crack, discoloration or vision reducing matter except: (1) coloring or tinting applied at time of manufacture; (2) any crack not over $1/4$ inch wide, if not intersected by any other crack; (3) any damaged area not more than $3/4$ inch in diameter, if not closer than 3 inches to any other such damaged area; (4) labels, stickers, decalcomania, etc. (see 393.60 for exceptions).

13. Windshield Wipers.

Any power unit that has an inoperative wiper, or missing or damaged parts that render it ineffective.

Comparison of Appendix G, and the new North American Uniform Driver-Vehicle Inspection Procedure (North American Commercial Vehicle Critical Safety Inspection Items and Out-Of-Service Criteria)

The vehicle portion of the FMCSA's North American Uniform Driver-Vehicle Inspection Procedure (NAUD-VIP) requirements, CVSA's North American Commercial Vehicle Critical Safety Inspection Items and Out-Of-Service Criteria and Appendix G of subchapter B are similar documents and follow the same inspection procedures. The same items are required to be inspected by each document. FMCSA's and CVSA's out-of-service criteria are intended to be used in random roadside inspections to identify critical vehicle inspection items and provide criteria for placing a vehicle(s) out-of-service. A vehicle(s) is placed out-of-service only when by reason of its mechanical condition or loading it is determined to be so imminently hazardous as to likely cause an accident or breakdown, or when such condition(s) would likely contribute to loss of control of the vehicle(s) by the driver. A certain amount of flexibility is given to the inspecting official whether to place the vehicle out-of-service at the inspection site or if it would be less hazardous to allow the vehicle to proceed to a repair facility for repair. The distance to the repair facility must not exceed 25 miles. The roadside type of inspection, however, does not necessarily mean that a vehicle has to be defect-free in order to continue in service.

In contrast, the Appendix G inspection procedure requires that all items required to be inspected are in proper adjustment, are not defective and function properly prior to the vehicle being placed in service.

Differences Between the Out-Of-Service Criteria & FMCSA's Annual Inspection

1. **Brake System.**
    The Appendix G criteria rejects vehicles with any defective brakes, any air leaks, etc. The out-of-service criteria allows 20% defective brakes on non-steering axles and a certain latitude on air leaks before placing a vehicle out-of-service.

2. **Coupling Devices.**
    Appendix G rejects vehicles with any fifth wheel mounting fastener missing or ineffective. The out-of-service criteria allows up to 20% missing or ineffective fasteners on frame mountings and pivot bracket mountings and 25% on sliderlatching fasteners. The out-of-service criteria also allows some latitude on cracked welds.

3. **Exhaust System.**
    Appendix G follows Section 393.83 verbatim. The CVSA out-of-service criteria allows vehicles to exhaust forward of the dimensions given in Section 393.83 as long as the exhaust does not leak or exhaust under the chassis.

4. **Fuel System.**
    Same for Appendix G and the out-of-service criteria.

5. **Lighting Devices.**
   Appendix G requires all lighting devices required by section 393 to be operative at all times. The out-of-service criteria only requires one stop light and functioning turn signals on the rear most vehicle of a combination vehicle to be operative at all times. In addtion one operative head lamp and tail lamp are required during the hours of darkness.

6. **Safe Loading.**
   Same for both Appendix G and the out-of-service criteria.

7. **Steering Mechanism.**
   Steering lash requirements of Appendix G follows the new requirements of §393.209.

8. **Suspension.**
   Appendix G follows the new requirements of §393.207 which does not allow any broken leaves in a leaf spring assembly. The out-of-service criteria allows up to 25% broken or missing leaves before being placed out-of-service.

9. **Frame.**
   The out-of-service criteria allows a certain latitude in frame cracks before placing a vehicle out-of-service. Appendix G follows the new requirements of 393.201 which does not allow any frame cracks.

10. **Tires.**
    Appendix G follows the requirements of 393.75 which requires a tire tread depth of $4/32$ inch on power unit steering axles and $2/32$ inch on all other axles. The out-of-service criteria only requires $2/32$ inch tire tread depth on power unit steering axles and $1/32$ inch on all other axles.

11. **Wheel and Rims.**
    The out-of-service criteria allows a certain amount latitude for wheel and rim cracks and missing or defective fasteners. Appendix G meets the requirements of the new 393.205 which does not allow defective wheels and rims non-effective nuts and bolts.

12. **Windshield Glazing.**
    The out-of-service criteria places in a restricted service condition any vehicle that has a crack or discoloration in the windshield area lying within the sweep of the wiper on the drivers side and does not address the remaining area of the windshield. Appendix G addresses requirements for the whole windshield as specified in 393.60.

13. **Windshield Wipers.**
    Appendix G requires windshield wipers to be operative at all times. The out-of-service criteria only requires that the windshield wiper on the driver's side to be inspected during inclement weather.

FEDERAL TRANSIT AUTHORITY

Note: The Following Part 655 has been issued by the Federal Transit Authority and pertains **only** to mass transit operations. It is not part of the Federal Motor Carrier Safety Regulations.

PART 653 — [Removed]

PART 654 — [Removed]

PART 655 — PREVENTION OF ALCOHOL MISUSE AND PROHIBITED DRUG USE IN TRANSIT OPERATIONS

Subpart A — General

Subpart D — Prohibited Alcohol Use

655.31   Alcohol testing.
655.32   On-duty use.
655.33   Pre-duty use.
655.34   Use following an accident.
655.35   Other alcohol-related conduct.
655.36–655.40   [Reserved]

Subpart E — Types of Testing

655.41   Pre-employment drug testing.
655.42   Pre-employment alcohol testing.
655.43   Reasonable suspicion testing.
655.44   Post-accident testing.
655.45   Random testing.
655.46   Return to duty following refusal to submit to a test, verified positive drug test result and/or breath alcohol test result of 0.04 or greater.
655.47   Follow-up testing after returning to duty.
655.48   Retesting of covered employees with an alcohol concentration of 0.02 or greater but less than 0.04.
655.49   Refusal to submit to a drug or alcohol test.
655.50   [Reserved]

Subpart F — Drug and Alcohol Testing Procedures

655.51   Compliance with testing procedures requirements.
655.52   Substance abuse professional (SAP).
655.53   Supervisor acting as collection site personnel.
655.54–655.60   [Reserved]

Subpart G — Consequences

655.61   Action when an employee has a verified positive drug test result or has a confirmed alcohol test result of 0.04 or greater, or refuses to submit to a test.
655.62   Referral, evaluation, and treatment.
655.63–655.70   [Reserved]

Subpart H — Administrative Requirements

655.71   Retention of records.
655.72   Reporting of results in a management information system.
655.73   Access to facilities and records.
655.74–655.80   [Reserved]

Subpart I — Certifying Compliance

655.81   Grantee oversight responsibility.
655.82   Compliance as a condition of financial assistance.
655.83   Requirement to certify compliance.

AUTHORITY: 49 U.S.C. 5331; 49 CFR 1.51.

Subpart A — General

§655.1 Purpose.

The purpose of this part is to establish programs to be implemented by employers that receive financial assistance from the Federal Transit Administration (FTA) and by contractors of those employers, that are designed to help prevent accidents, injuries, and fatalities resulting from the misuse of alcohol and use of prohibited drugs by employees who perform safety-sensitive functions.

§655.2 Overview.

(a) This part includes nine subparts. Subpart A of this part covers the general requirements of FTA's drug and alcohol testing programs. Subpart B of this part specifies the basic requirements of each employer's alcohol misuse and prohibited drug use program, including the elements required to be in each employer's testing program. Subpart C of this part describes prohibited drug use. Subpart D of this part describes prohibited alcohol use. Subpart E of this part describes the types of alcohol and drug tests to be conducted. Subpart F of this part addresses the testing procedural requirements mandated by the Omnibus Transportation Employee Testing Act of 1991, and as required in 49 CFR Part 40. Subpart G of this part lists the consequences for covered employees who engage in alcohol misuse or prohibited drug use. Subpart H of this part contains administrative matters, such as reports and recordkeeping requirements. Subpart I of this part specifies how a recipient certifies compliance with the rule.

(b) This part must be read in conjunction with 49 CFR Part 40, Procedures for Transportation Workplace Drug and Alcohol Testing Programs.

§655.3 Applicability.

(a) Except as specifically excluded in paragraph (b) of this section, this part applies to:

(1) Each recipient and subrecipient receiving Federal assistance under:

(i) 49 U.S.C. 5307, 5309, or 5311; or

(ii) 23 U.S.C. 103(e)(4); and

(2) Any contractor of a recipient or subrecipient of Federal assistance under:

(i) 49 U.S.C. 5307, 5309, or 5311; or

(ii) 23 U.S.C. 103(e)(4).

(b) A recipient operating a railroad regulated by the Fedeal Railroad Administration (FRA) shall follow 49 CFR Part 219 and §655.83 for its railroad operations, and shall follow this part for its non-railroad operations, if any.

§655.4 Definitions.

For this part, the terms listed in this section have the following definitions. The definitions of additional terms used in this part but not listed in this section can be found in 49 CFR Part 40.

Accident means an occurrence associated with the operation of a vehicle, if as a result:

(1) An individual dies; or

(2) An individual suffers bodily injury and immediately receives medical treatment away from the scene of the accident; or

(3) With respect to an occurrence in which the mass transit vehicle involved is a bus, electric bus, van, or automobile, one or more vehicles (including non-FTA funded vehicles) incurs disabling damage as the result of the occurrence and such vehicle or vehicles are transported away from the scene by a tow truck or other vehicle; or

(4) With respect to an occurrence in which the mass transit vehicle involved is a rail car, trolley car, trolley bus, or vessel, the mass transit vehicle is removed from operation.

Administrator means the Administrator of the Federal Transit Administration or the Administrator's designee.

Anti-drug program means a program to detect and deter the use of prohibited drugs as required by this part.

Certification means a recipient's written statement, authorized by the organization's governing board or other authorizing official that the recipient has complied with the provisions of this part. (See §655.82 and §655.83 for certification requirements.)

§655.4

Contractor means a person or organization that provides a safety-sensitive service for a recipient, subrecipient, employer, or operator consistent with a specific understanding or arrangement. The understanding can be a written contract or an informal arrangement that reflects an ongoing relationship between the parties.

Covered employee means a person, including an applicant or transferee, who performs or will perform a safety-sensitive function for an entity subject to this part. A volunteer is a covered employee if:

(1) The volunteer is required to hold a commercial driver's license to operate the vehicle; or

(2) The volunteer performs a safety-sensitive function for an entity subject to this part and receives remuneration in excess of his or her actual expenses incurred while engaged in the volunteer activity.

Disabling damage means damage that precludes departure of a motor vehicle from the scene of the accident in its usual manner in daylight after simple repairs.

(1) Inclusion. Damage to a motor vehicle, where the vehicle could have been driven, but would have been further damaged if so driven.

(2) Exclusions. (i) Damage that can be remedied temporarily at the scene of the accident without special tools or parts.

(ii) Tire disablement without other damage even if no spare tire is available.

(iii) Headlamp or tail light damage.

(iv) Damage to turn signals, horn, or windshield wipers, which makes the vehicle inoperable.

DOT or The Department means the United States Department of Transportation.

DOT agency means an agency (or "operating administration") of the United States Department of Transportation administering regulations requiring drug and alcohol testing. See 14 CFR part 121, appendices I and J; 33 CFR part 95; 46 CFR parts 4, 5, and 16; and 49 CFR parts 199, 219, 382, and 655.

Employer means a recipient or other entity that provides mass transportation service or which performs a safety-sensitive function for such recipient or other entity. This term includes subrecipients, operators, and contractors.

FTA means the Federal Transit Administration, an agency of the U.S. Department of Transportation.

Performing (a safety-sensitive function) means a covered employee is considered to be performing a safety-sensitive function and includes any period in which he or she is actually-performing, ready to perform, or immediately available to perform such functions.

Positive rate means the sum of the annual number of positive results for random drug tests conducted under this part plus the annual number of refusals to submit to a random drug test authorized under this part divided by the sum of the annual number of random drug tests conducted under this part plus the annual number of refusals to submit to a random drug test authorized under this part.

Railroad means:

(1) All forms of non-highway ground transportation that run on rails or electromagnetic guideways, including:

(i) Commuter or other short-haul rail passenger service in a metropolitan or suburban area, as well as any commuter rail service that was operated by the Consolidated Rail Corporation as of January 1, 1979; and

(ii) High speed ground transportation systems that connect metropolitan areas, without regard to whether they use new technologies not associated with traditional railroads.

(2) Such term does not include rapid transit operations within an urban area that are not connected to the general railroad system of transportation.

Recipient means an entity receiving Federal financial assistance under 49 U.S.C. 5307, 5309, or 5311; or under 23 U.S.C. 103(e)(4).

Refuse to submit means any circumstance outlined in 49 CFR 40.191 and 40.261.

Safety-sensitive function means any of the following duties, when performed by employees of recipients, subrecipients, operators, or contractors:

(1) Operating a revenue service vehicle, including when not in revenue service;

(2) Operating a nonrevenue service vehicle, when required to be operated by a holder of a Commercial Driver's License;

(3) Controlling dispatch or movement of a revenue service vehicle;

(4) Maintaining (including repairs, overhaul and rebuilding) a revenue service vehicle or equipment used in revenue service. This section does not apply to the following: an employer who

receives funding under 49 U.S.C. 5307 or 5309, is in an area less than 200,000 in population, and contracts out such services; or an employer who receives funding under 49 U.S.C. 5311 and contracts out such services;

(5) Carrying a firearm for security purposes.

Vehicle means a bus, electric bus, van, automobile, rail car, trolley car, trolley bus, or vessel. A mass transit vehicle is a vehicle used for mass transportation or for ancillary services.

Violation rate means the sum of the annual number of results from random alcohol tests conducted under this part that have alcohol concentrations of .04 or greater plus the annual number of refusals to submit to alcohol tests authorized under this part, divided by the sum of the annual number of random alcohol tests conducted under this part plus the annual number of refusals to submit to a drug test authorized under this part.

§655.5 Stand-down waivers for drug testing.

(a) An employer subject to this part may petition the FTA for a waiver allowing the employer to stand down, per 49 CFR Part 40, an employee following a report of a laboratory confirmed positive drug test or refusal, pending the outcome of the verification process.

(b) Each petition for a waiver must be in writing and include facts and justification to support the waiver. Each petition must satisfy the requirements for obtaining a waiver, as provided in 49 CFR 40.21.

(c) Each petition for a waiver must be submitted to the Office of Safety and Security, Federal Transit Administration, U.S. Department of Transportation, 400 Seventh Street, SW. Washington, DC 20590.

(d) The Administrator may grant a waiver subject to 49 CFR 40.21(d).

§655.6 Preemption of state and local laws.

(a) Except as provided in paragraph (b) of this section, this part preempts any state or local law, rule, regulation, or order to the extent that:

(1) Compliance with both the state or local requirement and any requirement in this part is not possible; or

(2) Compliance with the state or local requirement is an obstacle to the accomplishment and execution of any requirement in this part.

(b) This part shall not be construed to preempt provisions of state criminal laws that impose sanctions for reckless conduct attributed to prohibited drug use or alcohol misuse leading to actual loss of life, injury, or damage to property, whether the provisions apply specifically to transportation employees or employers or to the general public.

§655.7 Starting date for testing programs.

An employer must have an anti-drug and alcohol misuse testing program in place by the date the employer begins operations.

Subpart B — Program Requirements

§655.11 Requirement to establish an anti-drug use and alcohol misuse program.

Each employer shall establish an anti-drug use and alcohol misuse program consistent with the requirements of this part.

§655.12 Required elements of an anti-drug use and alcohol misuse program.

An anti-drug use and alcohol misuse program shall include the following:

(a) A statement describing the employer's policy on prohibited drug use and alcohol misuse in the workplace, including the consequences associated with prohibited drug use and alcohol misuse. This policy statement shall include all of the elements specified in §655.15. Each employer shall disseminate the policy consistent with the provisions of §655.16.

(b) An education and training program which meets the requirements of §655.14.

(c) A testing program, as described in Subparts C and D of this part, which meets the requirements of this part and 49 CFR Part 40.

(d) Procedures for referring a covered employee who has a verified positive drug test result or an alcohol concentration of 0.04 or greater to a Substance Abuse Professional, consistent with 49 CFR Part 40.

§655.13 [Reserved]

§655.14 Education and training programs.

Each employer shall establish an employee education and training program for all covered employees, including:

(a) **Education.** The education component shall include display and distribution to every covered employee of: informational material and a community service hot-line telephone number for employee assistance, if available.

(b) **Training.** (1) Covered employees. Covered employees must receive at least 60 minutes of training on the effects and consequences of prohibited drug use on personal health, safety, and the work environment, and on the signs and symptoms that may indicate prohibited drug use.

(2) Supervisors. Supervisors and/or other company officers authorized by the employer to make reasonable suspicion determinations shall receive at least 60 minutes of training on the physical, behavioral, and performance indicators of probable drug use and at least 60 minutes of training on the physical, behavioral, speech, and performance indicators of probable alcohol misuse.

§655.15 Policy statement contents.

The local governing board of the employer or operator shall adopt an anti-drug and alcohol misuse policy statement. The statement must be made available to each covered employee, and shall include the following:

(a) The identity of the person, office, branch and/or position designated by the employer to answer employee questions about the employer's anti-drug use and alcohol misuse programs.

(b) The categories of employees who are subject to the provisions of this part.

(c) Specific information concerning the behavior and conduct prohibited by this part.

(d) The specific circumstances under which a covered employee will be tested for prohibited drugs or alcohol misuse under this part.

(e) The procedures that will be used to test for the presence of illegal drugs or alcohol misuse, protect the employee and the integrity of the drug and alcohol testing process, safeguard the validity of the test results, and ensure the test results are attributed to the correct covered employee.

(f) The requirement that a covered employee submit to drug and alcohol testing administered in accordance with this part.

(g) A description of the kind of behavior that constitutes a refusal to take a drug or alcohol test, and a statement that such a refusal constitutes a violation of the employer's policy.

(h) The consequences for a covered employee who has a verified positive drug or a confirmed alcohol test result with an alcohol concentration of 0.04 or greater, or who refuses to submit to a test under this part, including the mandatory requirements that the covered employee be removed immediately from his or her safety-sensitive function and be evaluated by a substance abuse professional, as required by 49 CFR Part 40.

(i) The consequences, as set forth in §655.35 of subpart D, for a covered employee who is found to have an alcohol concentration of 0.02 or greater but less than 0.04.

(j) The employer shall inform each covered employee if it implements elements of an anti-drug use or alcohol misuse program that are not required by this part. An employer may not impose requirements that are inconsistent with, contrary to, or frustrate the provisions of this part.

§655.16 Requirement to disseminate policy.

Each employer shall provide written notice to every covered employee and to representatives of employee organizations of the employer's anti-drug and alcohol misuse policies and procedures.

§655.17 Notice requirement.

Before performing a drug or alcohol test under this part, each employer shall notify a covered employee that the test is required by this part. No employer shall falsely represent that a test is administered under this part.

§§655.18-655.20 [Reserved]

Subpart C — Prohibited Drug Use

§655.21 Drug testing.

(a) An employer shall establish a program that provides testing for prohibited drugs and drug metabolites in the following circumstances: pre-employment, post-accident, reasonable suspicion, random, and return to duty/follow-up.

(b) When administering a drug test, an employer shall ensure that the following drugs are tested for:

(1) Marijuana;

(2) Cocaine;

(3) Opiates;

(4) Amphetamines; and

(5) Phencyclidine.

(c) Consumption of these products is prohibited at all times.

§§655.22-655.30 [Reserved]

Subpart D — Prohibited Alcohol Use

§655.31 Alcohol testing.

(a) An employer shall establish a program that provides for testing for alcohol in the following circumstances: post-accident, reasonable suspicion, random, and return to duty/follow-up. An employer may also conduct pre-employment alcohol testing.

(b) Each employer shall prohibit a covered employee, while having an alcohol concentration of 0.04 or greater, from performing or continuing to perform a safety-sensitive function.

§655.32 On duty use.

Each employer shall prohibit a covered employee from using alcohol while performing safety-sensitive functions. No employer having actual knowledge that a covered employee is using alcohol while performing safety-sensitive functions shall permit the employee to perform or continue to perform safety-sensitive functions.

§655.33 Pre-duty use.

(a) General. Each employer shall prohibit a covered employee from using alcohol within 4 hours prior to performing safety-sensitive functions. No employer having actual knowledge that a covered employee has used alcohol within four hours of performing a safety-sensitive function shall permit the employee to perform or continue to perform safety-sensitive functions.

(b) On-call employees. An employer shall prohibit the consumption of alcohol for the specified on-call hours of each covered employee who is on-call. The procedure shall include:

(1) The opportunity for the covered employee to acknowledge the use of alcohol at the time he or she is called to report to duty and the inability to perform his or her safety-sensitive function.

(2) The requirement that the covered employee take an alcohol test, if the covered employee has acknowledged the use of alcohol, but claims ability to perform his or her safety-sensitive function.

§655.34 Use following an accident.

Each employer shall prohibit alcohol use by any covered employee required to take a post-accident alcohol test under §655.44 for eight hours following the accident or until he or she undergoes a post-accident alcohol test, whichever occurs first.

§655.35 Other alcohol-related conduct.

(a) No employer shall permit a covered employee tested under the provisions of subpart E of this part who is found to have an alcohol concentration of 0.02 or greater but less than 0.04 to perform or continue to perform safety-sensitive functions, until:

(1) The employee's alcohol concentration measures less than 0.02; or

(2) The start of the employee's next regularly scheduled duty period, but not less than eight hours following administration of the test.

(b) Except as provided in paragraph (a) of this section, no employer shall take any action under this part against an employee based solely on test results showing an alcohol concentration less than 0.04. This does not prohibit an employer with authority independent of this part from taking any action otherwise consistent with law.

Subpart E — Types of Testing

§655.41 Pre-employment drug testing.

(a)(1) Before allowing a covered employee or applicant to perform a safety-sensitive function for the first time, the employer must ensure that the employee takes a pre-employment drug test administered under this part with a verified negative result. An employer may not allow a covered employee, including an applicant, to perform a safety-sensitive function unless theemployee takes a drug test administered under this part with a verified negative result.

(2) When a covered employee or applicant has previously failed or refused a pre-employment drug test administered under this part, the employee must provide the employer proof of having successfully completed a referral, evaluation and treatment plan as described in §655.62.

(b) An employer may not transfer an employee from a non-safety-sensitive function to a safety-sensitive function until the employee takes a pre-employment drug test administered under this part with a verified negative result.

(c) If a pre-employment drug test is canceled, the employer shall require the covered employee or applicant to take another pre-employment drug test administered under this part with a verified negative result.

(d) When a covered employee or applicant has not performed a safety-sensitive function for 90 consecutive calendar days regardless of the reason, and the employee has not been in the employer's random selection pool during that time, the employer shall ensure that the employee takes a pre-employment drug test with a verified negative result.

§655.42 Pre-employment alcohol testing.

An employer may, but is not required to, conduct pre-employment alcohol testing under this part. If an employer chooses to conduct pre-employment alcohol testing, the employer must comply with the following requirements:

(a) The employer must conduct a pre-employment alcohol test before the first performance of safety-sensitive functions by every covered employee (whether a new employee or someone who has transferred to a position involving the performance of safety-sensitive functions).

(b) The employer must treat all covered employees performing safety-sensitive functions the same for the purpose of pre-employment alcohol testing (i.e., you must not test some covered employees and not others).

(c) The employer must conduct the pre-employment tests after making a contingent offer of employment or transfer, subject to the employee passing the pre-employment alcohol test.

(d) The employer must conduct all pre-employment alcohol tests using the alcohol testing procedures set forth in 49 CFR Part 40.

(e) The employer must not allow a covered employee to begin performing safety-sensitive functions unless the result of the employee's test indicates an alcohol concentration of less than 0.02.

§655.43 Reasonable suspicion testing.

(a) An employer shall conduct a drug and/or alcohol test when the employer has reasonable suspicion to believe that the covered employee has used a prohibited drug and/or engaged in alcohol misuse.

(b) An employer's determination that reasonable suspicion exists shall be based on specific, contemporaneous, articulable observations concerning the appearance, behavior, speech, or body odors of the covered employee. A supervisor(s), or other company official(s) who is trained in detecting the signs and symptoms of drug use and alcohol misuse must make the required observations.

(c) Alcohol testing is authorized under this section only if the observations required by paragraph (b) of this section are made during, just preceding, or just after the period of the workday that the covered employee is required to be in compliance with this part. An employer may direct a covered employee to undergo reasonable suspicion testing for alcohol only while the employee is performing safety-sensitive functions; just before the employee is to perform safety-sensitive functions; or just after the employee has ceased performing such functions.

(d) If an alcohol test required by this section is not administered within two hours following the determination under paragraph (b) of this section, the employer shall prepare and maintain on file a record stating the reasons the alcohol test was not promptly administered. If an alcohol test required by this section is not administered within eight hours following the determination under paragraph (b) of this section, the employer shall cease attempts to administer an alcohol test and shall state in the record the reasons for not administering the test.

§655.44 Post-accident testing.

(a) Accidents. (1) Fatal accidents. (i) As soon as practicable following an accident involving the loss of human life, an employer shall conduct drug and alcohol tests on each surviving covered employee operating the mass transit vehicle at the time of the accident. Post-accident drug and alcohol testing of the operator is not required under this section if the covered employee is tested under the fatal accident testing requirements of the Federal Motor Carrier Safety Administration rule 49 CFR 389.303(a)(1) or (b)(1).

(ii) The employer shall also drug and alcohol test any other covered employee whose performance could have contributed to the accident, as determined by the employer using the best information available at the time of the decision.

(2) Nonfatal accidents. (i) As soon as practicable following an accident not involving the loss of human life in which a mass

transit vehicle is involved, the employer shall drug and alcohol test each covered employee operating the mass transit vehicle at the time of the accident unless the employer determines, using the best information available at the time of the decision, that the covered employee's performance can be completely discounted as a contributing factor to the accident. The employer shall also drug and alcohol test any other covered employee whose performance could have contributed to the accident, as determined by the employer using the best information available at the time of the decision.

(ii) If an alcohol test required by this section is not administered within two hours following the accident, the employer shall prepare and maintain on file a record stating the reasons the alcohol test was not promptly administered. If an alcohol test required by this section is not administered within eight hours following the accident, the employer shall cease attempts to administer an alcohol test and maintain the record. Records shall be submitted to FTA upon request of the Administrator.

(b) An employer shall ensure that a covered employee required to be drug tested under this section is tested as soon as practicable but within 32 hours of the accident.

(c) A covered employee who is subject to post-accident testing who fails to remain readily available for such testing, including notifying the employer or the employer representative of his or her location if he or she leaves the scene of the accident prior to submission to such test, may be deemed by the employer to have refused to submit to testing.

(d) The decision not to administer a drug and/or alcohol test under this section shall be based on the employer's determination, using the best available information at the time of the determination that the employee's performance could not have contributed to the accident. Such a decision must be documented in detail, including the decision-making process used to reach the decision not to test.

(e) Nothing in this section shall be construed to require the delay of necessary medical attention for the injured following an accident or to prohibit a covered employee from leaving the scene of an accident for the period necessary to obtain assistance in responding to the accident or to obtain necessary emergency medical care.

(f) The results of a blood, urine, or breath test for the use of prohibited drugs or alcohol misuse, conducted by Federal, State, or local officials having independent authority for the test, shall be considered to meet the requirements of this section provided such test conforms to the applicable Federal, State, or local testing requirements, and that the test results are obtained by the employer. Such test results may be used only when the employer is unable to perform a post-accident test within the required period noted in paragraphs (a) and (b) of this section.

§655.45 Random testing.

(a) Except as provided in paragraphs (b) through (d) of this section, the minimum annual percentage rate for random drug testing shall be 50 percent of covered employees; the random alcohol testing rate shall be 10 percent. As provided in paragraph (b) of this section, this rate is subject to annual review by the Administrator.

(b) The Administrator's decision to increase or decrease the minimum annual percentage rate for random drug and alcohol testing is based, respectively, on the reported positive drug and alcohol violation rates for the entire industry. All information used for this determination is drawn from the drug and alcohol Management Information System (MIS) reports required by this part. In order to ensure reliability of the data, the Administrator shall consider the quality and completeness of the reported data, may obtain additional information or reports from employers, and may make appropriate modifications in calculating the industry's verified positive results and violation rates. Each year, the Administrator will publish in the *Federal Register* the minimum annual percentage rates for random drug and alcohol testing of covered employees. The new minimum annual percentage rate for random drug and alcohol testing will be applicable starting January 1 of the calendar year following publication.

(c) Rates for drug testing. (1) When the minimum annual percentage rate for random drug testing is 50 percent, the Administrator may lower this rate to 25 percent of all covered employees if the Administrator determines that the data received under the reporting requirements of §655.72 for the two preceding consecutive calendar years indicate that the reported positive rate is less than 1.0 percent.

(2) When the minimum annual percentage rate for random drug testing is 25 percent, and the data received under the reporting requirements of §655.72 for the calendar year indicate that the reported positive rate is equal to or greater than 1.0

percent, the Administrator will increase the minimum annual percentage rate for random drug or random alcohol testing to 50 percent of all covered employees.

(d) Rates for alcohol testing. (1)(i) When the minimum annual percentage rate for random alcohol testing is 25 percent or more, the Administrator may lower this rate to 10 percent of all covered employees if the Administrator determines that the data received under the reporting requirements of §655.72 for two consecutive calendar years indicate that the violation rate is less than 0.5 percent.

(ii) When the minimum annual percentage rate for random alcohol testing is 50 percent, the Administrator may lower this rate to 25 percent of all covered employees if the Administrator determines that the data received under the reporting requirements of §655.72 for two consecutive calendar years indicate that the violation rate is less than 1.0 percent but equal to or greater than 0.5 percent.

(2)(i) When the minimum annual percentage rate for random alcohol testing is 10 percent, and the data received under the reporting requirements of §655.72 for that calendar year indicate that the violation rate is equal to or greater than 0.5 percent, but less than 1.0 percent, the Administrator will increase the minimum annual percentage rate for random alcohol testing to 25 percent of all covered employees.

(ii) When the minimum annual percentage rate for random alcohol testing is 25 percent or less, and the data received under the reporting requirements of §655.72 for that calendar year indicate that the violation rate is equal to or greater than 1.0 percent, the Administrator will increase the minimum annual percentage rate for random alcohol testing to 50 percent of all covered employees.

(e) The selection of employees for random drug and alcohol testing shall be made by a scientifically valid method, such as a random number table or a computer-based random number generator that is matched with employees' Social Security numbers, payroll identification numbers, or other comparable identifying numbers. Under the selection process used, each covered employee shall have an equal chance of being tested each time selections are made.

(f) The employer shall randomly select a sufficient number of covered employees for testing during each calendar year to equal an annual rate not less than the minimum annual percentage rates for random drug and alcohol testing determined by the Administrator. If the employer conducts random drug and alcohol testing through a consortium, the number of employees to be tested may be calculated for each individual employer or may be based on the total number of covered employees covered by the consortium who are subject to random drug and alcohol testing at the same minimum annual percentage rate under this part.

(g) Each employer shall ensure that random drug and alcohol tests conducted under this part are unannounced and unpredictable, and that the dates for administering random tests are spread reasonably throughout the calendar year. Random testing must be conducted at all times of day when safety-sensitive functions are performed.

(h) Each employer shall require that each covered employee who is notified of selection for random drug or random alcohol testing proceed to the test site immediately. If the employee is performing a safety-sensitive function at the time of the notification, the employer shall instead ensure that the employee ceases to perform the safety-sensitive function and proceeds to the testing site immediately.

(i) A covered employee shall only be randomly tested for alcohol misuse while the employee is performing safety-sensitive functions; just before the employee is to perform safety-sensitive functions; or just after the employee has ceased performing such functions. A covered employee may be randomly tested for prohibited drug use anytime while on duty.

(j) If a given covered employee is subject to random drug and alcohol testing under the testing rules of more than one DOT agency for the same employer, the employee shall be subject to random drug and alcohol testing at the percentage rate established for the calendar year by the DOT agency regulating more than 50 percent of the employee's function.

(k) If an employer is required to conduct random drug and alcohol testing under the drug and alcohol testing rules of more than one DOT agency, the employer may—

(1) Establish separate pools for random selection, with each pool containing the covered employees who are subject to testing at the same required rate; or

(2) Randomly select such employees for testing at the highest percentage rate established for the calendar year by any DOT agency to which the employer is subject.

§655.46 Return to duty following refusal to submit to a test, verified positive drug test result and/or breath alcohol test result of 0.04 or greater.

Where a covered employee refuses to submit to a test, has a verified positive drug test result, and/or has a confirmed alcohol test result of 0.04 or greater, the employer, before returning the employee to duty to perform a safety-sensitive function, shall follow the procedures outlined in 49 CFR Part 40.

§655.47 Follow-up testing after returning to duty.

An employer shall conduct follow-up testing of each employee who returns to duty, as specified in 49 CFR Part 40, subpart O.

§655.48 Retesting of covered employees with an alcohol concentration of 0.02 or greater but less than 0.04.

If an employer chooses to permit a covered employee to perform a safety-sensitive function within 8 hours of an alcohol test indicating an alcohol concentration of 0.02 or greater but less than 0.04, the employer shall retest the covered employee to ensure compliance with the provisions of §655.35. The covered employee may not perform safety-sensitive functions unless the confirmation alcohol test result is less than 0.02.

§655.49 Refusal to submit to a drug or alcohol test.

(a) Each employer shall require a covered employee to submit to a post-accident drug and alcohol test required under §655.44, a random drug and alcohol test required under §655.45, a reasonable suspicion drug and alcohol test required under §655.43, or a follow-up drug and alcohol test required under §655.47. No employer shall permit an employee who refuses to submit to such a test to perform or continue to perform safety-sensitive functions.

(b) When an employee refuses to submit to a drug or alcohol test, the employer shall follow the procedures outlined in 49 CFR Part 40.

§655.50 [Reserved]

Subpart F — Drug and Alcohol Testing Procedures

§655.51 Compliance with testing procedures requirements.

The drug and alcohol testing procedures in 49 CFR Part 40 apply to employers covered by this part, and must be read together with this part, unless expressly provided otherwise in this part.

§655.52 Substance abuse professional (SAP).

The SAP must perform the functions in 49 CFR Part 40.

§655.53 Supervisor acting as collection site personnel.

An employer shall not permit an employee with direct or immediate supervisory responsibility or authority over another employee to serve as the urine collection person, breath alcohol technician, or saliva-testing technician for a drug or alcohol test of the employee.

§§655.54–655.60 [Reserved]

Subpart G — Consequences

§655.61 Action when an employee has a verified positive drug test result or has a confirmed alcohol test result of 0.04 or greater, or refuses to submit to a test.

(a) (1) Immediately after receiving notice from a medical review officer (MRO) or a consortium/third party administrator (C/TPA) that a covered employee has a verified positive drug test result, the employer shall require that the covered employee cease performing a safety-sensitive function.

(2) Immediately after receiving notice from a Breath Alcohol Technician (BAT) that a covered employee has a confirmed alcohol test result of 0.04 or greater, the employer shall require that the covered employee cease performing a safety-sensitive function.

(3) If an employee refuses to submit to a drug or alcohol test required by this part, the employer shall require that the covered employee cease performing a safety-sensitive function.

(b) Before allowing the covered employee to resume performing a safety-sensitive function, the employer shall ensure the employee meets the requirements of 49 CFR Part 40 for returning to duty, including taking a return to duty drug and/or alcohol test.

§655.62 Referral, evaluation, and treatment.

If a covered employee has a verified positive drug test result, or has a confirmed alcohol test of 0.04 or greater, or refuses to submit to a drug or alcohol test required by this part, the employer shall advise the employee of the resources available for evaluating and resolving problems associated with prohibited drug use and alcohol misuse, including the names, addresses, and telephone numbers of substance abuse professionals (SAPs) and counseling and treatment programs.

§§655.63-655.70 [Reserved]

Subpart H — Administrative Requirements

§655. 71 Retention of records.

(a) General requirement. An employer shall maintain records of its anti-drug and alcohol misuse program as provided in this section. The records shall be maintained in a secure location with controlled access.

(b) Period of retention. In determining compliance with the retention period requirement, each record shall be maintained for the specified minimum period of time as measured from the date of the creation of the record. Each employer shall maintain the records in accordance with the following schedule:

(1) Five years. Records of covered employee verified positive drug or alcohol test results, documentation of refusals to take required drug or alcohol tests, and covered employee referrals to the substance abuse professional, and copies of annual MIS reports submitted to FTA.

(2) Two years. Records related to the collection process and employee training.

(3) One year. Records of negative drug or alcohol test results.

(c) Types of records. The following specific records must be maintained:

(1) Records related to the collection process:

(i) Collection logbooks, if used.

(ii) Documents relating to the random selection process.

(iii) Documents generated in connection with decisions to administer reasonable suspicion drug or alcohol tests.

(iv) Documents generated in connection with decisions on post-accident drug and alcohol testing.

(v) MRO documents verifying existence of a medical explanation of the inability of a covered employee to provide an adequate urine or breathe sample.

(2) Records related to test results:

(i) The employer's copy of the custody and control form.

(ii) Documents related to the refusal of any covered employee to submit to a test required by this part.

(iii) Documents presented by a covered employee to dispute the result of a test administered under this part.

(3) Records related to referral and return to duty and follow-up testing: Records concerning a covered employee's entry into and completion of the treatment program recommended by the substance abuse professional.

(4) Records related to employee training:

(i) Training materials on drug use awareness and alcohol misuse, including a copy of the employer's policy on prohibited drug use and alcohol misuse.

(ii) Names of covered employees attending training on prohibited drug use and alcohol misuse and the dates and times of such training.

(iii) Documentation of training provided to supervisors for the purpose of qualifying the supervisors to make a determination concerning the need for drug and alcohol testing based on reasonable suspicion.

(iv) Certification that any training conducted under this part complies with the requirements for such training.

(5) Copies of annual MIS reports submitted to FTA.

§655.72 Reporting of results in a management information system.

(a) Each recipient shall annually prepare and maintain a summary of the results of its anti-drug and alcohol misuse testing programs performed under this part during the previous calendar year.

(b) When requested by FTA, each recipient shall submit to FTA's Office of Safety and Security, or its designated agent, by March 15, a report covering the previous calendar year (January 1 through December 31) summarizing the results of its anti-drug and alcohol misuse programs.

(c) Each recipient shall be responsible for ensuring the accuracy and timeliness of each report submitted by an employer, contractor, consortium or joint enterprise or by a third party service provider acting on the recipient's or employer's behalf.

(d) Drug use information: Long Form. Each report that contains information on verified positive drug test results shall be submitted on the FTA Drug Testing Management Information System (MIS) Data Collection Form (Appendix A of this part) and shall include the following informational elements:

(1) Number of FTA covered employees by employee category.

(2) Number of covered employees subject to testing under the anti-drug regulations of the other DOT operating administrations subject to 49 CFR Part 40.

(3) Number of specimens collected by type of test (i.e., pre-employment, follow-up, random, etc.) and employee category.

(4) Number of positives verified by a Medical Review Officer (MRO) by type of test, type of drug, and employee category.

(5) Number of negatives verified by an MRO by type of test and employee category.

(6) Number of persons denied a position as a covered employee following a verified positive drug test.

(7) Number of covered employees verified positive by an MRO or who refused to submit to a drug test, who were returned to duty in covered positions during the reporting period (having complied with the recommendations of a substance abuse professional as described in §655.61).

(8) Number of employees with tests verified positive by an MRO for multiple drugs.

(9) Number of covered employees who were administered drug and alcohol tests at the same time, with both a verified positive drug test result and an alcohol test result indicating an alcohol concentration of 0.04 or greater.

(10) Number of covered employees who refused to submit to a random drug test required under this part.

(11) Number of covered employees who refused to submit to a non-random drug test required under this part.

(12) Number of covered employees and supervisors who received training during the reporting period.

(13) Number of fatal and nonfatal accidents which resulted in a verified positive post-accident drug test.

(14) Number of fatalities resulting from accidents which resulted in a verified positive post-accident drug test.

(15) Identification of FTA funding source(s).

(e) Drug Use Information: Short Form. If all drug test results were negative during the reporting period, the employer must use the "EZ form" (Appendix B of this part). It shall contain:

(1) Number of FTA covered employees.

(2) Number of covered employees subject to testing under the anti-drug regulation of the other DOT operating administrations subject to 49 CFR Part 40.

(3) Number of specimens collected and verified negative by type of test and employee category.

(4) Number of covered employees verified positive by an MRO or who refused to submit to a drug test prior to the reporting period and who were returned to duty in covered positions during the reporting period (having complied with the recommendations of a substance abuse professional as described in §655.62).

(5) Number of covered employees who refused to submit to a non-random drug test required under this part.

(6) Number of covered employees and supervisors who received training during the reporting period.

(7) Identification of FTA funding source(s).

(f) Alcohol misuse information: Long Form. Each report that contains information on an alcohol screening test result of 0.02 or greater or a violation of the alcohol misuse provisions of this part shall be submitted on the FTA Alcohol Testing Management (MIS) Data Collection Form (Appendix C of this part) and shall include the following informational elements:

(1) Number of FTA covered employees by employee category.

(2) (i) Number of screening tests by type of test and employee category.

(ii) Number of confirmed tests, by type of test and employee category.

(3) Number of confirmed alcohol tests indicating an alcohol concentration of 0.02 or greater but less than 0.04, by type of test and employee category.

(4) Number of confirmed alcohol tests indicating an alcohol concentration of 0.04 or greater, by type of test and employee category.

(5) Number of covered employees with a confirmed alcohol test indicating an alcohol concentration of 0.04 or greater who

§655.72

were returned to duty in covered positions during the reporting period (having complied with the recommendation of a substance abuse professional as described in §655.61).

(6) Number of fatal and nonfatal accidents which resulted in a confirmed post-accident alcohol test indicating an alcohol concentration of 0.04 or greater.

(7) Number of fatalities resulting from accidents which resulted in a confirmed post-accident alcohol test indicating an alcohol concentration of 0.04 or greater.

(8) Number of covered employees who were found to have violated other provisions of subpart B of this part and the action taken in response to the violation.

(9) Number of covered employees who were administered alcohol and drug tests at the same time, with a positive drug test result and an alcohol test result indicating an alcohol concentration of 0.04 or greater.

(10) Number of covered employees who refused to submit to a random alcohol test required under this part.

(11) Number of covered employees who refused to submit to a non-random alcohol test required under this part.

(12) Number of supervisors who have received training during the reporting period in determining the existence of reasonable suspicion of alcohol misuse.

(13) Identification of FTA funding source(s).

(g) Alcohol Misuse Information: Short Form. If an employer has no screening test results of 0.02 or greater and no violations of the alcohol misuse provisions of this part, the employer must use the "EZ" form (Appendix D of this part). It shall contain (This report may only be submitted if the program results meet these criteria.):

(1) Number of FTA covered employees.

(2) Number of alcohol tests conducted with results less than 0.02 by type of test and employee category.

(3) Number of employees with confirmed alcohol test results indicating an alcohol concentration of 0.04 or greater prior to the reporting period and who were returned to duty in a covered position during the reporting period.

(4) Number of covered employees who refused to submit to a random alcohol test required under this part.

(5) Number of supervisors who have received training in determining the existence of reasonable suspicion of alcohol misuse during the reporting period.

(6) Identification of FTA funding source(s).

§655.73 Access to facilities and records.

(a) Except as required by law, or expressly authorized or required in this section, no employer may release information pertaining to a covered employee that is contained in records required to be maintained by §655.71.

(b) A covered employee is entitled, upon written request, to obtain copies of any records pertaining to the covered employee's use of prohibited drugs or misuse of alcohol, including any records pertaining to his or her drug or alcohol tests. The employer shall provide promptly the records requested by the employee. Access to a covered employee's records shall not be contingent upon the employer's receipt of payment for the production of those records.

(c) An employer shall permit access to all facilities utilized and records compiled in complying with the requirements of this part to the Secretary of Transportation or any DOT agency with regulatory authority over the employer or any of its employees or to a State oversight agency authorized to oversee rail fixed guideway systems.

(d) An employer shall disclose data for its drug and alcohol testing programs, and any other information pertaining to the employer's anti-drug and alcohol misuse programs required to be maintained by this part, to the Secretary of Transportation or any DOT agency with regulatory authority over the employer or covered employee or to a State oversight agency authorized to oversee rail fixed guideway systems, upon the Secretary's request or the respective agency's request.

(e) When requested by the National Transportation Safety Board as part of an accident investigation, employers shall disclose information related to the employer's drug or alcohol testing related to the accident under investigation.

(f) Records shall be made available to a subsequent employer upon receipt of a written request from the covered employee. Subsequent disclosure by the employer is permitted only as expressly authorized by the terms of the covered employee's request.

(g) An employer may disclose information required to be maintained under this part pertaining to a covered employee to the employee or the decisionmaker in a lawsuit, grievance, or other proceeding initiated by or on behalf of the individual, and arising from the results of a drug or alcohol test under this part (including, but not limited to, a worker's compensation, unemployment compensation, or other proceeding relating to a benefit sought by the covered employee.)

(h) An employer shall release information regarding a covered employee's record as directed by the specific, written consent of the employee authorizing release of the information to an identified person.

(i) An employer may disclose drug and alcohol testing information required to be maintained under this part, pertaining to a covered employee, to the State oversight agency or grantee required to certify to FTA compliance with the drug and alcohol testing procedures of 49 CFR parts 40 and 655.

§§655.74-655.80 [Reserved]

Subpart I — Certifying Compliance

§655.81 Grantee oversight responsibility.

A grantee shall ensure that the recipients of funds under 49 U.S.C. 5307, 5309, 5311 or 23 U.S.C. 103(e)(4) comply with this part.

§655.82 Compliance as a condition of financial assistance.

(a) General. A recipient may not be eligible for Federal financial assistance under 49 U.S.C. 5307, 5309, or 5311 or under 23 U.S.C. 103(e)(4), if a recipient fails to establish and implement an anti-drug and alcohol misuse program as required by this part. Failure to certify compliance with these requirements, as specified in §655.83, may result in the suspension of a grantee's eligibility for Federal funding.

(b) Criminal violation. A recipient is subject to criminal sanctions and fines for false statements or misrepresentations under 18 U.S.C. 1001.

(c) State's role. Each State shall certify compliance on behalf of its 49 U.S.C. 5307, 5309, 5311 or 23 U.S.C. 103(e)(4) subrecipients, as applicable. In so certifying, the State shall ensure that each subrecipient is complying with the requirements of this part. A section 5307, 5309, 5311 or 103(e)(4) subrecipient, through the administering State, is subject to suspension of funding from the State if such subrecipient is not in compliance with this part.

§655.83 Requirement to certify compliance.

(a) A recipient of FTA financial assistance shall annually certify compliance, as set forth in §655.82, to the applicable FTA Regional Office.

(b) A certification must be authorized by the organization's governing board or other authorizing official, and must be signed by a party specifically authorized to do so.

(c) A recipient will be ineligible for further FTA financial assistance if the recipient fails to establish and implement an anti-drug and alcohol misuse program in accordance with this part.

NOTES

NOTES

NOTES

NOTES

NOTES

NOTES

NOTES

NOTES